P9-CCC-916

T H E
Fusion of Psychiatry and Social Science

By HARRY STACK SULLIVAN, M.D.

Conceptions of Modern Psychiatry
The Interpersonal Theory of Psychiatry
The Psychiatric Interview
Clinical Studies in Psychiatry
Schizophrenia as a Human Process
The Fusion of Psychiatry and Social Science

Prepared under the auspices of
THE WILLIAM ALANSON WHITE PSYCHIATRIC FOUNDATION
COMMITTEE ON PUBLICATION OF SULLIVAN'S WRITINGS
Mabel Blake Cohen, M.D.   Dexter M. Bullard, M.D.
David McK. Rioch, M.D.   Otto Allen Will, M.D.

301.
15
S94

HARRY STACK SULLIVAN, M.D.

THE
Fusion of Psychiatry
and Social Science

With Introduction and Commentaries

by HELEN SWICK PERRY

79-300
PROVINCE OF ST. JOSEPH
CAPUCHIN
THEOLOGY LIBRARY

The Norton Library

W · W · NORTON & COMPANY · INC · *New York*

COPYRIGHT © 1964 BY THE WILLIAM ALANSON WHITE
PSYCHIATRIC FOUNDATION
First published in the Norton Library 1971

All Rights Reserved
Published simultaneously in Canada by
George J. McLeod Limited, Toronto

W. W. Norton & Company, Inc. is also the publisher of
the works of Erik H. Erikson, Otto Fenichel, Karen Horney and
Harry Stack Sullivan, and the principal works of Sigmund Freud.

ISBN 0 393 00603 3

PRINTED IN THE UNITED STATES OF AMERICA

2 3 4 5 6 7 8 9 0

Contents

Preface

Plan of book.—This book should be viewed as a companion piece to *Schizophrenia as a Human Process* (Norton, 1962). The earlier book, covering Sullivan's work at the Sheppard and Enoch Pratt Hospital, reports mainly on Sullivan's career before he moved to New York in 1930, with actual publication dates extending to 1935—the usual lag between completion of research and date of publication. The present book reports on the period after the move to New York. The publication dates (with the exception of the first article, published in 1934) begin with the year 1937, showing of course the same general lag. In the Commentaries, I have attempted to bridge the change in pace between the two periods by dipping back into the Sheppard years, and I have covered the New York and Washington years in some detail. Thus the two books form a fairly complete record of Sullivan's total professional career.

In the earlier book, I was able through the Commentaries to give a rather complete bibliography of the major writings for the period covered. In this book, the bibliography is less complete for a number of reasons pertinent to understanding the scope of Sullivan's diverse activities after he left Sheppard. In these years, he was busy lecturing in New York, Washington, and elsewhere, often speaking to widely different audiences within the same general period; and he would occasionally borrow from one article for another in order to give a new audience some quick glimpse of his overriding theory before proceeding to some new application. But the theory was itself in transition, so that the borrowing sometimes included modifications. Systematic analysis of the duplication and modification that exist between one article and another would be necessary to prepare a useful and complete bibliography. Also Sullivan's bibliography is considerably more extensive than his formal authorship, since he often wrote unsigned memoranda, editorials, or frontispiece material for the journal *Psychiatry*. These unsigned writings appeared in a period when there was a three-man publications committee for *Psychiatry*—Sullivan, Thomas Harvey Gill, and Ernest E. Hadley; thus, unless the authorship is ascribed in some other way in a subsequent journal or in Sullivan's own bibliography as compiled by him, it would be necessary to assign formal authorship to the three men. Only a few of these unsigned writings appear in this book; in each case, I have some clear indication that Sullivan had claimed sole authorship, but I have also indicated the fact that the material was unsigned, as originally published. The list of these writings is extensive indeed, and it is quite clear that a large proportion of them were authored by Sullivan.

Anyone interested in a fuller record of Sullivan's published writings should review the issues of *Psychiatry* between 1938 and 1946, looking closely at unsigned material found anywhere throughout each issue. Such a task is rewarding indeed, once the student has learned to read lightly over topical material and concentrate on the more timeless insights into human behavior and the rich splattering of largely unexplored ideas and hypotheses on a multitude of subjects, many of them still as fresh as they were twenty years ago. The student of Sullivan will recognize his unmistakable style in literally hundreds of passages, unsigned and largely unknown to most social scientists today. It is my hope that this book will create interest in this unrecognized material and that eventually some detailed and annotated bibliography of all of Sullivan's writings, signed and unsigned, will be available. Within the scope of this book and my own resources, such a bibliography was regrettably unrealistic at this time.

The Use of Single Quotation Marks.—In this period, Sullivan began his distinctive use of single quotation marks to express fringe meanings for words and phrases, alerting the reader to certain implicit assumptions in those particular words as they are commonly used. (See the footnote on page 315 of this book.) But he was not able to convince other editors of the importance of this distinction between single quotation marks and the ordinary use of double ones; only in his own journal *Psychiatry* was he able to evade the pencil of the copy editor eager to maintain consistency at any cost. There is therefore considerable unevenness in the use

of single quotation marks in this book, following his own criteria. Only articles that originally appeared in *Psychiatry* during
his lifetime accurately reflect his use; posthumous articles from
Psychiatry do not carry the single quotation marks, unless Sullivan, in the recordings from which the articles were taken, specified their use. In all other articles, single quotation marks had
obviously been changed by other editors to double ones, and I
have no original manuscripts to follow in re-editing them back to
his original style.

Acknowledgements.—As in the previous book, my chief consultant has been my husband, Stewart E. Perry; his particular background in social science and psychiatry was especially useful as
a supplement to my own, in our joint effort to understand the
place of Sullivan in the history of American social science. For
insight into the early collaboration and the personal relationships
between Sullivan and various social scientists, I am profoundly
indebted to Harold D. Lasswell; on a trip to Cambridge made
especially for the purpose in June, 1963, he reminisced all one
afternoon and long into the night, and again on the next day, to
give us an intensive and unforgettable view of the period covered
in this book. Lawrence K. Frank has also been most generous in
discussing this same period of collaboration between psychiatry
and social science. An important and more general adjunct for seeing this historical development in psychiatry and the social sciences
against the background of American ideas has been a series of lectures entitled "American Intellectual History, 1789 to the Present,"
given at Harvard University by Professor Donald Harnish Fleming, Chairman of the History Department; while he is in no wise
responsible for my interpretation of the fusion herein reported,
his approach has been central to my thinking. In the Spring of
1963, Professor Fleming invited me to present some of my materials on Sullivan for discussion in his "Seminar in American Intellectual History," concerned that year with "Freud and the Neo-
Freudians in America"; and the stimulation from that opportunity
was especially useful. I am also indebted to a graduate student
from the History Department, Mrs. Joan T. Mark, who interviewed me in connection with her dissertation; her questions

forced me to clarify my thinking about some of the intellectual aspects of the collaborative relationship between Edward Sapir and Sullivan.

In connection with tracing out the early history of the journal *Psychiatry*, I should like to express my indebtedness to Katherine P. Olinick, Mrs. Marjorie Luke Clarkson, and Thomas Harvey Gill, one of the original members of the Publications Committee.

Since the book was begun on the East Coast and completed on the West, a number of people have been peripherally but importantly connected with the usual tasks of making a book. Again, as in the previous book, Mary Ladd Gavell and her staff at *Psychiatry*—Gloria H. Parloff and Benita S. Harris—have been supportive of this effort in a variety of ways. In Cambridge, Sheila Scanlon, Astrid Anderson, and Anna Girouard helped me with typing and proofing of manuscript. In San Francisco, Miss Joanne Clarke, a medical illustrator at the University of California Medical Center, redrew illustrations for one of the articles, under emergency conditions; and Mrs. Victoria Hicks has ably assisted me with the indexing.

Again librarians have been of memorable assistance in the task, particularly the staff at Widener Library at Harvard, and in San Francisco, the staff at the Medical Center Library of the University of California and the Langley Porter Neuropsychiatric Institute Library.

On behalf of the William Alanson White Psychiatric Foundation, I wish to make grateful acknowledgement to the following publishers and journals:

The American Council on Education, for permission to publish "Memorandum on a Psychiatric Reconnaissance" and "Discussion of the Case of Warren Wall."

The *American Journal of Sociology*, published by the University of Chicago Press, for permission to publish "A Note on the Implications of Psychiatry, the Study of Interpersonal Relations, for Investigations in the Social Sciences" and "A Note on Formulating the Relationship of the Individual and the Group."

The Macmillan Company, for "Psychiatry," from the *Encyclopaedia of the Social Sciences*, Volume 12, Copyright 1934 by

The Macmillan Company and used with their permission.

Charles C Thomas, for permission to publish "Psychiatry and Morale."

The University of Illinois Press, for permission to publish "Tensions Interpersonal and International: A Psychiatrist's View."

Other articles included in the book have been taken from the Foundation's own publication *Psychiatry*.

Full bibliographic information on each of these articles will be found at the beginning of each selection in this book.

H. S. P.

Introduction

THE TITLE of this book is taken from Gordon Allport's statement that ". . . Sullivan, perhaps more than any other person, labored to bring about *the fusion of psychiatry and social science*."[1] In this book, I have attempted to document this statement by bringing together some of Sullivan's writings published mainly between 1936 and 1949. While the papers in this period represent a *change in emphasis* from the papers reporting on Sullivan's work in the twenties with schizophrenic patients at the Sheppard and Enoch Pratt Hospital, I should like to note specifically that Sullivan's progression of ideas must be considered as a unit, for no sharp cleavage exists between the periods covered in this book and *Schizophrenia as a Human Process*, the earlier book of selected writings. At the same time, this book provides a new focus for viewing Sullivan's early relationships with social scientists—a liaison begun in the twenties while he was still at Sheppard and previously reported on within a more clinical purview.[2]

The psychiatrist sees the papers from the Sheppard period as basically clinical. But the social scientist tends to see the Sheppard experience as action research in human behavior that brought new and fresh insights to the social sciences. As early as 1927, for instance, W. I. Thomas as President of the American Sociological Society had described Sullivan's work at Sheppard in sociological terms: "Dr. Harry Stack Sullivan and his associates, working at the Sheppard and Enoch Pratt Hospital, Baltimore, are experimenting with a small group of persons now or recently actively disordered, from the situational standpoint, and among other re-

---

[1] Italics are mine. From *Tensions That Cause Wars*, edited by Hadley Cantril; Urbana, Ill.: University of Illinois Press, 1950; see footnote on pp. 135–136.

[2] For a relatively complete documentation of Sullivan's early collaboration with social scientists, the interested reader should read the commentaries for *Schizophrenia as a Human Process* in conjunction with this book.

sults this study reveals the fact that these persons tend to make successful adjustments in groupwise association between themselves. . . ." [3] In this book, I shall focus more sharply on the social scientist's evaluation of Sullivan's work.

In tracing out Sullivan's work at Sheppard in the twenties, the intellectual historian would find certain obvious anchor points to simplify his task. While Sullivan appeared at a number of interdisciplinary conferences during this period, his professional activities centered about his patients at Sheppard, and his data were almost exclusively derived from them. By comparison, the period represented by the writings in this book is much more complex. This period began late in 1929 when Sullivan left Sheppard and opened an office on Park Avenue for the express purpose of studying the obsessional process in office patients; this was followed in the late thirties by a move to the environs of Washington, D.C., in connection with the activating of the Washington School of Psychiatry and the journal *Psychiatry*. In this period, centering around New York and Washington, the scope of Sullivan's activities, writings, and data becomes increasingly wide and difficult to present in any unified way. To trace it out, even at a modest level, would require a major research effort and would involve a series of disciplines, including some look at the influence of modern physics in his developing theoretical statement. In addition, his roles during this period were multifold and intricate: clinician still, although he labored increasingly to free himself for writing and research; teacher in both the Washington and New York areas; editorial writer and political commentator par excellence for the new journal *Psychiatry;* a training and/or consulting psychiatrist for scores of junior and senior colleagues on the East Coast; consultant to Selective Service in the World War II effort; participant at various international conferences, often carrying a major responsibility for organizing them; and so on. Thus the anchor points for viewing the intellectual history of this part of Sullivan's life are complex and overlapping, and do not

[3] See "The Behavior Pattern and the Situation" in *Social Behavior and Personality: Contributions of W. I. Thomas to Theory and Social Research,* edited by Edmund H. Volkart; New York: Social Science Research Council, 1951; p. 65.

automatically emerge from the experience itself; over the years, I have fashioned a few such points for myself, and I present them here not in any definitive way but as, perhaps, orienting departures for others.

Sullivan's Move to New York

The move from an institutional setting to private practice, exemplified in Sullivan's move from Sheppard to New York City, is a relatively usual path for the psychiatrist or the psychoanalyst in his early professional life. But the implications of this move for Sullivan were by no means usual. There must, of course, have been a certain glamour involved in the self-picture of the Irish farm boy from Chenango Country in central New York State moving into a Park Avenue office, with some overtones of a wish for a fashionable practice. But the glamour was a small part of the motivation; Sullivan's concern with the world's dispossessed seemed if anything to increase in intensity after the New York experience. To some extent, one must accept Sullivan's definition of his research interest in opening an office in New York: He hypothesized that the obsessional process could best be observed in the ordinary office patient and that the study of this process would clarify some ideas about the schizophrenic process which he had studied at Sheppard; he felt that somehow the neurotic, or the office patient, had escaped a schizophrenic break in the culturally dangerous years of preadolescence and adolescence; such a patient had found defenses to avoid the omnipresent threat of schizophrenia in any life crisis. In this manner Sullivan was expanding considerably the field of his research interest by going into private practice; in the course of this book, the reader can see the ever-widening field of data that he gained access to as the years proceeded, until he was finally groping indeed "towards a psychiatry of peoples." In New York, for instance, he probably first treated a Negro patient, and this clinical experience again moved him toward a wider research interest, particularly in the Washington years, as I shall attempt to document in the book.

In addition, Sullivan had probably largely explored the avenues for growth in the Baltimore area by 1929; these avenues were, of course, considerable—William Welch, though an old man, was still at Johns Hopkins Medical School and Adolf Meyer was still active in psychiatry. But New York City offered new possibilities for varying contacts with European psychiatry and psychoanalysis that were not immediately available in and around Baltimore. That Sullivan was aware of this intellectual need can be documented in part by his first trip abroad—a short visit to Berlin during the Christmas vacation of 1928. During this vacation, Sullivan first met, however briefly, some of the members of the psychiatric and psychoanalytic community in Berlin, including Franz Alexander and Karen Horney. These face-to-face encounters considerably broadened Sullivan's interests and perspectives. During this same hurried trip, Sullivan went to Madrid to see what he could learn of the manifestations of catatonia in hospitals there. He had heard that catatonia was largely unknown in Spain, and he found this indeed to be true in the hospitals he visited. Did this mean, then, that culture might determine symptoms in schizophrenia? [4]

It is obvious in many ways that this trip at least partially reinforced Sullivan's move to New York City, for wider access to European influences existed there than elsewhere in America in the late twenties and thirties. For instance, Clara Thompson had left Johns Hopkins for private practice in New York City by 1925; she had trained under Ferenczi in Europe, and Sullivan hoped to learn something of Ferenczi's ideas from her. As it turned out, life in New York City in the thirties provided some perhaps unanticipated access to European thought, for it was in this period that the European refugees began to arrive—Karen Horney, Erich Fromm, Frieda Fromm-Reichmann, and so on.

Finally—and most important for the purposes of this book—New York provided Sullivan with access to American social scientists and their ideas, which at that time were centrally influenced by what I shall term *the mosaic of Chicago social science*. It is this nexus of influences, of face-to-face and mediate relationships, that I should like to outline here. Sullivan's subsequent move from New York to Washington in the late thirties

---

[4] The account of this trip is based mainly on a personal communication with Harold D. Lasswell.

was a direct outcome of this collaboration with social scientists in and around New York; in Washington, Sullivan and his social-science colleagues of the twenties and thirties—particularly Sapir and Lasswell—hoped to found an institution that would significantly collaborate on a formal or an informal basis with government in an ameliorative plan for a broad program of preventive psychiatry, politically informed and dynamic. By the end of 1933, these plans were already afoot, and the William Alanson White Psychiatric Foundation was incorporated that year in the District of Columbia, although it did not become active through its school and journal until considerably later. Such plans were undoubtedly part of the same climate that produced the dedicated men and women throughout the nation who followed Franklin D. Roosevelt and his New Deal into Washington, in the hope that government could offer some meaningful help to "one-third of the nation."

Sullivan's introduction to American social science was undoubtedly facilitated by a trip to New York in the middle twenties when he first met Lawrence K. Frank through a mutual friend. If Sullivan, more than anyone else, brought about the fusion of psychiatry and social science, Frank has for many decades represented the dedicated middleman in the process of fusion, chairing scores of conferences on mental health throughout the world and gaining the respect and trust of both disciplines. At the time of their meeting, Frank was with the Laura Spelman Rockefeller Memorial Foundation, then under the directorship of Beardsley Ruml, who had received his doctorate in psychology from the University of Chicago (1917). This was the period when the various great foundations were moving from philanthropic enterprises into the support of social science research, and Ruml was an important figure in this changeover. From the beginning of the friendship between Frank and Sullivan, they recognized a common interest: the urgent necessity for bringing the dynamic findings of psychiatry into a meaningful relationship with social science, for the benefit of both disciplines. Increasingly they felt that remedial attempts in the society were necessary and anticipated the ultimate inability of the casework approach, then developing in various outpatient clinics, to meet the over-all problem at all class levels. In the beginning, these meetings between Frank and Sullivan were informal; but eventually, particularly after the addition of Lasswell to their group, the meetings became more formal planning sessions concerned with ways for creating awareness in American society of the necessity for dynamic approaches to social and political problems.

As a result in large part of these early conversations between Frank, Sullivan, and Lasswell, and with the blessing of William Alanson White, "the great encourager," [5] there emerged two larger formal meetings between social scientists and psychiatrists, the First and Second Colloquia on Personality Investigation held in 1928 and 1929, under the auspices of the American Psychiatric Association, and financed by a grant from the Laura Spelman Rockefeller Memorial Foundation.[6] I have already made numerous comments on these two Colloquia in the book covering the earlier period, *Schizophrenia as a Human Process;* but these meetings are so important for evaluating Sullivan's work in the thirties and forties—and indeed in the whole history of the fusion of psychiatry and social science—that it is necessary to look at them again for the purposes of this book.

The participants in the meetings were directed by the APA to "survey the field of interrelations of psychiatry and the social sciences, with view to greater cooperation among those concerned in studying *the nature and influence of cultural environments.*" [7] Before the Colloquia, Sullivan had already met and had significant contact with both W. I. Thomas and Edward Sapir,

[5] I am indebted to Lasswell for this felicitous description of White's role in this whole movement.

[6] For a record of these meetings, see *Proceedings: First Colloquium on Personality Investigation* (held under the auspices of the American Psychiatric Association: Committee on Relations with the Social Sciences, December 1–2, 1928, New York City); Baltimore: The Lord Baltimore Press, 1929(?). And *Proceedings: Second Colloquium on Personality Investigation* (held under the joint auspices of the American Psychiatric Association, Committee on Relations of Psychiatry, and the Social Science Research Council, November 29–30, 1929, New York City); Baltimore: The Johns Hopkins Press, 1930.

[7] See first page (unnumbered) of the *Proceedings: First Colloquium, op. cit.*

then a professor at the University of Chicago (1925–1931); but the *Proceedings* of the Colloquia supply a formal statement on the kind of collaborative thinking that was going on between Sullivan and these representatives from the Chicago social-science tradition. Indeed, much of the important information at the Colloquia on the "nature and influence of cultural environments" came out of those who had some contact with the city and university tradition in Chicago, as it had been developing for forty years: in addition to Thomas, Sapir, and Lasswell, there were present at one or both of the Colloquia, Robert E. Park, Ernest W. Burgess, Charles E. Merriam, William Healy (then in Boston, but founder of the Institute for Juvenile Research in Chicago), and others—all from the Chicago milieu. There were certain other key figures in this durable collaborative enterprise—such as Gordon W. Allport, Elton Mayo, and James Plant—and I do not mean to minimize their importance. At the same time, it was the Chicago group in collaboration principally with Sullivan that succeeded in forging a new unit for study for the whole of social science and psychiatry—*the interpersonal event or relationship*— and this is documented in the *Proceedings* of the Colloquia. The term *interpersonal* used in this way was probably Sullivan's; but all the richness of theory and empirical knowledge coming out of the Chicago mosaic informed the unit for study. It is of this patterned and rich Chicago social science, both face-to-face and mediate for Sullivan, stretching from Hull-House to George Herbert Mead, from Robert Park to Charles Johnson that I wish now to address myself.

The Mosaic of Chicago Social Science (1889–1930)

It was mainly a mosaic of Chicago social science that seemed to fit Sullivan's clinical and life experience. I use the word *mosaic* to describe the apparently dissimilar ideas, people, interests, and experiences that grouped together in and around Chicago to form a patterned whole in the historical development of American social science. After 1930, the Chicago experience seemed to blend into a more total American experience, and many urban universities had their own contributions to make to a more diversified social science. Perhaps the period of Chicago social science as a distinguishable phenomenon was more or less at an end with the publication of the *Encyclopaedia of the Social Sciences* in the early thirties.

I have dated the beginnings of this Chicago phenomenon with the opening of Hull-House in 1889, in a deliberate attempt to focus on the importance of Jane Addams and her collaborators in this Chicago pattern of ideas.[8] As Henry Steele Commager has said: "It was no accident that the new University of Chicago, which was founded just a few years after Hull-House, came to be the center of sociological study in America, and that so many of its professors were intimately associated with Hull-House." [9] It would require a major research effort to trace out the connections between Hull-House and the social scientists at the University of Chicago; I shall have to confine myself here to a brief look at a few figures in this emergent pattern of ideas and people.

I shall begin with George Herbert Mead.[10] From 1894 until his death in 1931, Mead was an important figure at the University of Chicago—a self-styled social psychologist who represented an important bridge between sociology and an emergent American philosophy. Shortly after he and his wife came to Chicago from the University of Michigan in 1894, they met Jane Addams;

[8] I am indebted to Professor Donald Harnish Fleming, Chairman of the History Department at Harvard University, for alerting me to the importance of Jane Addams in the history of American thought.

[9] See p. ix of Commager's Foreword to Jane Addams, *Twenty Years at Hull-House;* Signet Classic edition, 1961.

[10] In the discussion of Mead, I have relied on many sources in addition to his own writings. My chief sources are as follows: T. V. Smith, "The Social Philosophy of George Herbert Mead," *Amer. J. Sociology* (1931–32) 37: 368–385. Biographical note by H.C.A.M. (Mead's son) in George Herbert Mead, *The Philosophy of the Act*, edited by Charles W. Morris, *et al.;* Chicago: University of Chicago Press, 1938. Maurice Natanson, *The Social Dynamics of George H. Mead;* Washington, D.C.: Public Affairs Press, 1956. T. V. Smith, "George Herbert Mead and the Philosophy of Philanthropy," *Soc. Service Rev.* (1932) 6: 39–54.

By far the most useful document I found, however, was a privately printed book of letters by Henry Northrup Castle, with a beginning essay by Helen Castle Mead ("A Few Recollections of Henry's Childhood") and an end essay by Mead ("Recollections of Henry in Oberlin, and After"). (Copy no. 17 from a printing of 51 can be found in the Houghton Library, Harvard University; see *Henry Northrup Castle Letters,* printed by Mary Castle for her children; London: Sands and Co., 1902.)

and a close personal relationship grew up between the Meads and Jane Addams. John Dewey and his wife were also members of this nuclear group. This group had more than informal social and intellectual interchange; for many years, for instance, Mead was an active and successful treasurer for Chicago settlement houses.

In Ann Arbor, Mead had met Charles H. Cooley and had familiarized himself with Cooley's work on the genesis of the self; at Chicago, Mead set himself the task of extending and modifying this theory of the self. In this emergent theory, the central motif was "amelioration through understanding," as T. V. Smith has characterized it. This hopefulness, which actually can be found in Cooley, too, emerged, in part, for both Cooley and Mead, from their knowledge of what was happening at Hull-House. Jane Addams and her collaborators were concerned with averting personal disaster in the lives of immigrants in transition. At a kind of rough-and-ready action-research level, the settlement-house worker in Chicago, as elsewhere, came to understand that effective legislation could accomplish amelioration of critical human conditions; and that man of all the biological creatures did not have to wait idly by while the law of natural selection took its wasteful and painful way. The immigrant in transition, bridging two cultures, faced a crisis in which his very survival was at stake; yet potentially this "marginal man," as Robert Park came to name him, had a sturdiness that was not biological but cultural.

Mead's wife, Helen Castle Mead, was also an important figure in the development of the theme of "amelioration through understanding." The Castles were a missionary family in Hawaii. Both Helen and her brother, Henry Castle, who died tragically in his twenties, made important contributions to Mead's thinking; these contributions were again in areas of living that might otherwise have represented scotoma in Mead's experience. Helen and Henry Castle had met Mead at Oberlin College, where they were all undergraduates. The Castles brought with them from Hawaii an ease with people of color—an ability still seldom found in a member of the white race in mainland America. Near the end of her life, Jane Addams specifically commented on this ability, noting with some wonderment that Negroes moving into Chicago's South Side never affected Helen Mead. She was the "absolute democrat," Jane Addams states, relating this to the fact that Helen Mead came from Hawaii, a place in which races mingle both politically and socially.[11]

There were, of course, other important elements in Mead's experience and training that made him central to this Chicago mosaic. As young men, Mead and Henry Castle had spent considerable time in Germany studying philosophy. Later they had both been at Harvard University together and had come under the influence of William James.[12] The same climate in Europe that produced Freud had profoundly affected Mead as a young man; Freud and Mead were, of course, contemporaries. It is safe to say that the same kind of seminal mind was at work on both sides of the Atlantic, at much the same time, and with much the same exposure to European philosophy. Freud had an advantage in one important particular; as a doctor, he had data from his patients. Mead's development was more theoretical, until his exposure to the insights of Hull-House. But Mead's theory was joined with the psychology of William James, who spoke in the American idiom and thought within the New England experience. The difference between European and American words, like *ego* versus *self*, was more than a simple semantic one. The word *self* was deep in the American experience. The German concept of *ego* expanded somewhat Mead's concept of *self;* but it expanded the word *self* without supplanting it. Mead spoke of the *self* in his writings, as did Cooley; eventually Sullivan did,

[11] See "Helen Castle Mead" (a memorial, including words spoken by Edward Scribner Ames and Jane Addams, December 27, 1929). This is a 38-page monograph which I found in Widener Library, Harvard University; there is no date or place of publication.

It is interesting to note that Hawaii still represents a symbol for the white American in his quest for the ability to see the American Negro as simply and humanly a person and an American. President Kennedy's first major address on human rights for the American Negro was made on a hurried trip to Honolulu, and this was, of course, more than happenstance.

[12] Actually Mead tutored one of the James children and lived in their household during 1887–1888.

too. There was a certain assurance implicit in using the word that emerged from one's own native tongue and experience.

One can be misled by the understatement of Mead's thinking and writing, it seems to me. The idiom is American, but Mead is familiar with the thinking of Freud, Marx, Darwin, and Hegel, as T. V. Smith notes. In Mead's writings, Freud's concepts are couched in a new idiom and placed in a social-interactional context; the Freudian idea of emotional catharsis through understanding seems to have influenced Mead more than the unconscious, Smith states. But both appear in Mead's writings, as social-process concepts. The catharsis is a social amelioration through understanding; and the unconscious appears in part as "selective attention," which Sullivan deftly changed into "selective inattention." In both Sullivan's and Mead's terms, elements of the repressed, the unconscious, the preconscious, and so on, are included; but the area of control is exerted by the participants in the situation, even if the other person is only fantasied. Both Mead and Sullivan learned to avoid the geographic island of the intrapsychic for purposes of social-interactional theory.

The importance of Mead to sociologists and social scientists at Chicago seems to me to lie precisely in the field of the fusion that had taken place in his own thinking. The sociologist did not have to be trapped into explaining whether his sociology was Freudian or anti-Freudian, Marxian or non-Marxian. The useful insights from European and American thinkers of the nineteenth century had been sorted out and placed into a meaningful whole, a consistent and intellectually vigorous social psychology. This was Mead's gift to Chicago social science. Once Sullivan had incorporated some of this thinking into his own theory, he too was able to avoid some of the needless competition between various cults and simply try to place his own observations within a central body of American knowledge and philosophy.

While Mead's theory was not prevailingly concerned with the deviant, or the psychiatric casualty, some provision had been made for this theoretically; it was not inimical to his philosophy.[13]

[13] In one passage, for instance, Mead states: "To a person who is somewhat unstable nervously and in whom there is a line of cleavage, certain activities become impossible, and that set of activities may separate and

An awareness of needless waste in human living pervaded all of Mead's thinking, and this seemed to come centrally from his association with both John Dewey and Jane Addams. At the same time, Sullivan's clinical experience supplies some element missing in Mead's theory, as Mead's theory came to give substance and continuity to Sullivan's thinking.

Mead was known to Sullivan through his writings and through other Chicago thinkers; but as far as I know, Mead and Sullivan never met personally. It is even more unlikely that Sullivan knew Jane Addams or her writings; he never makes reference to her in his published papers, or as far as I remember in his unpublished writings. Yet Jane Addams and Sullivan are obviously part of the same main stream of American thought. Indeed, parts of Jane Addams' books could have been written by Sullivan, and vice versa. At some level, they had participated in a common experience that had wrung from them the same kinds of words. "We are all much more simply human than otherwise . . ." Sullivan wrote in his one-genus postulate. Jane Addams reported that she and her co-workers at Hull-House gained the conviction "that the things which make men alike are finer and better than the things that keep them apart, and that these basic likenesses, if they are properly accentuated, easily transcend the less essential differences of race, language, creed, and tradition." [14] Or again, Sullivan writes: " . . . I believe that for a great majority of our people [Americans], preadolescence is the nearest that they come to untroubled human life—that from then on the stresses of life distort them to inferior caricatures of what they might have been." [15] How little difference there is between this and the statement by Jane Addams that there are many people in poorer neighborhoods "who are caricatures of what they meant to be . . ." [16]

---

evolve another self. Two separate 'me's' and 'I's,' two separate selves, result and that is the condition under which there is a tendency to break up the personality." See George Herbert Mead, *Mind, Self and Society*, edited by Charles W. Morris; Chicago: University of Chicago Press, 1934; see p. 143.

[14] See Jane Addams, *Twenty Years at Hull-House, op. cit.,* p. 89.

[15] This statement, in essence, is found in several of Sullivan's books and papers. See *Conceptions of Modern Psychiatry;* Norton edition, p. 56.

[16] Jane Addams, *op. cit.,* p. 83.

The influence of the sociologist Robert E. Park [17] on Sullivan was more direct than Mead's. Sullivan and Park probably met for the first time at the First Colloquium in 1928, in New York City. At about the same time, Sullivan read the *Introduction to the Science of Sociology* by Park and Burgess,[18] and termed it "a richly documented sociological text." [19] The impact of this book on Sullivan can only be appreciated by actually going through it in the light of his later theoretical development.

Park's vigor as a participant observer came in part from his training in journalism; and his curiosity about all aspects of life must have stimulated Sullivan's own interest in exploring beyond the hospital and the office. In many ways, Mead and Park, who were contemporaries, had somewhat similar training. Park had met John Dewey at the University of Michigan, where Park had done his undergraduate work, and Dewey had convinced Park of the importance of the newspaper in historical process. Interestingly enough, Mead, too, had had an early interest in the important function of the newspaper in a developing democracy.[20] As a result of Dewey's stimulation, Park had gone back to graduate school to study philosophy under William James at Harvard; this was followed by four years of study in Germany, roughly comparable to Mead's work in Germany, although Park was there at a somewhat later period. After a period of study of both the African and the American Negro, Park had finally become a full-

[17] Unless otherwise stated, my information on Robert Park is derived largely from prefatory material in *Race and Culture* (Volume I of the *Collected Papers of Robert Ezra Park,* edited by Everett Cherrington Hughes, *et al.;* Glencoe, Ill.: The Free Press, 1950; see Park's "An Autobiographical Note," and Hughes' Preface). This has been importantly supplemented by conversations with Harold D. Lasswell, and by Park's own writings, of course.

[18] Robert E. Park and Ernest W. Burgess, *Introduction to the Science of Sociology;* Chicago: University of Chicago Press, 1921.

[19] See *Proceedings* of Second Colloquium, *op. cit.,* p. 204.

[20] In Mead's essay included in the Castle Letters (*op. cit.*), he reports that he and Henry Castle had planned some day to have a newspaper of their own: "We had a dream of our own newspaper, which was to correspond to our ideas, not to the demands of the American press." Before his death, Castle did edit a newspaper briefly in Honolulu; and Mead and Castle hoped that Mead's theoretical work would be contributory to Castle's more practical endeavor.

fledged academician, teaching sociology at the University of Chicago; by then he was "nearly fifty," Everett Hughes reports. Park states that his only formal training in sociology came in Germany, "listening to the lectures of Georg Simmel, at Berlin." Actually Park's training in sociology had largely come from his close observation of life.

Lasswell has described Park as the empiricist of the Chicago group. Certainly, Park had a first-hand knowledge of the social organism of the city—and of Chicago—that few other social scientists have ever achieved. "I expect that I have actually covered more ground, tramping about in cities in different parts of the world, than any other living man," Park reports. As a journalist, Park was aware of the fact that most formal research did not give an adequate picture of the nature and process of the city. In 1921, he stated that the most sympathetic and arresting pictures of city life had been written by residents of settlements. He mentions particularly Jane Addams' *The Spirit of Youth and the City Streets* as throwing a "flood of light upon the contrasts between the warmth, the sincerity, and the wholesomeness of primary human responses and the sophistication, the coldness, and the moral dangers of the secondary organization of urban life." [21]

One of Park's early encounters with the American scene other than the big city was made possible by the invitation of Booker T. Washington to visit Tuskegee. In an autobiographical note written shortly before his death, Park reports that he learned more about "human nature and society, in the South under Booker Washington, than I had learned elsewhere in all my previous studies." In turn, two younger sociologists, both Negroes—Charles Johnson and E. Franklin Frazier—have reported that Park significantly influenced them when they were students at the University of Chicago. It is important to note that Sullivan's first significant knowledge of the American Negro came in 1938, as a result of his participation, at Johnson's invitation, in a joint study of Negro youth in the rural black belt.[22] Johnson comments on this early collaboration in his evaluation

[21] Park and Burgess, *op. cit.*, pp. 329, 331.
[22] See "Memorandum on a Psychiatric Reconnaissance" in this book, for Sullivan's report on his work with Johnson.

of Sullivan as a social scientist, which I have included at the beginning of this book.

I have attempted here to fit in only a few pieces of the Chicago mosaic of thought that so centrally fused with Sullivan's thinking through the years. In the collaborative effort that came out of Chicago, there was a real division of intellectual labor. There was the viable, natural microscope of Hull-House through which the social scientist could observe the dormant hope of the marginal man for a better way of life, as this hope was stimulated by Jane Addams and her co-workers. There was Mead's social philosophy that had achieved some significant synthesis of American and European thought and experience, in an American idiom. And there were the great pragmatically oriented empiricists, too numerous to mention—men like W. I. Thomas and Robert Park —who sought through endless participant observation and restless inquiry to provide reality for the drive toward amelioration of the American scene. Sullivan's clinical knowledge and action-research techniques provided this Chicago social science with important new data and, eventually, new theory; but Sullivan's work joined a central body of knowledge in American social science that was pragmatic and hopeful.

By contrast, Freud's theory—viewed in terms of social psychology—had begun to emerge in an earlier historical period and in an older society. Freud had an advantage over Mead, for instance, in that he was a physician and had as data clinical observations from his own patients. Yet Freud remained an early and lonely pioneer in terms of social psychological theory, trying singlehanded to synthesize European social science and philosophy with his own clinical discoveries. Freud's help largely came from disciples in his own profession and not from collaborators in other disciplines. Obviously Sullivan's position in American social psychology was completely different. For Sullivan's clinical insights were fused with the work of many social scientists who participated with him in a relatively new society; and in this society, optimism—no matter how battered by world-wide strife— continued to assert itself from time to time.

The Plans for Institutionalization of the Fusion

From a variety of directions, too numerous to document here, the need for some fusion between social science and the new dynamic psychiatry was clear by the early thirties. An interesting illustration of Sullivan's eagerness for some proof that such a fusion was taking place is found in an article by Sapir, "Observations on the Sex Problem in America," published in the *American Journal of Psychiatry* in 1928; it was Sapir's first article in a psychiatric journal, and it was written "rather reluctantly" after considerable prodding from Sullivan, according to Sapir.[23] The subject matter was very close to Sullivan's own thinking and writing at that period; it was obviously important to Sullivan that Sapir, a senior cultural anthropologist, should take a stand similar to his own.

From the early thirties, Sullivan's interest took the form of plans for an institution that would expedite the fusion in terms of both research and training. While there were several eminent psychiatrists and social scientists who furthered and encouraged such an undertaking, the main collaboration for formulating the interdisciplinary character of the undertaking probably centered around three figures—Sapir, Sullivan, and Lasswell. The institution was to be named the William Alanson White Psychiatric Foundation—undoubtedly at Sullivan's insistence; White was a very important person in Sullivan's early career. The training and research arm of the Foundation would have two branches to begin with—in Washington and New York. And there would be a publication; Sullivan's early interest in publications was undoubtedly reinforced considerably by Park's remarkable career and interests. Some of these plans reached fruition: The Washington School of Psychiatry, the William Alanson White Psychiatric Institute in New York (formerly the New York branch of the Washington School), and the journal *Psychiatry* are of course living evidence. For the purposes of this discussion, it is not important to trace out the history of these various activities

[23] See Sapir's letter to Ruth Benedict, found in *An Anthropologist at Work: The Writings of Ruth Benedict*, by Margaret Mead; Boston: Houghton Mifflin, 1959; p. 195. Sapir's article is found in *Amer. J. Psychiatry* (1928–29) 85: 519–534.

as they evolved and to document the modifications, through the years, of the original plans. Actually the collaboration between Sapir, Sullivan, and Lasswell was cut short by Sapir's fatal illness and death, in 1939, and by the implications of the Munich Pact in 1938. Almost as soon as the Journal and the Washington School were activated, the collaboration between these three men was largely over. But their collaboration still reverberates in the world of ideas, and it is for this reason that I wish to examine it briefly.

Lasswell was the junior member of this threesome. He had done his undergraduate and graduate work in political science under Charles E. Merriam at the University of Chicago, in the twenties, and he had then been formally trained in the new psychoanalysis. He was therefore one of the early social scientists to have rigorous training in the two general areas under process of fusion. Lasswell had met Sapir shortly after Sapir, as a distinguished linguist, went to the University of Chicago in 1925. Undoubtedly this was crucial in the development of the collaborative relationship with Sullivan, for Lasswell could see the importance of an interchange between Sapir and Sullivan. More importantly, Lasswell probably represented a discipline which offered significant fusion possibilities for both Sullivan and Sapir. For all three of them felt that psychiatry had something to offer to politics and the affairs of men. In the course of this book, the reader can watch Sullivan shift from a psychiatry of politics (broadly conceived), to a psychiatry of the state (in terms of the World War II crisis), to a psychiatry of peoples and enduring peace.

Sapir was the senior member of the group. As an American cultural anthropologist he had moved toward the new dynamic psychiatry at a relatively early period, and the years at Chicago readied him for a cultural anthropology that would be available for the study of American subcultural groups. This cultural anthropology was very close indeed to the kind of sociology that W. I. Thomas was developing; Sapir saw that cultural anthropology need no longer confine itself to the study of the languages, customs, and so on, of primitive cultures; it could, like sociology, study various cultural groups in transition.

Although the Chicago years probably underlined for Sapir the ameliorative possibilities of the new dynamic psychiatry in terms of various cultural groups in transition, his interest in it predated his Chicago experience. In many particulars, Sapir approached Freudian psychology with the same scientific acumen displayed by Malinowski in his study of the Trobriand Islanders: Freud was an important thinker with seminal ideas, but these ideas must be examined in terms of other knowledge and other data. Even before Malinowski had reported that Freud's hypothesis of the omnipresence of the Oedipus complex did not apply to the Trobriand Islanders,[24] Sapir had warned in 1917 of the danger of the overpopularity of Freud's discoveries, in terms of scientific progress. Sapir hoped that this

. . . not altogether healthy overpopularity of the subject [would] prove no hindrance to the study of the perplexing problems with which the Freudian psychology bristles. What is sorely needed at the present time, or will be before many years, is a thoroughly objective probing into the new psychology with a special view to seeking out the paths of reconciliation with the older orthodox psychology of conscious states and to the rigorous elimination of all aspects of Freudian theory that seem dispensable or ill-substantiated. The present militant attitude of the psychoanalysts toward their skeptical schoolmasters is naturally but a passing phase. The opposed schools of psychological interpretation will have to meet each other halfway and effect a common *modus vivendi*.[25]

Sullivan's experience with psychotic patients at Sheppard was within the tradition of Malinowski's test of certain of Freud's hypotheses by data collected from another culture. Sullivan had used part of Freud's theory in establishing therapeutic contact with a new population of patients—psychotics; but Freud's theory held that his discoveries could not be used with psychotic patients. Thus Sullivan had extended the application of Freud's theory in line with new observation; but at the same time, he had

[24] Malinowski's work in the Trobriand Islands was carried out, off and on, between 1915 and 1918. See *Sex and Repression in Savage Society;* New York: Harcourt, Brace, 1927. And *Sexual Life of Savages* (2 vols.); New York: Horace Liveright, 1929.

[25] From Sapir's review of Oskar Pfister, "The Psychoanalytic Method," excerpted in *Selected Writings of Edward Sapir,* edited by David G. Mandelbaum (University of California Press, 1958); see p. 522. The original review appeared in *The Dial* in 1917.

found the necessity for important modifications. Within the American culture, for instance, Sullivan did not find a ubiquitous death instinct. In some such fashion, Sullivan was fulfilling Sapir's 1917 prediction that the militant attitude of the psychoanalysts would pass, for Sullivan was willing to continue to pursue in a scientific manner the task of extending knowledge. Some of Sapir's scholarly caution—his awareness of the necessity for evaluating any new discovery in terms of its position in the history of ideas—seems to have rubbed off on Sullivan. Neither Sapir nor Sullivan had other than admiration for Freud's stature as a thinker. But Sullivan came to think with Sapir that if ideas were any good at all, they were in a mainstream of thought and process that would eventually lead to important modifications and important discards.

Fortunately, some record of the collaboration between Sullivan, Sapir, and Lasswell remains and can be reconstructed. They came to think of themselves as having a core discipline in common, for instance. This is reflected in part by Sullivan's description of Sapir's areas of competence: "He was a social psychologist and a psychiatrist." [26] Occasionally in the last years of his life Sullivan called himself a social psychologist. In essence, the Washington School of Psychiatry sought to combine these two disciplines in a variety of ways, reflected particularly in the School's bulletins during Sullivan's lifetime. The purpose of the Journal as initially stated by Sullivan also encapsulated this collaboration.[27]

There are also several papers that report the essence of this collaboration. Sapir's article "Why Cultural Anthropology Needs the Psychiatrist" appeared in the first issue of *Psychiatry* (1938), and is a good example of the consensus that had been achieved. A further example of their collaborative effort is found in papers by Lasswell and Sapir given at the 1939 Richmond meeting of the American Association for the Advancement of Science, chaired by Sullivan.[28] Perhaps the best short statement of Sapir's

[26] Sullivan, "Edward Sapir (1884–1939)," *Psychiatry* (1939) 2: 159.

[27] For the interested reader, copies of the School's bulletin can be found in Volumes 1–10 of *Psychiatry*. The purpose of the Journal is stated in the inside front cover.

[28] See the fourth commentary in this book.

evaluation of Sullivan's contribution to their collaboration is found in a 1937 paper by Sapir on "The Contribution of Psychiatry to an Understanding of Behavior in Society":

> The conceptual reconciliation of the life of society with the life of the individual can never come from an indulgence in metaphors. It will come from the ultimate implications of Dr. Sullivan's "interpersonal relations." Interpersonal relations are not finger exercises in the art of society. They are real things, deserving of the most careful and anxious study. We know very little about them as yet. If we could only get a reasonably clear conception of how the lives of A and B intertwine into a mutually interpretable complex of experiences, we should see far more clearly than is at present the case the extreme importance and the irrevocable necessity of the concept of personality. We should also be moving forward to a realistic instead of a metaphorical definition of what is meant by culture and society. One suspects that the symbolic role of words has an importance for the solution of our problems that is far greater than we might be willing to admit. After all, if A calls B a "liar," he creates a reverberating cosmos of potential action and judgment. And if the fatal word can be passed on to C, the triangulation of society and culture is complete.[29]

Most of the papers in this book were written against the backdrop of the "reverberating cosmos" of World War II—impending, happening, and echoing. The plans made by Sullivan in the twenties and thirties were only prologue for the reality of the forties. For Sullivan's years of fruition coincided with years of world-wide crisis; in the tragic decade following the Munich Pact, most of Sullivan's major work was accomplished. The plans changed, but his sense of scientific and human responsibility did not falter. And his black despair over the urgency of the world-wide task at the end of World War II—measured against the dearth of informed people to help avert another catastrophe—only seemed to underline his determination to find a way.

H.S.P.

Cambridge, Massachusetts
July 14, 1963

[29] Edward Sapir, "The Contribution of Psychiatry to an Understanding of Behavior in Society," *Amer. J. Sociology* (1936–37) 42: 862–870.

Harry Stack Sullivan, Social Scientist

by CHARLES S. JOHNSON *

IN A LOUD and frightened world, the quiet passing of a quiet man who made a science of the interplay of human emotions could easily escape the attention of the multitude. But this multitude, as surely as the coming of death itself, must inevitably feel the influence, if it never learns the name, of one who pointed through a confusing maze of human elements to a way of survival.

As a social scientist I am indebted to the insights and wisdom and friendship of Dr. Sullivan in ways that can be no more fully expressed than they can be repaid. Tradition as well as calculated organization has kept in separated cells the vested disciplines which would describe and systematize in one universe the behavior, and in still another the motivations of peoples. Psychiatry has been, at least from the knowledge and point of view of the social scientist, a closed and almost mystical world. The skills and brilliant intuitions and inductions of its great practitioners have been very largely lost to the empirical observers and classifiers of human behavior.

The penetration of this social world of reality required daring and originality of the sort that few men possess, and fewer still can make intelligible to others. This was the genius of Dr. Harry Stack Sullivan. He had an instinctive sympathy with the inner tensions and turmoils of lost and lonely and frightened people— a way of giving life by finding meaning for it in the very world of reality from which this life had sought so frantically to escape. This world of reality, which he knew so well and respected so profoundly—the social setting, the culture milieu—was so completely a part of his whole that no other construction could have meaning for him, or for anyone following him.

[* This is the text of an address given by Dr. Charles S. Johnson, then President of Fisk University, at memorial services for Sullivan on February 11, 1949, following his death in Paris on January 14, 1949. H.S.P.]

This carrying over of the rich insights of psychiatry into the actual relations between people—between persons—has made possible a new and expanding field of usefulness to both psychiatry and the social sciences. It has placed new tools and materials at the service of students of society that offer, perhaps, the first bright hope of understanding and controlling those group tensions and international conflicts by which our civilization is now so darkly endangered.

This is a personal as well as a professional tribute. Wherever there was a common interest in a human problem, and the rare and precious opportunity of association with Dr. Sullivan, its most enviable reward was the friendship that enriched the inevitable respect and admiration. The catholicity of his interest and concern seems to me to be well marked by the manner in which he gave so much of himself to a problem in group tensions which brought me first to his door. It was in 1938 in the interlude between private practice in New York and institutional responsibilities. Mine was not a generously supported research or one that gave any particular promise of becoming a distinguished contribution. The problem centered in the deep South and involved the personality development of one of the most neglected, if not the most discounted elements in our American society— Negro youth in the rural black belt.* But he was interested, and with no other incentive but the prompting of his own heart and head, and no other reward than the satisfaction that might come from this reconnaissance into a lowly but very real world, he spent three weeks away from his urgent practice, in the deep South.

One of the most important values from his formulations has been his utilization of positive and understandable elements in the interpretation of personal or interpersonal relationships. For him the purpose of psychiatry was the understanding of living to the end that it might be facilitated. He was neither a defeatist nor a mystic. There was for him a lively possibility and hope that controllable social rather than impersonal natural forces were in the end the strongest influences in the fashioning of personality.

[* See "Memorandum on a Psychiatric Reconnaissance" in this book for a record of this collaboration between Johnson and Sullivan. H.S.P.]

It was this conviction, made urgent by world disorder and the tensions of war, that extended his concern to the spreading virus of racial and religious prejudices and of international antagonisms. The roots lie deep in the fears and illusions that keep men lonely and distrustful in our bewildering modern society. These are the same roots that isolated the black-belt plantation Negro in what Dr. Sullivan referred to as the nexus of fields of hostility.

It is tragically fitting that he should have reached the end of his life and work in Europe, where the last bright fires of his zeal and skill have been devoted to the analysis of those tensions between nations and groups that lead men to war and to futile killings, that are leading the nations of the world into a new and perhaps last remaining great effort at mutual self-destruction.

We are permitted so rarely to see life and its highest purpose illumined by a truly great personality; we can only stand silent and reverent before the beauty and excellence of it. It is one of the strangest paradoxes of our civilization that the simplest human virtues and those which alone give us the right to call ourselves civilized are precisely those which demand the highest courage to translate into life and honest social action. . . .

THE
Fusion of Psychiatry and Social Science

1

Commentary

THE FIRST PAPER in this book, Sullivan's article "Psychiatry" (1934), written for the *Encyclopaedia of the Social Sciences,* has significance for the history of psychiatry in a variety of ways. The *Encyclopaedia* in itself represents a great watershed of thought in the social sciences in America; from the time of its publication, with gathering momentum, most of American social science has become clearly interdisciplinary in character, and psychiatry is explicitly joined with the social sciences in the thinking of many major theoreticians. Sullivan's formulation of psychiatry as including "all that is known of persons and their interactions" can be seen from our present vantage point as a crucial step in this redefinition of psychiatry within the framework of a new science of man. Now, thirty years later, the process of fusion between social science and the medical discipline of psychiatry is by no means complete or satisfactory; but the reference point provided by Sullivan's definition of psychiatry as the study of interpersonal relations is noteworthy. Even if psychiatry today still deals—perhaps all too frequently—with "aggravated instances of personal disharmony" from which society seeks protection, the field of psychiatry has become much more encompassing and preventive in scope and is respected as an important source of data by the social scientist generally.

In the broader social scene, the article should be looked at within the temper of the political scene that produced Franklin D. Roosevelt, the New Deal, and an awareness of the people who made up "one-third of the nation." The psychiatrist of the thirties was faced with many of the same dilemmas as the politician and the statesman, Sullivan thought: ". . . some of the problems which come to the psychiatrist arise primarily from the difficulties of gifted individuals in an

3

unsuitable milieu, and these are sometimes insoluble because of factors inhering in the contemporary social and economic organization." In 1934, this kind of thinking was unusual in psychiatry.

It is no coincidence that the article bears the same name as the journal that would begin publication four years later, for this article clearly foreshadows the scope of the journal *Psychiatry*. This psychiatry not only offered an integrating discipline for such disparate practitioners as the alienist of the thirties, the state-hospital psychiatrist struggling with largely custodial attitudes in state legislatures, the European-trained psychoanalyst just beginning to arrive in this country, and so on; more importantly this psychiatry looked to all of the social sciences for "valid contributions" to its data. This broader use of the term "psychiatry" was one that Edward Sapir also furthered, as noted in my Introduction. In a paper written shortly before his death, Sapir gives his definition of *psychiatry* and *psychiatric*:

As some of my readers have from time to time expressed their difficulty with my non-medical use of the terms "psychiatry" and "psychiatric," I must explain that I use these terms in lieu of a possible use of "psychology" and "psychological" with explicit stress on the total personality as the central point of reference in all problems of behavior and in all problems of "culture" (analysis of socialized patterns). Thus, a segmental behavior study, such as a statistical inquiry into the ability of children of the age group 7–11 to learn to read, is not in my sense a properly "psychiatric" study because the attention is focused on a fundamentally arbitrary objective, however important or interesting, one not directly suggested by the study of personality structure and the relations of defined personalities to each other. Such a study may be referred to as "psychology" or "applied psychology" or "education" or "educational psychology." . . .

On the other hand, a systematic study of the acquirement of reading habits with reference to whether they help or hinder the development of fantasy in children of defined personality type is a properly "psychiatric" study because the concept of the total personality is necessarily utilized in it. . . . My excuse for extending the purely "medical" connotation of the terms "psychiatry" and "psychiatric" is that psychiatrists themselves, in trying to understand the wherefore of aberrant behavior, have had to look far more closely into basic problems of personality structure, of symbolism, and of fundamental human interrelationships than have either the "psychologists" or the various types of "social scientists." [1]

[1] "Psychiatric and Cultural Pitfalls in the Business of Getting a Living," in *Selected Writings of Edward Sapir in Language, Culture and Personality*,

In the earlier book of selected papers, *Schizophrenia as a Human Process*, I have included another article by Sullivan from the *Encyclopaedia*—"Mental Disorders" (1933). That article represents, in part, Sullivan's summary of his work at Sheppard-Pratt with schizophrenic disorders; it can be seen as a *l'envoi* to his almost exclusive concern with patients in the hospital. But the entry in the *Encyclopaedia* for "Psychiatry" opens the door to a wider view of his subsequent work; it can be seen as a preamble to a "psychiatry of peoples."

For the reader who wishes a further identification of the historical figures mentioned in the first two paragraphs of Sullivan's paper, the following alphabetically arranged list is provided: *Hippolyte-Marie Bernheim* (1840–1919), French psychotherapist specializing in hypnotism and suggestibility; *Alexandre Bertrand* (1795–1831), French physician who conducted studies of somnambulism, magnetism, and hypnotism; *Thomas Bond* (1712–1784), a founder of what was to become the University of Pennsylvania Medical School and its teaching hospital; *Joseph Breuer* (1841–1925), Viennese neurologist; *Marcel Briand* (1853–1927), French alienist and hospital director; *Vincenzo Chiarugi* (1759–1820), physician who with Daquin is credited in Italian psychiatric history with anticipating the humanitarian reforms of the Frenchman Pinel; *Giuseppe Daquin* or *d'Aquin* (dates not ascertained), Italian physician, generally less well known than Chiarugi but sharing honors with him as the first psychiatric humanitarian reformers in Italy; *Dorothea Lynde Dix* (1802-1887), American reformer in the care of psychiatric patients; *Jean Étienne Dominique Esquirol* (1772–1840), French physician who carried on Pinel's work; *Johann Karl Georg Fricke* (1790–1841), German physician, foremost surgeon of his time and hospital reformer; *Pierre Janet* (1859–1947), French psychiatrist; *Kayssler*, apparently a minor German philosopher; *Thomas Story Kirkbride* (1809–1883), an American psychiatrist who was specially interested in the therapeutic aspects of hospital architecture; *William Maxwell*, a Scottish physician who published his studies of hypnotic phenomena in Frankfort in 1679; *Giovanni Battista Morgagni* (1682–1771), Italian physician and founder of scientific pathological anatomy; *Philippe Pinel* (1745–1826), generally

edited by David G. Mandelbaum; Berkeley and Los Angeles: University of California Press, 1958; pp. 578–589, see p. 579.

considered as the first physician to organize the humane hospital care of the mentally ill; *Morton Prince* (1854–1929), American psychiatrist and neurologist; *Johann Christian Reil* (1759–1813), German physician and educator who conducted research on the structure of the nervous system; *Benjamin Rush* (1745–1813), an American physician renowned for reforms in the teaching and practice of medicine in general and a signer of the Declaration of Independence; and *William Tuke* (1732–1822), founder of the first English hospital for the humane treatment of the mentally ill—the famous Retreat at York, associated with the Society of Friends.

Psychiatry†

PSYCHIATRY, long the art of observing and perhaps influencing the course of mental disorders, has recently tended to become the scientific study of peculiarities of personality and of interpersonal relations. It appeared as a medical discipline in the Hippocratic writings, about 400 B.C. The Greek physicians made good clinical observations and evolved some rational therapeutic techniques, but psychiatry as such survived the demonology and witchcraft of the Middle Ages only in Arabian medicine. It began anew in western Europe with the humanitarian reforms of Pinel and was furthered by his pupil Esquirol in France, by Rush, Bond, and Kirkbride in the United States, by Tuke in England, by Fricke and Reil in Germany and by Morgagni, Chiarugi, and d'Aquin in Italy.* The first periodical in psychiatry, *Magasin für die psychische Heilkunde*, was founded by Reil and Kayssler in 1805. The *Annales médico-psychologiques* appeared in 1843, the *Allgemeine Zeitschrift für Psychiatrie* and the *American Journal of Insanity* (now the *American Journal of Psychiatry*) followed in 1844. About this time Dorothea Lynde Dix was spreading humanitarian attitudes toward persons suffering from mental disorders. By 1860 nursing personnel was being trained in England, and the era of the modern mental hospital had begun. Mechanical restraint of patients by chains, handcuffs, and cami-

† Reprinted from *Encyclopedia of the Social Sciences*, 12: 578–580; New York: Macmillan, 1934. [In the original, a bibliography is included at the end of the article, which has been omitted here.]

[* Historical figures mentioned here and following are briefly identified at the end of the preceding commentary, H.S.P.]

soles gave way to seclusion. Here and there a beginning was made in the classification of patients on the basis of their mental condition and probable development, and special facilities were provided for patients in the early stages of mental disorders and those whose cases were considered hopeful.

What there was of treatment in the institutions of the nineteenth century was in principle physiological. The affiliation of psychiatry in medicine was with neurology, on the assumption that mental disorders manifested perhaps obscure but none the less definite diseases of the nervous system. Of late the association of psychiatry with physiology is also reflected in the work of psychiatrists who specialize in glandular therapy. As early as the seventeenth century Maxwell was accumulating data on hypnosis, which Mesmer expanded greatly in the eighteenth century, and Bertrand and Briand rendered reputable in the early years of the nineteenth. Charcot undertook to give a physiological explanation to hypnotic phenomena, an attempt which Bernheim successfully contested in favor of the hypothesis of suggestion, which is personal rather than physiological. Meanwhile Janet attacked the problem of the milder mental disorders by the experimental method and convincingly demonstrated the actuality of alternating (multiple) personality, extraconscious mental processes ("subconscious") and psychogenetic amnesias (specific losses of memory arising from factors significant to the person). This work was expanded, particularly in the matter of multiple personality, by Prince. Following the current medical ideals, much effort was wasted in attempting to square these phenomena with the terms of neurophysiology, the irrelevancy of which was first clearly indicated by Breuer and Freud in the *Studien über Hysterie*.

Shortly after the publication of this volume Freud invented the method of investigating by free association and began the elaboration of psychoanalysis, the effects of which on psychiatry, although still somewhat circumscribed, promise to be profound. The psychoanalytic work on the milder mental disorders paralleled a tendency inaugurated in the United States by Adolf Meyer, who enunciated in 1906 the dynamic conception of dementia praecox by emphasizing the explanatory importance of symbolic operations by the person rather than the physiological activity of his neurones. These developments, not fundamentally divergent, went far to raise psychiatry from a subordinate position in medicine. The emphasis placed on the crucial conception of personality then brought psychiatry nearer to the social sciences.

These twentieth-century changes, which include as practical consequences therapy of many mild and some severe mental disorders, also fostered the mental hygiene movement and a growing appreciation of the possibilities of psychiatry for individual and social welfare. The medical profession, however, emerging from a phase of biochemical investigations following on the failure of microscopic pathology to resolve its problems, has been rather slow to appreciate the new role of this discipline. Medical education, heavily biological in its foundations, has become depersonalized, and medical curricula have little place for the social sciences and psychobiology. As a result well-trained psychiatrists are largely products of postgraduate training, and their proportion among those dealing with mental disorders and related problems and among the teachers of psychiatry is still rather small. The American Psychiatric Association has recently taken active interest in the problem of training and competence for practice and is seeking to improve standards and to encourage appropriate modifications in the medical curricula.

The theoretical background of psychiatry includes all that is known of persons and their interactions. In practice, however, it has dealt largely with aggravated instances of personal disharmony, the social demand for its services being based on a desire to obtain security from dangerous persons and to restore the unusually aberrant to commonplace living. So far as psychiatry has been preoccupied with the mental life, it has tended to follow the prevailing schools of psychology, with increasing interest in conative systems. Disorder of the emotional life in the mentally deranged is too striking to be ignored, but there are at present some who adhere to fundamentally cognitive approaches. The psychoanalytic and related schools, however, have accomplished such solid results by dealing with the evolution of motives in those who suffer from mental disorders that this principle bids fair to dominate the psychiatry of the future. Current dynamic psychiatry sees the person as the resultant of physiological, psychobiological and situational factors. Physiological factors include native endowment, the interplay of nutrition and needs, and disease and injury. The psychobiological factors comprise the evolution of differentiated personality; acculturation in successive epochs of personality growth; inhibitions and facilitations historically effective and manifesting themselves in the present in conflicts of motivations; characterizing drives; energy partition in activities; sensitivity to events; ease of personal contacts; speech and gesture, including emotional expression. The situational factors include the actual interpersonal opportunities and handicaps in turn reflecting the interplay of culture and its participants, the changing institutional setting of life, and the abundance or restriction of opportunity for new experience. Mental health, meaningful only when it refers to interpersonal adjustment, is that balance among these factors which permits a positive progression in terms of the total situations through which the individual * lives. Mental disorder, an aberration from the state of mental health, can result from factors in any or all of the categories mentioned. Defective endowment may limit or arrest growth of personality or bring on premature senescence; defective nutrition may halt development or lead to recessive changes; disease may disable the organism. The psychobiological factors making for mental disorder arise from specific warping influences bearing upon the person at any time from birth onward; these may bring about such imbalance of growth by experience that unfortunate motivation may develop; and explicit and implicit interpersonal activity may cause lack of self-esteem, dissatisfaction with life, chronic anxiety, or persistent fatigue and inertia, which may manifest themselves objectively in symptoms of mental disorder. The situational factors are involved most simply in the cases of defectively endowed individuals subjected to excessive demands and of superior individuals subjected to privation. They are present more ob-

[* The word "individual" appears infrequently in this paper as compared with "person." As time goes on, "individual" disappears almost completely from Sullivan's writings. H.S.P.]

scurely in instances in which the adolescent finds himself incapaci-
tated for the demanded adjustive growth because of powerful
inhibitions incorporated in him beyond his remedy. As long as
the culture configuration of a group is relatively static and the
young do not leave its area, mental disorders from situational
causes appear to be few. In the contemporary scene, however,
particularly in the case of those who come from remote parts
to the great urban centers or who undergo abrupt change of
social status, the effects of personality warp and the new situational factors may be disastrous. Also because of factors in the
culture pattern, problems of adjustment of both heterosexual
and homosexual motivations assume singular importance for
psychiatry.

For many years psychiatry was largely preoccupied with
humanizing the treatment of persons confined in asylums and
mental hospitals, a work by no means finished; it has only gradually entered upon the tasks of public enlightenment and prevention. The experience of hospitals for convicted criminals suffering
mental disorders turned the attention of psychiatrists to the
problem of the personal origins of criminal behavior, and concomitantly, following pioneering work by Healy,* juvenile
delinquency became an object of psychiatric study. Correctional
schools, penitentiaries, and parole departments now seek the aid
of psychiatrists, and child guidance clinics supervised by psychiatrists have spread rapidly. Specially trained social workers have
become an indispensable part of these clinics, and mental hospitals
and dispensaries are beginning to employ them to secure the
extensive data needed by the psychiatrists and in some cases to
aid in treatment. The field of general social work is being
permeated by the psychiatric viewpoint; like all other fields of
psychiatric endeavor it suffers from dearth of competent instruction and [from] inadequate preparation of personnel. Education
has evinced some curiosity as to the possible contributions of
psychiatry, and special schools and special classes for maladjusted
children have been organized, with or without psychiatric direction. As a result of these developments the demand for psychiatric

[* See, for instance, William Healy, *The Individual Delinquent*; Boston:
Little, Brown, 1915. H.S.P.]

services exceeds the available personnel, the more so in that the specialty has become a fairly attractive field of private practice since the public has grown less superstitious about mental disorders.

Psychiatry has many limitations, not the least of which is the enthusiasm that has led to exaggerated claims as to current accomplishments. The best psychiatry is still more of art than of science; and however much this may be deplored, it can be remedied only by extensive research. Many disorders can be remedied by competent psychiatrists, but the process is difficult and the costs are often prohibitive. The prolonged interview method of psychoanalysis can scarcely achieve a durable result in the simplest problem under sixty-five to ninety hours, and in difficult cases of obsessional and parergastic disorders * five hundred or even a thousand hours may be required. Much can often be accomplished in the way of improving maladjustments, without completely eradicating them, by methods derived from psychoanalysis, for example, "attitude therapy," and in the socialization techniques worked out in the institutional care of parergastic patients. But some of the problems which come to the psychiatrist arise primarily from the difficulties of gifted individuals in an unsuitable milieu, and these are sometimes insoluble because of factors inhering in the contemporary social and economic organization. Moreover it is often impossible to correct personality warp in the less gifted because there is nothing attractive to offer the sufferer. Therefore the psychiatrist, primarily concerned with needless wastage of human ability, cannot but envisage a changed social order under which these problems will no longer exist.

[* Sullivan is here using Adolf Meyer's term for schizophrenia and schizophrenic processes, which he later discarded. H.S.P.]

2

Commentary

IN THE NEXT ARTICLE, which appeared as part of a symposium on psychiatry in the *American Journal of Sociology*, Sullivan first formally addressed himself to the professional sociologists in America. Alfred Adler, Franz Alexander, Elton Mayo, and Edward Sapir had articles in the same issue, with a summing-up by the sociologist, Herbert Blumer.

Sullivan notes that the psychiatrist sees "society" as

a matter of two-groups and three-groups, real or illusory or a blend, and of larger, less durable integrations of two-groups and three-groups having members in common. If the sociologist, in studying the molar movements that concern him, looks to the individuals concerned and not to the processes integrating him with some of them, his data are incomprehensible. If his awareness is governed by a belief that he is standing off detached from participation and seeking statistical norms of the group behavior, his alertness is so inhibited that he cannot observe any parataxically concomitant processes that are influencing the evolution of belief from his reverie. "Discovery" under these circumstances bears a most intimate relation to the habitual, unwitting preoccupations of the investigator; tends to remedy his insecurities, so to speak, rather than to illuminate social reality.

Several points made in this paper seem important to single out. I believe that this is the first major paper by Sullivan in which the word "schizophrenia" (or "parergasia") does not appear; this probably represents a firm decision to redefine the area of his interest. Moreover, while Sullivan is still using the developmental approach in this paper, which is primarily concerned with the role of the scientific *observer*, he is specifically commenting on the general training for life that restricts our abilities as observers of life. That is, he is selecting the particular life events, as they occur in the developmental eras, that affect personifications, distortions, illusions, communication patterns, and so on, as a preliminary for the definition of the main task in the social sciences—the training of competent observers: "The crying need is for observers who are growing observant of their observing." He is describing here an ongoing process, not any final possible achievement of a 'perfect' observer.

Here, for the first time, he clearly posits the necessity for some improvement on the psychoanalytic procedures for training observers. Free-associational techniques borrowed from psychoanalysis are necessary, Sullivan says, but facts and observations from the social sciences must be synthesized with psychoanalytic techniques.

This paper offers one of the best expositions on Sullivan's thinking on so-called personal individuality. He felt that the psychiatrist, and to some degree the social scientist, is able to find out about human beings to the extent that he has experienced life himself; therefore, any real, instead of fancied, improvement in society or the patient must be based on the process of working out the me-you patterns implicit in each; understanding has to be based on the ability of the expert to use his own experience in understanding the other. For this reason, Sullivan states, "The psychiatrist cannot be concerned with the unique individuality of the persons underlying the interpersonal relations in which he comes to be involved with his patient."

Sullivan cites W. I. Thomas in this paper but does not comment specifically on how Thomas' early work on the problem of internal versus external determinants of behavior influenced him.[1] Thomas' early formulation emphasized the importance of the situation, but in addition postulated "four wishes" found 'in' the person.[2] Sullivan has simplified this interaction between the person and his environment in his interpersonal or field theory, postulating that the pattern of the developing person arises out of the need for satisfactions (physiological) as it collides, beginning early in life, with the need for security (interpersonal). Three of the wishes formulated by Thomas —the wish for "security," for "response," and for "recognition"—are clearly involved in Sullivan's concept of interpersonal security.

[1] I base my comments here on an unpublished paper by Stewart E. Perry, "Interrelations in the Concepts of Personality Held by Mead, Thomas, and Sullivan."

[2] See, for example, William I. Thomas and Florian Znaniecki, *The Polish Peasant in Europe and America;* New York: Knopf, 1927; p. 73.

A Note on
the Implications of Psychiatry,
the Study of Interpersonal
Relations, for Investigations
in the Social Sciences†

NEITHER the students of individual and social psychology nor the students of social entities and processes have been able thus far to evolve any very powerful generalizations for the organization of their data and the formulation of their investigations. Many of the difficulties that have been encountered in these directions arise from the fact that the investigator is immersed in his investigation and participates more or less unwittingly in the data which he is assembling. This participation in the data cannot be avoided if one is to do more than count noses or other crude indices of human existence and functional activity. The skill of the investigator resides not in achieving some fancied aloofness but in being free from serious inhibitions of his awareness as to the stream of events which involve him.[1]

† Reprinted from *Amer. J. Sociology* (1936–37) 42:848–861.
[1] While the processes of deconditioning and reconditioning—to use Pavlovian terms—that one would have to undergo in order to delete all of one's inhibitions of alertness would certainly be of an unparalleled complexity and subtlety, we have recently been able to proceed some distance

15

The most general category of these inhibitions of awareness is the overweening conviction of authentic individual selfhood which permeates all the implicit and explicit communicative efforts of nearly everyone. This amounts to a delusion of unique individuality, related to beliefs in one's omnipotence and omniscience, and is only a very complex and personally misleading expression of the real unique individuality of each psychobiological organism—an individuality that must always escape the methods of science.

One must realize that man is in communal existence with the physicochemical, the biological, and the personal or psychobiological worlds—the [last] including adaptive, normative, and material culture. His organization includes excerpts from these several worlds, and a human being can no more exist without communality with a psychobiological (personal-cultural) medium than without oxygen or water. We are inclined to refer to the physicochemical and biological elements of man's organization in one way and to the psychobiological elements in another. The latter we call his mind or his symbol equipment. We also tend to abstract the more psychobiological of his functional activities

---

toward this ideal. The psychoanalysis of Freud, as transplanted in the American field [and] rendered fertile by the psychobiology of Adolf Meyer, has been developed in some degree toward the sort of disintegrative and reintegrative techniques of interpersonal operation that are proving useful in improving one's alertness and in dissipating some of the more troublesome of one's conventional delusions. This paper is intended to be a succinct preliminary communication of some of the more striking results that seem to stem from this approach toward a scientific study of the life-processes of human personality.

In the history of this development one comes first to Sigmund Freud, Adolf Meyer, and William A. White; thereafter, among the psychiatrists, to Albert M. Barrett, E. Bleuler, A. A. Brill, Edward N. Brush, C. B. Dunlap, Richard Dewey, G. Stanley Hall, William Healy, August Hoch, Smith Ely Jelliffe, Carl G. Jung, George Kirby, and Thomas W. Salmon. The parallel growth of cultural anthropology, the life-history method in sociology, and the dynamic-genetic-experimental methods in psychology contributed greatly to making possible a new orientation of our study, when finally these several disciplines were embodied in people who could share their preoccupations and viewpoints. In this connection one looks to contemporary specialists: e.g., Gordon Allport, Ruth Benedict, Erich Fromm, Harold D. Lasswell, Kurt Lewin, Mark A. May, Charles E. Merriam, B. Malinowski, Hortense Powdermaker, Paul Radin, Edward Sapir, Dorothy S. Thomas, William I. Thomas, and Kimball Young.

and refer to them as his mentation, his operations with symbols and meanings. Within limits this sort of formulation is useful.

People are a necessary environing medium for the human being; but people, including the person concerned, are organized in very significant part out of the materials studied by the anthropologist as culture. Just as a locality deficient in iodides may be related to endemic goiter—a specific deviation of development —so the surpluses and deficits in the personal environment of the growing person determine peculiarities and deviations of personality development. Besides the more local factors, there are also factors affecting all of the members of an ethnic group, all the denizens of a particular culture area. The effects are varied, depending on many factors; e.g., the complexity of the culture, contiguity with other culture areas,[2] and individual differences in ability to organize, and in ability to manifest, the various entities of the culture. The most pervasive of all adaptive culture is that which pertains to communication with similar organisms, the most obvious part of which is language. The linguistic elements organized in each person are extremely important, for, as should presently appear, information can arise only from explicit or implicit attempts toward communication with other persons. One has information only to the extent that one has *general* tended to communicate one's states of being, one's experience.

Every person develops from an adaptive state called infancy, in which linguistic processes are only beginning to be organized and in which the simplest patterns of interpersonal processes hold sway. In brief, physicochemical and biological needs appear and make their presence felt by concomitant increases of tension in muscular tissues. The satisfaction of these needs is attended by reduction or abolition of these tensions and a withdrawal of alertness or vigilance from circumambient reality. Throughout life the pursuit of satisfaction is somatically a seeking to reduce

[2] Consider in this connection the important concept of the marginal man as developed by Robert E. Park. [See Park's introduction to Everett V. Stonequist's *The Marginal Man: A Study in Personality and Culture Conflict;* New York: Scribner's, 1937. The marginal man originally referred to a man of mixed cultures, and this is how Park used it here. While the marginal man is at a disadvantage psychologically in a number of ways, he is still "relatively the more civilized human being," according to Park. H.S.P.]

Don't follow this at all— Moves from speaking of infancy to generalisations of Life

or abolish some particular muscular tensions or heightenings of tonus.

In the next genetic epoch of childhood a new sort of necessity that has already been acquired from the world of people begins to be invested with words, begins to be the subject of information and misinformation. I refer to the need for security, primarily a security from noxious emotional states empathized from the personal environment. The infant learns to seek personal security by reversing the pattern of seeking satisfactions. He is preserved from primitive insecurity by virtue of maintaining tensions in various of his muscular tissues. Throughout life the seeking of security or the need to escape insecurity is somatically a matter of tensing various muscle groups, of maintaining some tissues in a state of heightened tonus, the very opposite of the end-state sought in pursuing satisfactions. The more acute one's insecurity becomes, the greater becomes the tonus in some muscular organs —often in the alimentary tract—unless or until panic (personal disorganization) ensues.

This dichotomy, security-satisfaction, is of profound significance for psychopathology, for it organizes a swiftly widening body of data in a fundamental way; in particular, for our present purpose, it permits some insight into the vicissitudes of information as to one's personal reality. The character of experience had by almost all denizens of our culture includes a great body of forbidding gestures, the experiencing of which gestures inspires a feeling of personal insecurity. In the epoch of childhood one learns to adjust to superior authorities [and] to avoid as well as one can the occurrence of these forbidding gestures and the ensuing tension states. As a part of this learning, one develops sundry language performances which help to ward them off and often spare one more or less discomfort. These verbalizations, comprising information and misinformation, come rapidly to pertain to conceptual "me" and "you," figments of mentation chiefly useful in warding off insecurity and secondarily useful in securing satisfactions.

Much of the child's life goes on without any necessity for alertness. Needs call out adjustive movements and achieve satisfactions without particular attention from the authorities, and therefore without implicit or explicit communicative processes. They tend to be unnoticed, to remain outside of the realm of information and misinformation, outside of the growing elaboration of conceptual "me" and "you." These adjustive performances are a part of the experience of the organism, are a part of the growth process, and contribute, like all other experience, to the refinement and differentiation of behavior of the individual. But they are a part of experience the memory of which is not readily accessible to subsequent states of awareness. As one proceeds toward adulthood, one's more lucid states of consciousness tend more and more completely to be concerned with experiences definitely involving the conceptual "me" and "you"—experiences about which there has been at least a tendency to communicate. It is usual to be able to recall a great deal of one's experience of which one was clearly aware at the time it occurred; it generally requires a special set of circumstances, a peculiarly characterized interpersonal situation, to provoke the mnemonic reproduction of previously unnoticed experience.

In childhood—arbitrarily defined as the era from the appearance of the capacity to acquire language habits to the appearance of the capacity to learn cooperative adjustments with compeers —implicit and explicit symbol activities are strikingly autistic-magical; i.e., presumptively invested with powers that the adult recognizes as transcendental—exceedingly improbable as a matter of fact. The prehensions [3] of the child are only beginning to reveal the principles of reality as we come to know it, and the family group more often than not supplies experience that is retarding rather than facilitating to this development. Parents, their surrogates, and other significant older people often in the environment of the child are the culture-carriers through whom he is supplied his earlier accessions of the psychobiological world. Their patterns of behavior-toward-a-child are generally far from simple; their restraints and facilitations of behavior are usually much less adequate than is the case in their interpersonal relations with compeers. All too generally they inculcate a great deal that

[3] To prehend is to have potential information or misinformation about something; to perceive is to have information or misinformation in or readily accessible to awareness.

is incoherent and incapable of unitary integration. Almost universally they encourage the continuance of autistic-magical processes in the field of speech behavior. For example, "You are a naughty boy; say that you are sorry" includes being naughty as an addition to [a] conceptual "me" that has its real basis in empathized hostile-disapproving attitudes of the authoritative individual, with somatic heightenings of muscle tonus; [and] saying-I-am-sorry comes to have the power of reducing or dissipating the hostile-disapproving attitude, without in any way undoing the activity which comes presently to be seen to be the exciting cause for the disapproval. When one considers how much of this sort of thing almost every child experiences, it does not seem so peculiar (or inevitable) that, while some considerable proportion of our people develop aptitudes for manipulating machinery and scientific concepts in a practical way, very few people show much "sense" in interpersonal relations, and almost everyone deals with other people with a wonderful blend of magic, illusions, and incoherent irrelevancy. Childhood is the incubator of man's evil genius for rationalizing—a special aspect of the delusion of unique individuality which is necessitated by the peculiar limitations of conceptual "me" and "you" as a governor of one's perceptions, [that is,] a reference frame that determines the accessibility of one's experience to awareness.[4]

In the juvenile era—arbitrarily defined as the era from the appearance of the capacity for give-and-take adjustments with compeers to the appearance of the capacity for interpersonal intimacy—new culture-carriers of the authoritative adult type effect some modification of the results achieved by the family group. The capacity and (obverse) need for cooperation with compeers usually brings about considerable modification of the autistic-magical behavior complexes which have been developed in dealing with adults, and conceptual "me" and "you" is usually

[4] An understanding of interpersonal relations requires a clear grasp of the serial order of development through the successive stages—infancy, childhood, the juvenile era, preadolescence, and the several stages of adolescence—to some point in which the motives (integrating tendencies) manifesting in any given situation have been evolved. The all-too-general "scientific" notion of one's being translated rather casually from birth to adolescence is thoroughly misleading. . . .

brought at least to a competitive-cooperative differentiation of personal reality. A great deal of the culture accessions of each juvenile, however, is likely to be closely similar to that of every other juvenile in his milieu (the various family groups being denizens of the same culture area); or, when this is not the case, profit from contact with a wider experience is prohibited or restricted by already inculcated fear of the stranger in its various forms and disguises. Moreover, there is only a limited interest in other people at this stage of development; the delusion of unique individuality cuts off all communion that is not absolutely re-quired by maturing necessities (growth of integrating tenden-cies). We see quite a number of people in whom effectual development of personality was arrested at this stage—the later matured needs for intimacy (inhering in the human biological equipment) having then been tortured into strange channels of maladaptive expression, and the autistic-magical interpersonal behavior [having] evolved [into] delusions of reference, of persecution, and of grandeur, or along an uncertain course in which other people are treated as troublesome units transiently more or less useful to a flaming ambition to outdo everyone else in some particular field of accomplishment.

In this connection it must be understood that the effectual development of personality, of capacities (and obverse needs) for integrating interpersonal relations, may be arrested in any of the stages of personality development, with characteristic pathological results on the further maturations of the psycho-biological organism. The progression through infancy and child-hood is usually rather successful, although the vicissitudes of the unwanted infant are all too well demonstrated to the psychiatrist, and the characteristics of people who in childhood struggled against principally destructive influences are not hard to find exemplified. By and large, however, the adjustive patterns wide-spread among American families and American grammar-school communities are adequate to see most young people of mediocre abilities safely up to the threshold of preadolescence. With the appearance of integrating tendencies that elevate the satisfactions and security of a specific "other fellow" to much the same im-portance as are one's own, the differentiations of personality become very striking, and, unless one quickly stabilizes on one of the more conventional quasi-human forms of community life, one goes on toward adulthood quite as uniquely in a world of significantly different personalities as the most deluded "self" might wish. The growth and characteristics of the patterns of one's interpersonal relations are from preadolescence onward the problem of science, and, since almost universally among us, these include much that is overcomplicated (if not directly destructive), the task of this study has fallen to the lot of psychiatry.

The psychiatrist cannot be concerned with the unique individuality of the persons underlying the interpersonal relations in which he comes to be involved with his patient. In a word, he has to make the substantiality of his own and the other personality concerned yield their all too self-evident foci of attention, so that the processes in the interpersonal contexts may emerge as the tangible field for his study. As a listener, he must realize that he is participating in speech behavior that pertains chiefly to the conceptual "me" and "you," with corresponding manifestation of the factors that have distorted and continue to complicate the interpersonal relations of the subject personality. As one who speaks, he is keenly aware that he is using linguistic processes in a configuration in which the hearer enters most significantly into the outcome of the attempt at communication.[5]

In the interpersonal contexts through which the writer has passed, it is recurrently necessary to dissipate the importance of statements allegedly indicative of various aspects of reality, but

[5] The removal of other than conceptual substance from the "me" and "you" in our discourse is rather catastrophic to the language process as we presume we know it, and verbal communicative efforts under this set of circumstances have to be recognized as a decidedly tentative kind of performance. The current effort is no exception to the insight just mentioned, and the writer must beg of the reader a more than "reflex" consideration of the matter herein stated—or at least invested with words. There "comes to mind" in this connection an experience with Dr. Charles Merriam concerned with a committee report the writer had drafted. Dr. Merriam indicated by a mark each word used in a "special" meaning—the proportion was roughly one in every fourteen. The statistically common sense of meaning per word thus implied seemed at that time a Dunsanian vision of sad, far-off things; and now seems even more remote and sadly wanting in psychiatry.

actually far too complex to accomplish anything more than self-deception of the speaker. Some insight has developed as to the function performed by uncommunicative, unintelligible, and misleading statements in allegedly communicative interpersonal contexts. These have been observed to occur when the integration is parataxic; [6] i.e., when, besides the interpersonal situation as defined within the awareness of the speaker, there is a concomitant interpersonal situation quite different as to its principal integrating tendencies, of which the speaker is more or less completely unaware.

Besides the two-group integrated of psychiatrist and subject there is in the parataxic situations also an illusory two-group integrated of psychiatrist-distorted-to-accommodate-a-special-"you"-pattern and subject-reliving-an-earlier-unresolved-integration-and-manifesting-the-corresponding-special-"me"-pattern. The shift of communicative processes from one to another of these concomitant integrations may be frequent or only occasional; in any case the alertness of the speaker is usually sufficient to insure the weaving of word patterns and other linguistic elements into grammatical speech. There therefore ensues an apparently coherent discussion, and one usually rather clearly addressed to the hearer. Only under great stress from the surviving unresolved situation does the "me" and "you" performance suffer such strain that the hearer is warned of his factual submergence in the illusory distortions of the speaker. Generally, the hearer receives no direct clue to the complexity of the situation in which he is participating. The chief detectable peculiarity of the situation is the tension of the performances, showing as an incongruity of effort to effects, so to speak. Sometimes there is an undertone of insecurity when there is nothing hostile or negative in the more real aspects of the integration; sometimes there are signs of the pursuit of satisfactions that are irrelevant or factually impossible in the current integration. There seem always to be some objective signs, when the whole context is available for minute study; with the most active interest in uncovering these very

[6] This term, I believe, was first utilized in a psychiatric sense by Dom Thomas V. Moore, M.D., in his paper, "The Parataxes" (*Psychoanalytic Rev.* [1921] 8: 252–283).

data, the writer has often found himself without any information as to actual incidence of the overcomplicating processes in the interpersonal contexts. Only in retrospect he sees that the parataxic situation must have evolved out of the consensually valid one some little time prior to his becoming aware of its presence.

If now we consider the parataxic situations in which the alertness of both people concerned is seriously inhibited (neither is "possessed of personal insight"), we see literally a play of cross-purposes—but one of great subtlety and obscurity as to the processes actually present. It might be thought that a two-group thus integrated would be short-lived, would break up from mutual misunderstanding. This is very far from necessarily the case. The integrating tendencies that create an interpersonal situation are relatively powerful compared with the disintegrative complicating factors included in the surviving unresolved situations that involve the persons concerned. The parataxic situation includes a prevailingly positive group of integrating tendencies, and the persons concerned accommodate each other in the plural roles—by shifts of attention, inhibition of inquiry, and otherwise—in subserving the complex motivation, sometimes over very long stretches of time. As a matter of brute fact, these bilateral parataxic interpersonal situations are the rule rather than the exception among us, and the average person magically stripped of his illusions about his friends and acquaintances would find himself surrounded by strangers.[7] Certainly, this surviving unresolved past of the person—the underlying reality of the "transference" and "repetition compulsion" of Freud—is a ubiquitous complicating factor in interpersonal relations which

[7] The facts that people do on occasion cooperate meaningly and even sometimes collaborate successfully in achieving distant goals are the proper source for wonder and a sufficient basis for optimism about the future of humanity. Of the thirty people enumerated in the second paragraph of the first footnote hereto, I believe that I have been in direct consensually valid communicative integration from time to time with each of a total of nine. Of my readers, I confidently anticipate a really understanding concomitance of reverie processes (mediate communication) in certainly ten or fifteen more. My thanks go chiefly to Professor W. I. Thomas for teaching me to appreciate the extraordinary good fortune in being so widely successful.

cannot safely be ignored in any inquiry into human relations.

Every interpersonal context seems, then, to include two or three human organisms, and/or reverie-toned simulacra or illusions thereof, integrated into a single more or less discrete if transient entity by forces tending to produce cooperative, collaborative, antagonistic, and/or disjunctive movements.* The interpersonal situation, this rather discrete if transient entity, is characterizable on the basis of the effective alertness of each of the organisms concerned. The effective alertness of one of the organisms thus integrated into an interpersonal situation may be considerably greater (in scope, freedom from inhibitions, instabilities of attention, etc.) than is the effective alertness of the other organism or organisms concerned. The more lucid organism is at least potentially more aware of the real character of the interpersonal processes going on in the situation than are the other organisms concerned. His verbalization of the situation, his expression by linguistic processes of what might "come to [my] mind" as to "what is going on," will be of correspondingly greater probability as to correctness. If he is chiefly motivated toward constructive resolution of the situation, his greater alertness permits his awareness of both the explicit (witting, at least potentially conscious) situation and the parataxically concomitant and complicating situation. If he is a student of personality or other interested scientific observer (not dominated by some reverie formation as to the nature of what should be going on), his participation in the situation is characterized by explicit or implicit communicative processes which tend to expand the awareness of all the organisms concerned as to the interpersonal processes manifesting in the situation. If he is a practicing psychiatrist, his verbalizations tend to "interpret the situation" so that the degree of awareness ("personal insight") of the patient increases. If his preoccupation is one of the social sciences, there go on "in him"

[* The working paper which I used in preparing this book came from Sullivan's own files and contained comments written in by some colleague who is unidentified. This sentence in particular was commented on as follows: "The most difficult sentence I ever read. It puts such a burden on the reader that it is almost code." Another note is added: "Read this over several days later and it didn't seem so difficult." This is such a cogent commentary on some of Sullivan's ideas and words that I felt it should be preserved. H.S.P.]

processes that tend to eventuate in communicable information as to the particular situation, and more or less significantly similar situations within his experience.

To the student of culture, of social environments, of social organization, of social processes, or of special aspects of any of these, the psychiatrist would then seem able to offer some generalization of his experience in dealing with those difficulties of living that are to be referred to inadequacies or eccentricities of personality or to minor or major mental disorders. The generalization would seem to bear primarily on the locus of the scientist's study; secondarily, on the evaluation and interpretation of the data obtained by the study; and, third, on the limiting factors that should control the scientist's building of working hypotheses within the general framework of his special preoccupation. To the psychiatrist, the fully human is always embodied and made manifest in an interpersonal situation, real or illusory, or a blend of both. For example, for the anthropologist, the data of a language may be usefully abstracted from the concrete uses of the language, and linguistic processes may be traced without immediate regard to the fact that people using the language throughout its various developmental vicissitudes gave rise to all the extant data on its history. In common, however, with others who are devoted to rational processes, the anthropologist is likely to overlook the fact that "the data" are made philological data by virtue of certain reverie processes in which he is integrated with other (illusory) persons with whom he is (in reverie) engaged in language behavior of a communicative character. Without alertness in this particular, there is not likely to be alertness as to any parataxically concomitant processes, and it thus comes about that any belief that may arise from his study may be delusive rather than consensually valid information.

Again, to the psychiatrist, "society" is practically a matter of two-groups and three-groups, real or illusory or a blend, and of larger, less durable integrations of two-groups and three-groups having members in common. If the sociologist, in studying the molar movements that concern him, looks to the individuals concerned and not to the processes integrating him with some of them, his data are incomprehensible. If his awareness is governed by a belief that he is standing off detached from participation and seeking statistical norms of the group behavior, his alertness is so inhibited that he cannot observe any parataxically concomitant processes that are influencing the evolution of belief from his reverie. "Discovery" under these circumstances bears a most intimate relation to the habitual, unwitting preoccupations of the investigator; tends to remedy his insecurities, so to speak, rather than to illuminate social reality.

It thus comes about that a pessimistic student finds in the current scene of widening social disorganization the promise of an early eclipse of Western culture. It is now rather widely held that the person, considered individually, evolves on the combined bases of his more or less serially maturing inborn capacities and the temporally corresponding environmentally conditioned facilitations and restrictions. One would seem secure in inferring, then, in this individualistic framework, that the spread of social disorganization will increase the probability of eccentric developments of personality. An accelerating vicious circle becomes apparent as soon as one introduces the assumption that the novel in personality is disorganizing to those influenced by it. The twilight of the Western world thus becomes all but an accomplished fact—when such a vision is useful in the parataxic integrations of the thinker, in which unresolved interpersonal situations survive from an earlier time.

It is clear that we are proceeding with positive acceleration into an unknown future, and it is clear that many people are on occasion at least dimly aware of the increasing uncertainty of things to come. It is probable that the adaptive capacities of man are greatly in excess of the demands of current life, and it is clear that consensually valid information is useful in meeting the contingencies of living. The general outline of the useful task of the psychiatrist and the social scientist would seem to be the amassing of valid information about living, and the changing velocity of social processes would seem to give increasing opportunity for accomplishing this. The experiments of nature (Adolf Meyer) are increasing in number and variety. The crying need is for observers who are growing observant of their observing.

It would seem that interpersonal processes free from parataxic elements are either positive-constructive movements toward intimacy, with the securing of satisfactions and the maintenance of ("personal") security, or negative-destructive movements of hostile avoiding, ostracizing, or dominating of persons more or less clearly identified as the sources of insecurity, and thus barriers to the securing of satisfactions. An indeterminate but certainly very great part of the manifest negative-destructive motivation in the world today must be identical in character with the instances that come to the attention of the psychiatrist. The latter include without exception important parataxic elements. In other words, there is every apparent justification for questioning the inevitable, necessary, character of some great part of the hostile-destructive interpersonal processes that are so conspicuous a feature of current life; and therefore [there is] a notable implication as to the possibility of a social order in which they would have at most a minor role.

If it were not for the parataxic concomitance of unresolved interpersonal situations of the chronological past that survive in and complicate temporally present interpersonal situations, the study of human relations would be much less recondite than it is. In the presence of this ubiquitous factor, however, the elucidation of the fundamental characteristics of interpersonal relations ("personality processes") in the form of scientific laws requires the extended collaboration of investigators along many approaches. These investigators must be relatively free from the more serious inhibitions of their alertness in the interpersonal situations that supply their real data; and significant freedom from inhibitions of alertness is but rarely the outcome of personality development as it is likely to occur among us. In other words, it has usually to be acquired by way of special training in interpersonal relations by methods related to the best of current psychoanalytic practices,[8] perhaps now only beginning to be evolved.[9] With this superior alertness the observer may become

[8] That "a personal psychoanalysis" is all that is required is vividly contradicted by the performances of some few of my colleagues, who would seem either to have had singularly little in the way of native abilities or to have acquired handicaps rather than benefits in the course of their "psychoanalytic training."

[9] In this connection it may be noted that a promising plan for the

aware of the experience that would arise, for example, in his integration with a member of a disorganized group, and would thus acquire valid data for generalizing some information as to the spread and recession of social disorganization. He would have augmented ability to discover "the private history of great events" (W. I. Thomas) and to comprehend the factors that extend and that restrict the diversification of interpersonal relations along seemingly constructive, and in apparently destructive, directions.*

---

postdoctoral training of psychiatrists and social scientists is being worked out at Washington, D.C. The Washington School of Psychiatry looks toward the evolution of techniques for personality study that will utilize free-associational processes and psychiatric methods on a growing foundation of consensually valid information to be refined and synthesized from the facts and observations of specialists in the several social sciences.

[* The last part of this sentence might be more clearly read as follows, although I am not certain this is its meaning: "in seemingly constructive directions as well as in apparently destructive ones." H.S.P.]

3

─────────

Commentary

THE NEXT SELECTION is found in the first issue of *Psychiatry: Journal of the Biology and the Pathology of Interpersonal Relations*, edited by a three-man publications committee—Thomas Harvey Gill, Ernest E. Hadley, and Harry Stack Sullivan. It is clear in the article that Sullivan is still pursuing his goal—a wider definition of the field of psychiatry in line with the avowed intention of the Journal: "The William Alanson White Psychiatric Foundation seeks to communicate the growing insights of psychiatry, the study of interpersonal relations, to a wide audience of those who can make valid contributions to the data of psychiatry, and correct use of its formulations. The Journal is addressed not alone to psychiatrists and psychiatric research personnel in the narrower sense, but to all serious students of human living in any of its aspects, and to those who must meet pressing social needs with current remedial attempts."

Much of the discussion of Mr. A and Mrs. A in this paper is within the experiential range of a 'normal' person. In the earlier papers (see *Schizophrenia as a Human Process*), the clinical data are from patients showing the schizophrenic process. In a footnote to this paper, Sullivan suggests that the words "neurotic" and "neurosis" be discarded and "relegated to medical history along with 'humors' and other monuments of discarded theories." He substitutes a process term, *parataxis*, describing behavior everyone shows from time to time—"the shift from a more or less adequate pattern of interpersonal relations to the parataxically intricate one [a change that happens] so swiftly and by steps so subtle that no trace of what is meant by volition can be discovered in the process." Here again the move is from a *diagnosis* (neurotic, schizophrenic) to a *process;* the schizophrenic process is less ubiquitous in 'normal' personality; by contrast the parataxic process is prevalent in the person living in our society. But, according to Sullivan, none of us is completely unfamiliar with either process.

The clinical data for this paper, information on the relationship of a married couple, are undoubtedly extrapolated and composited from his clinical experience as a private psychiatrist in New York City. Sullivan characterized this practice as being with patients showing obsessional processes—actually those within the span of 'normal' upper middle-class members of our society. Sullivan's practice in New York was largely with those who would seek private care. While he made good use of the data thus collected in the formulation of his expanding theory, it is notable that this kind of data from upper middle-class patients is seldom found in Sullivan's papers; [1] after the New York experience, he did not actively engage in this kind of practice again, although he characterized a good proportion of his trainees in psychiatry as showing obsessional preoccupations.

[1] Some of this kind of data was used in later lecture series given by Sullivan. See, for instance, the chapter on "Obsessionalism" in *Clinical Studies in Psychiatry* (Norton, 1956).

The Data of Psychiatry†

PSYCHIATRY as a science is concerned with the thinking and doings of persons, real and illusory. Everything personal is data for psychiatry, and relevant exactly to the extent that it is personal. Many of the phenomena of life that at first glance seem subpersonal or impersonal are found to have personal connections which make them of psychiatric interest. The whole subject of human biology is directly or indirectly psychiatric. All contemplations of human thinking and all study of social or group life are tributary to psychiatry. All that is man-made and used by man, all that the anthropologist calls culture, has personal and therefore psychiatric aspects and implications. The range of psychiatric relevance is vast indeed. The primary concern of psychiatry as a science, however, is relatively narrow. Psychiatry seeks to discover and formulate the laws of human personality. It is only indirectly concerned with the study of abstractions less or more inclusive than the person. Its peculiar field is the study of *interpersonal phenomena*. Personality is made manifest in interpersonal situations, and not otherwise. It is to the elucidation of interpersonal relations, therefore, that psychiatry applies itself.

1. The personality that can be studied by scientific method is neither something that can be observed directly nor something the unique individuality of any instance of which would be any

† Reprinted from *Psychiatry* (1938) 1: 121–134. [This article was originally published as a first chapter in a book to be titled *Psychiatry: Introduction to the Study of Interpersonal Relations;* the book was never completed as such. H.S.P.]

concern of the psychiatrist. The individuality of a particular electron is of no concern to the physicist; the individuality of the biologist's dog is not apt to confuse his biology of the dog. It is quite otherwise, however, with the traditionally emphasized individuality of each of us, "myself." Here we have the very mother of illusions, the ever pregnant source of preconceptions that invalidate almost all our efforts to understand other people. The psychiatrist may, in his more objective moments, hold the correct view of personality, that it is the hypothetical entity that one postulates to account for the doings of people, one with another, and with more or less personified objects. In his less specialized operations this same psychiatrist joins the throng in exploiting his delusions of unique individuality. He conceives himself to be a self-limited unit that alternates between a state of insular detachment and varying degrees of contact with other people and with cultural entities. He arrogates to himself the principal role in such of his actions as he "happens" to notice.

2. Psychiatry is the study of the phenomena that occur in interpersonal situations, in configurations made up of two or more people, all but one of whom may be more or less completely illusory. This study has obvious relevance for the doings of everyone under most of the circumstances that characterize human life. Habitual operations on inanimate objects are an exception, in so far as they have come to include nothing personal. They are not the only exceptions, and some people manifest a somewhat less striking preponderance of interpersonal actions than do others. In general, however, anything that one *notices* is apt to be interpersonal and thus within the field of valid psychiatric data. Few interpersonal phenomena may appear in a mechanic's "listening" to a strange noise that has appeared in one's automobile. When he formulates his opinion, however, and particularly when he discovers that he is mistaken, this is no longer the case. Interpersonal factors in·the latter situation may overshadow his technical competence to the serious detriment of one's car, may ensue in alterations in one's personal organization such that interpersonal factors seriously complicate all of one's subsequent dealings with auto mechanics, with any mechanics, or even with engineers and experts in all fields pertaining to machinery.

3. Human behavior, including the verbal report of subjective appearances (phenomena), is the actual matter of observation of the psychiatrist; it is important, however, to note that the act of observing is in itself human behavior and involves the observer's experience. That which one cannot experience cannot be observed, but people seem all much more simply human than otherwise, and the data of psychiatry are for the most part events of frequent occurrence. At the same time, these data are often matters the *personal significance* of which is veiled from the person chiefly concerned, and more or less obscured in the process of being observed by another. This is always the case with processes that go on in sleep; it is often the case in the mental disorders called *parergasia;* [1] and it is not infrequently the case in the doings of everyday life. Thus, the experience of weariness is often a veiled expression of resentment; and unreasonable worry about someone, the disguised expression of a hostile wish.[2] Neither resentment nor hostility would appear in the person's verbal report of his mental state, because they exist outside of his awareness: it is from observation of his

[1] "Mental disorder" as a term refers to interpersonal processes either inadequate to the situation in which the persons are integrated, or excessively complex because of illusory persons also integrated in the situation. It implies some—sometimes a great—ineffectiveness of the behavior by which the person is conceived to be pursuing the satisfactions that he requires. It is not, however, to be envisaged as an equivalent of *psychosis,* "insanity," or the like. The failure to remember the name of an acquaintance at the opportune moment is just as truly an instance of mental disorder as is a fixed delusion that one is Napoleon I.

The term *parergasia* is used throughout this text to refer to a group of serious mental disorders that make up the particular patterns of interpersonal maladjustment seen in more fully developed form in many patients diagnosed as suffering the *dementia praecox* of Kraepelin or the *schizophrenia* of Bleuler.

The term *parergasia* is a part of the psychiatric formulations of Professor Adolf Meyer, to whom the writer, like many another psychiatrist, is greatly indebted.

[2] So great are the difficulties in communicating the viewpoints of psychiatry—and so limited in particular are the capacities of the writer—that one may well distrust as a matter of principle the impressions gained on first reading of any part of this text. If the reader should seem to find something new and important, I must bespeak of him a rereading . . . of the whole. One of the sociologists who read the fourth version—this is the seventh—remarked that my ideas were contagious, but, like some other contagious things, they had a considerable incubation period.

continued behavior towards the other person that one may demonstrate their presence "in him." We say that he is motivated to punish or to harm, but judge that these motives are denied his recognition, and are absent from his intentions. When he uses the pronoun "I," he includes in its reference only those motives of which he is aware, and refers to his *self*, a much less inclusive entity than the hypothetical personality with which the psychiatrist invests him. This self is an entity that is of little service as a general explanatory principle in the study of interpersonal relations. The weariness and the worry are fully real to the self, and provoke no feeling of incompleteness or obscurity. If the weariness should suddenly disappear when some new activity is suggested by a third person, or the worry be entirely assuaged by a game of bowling, no suggestion of inconsistency arises to disturb one's feeling of completeness, no awareness of the missing motive ensues. Even if an observer should suggest the probable motivation, no extension of awareness is to be expected, but instead a series of *rationalizations;* that is, plausible statements, in general appealing to prejudices (unwarranted beliefs), held by many persons known to the speaker, without particular regard to probability but only to interpersonal expediency, to the end that the observer shall defer to the "explanations" and thus withdraw the challenge to the other's self-esteem.

4. Psychiatry concerns itself with the way in which each of us comes to be possessed of a self which he esteems and cherishes, shelters from questioning and criticism, and expands by commendation, all without much regard to his objectively observable performances, which include contradictions and gross inconsistencies. We know that these self-dynamisms,[3] clearly the referent[4] of a great part of our conversation and other social

---

[3] The term *dynamism* is used throughout this text to connote a *relatively enduring configuration of energy which manifests itself in characterizable processes in interpersonal relations.* It is to be preferred to "mental mechanism," "psychic system," "conative tendency," and the like, because it implies only *relatively enduring capacity to bring about change,* and not some fanciful substantial engines, regional organizations, or peculiar more or less physiological apparatus about which our present knowledge is nil.

[4] A *referent* is that to which something refers. As should presently appear, all our information is closely related to the formulation of experience in terms that *might be* used in an attempt to communicate with some other

behavior, are by no means inborn, relatively immutable, aspects of the person. Not only do they show significant differences between people from various parts of the world, and between the siblings of one family, but they change their characteristics in a more or less orderly fashion as one progresses from child-hood to maturity. Sometimes they undergo rather abrupt and extensive modification in the course of a personal crisis; e.g., a grave mental disorder. These latter in particular (the vicissitudes of the self among the events that make up a severe psychosis) indicate that the content—the expressible convictions and un-certainties—of the self has been acquired in the life of the person, chiefly by communication with others. Much of the praise and some of the blame that has come from parents, teach-ers, friends, and others with whom one has been significantly related, have been organized into the content of the self. A selecting and organizing factor determines what part of these observed judgments of one's personal value, what of the infor-mation that one secures through secondary channels (e.g., read-ing), and which of the deductions and inferences that occur in one's own thinking, shall be incorporated into the self. The growth of the self is regulated in much the same way as is the growth of an organic system of the body; it is kept in vital balance with the rest of the personality, in the functional activities of which it is peculiarly significant.

5. An outstanding activity involving the self is the having, organizing, and utilizing of *information*. Information is that part of our experience of which we are, or may easily become, aware. To be aware of something is to have information about it, and information varies from the merest hint within awareness to the most inclusive of abstract formulations. It is to be noted that information is never identical with any other aspect of reality and that, as in the case of the man's weariness in lieu of resentment, it is sometimes related in a most complicated fashion to the aspects of interpersonal reality of which it is a

---

person. The conception of referring pertains to the use in human mentation of abstractions from the events of life, the abstraction usually being closely related to verbal processes—secondary streams of events in which the characteristics of one's particular language are conspicuous factors.

function within awareness. The man in question may be defined as "one motivated by resentment." This implies that he will behave in such a fashion as to punish the other person, at the same time ideally being more or less clearly aware of (a) an event that called out the motivation, (b) the state of being resentful, (c) the punitive activity, (d) the activity of the other person, and (e) the satisfactory resolution of the situation integrated by the resentment when the second person shall have been discomfited. Our particular man's resentment, however, is represented in awareness as weariness. He does not formulate the resentment in any such form as "you make me tired"; he has no information about his resentment, and little or no information about the other person's relation to his weariness. If now his behavior *unwittingly* thwarts or humiliates the other, the dynamic system which we call his "motivation by resentment" may be discharged. His weariness disappears. He would still have no information as to the punitive character of his behavior and would regard as unjust and unreasonable any imputation that he had been unkind. Under pressure, he might be led to regret the discomfiture of the other, whereupon weariness would probably return. That night, he might dream of some disaster befalling a more or less disguised representation of the object of his unrecognized resentment. He would thus be seen to have undergone (experienced)—quite dissociated from his personal awareness—resentment, its satisfaction in reality, and its reactivation and secondary satisfaction in fantasy, in the dream. Also, he "himself" has experienced two episodes of weariness, about which he may have an indefinite number of (erroneous) convictions, astonishment, or even uncomfortable uncertainty; these representations within personal awareness amounting to definite misinformation about the interpersonal situation.

6. Suppose now that we review the events leading our hypothetical man to his "psychogenetic" weariness, and find that his wife made a derogatory remark to him a short time before he showed signs of his weariness. If it also appears that this weariness is interfering with some activity planned by his wife, we may be justified in surmising that the underlying resentment was aroused by her expressed disrespect for her husband. Let us now

offer this interpretation of the situation to him. We find him anything but open-minded; he shows a definite resistance to our attempt to correct his faults of awareness. He seems determined to remain misinformed. Perhaps he says, "I *never* mind anything like that; my wife means *nothing* by it," or turns the situation against us by expressing chagrin at our imputing such motives to him and his wife. If he is integrated with us by strong motives of affection or respect, he may be led to entertain our interpretation—usually after a series of unsuccessful rationalizations of his weariness. Even though he thus becomes somewhat aware of, "admits," the fact that he is hurt by his wife's apparent lack of respect for him, he may still maintain that "It is her way; she doesn't know any better; that's the way they treated each other in her home," and so forth. In other words, he is claiming that he was made unpleasantly emotional by a fixed type of reaction of his wife's, which is alleged to have no reference to him personally and which, moreover, is habitual—a sad state of affairs, if true. Let us assume that it is *not* true, that his wife demonstrates a nice discrimination in her more or less contemptuous remarks, reserving them exclusively for her husband. It then appears that, though we have been able to improve the accuracy of his awareness of the character of his motivation, we have failed to correct his information as to the motivation of the other person in provoking his previously misrepresented resentment. He has been punishing the offending person, not for merely existing, but for the specific contumely, though he has been doing so unwittingly. It is really difficult for him to become clearly aware of his prehension [5] of his wife's hostile action; there is a specific

---

[5] The term *to prehend* is used throughout this text to mean an intelligible alteration of the personality by an impinging event. Barring familiarity (similarity) of the event, that which is prehended *tends* to be apprehended or clearly noticed within awareness. Under various circumstances to be discussed later, the effect of a particular prehension on self-consciousness may vary from focal awareness of the event and its personal meaning to a suppression of the self-consciousness, "complete abstraction" or "unconsciousness," or a massive falsification of the event and its personal implications.

To prehend is to have potential information (or misinformation) about an event; to perceive is to have information or misinformation in, or readily accessible to, awareness.

limitation of his personal awareness of the manifestations of her negative attitude. Some supplementary process has been called out in the experiencing of her offense to his self-esteem which has interfered with his having information about it. The substitution of weariness for resentment is a part of this self-deceptive pattern, a way of eliminating awareness of the motive called out by the event, and thus of diminishing the tendency to become informed as to "what is going on" in the situation. His wife, as she is represented in his personal awareness—as an objectification of certain of the relatively persistent processes that make up his self-dynamism—does not manifest hostility towards him. Yet destructive interpersonal processes are to be observed, and the observer may well wonder as to the future course of the marriage.

7. One may perhaps question the propriety of referring to hostility and to destructive processes in the matter of our hypothetical man and wife—whom we shall henceforth identify as Mr. and Mrs. A. A genial neighbor who was present at the scene we observed—Mr. A's weariness after a slight by Mrs. A—would perhaps brush the whole incident aside as trivial, would task us with making mountains out of molehills, might even, if he is superficially acquainted with "psychoanalysis," surmise that we wished the couple ill and therefore grossly misinterpreted their attitudes toward each other. He might ask, for instance, if it is not more constructive for one to substitute weariness for resentment, if Mr. A was not in fact doing the very best he could to keep the peace between himself and his wife, and to avoid exposing his friends to a disagreeable scene. The general statement that bears on all these considerations runs somewhat as follows: Whenever two people are collaborating towards the achievement of a common goal, they and their interpersonal relations make up, compose, and are integrated into a *personal situation*. Factors in this two-group which improve the collaboration, which increase the probability of achieving the goal, are constructive; factors that hinder the collaboration, diminish the probability, are destructive —with reference to the personal situation. If Mrs. A makes remarks which, were they directed to the observer, would be offensive, but which have no unpleasant effect whatever on A, we may be permitted some curiosity as to the phenomenon, but

we would be in error in inferring the presence of destructive processes in the personal situation Mr.-and-Mrs.-A. If Mrs. A's remarks offend A and he is fully aware of his emotion (and retaliatory motivation towards her), the disintegrative effect on the personal situation might still be unimportant. He might resolve the subordinate and contradictory situation integrated by the hostility without particular damage to the major collaboration. In the given case, however, A is not aware of being offended; he is aware of being weary, without reference to Mrs. A or her provocative action. The situation of collaboration is attenuated or suspended by the weariness. He is more or less withdrawn from the A-and-Mrs.-A situation, which becomes subordinate to his preoccupation with himself and his weariness. Under cover, so to speak, of this preoccupation, the action of retaliation goes on in a dominantly hostile, noncollaborative, A-and-Mrs.-A situation. A and Mrs. A are not collaborating in an exchange of hostility. She has acted against him, perhaps with full awareness of her motivation; but he "suffers weariness" while unwittingly acting against her, in his weariness ceasing to be aware of her relevance in his motivation, to this extent passing from a personal to a *parataxic* situation, a much more complicated entity in that two of the *four* or more persons now concerned, while illusory, are real antagonists to any collaboration of A and Mrs. A. Our Mr. A has become multiplex. There is the perduring A who is much the same day after day. There is a transient A who has no awareness of Mrs. A's expressed hostility and of resenting it, much less of hostile motives towards her; the transient A is dimly aware of an illusory Mrs. A, who has an unwaveringly friendly attitude, and is focally aware of his own weariness. Perduring A has to be recognized in any adequate explanation of the total behavior that is to be observed; transient A, however, has no awareness of incompleteness or inadequacy. This, however, does not imply that transient A is comfortable; on the contrary, he is suffering weariness. And, in final answer to our genial friend of the family, perduring A did not consciously make, show, or choose to manifest, transient A and his weariness, in preference to being angered by his wife; the shift from a more or less adequate pattern of interpersonal relations to the parataxically intricate one happened

—and happened so swiftly and by steps so subtle that no trace of what is meant by volition can be discovered in the process.[6]

8. We have been content thus far in our discussion of hypothetical A and Mrs. A to refer to her showing some contempt for her husband, as a result of which he was in some obscure way hurt, slighted, humiliated, offended, angered, and moved to retaliation—although he was not aware of this, but instead felt weary. He *experienced*, lived, underwent, the hostile action; he manifested activity called out by it; but he was not clearly aware of either phase of this, rather avoided our efforts to correct his misinformation about it—and suffered an at first glance wholly irrelevant state, weariness. We have asserted that this course of events was not voluntary but parataxic, an automatic sequence resulting in a complex personal situation including an illusory Mr. A adjusted to an illusory Mrs. A. Let us again review our fancied observations of the sequence, with some extraordinary aids to our senses.

Let us observe Mr. A in the focus of a "slow-motion" camera. When we study our record, we discover that there is ample evidence that Mr. A experienced something connected with Mrs. A's remarks. He glanced sharply at her and looked away very swiftly. The postural tensions in some parts of his face—if not, indeed, in other of his skeletal muscles—changed suddenly, and then changed again, more slowly. The first change may be hard to interpret; the second is apt to reflect the reductions in tone that are habitual in Mr. A when he is tired. Yet farther, let us suppose that, some time prior to the event, we have caused him to drink some "barium milk" and that we are observing the tone of the muscles in his alimentary canal by aid of the fluoroscope at the time that Mrs. A disturbs him. We have noticed that the shadows cast by the barium in the fluid that fills his stomach and small

---

[6] The term *parataxis* to the writer's knowledge, was first used in a psychiatric sense by Dom Thomas V. Moore, M.D., in a paper entitled "The Parataxes" (*Psychoanalytic Rev.* [1921] 8:252–283). It is adopted for use in this text as a generic term with which to indicate sundry maladjustive or nonadjustive situations, some of which might be called in more conventional language "neurotic"—a misleading and much abused word which, with its substantive, "neurosis," might well be relegated to medical history along with "humors" and other monuments of discarded theories.

intestines are of a certain character. The insult comes. We observe, from change in the shape and position of the shadow, that the tone of his stomach walls is changing. His pylorus is becoming much more tense, may actually develop a spasm. The lumen or internal diameter of the small intestines is diminishing; their muscular walls are now more tense. Unlike the first changes in the skeletal muscles, these changes in the visceral muscles develop rather slowly but are persistent. We believe that they begin after the first fleeting shift of postural tension in the skeletal muscles, and that their persistence is connected with the continued feeling of weariness. One might surmise, from all these data, that the impulses which appeared in Mr. A, as he prehended the hostile action of Mrs. A, tended first to the ordinary expression of anger by changes of facial expression, and tensing of some of the other skeletal muscles—perhaps clenching a fist. It would seem that the impulses had very quickly been deflected from these objectively detectable expressive postures and movements, and that they had then discharged themselves by increasing the tension in the musculature of the alimentary tract.

Now if also in our apparatus for augmenting our observational abilities, we had included a device for phonographically recording the speech and adventitious vocal phenomena produced by Mr. A, we would have found interesting data in the field of this peculiarly expressive behavior. Here, too, there would appear a series of phenomena, beginning, perhaps, with an abrupt subvocal change in the flow of the breath. There might appear a rudimentary sort of a gasp. A rapid inhalation may be coincident with the shift in postural tension that we observed in the skeletal muscles. There may then have been a respiratory pause. When Mr. A speaks, we find that his voice has changed its characteristics considerably, and we may secure, in the record of his first sentence, phonographic evidence of a continuing shift of the vocal apparatus, first towards an "angry voice" and then to one somewhat expressive of a state of weary resignation. In brief, with refinements of observational technique applied to the performances of Mr. A as an organism, we find that we can no longer doubt that he experienced, even if he did not perceive, the personal significance of Mrs. A's hostile remark. We see rather impressive evidence of an *inhibition* of a direct, relatively simple, and presumably effective action on his part, and a series of phenomena that may represent the indirect, complicated, and only obscurely effective discharge of the situation. Along with this, we have already observed an inhibition of awareness of his wife's hostility, and the presence in his awareness of the parataxic, illusory, uniformly affectionate Mrs. A.

9. Some of the circumstances surrounding this illusory Mrs. A are peculiarly significant. She is not *all* that Mr. A perceives about his wife. He does not always deceive himself as to her amiability. He has learned, for example, that he cannot alter her dislike for one of his friends, Mr. B, nor can he persuade her to treat Mr. B civilly. Moreover, he has never inhibited his awareness of anger at his wife on occasions when she has been unpleasant to Mr. B. He has quarreled with her repeatedly about it; has condemned her insolence, her attitude of superiority, and her lack of consideration for his feelings for his friend; has finally informed her, with persisting unfriendly feeling, that he is continuing to see Mr. B at his club. In brief, we need assume that Mr. A has but the one illusion about his wife's disposition; namely, that she is uniformly amiable to him. "Of course, we have a spat now and then; but all married people do. We don't agree on everything, but we do agree on each other. We've been married ten years and she's never found a fault with me. And I—why, I'd do it over in a minute. She has made an ideal wife for me. In fact, I think she has been far too considerate of me, she never thinks of herself." As we hear these sentiments, we cannot doubt Mr. A's happiness, nor can we suspect his good faith. He believes; these are convictions that are a part of his self.

Let us explore farther into his views, and ask him, as tactfully as may be, to account for his wife's devotion to him. We learn that he married her because she was so keenly interested in his career. Even from the first, he had to remind himself that she came first, so self-effacing was she. She understands perfectly how exhausting his work can be; is perfectly content to stay at home when he is tired; of course, he sees to it that she has some good times; he has encouraged her to cultivate her natural gifts of musical appreciation and other artistic expression. He did not know this side of life, before marriage, but he has interested himself in it, for her sake, and is now able to enjoy the company of the artist friends that she has accumulated and, if he says it himself, to keep up his end in their conversations. It certainly has not been all on one side; he has gained quite as much as he has given, and his wife's influence has enriched his life very greatly. He did not know Bizet from Bach before he was married and could not tell a Corot from a Rembrandt. He goes with his wife to all the exhibitions now, is beginning a little collection. We recall, perhaps, at this point that the slighting remark that preceded his weariness showed his wife's contempt for his taste in painting. He almost never misses a symphony concert when he is in town, and has season tickets for the Opera. Here we recall to ourselves a friend's comment that Mr. A sleeps through everything but the "Habanera." In a word, while we know that Mr. A does not deceive himself as to his business abilities, does not make many errors of judgment in appraising himself as an executive, and errs rather on the side of underestimating the regard in which he is held by his men friends and acquaintances, it is quite otherwise when he thinks of himself as a husband. His conception of himself as his wife's husband is sadly awry, quite as much in error as is his conception of Mrs. A as his wife. With illusory Mrs. A there goes an illusory Mr. A—the gentleman who is never slighted by this embodiment of amiability and devotion, regardless of the data that our scrutiny of the A-and-Mrs.-A situation reveals. I seek by this fanciful tale to illustrate one of the specific *me-and-you conceptions* that we encounter in any exploration of a person's account of his relations with a (to him) significant person.

We shall now suppose that, instead of participating in the scene of domestic harmony, we are invisibly present at one of the family quarrels—perhaps about Mr. B. Mrs. A has just remarked on the number of evenings that she has had to shift for herself recently, owing, she remarks sarcastically, to her husband's devotion to his cronies. Up to this time, Mr. A has maintained equanimity in the face of her slightly veiled hostility. Now abruptly, he takes a deep breath, glares at her, flings down the newspaper, and in a frankly angry voice says that at least he does not have to listen to crackpots discussing art when he is with his friends. This acts as a cue to his wife, who now sheds all pretense of patience with him. "Don't judge my friends by the fools you spend your evenings with, telling each other what big shots you are and how you'd run the government." There follow sundry extravagant abuses about each other's apparently all-encompassing defects, about the imbecility of each other's friends and preoccupations, and, finally, as the heat mounts steadily, Mrs. A shouts, "And if I ever see that swine B around here again, I'll tell him to his face what he is; and what you are to go around with him." Mr. A undergoes an abrupt change. His color changes; his loud-voiced anger gives place to low-voiced rage. He speaks slowly, perhaps "thickly," as if he had difficulty in articulating his words. He is focally aware of a desire to strike, tear, kill, the illusory Mrs. A who is now before him. She is the epitome of malicious persecutions, a human viper whom the law protects while she taunts him with her ability to destroy his every chance of happiness. He says things about her that would shock him if he were to recall them when he is calm again. She laughs at him as he leaves the room. He is trembling as he goes to the hall closet for his coat and hat. He leaves the house, looks unseeingly at a taxi that pulls in towards the curb, and walks on towards the corner—to find a taxicab. A strange woman who passes him is startled by the hateful look he gives her. At the corner he enters the cab he had previously ignored, gives crisp instructions to take him to the club, and becomes lost in revery. Divorce, mayhem, finding his wife in the arms of a lover—whereupon he, in the presence of witnesses, kills both of them; these are some of the courses of action that flow through his mind. He begins to feel better, overtips the chauffeur at his destination, and orders himself a stiff drink. After sipping it in silence, lost in a revery so deep that he would scarcely be able to recall it, he bethinks himself of companionship, and joins in a game of bridge. In the course of his second rubber, Mr. B comes in and waves a greeting to him. Mr. A nods somewhat jerkily in return. In retrospect, he would have no information about having seen Mr. B. When the game is interrupted, he asks Mr. C to join him in a drink. As the evening wears on, they become immersed in a discussion of women. The views that A now expresses leave no place for the vaguely amiable, self-effacing woman that we encountered in the first of the illusory Mrs. A's. One gathers that women are the factual source of the belief in personal devils. As the refinements of his self-restraint become progressively beclouded, A proceeds to unfold his personal experiences with marriage. He has been deceived, exploited, cheated, humiliated, ignored, ridiculed. The self-confidence that is so necessary in his business has been undermined systematically. He has listened to so much "wishful thinking" that he is getting unrealistic himself. In short, Mr. A, as he now expresses himself, is quite as different from the happy benedict of his previous self-revelation, as is the second illusory Mrs. A from the first. A different "me" corresponds to the different illusory Mrs. A.

10. Each "me" and its appropriate "you" are part-aspects of different configurations that recur in the A-and-Mrs.-A situation as it is extended in time, as the two go on living together. We might speak of an A'-and-Mrs.-A' pattern which is characterized in his consciousness by mutual respect and affection, and an A"-and-Mrs.-A" pattern which is characterized by mutual contempt and hostility. Scrutiny might reveal a third, a fourth, a fifth of these me-you patterns in the interaction of A and his wife. Had we chosen to attend to the wife instead of the husband, we would have found a series of recurrent me-you patterns in her consciousness of herself and her husband. Her several me-conceptions would have been rather simply related to her several conceptions of A as "you." Each, too, would be a part-aspect of a configuration that recurs in their relations.

Let us now consider the circumstances that call out these various me-you patterns in the interactions of A and Mrs. A. We have seen A'-and-Mrs.-A' and A"-and-Mrs.-A". Let us assume a Mrs. A'-and-A' that is an illusion-pair of the tolerant wife-mother to a rather incompetent, absurdly conceited, but devoted husband; and a Mrs. A"-and-A", the disillusioned victim of an utterly selfish man who regards women as inferior creatures for whose services almost anything is extravagant overpayment. It will be apparent that these two sets of patterns can be fairly congruous aspects of two configurations in the A-and-Mrs.-A situation. Mrs. A has a me-you pattern that permits an approximate agreement of mutual illusion when A's motivation is friendly. She has a pattern that "suits" their integration in a frankly hostile relationship. This is usually the case, and the reader, considering his own relations with some intimate, may wonder why I have depicted the pairs of illusions as only imperfectly congruous. The series of me-you patterns and their more or less congruous me-you patterns in the awareness of one's intimate are seldom, severally or collectively, of much value as objectively verifiable descriptions of the two personalities concerned. All that A conceives of Mrs. A, or Mrs. A of A, may be beside the point, excepting in rationalizing their actions with each other. Moreover, the approach towards congruence that we have depicted need not be present; A'-and-Mrs.-A' may coincide with Mrs. A"-and-A". Mr. A will then feel that he is misunderstood, for this or that reason not to his wife's discredit; and Mrs. A, that she is penetrating one of his crafty attempts to mislead her. If situations of this kind recur fairly frequently, new sets of me-you patterns are apt to develop which are less incongruous aspects of the unitary interpersonal situation with which they are associated. This, however, need not be the case. The incongruity in the coincident me-you patterns may grow to such a point that A comes to think "something is wrong" with Mrs. A, and consults a psychiatrist about her. He reports that "she seems to have undergone a complete change. She misunderstands everything I do, thinks I deceive her about everything. The more I try to reassure her, the more suspicious she gets, the more firmly she believes I am doing underhanded things to her. It doesn't make any sense at all, and you can't reason with her." He speaks of a change having occurred in his relation with his wife. While she has always shown some suspiciousness about people, has attributed bad motives to them more frequently than he himself felt was justifiable, this tendency at first did not involve him. As he looks back, he sees that the tendency to think ill of others had been growing on Mrs. A for some considerable time before she centered her hostility on him.

11. The psychiatrist knows that the present state of the A-and-

Mrs.-A situation cannot possibly be formulated in meaningful terms until there are extensive data as to its history. He will wish to secure an outline of the whole history of the situation, will take pains to elucidate the events which culminated in the marriage, will inquire as to the circumstances in which the two became acquainted, the events leading up to their engagement, and the course of their relationship up to the marriage. He will ask as to the history of Mr. A's interest in women; was this his first love; if not, what of the earlier attachments. He will ask as to A's impressions regarding the wife's earlier attachments. He will want to know about the course of the courtship; did either of them have periods of uncertainty. He will ask particularly about their setting the date for marriage; was it precipitate, were there difficulties in deciding on it, did either of them have a change of mind once the date had been set—was the marriage perhaps actually postponed. He will inquire about instances of bad feeling between them that had preceded marriage. He will encourage Mr. A to talk about how these incidents affected him, as to how he disposed of his doubts as to her ideal suitability. He will be interested in almost anything that can be recalled from the very beginning of their relationship and will gradually clarify to himself the chronology (the order in time) of A's me-you patterns. Knowing that in most instances of durable relations there is a rather high degree of congruence in the me-you patterns that develop in the two or three people concerned, he will attend to any indications as to Mrs. A's series of me-you patterns about her husband. It will be evident that from early in their acquaintance, there have been me-you patterns that included some measure of hostility or unfriendliness. It will become clear that this type of me-you pattern has tended to increase in significance as they have gone on living together. Disagreeable scenes between them were originally quite infrequent. "Until my friend B began to visit us, we got on quite well together. My wife took a violent dislike to him. I could never understand it. We got so we never discussed him because it always led to a fight." Careful inquiry will cast some doubt on this peculiar significance given to Mrs. A's dislike of B. The psychiatrist may come to feel that the importance of this particular one of her negative attitudes resides chiefly in its disturbing effect on A. The increasing friction between them could be overlooked by the husband until it involved one of his close personal friends. Had their relations been as harmonious as A thinks, Mrs. A would have offered extensive rationalizations to "account for" her antipathy for Mr. B. Mr. A states that she never explained it, that she was entirely unreasonable about it. The psychiatrist then assumes that A's relationship up to the appearance of Mr. B included complex processes of the general type that we have seen in the substitution of weariness for felt resentment.

The probability that any A has imperfect information about his married life is in every case very considerable. A high degree of objectivity about someone who is important to one is as rare as the conviction is common that one is objective. The psychiatrist presumes that all the informant's accounts will be markedly one-sided, will show strong personal warp. He knows also that he cannot hope to separate truth and illusion unless his own integration with the informant is studied carefully. In securing this part of the history of the A-and-Mrs.-A relationship, the psychiatrist is integrated with Mr. A. Me-you patterns develop in this as in all significant relationships. Somewhere in their conversation, Mr. A may remark, "I do not have very much faith in doctors; and I have even less faith in psychiatrists." He then refers to the case of a relative who developed mental disorder which, he was told, was incurable. She had subsequently recovered, thereby demonstrating the unreliability of psychiatric prognosis. The story goes on to reveal that the patient was seen by several psychiatrists, all but the first of whom—an interne in a psychopathic hospital—having expressed opinions to the effect that she would probably recover. The one incorrect unfavorable opinion seems to have been especially significant in crystallizing A's lack of faith in psychiatry as presented in the current interview. As it is unfriendly to the psychiatrist, it must be recognized to be the presenting feature of a me-you pattern that will have something to do with the information which Mr. A imparts. This does not mean that Mr. A will wittingly omit significant data, will deliberately deceive the psychiatrist as to the facts. It suggests that certain data will not occur to him during the interview; if they occur to him afterwards, they will be dismissed as of no interest to a psychiatrist. Mr. A will have no sense of inadequacy to judge what is important and of interest to a psychiatrist, and the particular data, once recalled and dismissed between interviews, are not apt to appear subsequently.

Let us suppose now that the psychiatrist seeks to expand his acquaintance with the history of the A-and-Mrs.-A situation by consulting other informants. He will desire to confer with some personal friend of Mrs. A and of the husband. For purposes of exposition, we shall presume that these friends are unacquainted one with another. We shall have him confer with Mr. C, Mr. D, Mrs. E, and Miss F. It may become apparent that the impressions of Mrs. A which C has gained from years of acquaintance with the husband are strikingly different from the impressions gained by D during an equally extended acquaintance. Similarly, Mrs. E's impression of A gained over the years from the wife will be rather strikingly different from the impression that Miss F has formed. D's information about Mrs. A differs from C's. Mrs. E's information about A differs from Miss F's. A has never "happened to" tell D about events that he has related to C; and vice versa. Mrs. A has never "happened to" tell Mrs. E some of the things about A that she had told to Miss F; and vice versa.

Factors in the A-and-C situation have influenced the communication of information about the third person, Mrs. A. While there have been some two, three, or four illusory Cs in A's objectification of C; and several more or less congruous illusory As in C's objectification of A; the underlying configurations of the A-and-C situation have precluded the reporting of certain of his illusory Mrs. As in A's conversation with C. If we were able to call this to A's attention, he might say that C was not the sort of person to be interested in such and such attributes of Mrs. A. He might tell us that he had on certain occasions mentioned to C some matters concerning Mrs. A in these unrepresented aspects. Mr. C had paid no attention to this information, had forgotten it, or left it out of consideration in subsequent discussions of Mrs. A. C's opinion of A did not include the possibility of his feeling toward his wife in these unrepresented ways. C's objectification of the personality of Mrs. A, his illusory Mrs. A, is thus seen to be a fairly simple function of the A-and-C situation, but it is also a function of a C-imaginary-Mrs.-A situation; that is, it includes complex processes that are suggested when C says, "Well, if she were my wife . . . ." It might well seem that anything which C can offer as his impression of the to him actual unknown Mrs. A will be of little use in formulating an outline of her personality. The psychiatrist could perhaps make little headway if all of his information about A and Mrs. A came through these highly mediate interpersonal channels.

The mental disorder of Mrs. A, the psychiatrist's focal problem, has eventuated in the course of her life with A. While she has been living with A, A has been an important factor in her life. She knows something about his significance, and he knows something about his significance. Her accessible information is bound up in a series of me-you patterns, the variety of which has become restricted to a very hostile Mrs. A'''-and-A''' pattern. While the psychiatrist by appropriate steps could probably recover data on the whole series of A's illusory Mrs. A*s*, as they are recorded in his memory, a parallel recall could not be obtained in Mrs. A as she now is. In other words, among the changes that she has undergone, there is one that makes it difficult to remind her of the me-you patterns about her husband which are at striking variance with the now dominant pattern. Even though the psychiatrist, in the course of a long conversation, reminds her of an earlier me-you pattern in which Mr. A was represented as anything but a hostile and dangerous person—an achievement that may be quite difficult—he will be no nearer to convincing Mrs. A that she has undergone a striking change in the freedom with which she objectifies her husband. She will probably account for the earlier friendly illusions about her husband as mistakes which she has subsequently corrected. As an alternative, she may hold that Mr. A himself has undergone a marked change. In the first case, when next she sees the psychiatrist, Mrs. A will have elaborated some data with which to prove that her former favorable impressions were the result of the fraud and dishonesty in Mr. A which she has finally come to understand. While the psychiatrist may have made her somewhat uncomfortable when first she recalled the earlier personification, this is no longer possible in that connection. She believes entirely the correctness of her present me-you pattern, and the belief is not to be shaken.

In the face of so potent a factor, the psychiatrist in pursuit of information as to the history of Mrs. A's me-you patterns must have recourse to her friends. Again, in his conferences with Mrs. E and Miss F, he has to formulate the relation of each with him as best he can, [that is,] he must make some inquiries purposed to illuminate the characteristics of the illusory psychiatrist to whom each is addressing her remarks. He will seek mediate data on the Mrs. A-and-A situation. He will know that Mrs. E, for example, has developed an illusory A as a particular manifestation of some of the recurrent configurations that have characterized the enduring Mrs. E-and-Mrs.-A situation. His inquiry will bear significantly on the history of the latter. Without considerable information on this, Mrs. E's impressions about Mr. A would be practically beyond interpretation. As Mrs. E herself has a husband, the psychiatrist may encourage her to present contrasts between her married life and that of her friend, and between Mr. E and Mr. A as she knows him. Similarly, in his conferences with Miss F, having obtained some clues from time to time as to the illusory psychiatrist with whom she is communicating, he will develop the history of the Miss-F-and-Mrs.-A relationship. In all these conferences, he will attend to many phenomena besides the actual verbal contexts. He will note, for example, that whenever Miss F is discussing men, her voice, intonation, attitude, and set facial expression indicate something of a rigid attitude. Her replies to not too direct questions confirm his surmise that Miss F has an unfriendly view of men in general. This has value as collateral information concerning the configurations that have characterized the Miss-F-and-Mrs.-A situation. He comes ultimately to inquire as to Miss F's views of marriage, her preference for the single state, and how Mrs. A may have influenced her in this particular. He may ask finally if Mrs. A in bygone years urged Miss F to marry. She is surprised to recall that such was indeed the case. These contexts shed light on the factors which have resulted in the exclusion of some favorable illusions concerning A from the wife's discussion of him with her unmarried friend. For parallel reasons, Miss F in her account recalls certain facts that may have "escaped" not only Mrs. A herself, but also Mrs. E. In particular, the time-ordering of events—which preceded which—in the recollections respectively of Mrs. E and Miss F, may vary widely. Some of these discrepancies may be especially useful bases for exploration in subsequent conferences with any one of the informants.

12. Everyone with whom one has been in any significant relationship, from birth onward, is a potential informant about one. Informants are able to express a body of illusions that they have developed in the interpersonal situations in which they have been integrated. In the body of illusions that they can communicate, there are data capable of elaboration into more valid information than they themselves have formulated. This is chiefly because everyone prehends much more than he perceives; at the same time, one's behavior is affected by all that one has experienced, whether it was prehended or consciously perceived. The psychiatrist, in developing his skill in interrogating informants, learns to integrate situations the configurations of which provoke the elaboration of information that was previously potential. He thus obtains more data from the informant than the latter has clearly perceived. The informant, so to speak, tells more than he knows. The data are more significant to the psychiatrist because he has more experience and more freedom in formulating interpersonal processes. He is alert to implications; his alertness is oriented to understanding interpersonal processes; and he has many fewer specific inhibitions of alertness in the interpersonal configurations in which he participates. From the relative accessibility of his own past, and from intimate contact with the developmental history of a number of people, he has a considerable grasp on the actual dynamics of interpersonal relations. He knows more about the processes that can occur in these configurations; in particular, he knows that certain alleged processes are highly improbable. Reports of these alleged events are, therefore, most probably rationalizations, and he is able, from experience or by inquiry, to secure clues to the unwitting motivations that underlie these conventional statements.

Certainty about interpersonal processes is an ideal that should seldom concern one. Information about any situation should be considered as a formulation of probability. Information about a person may vary from very high probability—my companion is in the same room; to extremely low—my companion understands me perfectly. The physical factors in situations are often quite accurately measurable; they can be described in specialized language in a manner that contributes to an approximate *consensus* in the people who are considering the situation. This requires similarity of experience with the specialized language. Two people looking at this page may express different opinions as to the color of the paper. One may say it is yellow;* the other, that it is yellow-green. It is quite possible that a third observer may call it a deep orange; it is equally possible that a fourth may call it a vivid green. In the first pair of observers, the probability is that they had much the same initial prehensions, that the difference is primarily a difference in language. In the third and fourth observer, we must suspect differences in the initial prehensions. The spectral reflection of light by this paper includes green, yellow, orange, and red—the last three in approximately equal degree. The visual efficiency of light of different wave-lengths is rather widely variable in different people, the average maximum being in the yellow-green, falling off rather steeply in the green and orange. The long and the short waves producing relatively little effect when they impinge on the retina, the paper *looks* yellow (or yellow-green). In color-blind persons the experience caused by encountering colored light is markedly different from the average, and, while the meaning of their terms for these experiences are also necessarily different from the average, the more striking difference is in the initial prehension. A person in whom the prehension of green is lacking may, none the less, state that a green object is green. When we investigate this anomalous situation, we find that he has learned to call a particular gray appearance by the name of green—people have always been talking to him about how beautiful the green fields are, how bright this or that green is, how the traffic light is now green. Despite a fundamental defect in color-perception, he has come to talk

[* This was originally printed on the yellow paper of the journal *Psychiatry*. H.S.P.]

about colors much as others do. While he can be led to mention his color-blindness, he has found that it is a difference that does not enhance the regard in which he is held by others. It may make people "nervous" to ride with him when he is driving his car. Some people amuse themselves by testing his color-perception. His language behavior has been developed to shield him from these and many other unpleasant consequences of difference. A discussion with him of the merits of a Monet is obviously a much more complex process than an unsuspecting companion might believe.

When one has regard for the multiple me-you patterns that complicate interpersonal relations, for the possible differences in individual prehension of events, and for the peculiarities of language behavior which characterize each of us . . . the practical impossibility of one-to-one correspondence of mental states of the observer and the observed person should be evident. We never know all about another, we are fortunate when we achieve an approximate consensus and can carry on meaningful communication about relatively simple contexts of experience. Most of us spend the greater part of our social life in much less adequate contact with our interlocutors, with whom we manifest considerable skill at avoiding frank misunderstanding, with whom in fact we agree and disagree quite often with very little consensus as to subject of discussion. The psychiatrist of all people knows the relative character of his formulation of the other person, even if he has gained such skill that he is often quite correct.

4

Commentary

IN DECEMBER, 1938, the American Association for the Advancement of
Science, meeting in Richmond, Virginia, had six sections on Mental
Health, and Sullivan acted as chairman of the section on "Physical
and Cultural Environment in Relation to the Conservation of Mental
Health." Three symposia on public health had been previously
sponsored by the Association (the Cancer Problem, Tuberculosis and
Leprosy, and Syphilis). That the Association should have considered
Mental Health as the fourth subject for a public-health symposium at
this time was largely due to the energy and drive of Sullivan in
organizing it, according to Lawrence K. Frank.[1] Sullivan's section
included papers by Edward Sapir, Ruth Benedict, Charles C. Lim-
burg, Dorothy Swaine Thomas, Howard Rowland, and Harold D.
Lasswell.[2] It was the only section in which all the main contributions were from social scientists, although one other section, "The
Economic Aspects of Mental Health," had heavy representation from
the social sciences. The interdisciplinary nature of Sullivan's section
is self-evident from the names of the contributors, but the brilliance
of the contributions today after the lapse of almost twenty-five
years can only be appreciated by reading them as a group. Sullivan's
contribution to the symposium is mainly a summing-up of the
contributions made by the others, and it has not been included here
for that reason. The last paragraph of Sullivan's "Summary and

[1] Personal communication, Lawrence K. Frank.
[2] For the full text of these papers, see *Mental Health*, edited by Forest
Ray Moulton (AAAS Publication No. 9); Lancaster, Pa.: The Science Press,
1939; pp. 237–287. This section also includes formal and informal discussion
of the main contributions, including an interesting statement by Frank on
education and its relation to the promotion of mental hygiene.

Critique" (entitled "Man as Man") is, however, worth quoting to illustrate a perspective developed in the next selection:

This session of the symposium teaches us that we must study people as people, in the setting of the times and in their actual social-cultural environment, if we hope to uncover the factors that make for failure and mental disorder on the one hand, for success and mental health on the other. There are many fields of data that must be covered, many complex factors to be uncovered and assessed. The exploration calls for scientists who are intensely interested in man and his actual conduct among men and man-made institutions, rather than in parts of the human body or pale abstract formulae about people, or money, or work and play. The scientists of the future who will contribute most to these investigations will have rather broader training than has the average contemporary psychiatrist or social scientist. They will combine much that is best in the conceptual frameworks of these disciplines with greatly enhanced powers of participant observation.[3]

The 1938 presidential address at the Richmond meeting, given by a Harvard mathematician and physicist, George Birkhoff, was entitled "Intuition, Reason and Faith in Science." In an unsigned editorial in the February, 1939, issue of *Psychiatry*, Sullivan dueled with Birkhoff in a friendly fashion over some of the important issues raised by Birkhoff, and this editorial forms the next selection.

In his address to the AAAS, Birkhoff had insisted that man as scientist or thinker always uses a mixture of intuition, reason, and faith in dealing with reality or experience. In the most exact formulations of natural science, all three are present, for example. In a series of examples from mathematics, physics, biology, psychology, and sociology, Birkhoff showed that the limitations of reason are compensated for by intuition and faith.

In commenting on the address, Sullivan has extended Birkhoff's proposition logically as a way of criticizing some of Birkhoff's untutored notions about the nature of contemporary social science or psychiatry. Birkhoff had demonstrated, with illustrations from the history of mathematics, that from time to time generally accepted intuitions had been misleading and had occasioned reformulations. But mathematics is not unique in this respect, Sullivan thinks; in dealing with man's behavior in a scientific way, generally accepted intuitions can be just as misleading from time to time and demand

[3] *Mental Health, ibid.,* see p. 278.

reformulation. Sullivan proposes that the intuitive demarcation of the levels or realms of knowledge or reality (which Birkhoff has taken from Comte) requires reformulation so that there can be a greater place for reason (and scientific method) in the study of man. While we know relatively little about personality, "one at least begins to see," Sullivan notes, "that the facts of interpersonal relations are scarcely to be sought under the aegis of a personal faith appropriate to a student of *mind* or to a student of *society*. . . . It seems as if the basic concept *mind* characterizing the psychological level as a field superior in complexity to the biological (with basic concept of *organism*) may well be restudied on the basis of the intuition that the universe presents three aspects: the impersonal, the interpersonal, and the subjective." From this point on, through all his subsequent writings, it seems that Sullivan uses this three-fold classification of the universe in his thinking, although he is seldom explicit about it again. The *impersonal* is obviously closely related to the not-man of the cultural anthropologist; the *interpersonal* might be translated into the public mode of Bridgman; and the *subjective* into Bridgman's private mode.[4]

Sullivan again states in this editorial that the new level of knowledge for dealing with human beings is found somewhere between the disciplines of social psychology and psychiatry, both of which have assets and liabilities for the task. "The social psychologist is . . . not quite as naive as is the (biological) psychiatrist. It might appear that psychiatry should then become a satellite of social psychology, or otherwise identify itself as a social science." But no such simple solution is possible, Sullivan thinks, because sick people apply to the medical profession for help. There remains the problem of how the social scientist is to work with the psychiatrist in the interdisciplinary task without the social scientist feeling that he is being subordinated to the medical discipline—a task which Sullivan touches on but does not solve; this dilemma as posed by Sullivan in 1939 still remains a central one today.

In this paper for the first time Sullivan expresses clear discontent with Adolf Meyer's formulation. Meyer had made the *individual human organism* the unit for study, and this is common sense and

---

[4] Bridgman's public and private mode, and its relation to Sullivan's thinking, is discussed elsewhere in this book. See index entry for Public mode.

powerfully entrenched in the culture, Sullivan notes. Yet *interpersonal phenomena* are the units for study and "persons (personalities) are the entities which we infer in order to explain interpersonal events and relations."

Intuition, Reason, and Faith†

DEAN GEORGE D. BIRKHOFF's presidential address to the American Association for the Advancement of Science at its recent meeting at Richmond, Virginia, was entitled "Intuition, Reason and Faith in Science." [1] It merits most careful study by physicians, psychiatrists, and social scientists.

Dr. Birkhoff warns as to the distortion of viewpoint that arises if one chooses "to select . . . as somehow more real than the others" some particular one of the concepts respectively basic in the five-fold hierarchy of the mathematical, the physical, the biological, the psychological, and the social. Resymbolized in the special language appropriate to psychiatry as the study of interpersonal relations, one may be said to manifest a degree of parergasia if his personal necessities eventuate in thinking about facts on one of these levels of knowledge in the special language appropriate to another level. "Does it clarify our idea of social justice to try to explain it in terms of the reactions between protons and electrons in the brain?" asks Professor Birkhoff, in another connection stating "the basic belief of the professional psychologist is in the completeness of the physiological accompaniment of every psychical fact . . ." although nearly all of us "see all sorts of permanent values in personality, not adequately characterized in neural terms," that lead ". . . us to have deep affections and abiding personal loyalties, whether or not we are psychologists!" This contrast between the article of personal faith of the psychologist

† Reprinted from *Psychiatry* (1939) 2:129–132 [unsigned editorial].
[1] Printed in full in *Science* (1938) 88[o.s.2296]:601–609.

and his governance in living by the intuition of personal facts is exceedingly significant in psychiatric thinking. While one may agree that "as yet we know relatively little about the phenomena of personality," one at least begins to see that the facts of inter-personal relations are scarcely to be sought under the aegis of a personal faith appropriate to a student of *mind* or to a student of *society*.

Dr. Birkhoff remarks that the professional psychologist finds much illumination in the facts of abnormal psychology, although "even the psychiatrist, familiar with many concrete cases, must treat each new patient by the inductive method." He feels from a conviction natural to a mathematician that there is an infinity of hidden organization in our universe, wherefore "any broad conclusions concerning the nature of personality would seem altogether premature." We believe that this treatment of the subject is un-necessarily forbidding; that his conviction might more justifiably eventuate in a questioning of the levels of knowledge that he posits. It seems as if the basic concept *mind* characterizing the psychological level as a field superior in complexity to the biological (with basic concept of *organism*) may well be restudied on the basis of the intuition that the universe presents three aspects: the impersonal, the interpersonal, and the subjective.

It seems that in the distant centuries of prehistory, man came inevitably to the conviction that he himself and others like him included entities distinctive from the time-and-space-bound corporal body which ate, slept, and engaged in sundry other biological activities. His basic ideas in this field were variously *animus, spirit, soul*. Dream phenomena were doubtless the primary data from which arose these intuitions. In any case, he arrived at the conviction that the universe included embodied and disembodied entities of this sort. The advancement of knowledge, chiefly by the scientific method, has vastly complicated the data of reality and has for the most part removed this type of conviction from the realms of observation, experimentation, and reflective induction. Consensual validation—the technique by which intuitional truths are made safe premises for inference, and for that "careful application of impartial thoroughgoing analysis" which, as Dr. Birkhoff remarks, "is as important for everyday living as it is in the study and the laboratory"—has found much more ready application in the nonanimistic realm. The dichotomous attitude (faith, if you please), however, for the most part has persisted around the world. In the Western culture, it recently expressed itself in the belief in *alternative* methods of psychological investigation—the introspective and the objective. Freud and his students, whatever may be thought of their hypotheses about the "psychic apparatus" and society, did great service for Western thought in revealing the experiential origin of limitations of personal awareness. With the widening of our factual horizons through the work of the cultural anthropologists, this paved the way for the emergence of a new basic concept, the *person* or *personality*.

In the hierarchy of reality and knowledge, we now find between the psychological and the social levels, the psychiatric or social-psychological. Its basic concept is neither *mind* nor *society* but *person*. It requires and is slowly developing an appropriate special language. This language is essentially independent of the languages necessary and appropriate to the other levels.

Psychiatry is coupled with social psychology in naming this new level of reality and knowledge. Social psychology emerged on the relatively sterile grounds of the academic psychologies, while psychiatry has had a long development as a specialization of medicine. Each brings assets and liabilities from its source. Medicine as a science has been a biological science. Theories of physiology and pathology have become more perfect almost exactly to the extent that they are good biological theories. Disease, however, is manifested by concrete patients who are also people. Medical knowledge is applied to prevent and to remedy disease by physicians who are likewise people. The practice of medicine is a particular specialized field of interpersonal relations. As Dr. Louis Hamman, the Baltimore internist, said in a brilliant statement to the Richmond Symposium, the physician, consciously or otherwise, depends for success in his practice on his abilities as a psychiatrist.* Again, people who are sick are

[* See, for instance, Louis Hamman, "The Relation of Psychiatry to Internal Medicine," in *Mental Health*, edited by Forest Ray Moulton (AAAS Publication No. 9); Lancaster, Pa.: The Science Press, 1939. H.S.P.]

affected in the field of their interpersonal relations. Moreover, it is becoming evident that interpersonal factors often give rise to sickness which manifests much the same symptoms as do "organic" diseases. There are "functional" aggravations of somatically conditioned illness. Interpersonal factors undoubtedly facilitate or prevent recovery in many cases; abbreviate or prolong disability in many people. The conscientious physician needs, therefore, to have a considerable fund of accessible, practical psychiatric knowledge. As this aspect of medical education has been grossly neglected, he seeks to remedy his defect by reading and consultation with psychiatric authorities. He generally finds them incomprehensible. Their terminology is a barrier to communication and he often—now all too often, correctly—surmises that they have much less to offer him than he needs.

This attitude of the general medical man towards psychiatric terminology is not, however, entirely reasonable. Both he and many of the psychiatrists are misled by the biological orientation of medicine. The proper language of biology is not adequate to psychiatry and any attempt to make sense of interpersonal events and relations in strictly biological terms is foredoomed to "neurologizing tautology," obscurantist reification, or circular reasoning. The social psychologist is apt to be at a considerable advantage here, for psychology—for all its faith in a more or less realistic physiology—stems from a long history of theorizing about "human nature" and the human mind. Social psychology arose from this by way of functional and experimental psychology, and crystallized its interest in the interaction of the social order and the individual—at which point it benefited from the elaborations of the cultural anthropologist and other social scientists. The social psychologist is, therefore, not quite as naive as is the (biological) psychiatrist. It might appear that psychiatry should then become a satellite of social psychology, or otherwise identify itself as a social science.

No so simple solution of the problem is to be considered, however, for sick people apply to doctors and psychiatrists for help. The people to whom the ailing apply have need for medical knowledge, for the "organic" and the "functional" overlap as already stated, and there are many therapeutic tools that are useful adjuvants to more purely psychiatric techniques. Moreover, intercurrent illness may appear insidiously in the course of "neurotic" disorders, and more seriously disturbed patients may present a variety of acute medical problems at various stages of treatment. There is no practical solution other than equipping the general medical man with a sufficient working knowledge of psychiatry, and training a corps of psychiatrists for the effective treatment of involved and ominous mental states. An adequate formulation of psychiatry is, therefore, imperative, whereon the physician must add to his conceptual system the necessary breadth of view that psychiatry requires.

It is manifestly impossible to formulate all the difficulties of human adaptation in biological terms, in psychological terms, or in sociological terms; or, for that matter, in a meaningful blend of any or all of these. The psychobiology of Adolf Meyer is the most distinguished recent effort to find a new locus for problems, a new level of reality and knowledge, and new conceptual tools. Meyer recognizes the hierarchies of organization and proceeds from a consideration of organismic integrating factors—the nervous systems and autocoid dynamisms, in particular—to bridge the gap between biology and psychiatry by the concept of *mentation*, a peculiarly effective integrating activity by the use of symbols and meanings. So great is the power of his conceptual system that one may easily believe that he has in fact made a great refinement of psychology, has finally emancipated it from its medieval heritage. His primary entity, however, is still the *individual human organism* that in some fashion engages in the wonderfully effective integrative use of symbols and meanings.

This common-sense attitude interpenetrates the culture and is powerfully entrenched in almost everyone. Personality is manifest, however, in interpersonal situations, only. The phenomenal presence of personality *in or about* a discrete living being is not demonstrable and need not be assumed. Personality phenomena are conditional on the relevant personal situation, which always includes at least one other person—who need not be contemporarily real or immediately present as an embodied human organism. Persons (personalities) are the entities which we infer in order to explain interpersonal events and relations. We may believe that they are functional products of cultural entities *and* individuals of the species *homo sapiens*. Certainly, the occasional 'feral man' is not a person. Idiots also are not people. The relationship of personality and a particular type of career-line may be illuminating, as in the 'deterioration' of certain chronically psychotic people. In any case, the facts that are the data of psychiatry are perceived interpersonal events, and it is from the application of the scientific method to these data that the theory of psychiatry is to be evolved.

When this theory shall have been elaborated, it will synthesize much that is good in the biology of higher organisms, in the social psychology of the human young, in cultural anthropology and in linguistics, epistemology, scientific method, ecology, social geography, economics, social statistics, political science and administration. It will generalize much of this data and provide new orientations in all these fields of study. It will not be of any of them. It will be the general science of human living, and from it a body of specific techniques for living and for the improvement of inadequate living will be derived. In place of the relatively inexplicable successes and failures of our present psychiatric techniques, there will be precise communicable knowledge. Instead of more or less obviously prejudiced attitudes about eugenic, pediatric, educational, social, legal, penal, and religious reforms, we shall have dependable indications as to desirable goals and workable approaches. What Dr. Birkhoff says of the achievements of the quantum physics of today—"The process involved somehow reminds me of a record sea voyage made through a fog!"—is perfectly appropriate to the achievements of man in his sundry culture-complexes that have appeared thus far. Once we have evolved some superior formulations to make sense of the brute facts of everyday life, and somewhat uncovered the processes underlying these brute facts, we may discover consistencies and lawfulnesses in our universe of which we can today form no foresight whatever.

5

Commentary

THE NEXT PAPER, "A Note on Formulating the Relationship of the Individual and the Group," is a part of a symposium on "The Individual and the Group," in the May, 1939, issue of the *American Journal of Sociology*, with Louis Wirth commenting on the various contributions written by Florian Znaniecki, Kurt Lewin, Floyd H. Allport, Bronislaw Malinowski, and others. Sullivan has dutifully used the word "individual" in the title of the article, for the purpose of meeting the assignment, but it is a term he has already discarded in his thinking. In the article, Sullivan makes quite clear that the word "individual" is not scientifically accurate for the uses of the science psychiatry.

In commenting on Sullivan's contribution, Wirth notes that he "comes to the problem of the individual and society with a rich clinical experience which might be expected to predispose him to a view which emphasizes the primacy of the organism. It is therefore gratifying to note that the universe of interpersonal relations, which constitutes his central field of interest, is almost identical with the modern sociological approach."

A Note on Formulating
the Relationship of the
Individual and the Group †

WE THINK conventionally of ourself as a person and of others as individual persons or individuals. This is a convention of reference strongly intrenched in our language and widely disseminated in our culture. It seems to derive immediately from our observations of gross biological phenomena, and any other view would seem to be nothing short of absurd. I am here and not elsewhere. This is my hand, the expression of my thought. It is true that I must maintain recurrent communion with the environing supply of oxygen, water, and other substances. It may even be true that I cannot continue very long to manifest essentially human traits unless I maintain recurrent communion with other people. But my individuality as a concrete human being does not seem to be impaired by these perduring necessities which affect everyone in exactly the same way and to much the same degree that they affect me.

I may go farther and describe myself in generic terms: white, American, denizen of the Western culture in its transitional phase from the Industrial Era. I agree that I would not be myself if I were a Negro—American or African. I have no difficulty in understanding that as I, myself, I am largely a product of ac-

† Reprinted from *Amer. J. Sociology* (1938–39) 44:932–937.

culturation and as such not particularly different in many culturally controlled respects from a great many white Americans of approximately my somatic age and educational background. But I shall insist that, however like some average people I may be in many respects, I am nonetheless the product of a unique course of acculturation; I have undergone a unique series of events many of which have left their impress in my own personal memory. I know that I have come to have a relatively durable congeries of traits or characteristics (which I call my personality) which singles me out from everyone else. In a word, I am a person of some, however little, distinction; and there are at least a few other people who would be emphatic in supporting this judgment. They know me; they can tell you exactly what to expect if you have dealings with me. Should you confuse me with some other stranger about whom you have been told, you will gradually realize your error as you talk with me. You will see that my personality is different from the one with which you erroneously believed yourself to be dealing.

One may pause here to consider how often one has actually failed to observe these presumably specific differences of personality, has carried on serious conversation with the wrong person without any realization of the error in identification. These instances may not seem to have been at all numerous; this, however, in all likelihood is sheer illusion of memory. Most people would learn a great deal if they could study the negative instances of their identifying a stranger in terms of his reputed personality. So strongly ingrained in us is the conviction that we ought to be able to perceive the "personal traits" of other people that our feeling of personal security is involved in this norm of the "knower of men." In fact, the less secure one feels, the greater comfort one derives from a facile classifying of other people among various patterns of projection of one's own presumptively static traits—and their verbal opposites.

From infancy each of us is trained to think in this way. If one was fortunately born, the parents have been fairly consistent in their expressed appraisals, and one has elaborated a dependable self. However absurdly it may be related to one's manifest behavior, one is relatively secure in dealing with others. If one's parents have been less reassuring or if experience subsequent to childhood has demonstrated the serious deficiency of a once-trusted illusion as to one's personality, the case is quite otherwise. "I did not think you were *that* kind of a person" comes to be a very painful remark, the deeper implications of which do not engage one's attention. One becomes as realistically as possible a member of the group made up of the right kind of people and acts as rightly as possible in those restricted interpersonal contexts in which one still has freedom to participate.

The traits with which one believes one's self characterized are often amazingly fluid, if one's serious statements are to be taken as evidence. Discussing one's self with one person, one reports one perhaps only moderately consistent set. In an equally serious discussion with a different auditor the account is different. Some people are consistent in referring to certain outstanding traits about which a consensus could be obtained; some are consistent only in the breach—the traits that they generally claim are those which come near being merely ideal; the statements express wishful rather than factual data. Some know that their accounts vary with different auditors and can even rationalize noted differences —usually on the basis of the attitude of the auditor and one's wanting to make as good an impression as possible. The traits with which we endow others are also of varying certainty and sometimes subject to radical change under pressure of divergent opinion. The shift may not appear in the course of the particular controversy but may become evident in subsequent discussions. About all that seems perfectly certain about personal traits as subjects of opinion is that the having of such opinions seems important.

The interpretation of behavior is generally regarded as of a higher probability than is the analysis of conversation about one's self. It is easier to say the right thing than to keep on doing the right thing. This truism is not to be taken too seriously, however, for some people show high consistency over long periods in behavior that expresses a role which they feel is incongruous to them but demanded by the other person. Success in "acting like" this incongruous person does not excite them to much speculation about their "real" personality, perhaps for the good reason that it is but a particular, a clearly noticed, instance of something that has been going on from very early years.

The psychiatrist has to regard each personality (individual, unique person) as an indeterminate entity some significant characteristics of which may be inferred from the processes that occur in the group of persons—real and fantastic—in which the subject-individual participates. Participation is a pattern of processes and, in seeking to delimit the universe of interpersonal relations, the psychiatrist may begin with those psychobiological states in which interpersonal processes do not occur. These are chiefly two: deep sleep and panic. Panic is that condition which is beyond or in excess of complete insecurity. Deep sleep is antithetic in that it can appear only in the absence of insecurity or after neutralization of all insecurity-provoking factors. Behavior is impossible in either state, and the appearance of implicit (mental) activity marks the change alike from panic or from deep sleep toward a more characteristically human condition. Panic is the extreme of a series of states that grades through insecurity and fear to mild anxiety. Deep sleep is the extreme of a series including various levels of what may be called "active" sleep, somnolent detachment, and inattentive reverie states.

The reality of relevant other people is vestigial in severe insecurity and in all the sleep-states. Interpersonal phenomena are present, but the people concerned are largely fantastic, complexly related to real people. Characteristics of related real people have been magnified or minimized, moved from one personality to another, combined in poignantly artificial patterns. Experiences from long ago involving people but remotely related to those seemingly involved contribute elements to the fantastic personalizations. The novel and unreal are created out of items of actual experience, but the items are combined into patterns that reveal little about anyone except the subject-individual, himself in a state bordering on the primitive, if not, in fact, on the infrahuman, type of integration.

These are the minimal limits of interpersonal relations. What are the maximal? To find these limits of his field, the psychiatrist organizes his observations of the most durable and the most effective interpersonal situations. Duration is a directional function in time. Effectiveness is less easy to define but must, too, have some reference to vector quality.[1] Remembering that only inter-personal phenomena can be observed, an effective situation must be one that shows directional change in the interpersonal processes and hence in the series of interpersonal situations in which the subject-individual is involved. Maximal interpersonal relations must then be those that approach the span of a lifetime in duration and those that most powerfully alter the integrating tendencies of the person chiefly concerned.

Integrating tendencies are conceived to be the psychobiological substrata of the corresponding integrated interpersonal situations. Person A tends to integrate with Person B a situation to the more or less clearly envisaged end of improving his social status, thus relieving felt insecurity. Provisionally, we assume that, if any incipient A-B situation appears, Person B also tended to integrate a situation with a person such as Person A is apprehended to be. We need not assume that the integrating tendencies respectively of A toward B and of B toward A are in any sense comple-mentary. If they happen to be complementary—if B tends to integrate a situation of the vassalage [2] type with A—and if there are no stronger integrating tendencies that conflict, the A-B situation is consolidated and endures until its tensional aspect shall have been resolved. If the integrating tendencies that coincided in the incipient A-B situation are not complementary, B's inte-grating tendency is powerful, and there is no strong conflicting tendency, there will develop a $B-A_2$ situation which will have value to A, but is not likely to relieve the insecurity about status and deference. The incipient A-B situation will in any other

[1] The conception of an ultimate vector analysis of behavior was first for-mulated by the writer at the 1930 Hanover Conference of the Social Science Research Council and appears in abstract in its proceedings. Since that time some fairly extensive raids on the language of physics have been conducted by psychiatrists and psychologists (see in this connection an editorial, "Intuition, Reason, and Faith"). [See preceding article in this book.]

[2] The term "vassalage" is used to refer to the more completely dependent-identification situations in which one of the people concerned seems to act as if he were the source of decisive impulses, while the other (or others) act as if they were but effector organizations for realizing these impulses. This sort of situation grades through limited dependency relations and re-stricted identification-attachments to lucid (consensually valid) subordina-tions to competent leadership or example.

case disintegrate promptly, generally with increased feeling of insecurity on the part of A, who will tend somewhat more urgently to integrate a presumably reassuring situation with some other person apprehended by him as in the same class as B; that is, useful in improving A's status. The B-A_2 situation, on the other hand, may be effective in significantly changing this particular integrating tendency in A, so that his insecurity about status disappears.

One must observe that interpersonal situations may have multiple integration, and that durable situations may include more transient multiple integrated phases. Love situations often show recurrent episodes of lust and are not quite the same [in episodes of] mutual sexual excitement, [in episodes of] "untimely" excitement of one partner, and in the intervals [between the episodes]. The tendencies to integrate lustful-erotic situations should not be confused with those which eventuate in love situations. The latter may survive indefinitely the loss of prospective sexual satisfactions or the integration of sexual situations with persons not in the love relationship.[3]

I have now presented in extreme abstract the conceptual framework of the psychiatric study of interpersonal relations, which would seem to have relevance to the sociopsychological study of the relations of the individual and the various groups with which he is more or less identified. I hope that it is clear that the psychiatrist must usually confine his exploration to (1) situations in which he himself takes part—in which his trained alertness may help him to analyze the incipient situations—and (2) those other situations concerned in the life of his subject-individual which have been either very durable or clearly effective in changing the course of the individual's manifest interpersonal living. Verbal report and collateral evidence are useful in establishing the second category of data. In actual practice certainty is greatest in working back from the first type of data through the second. Without what we may call the immediate experimental situation and the historic view, it is often extremely difficult to get access to a

---

[3] See also "A Note on the Implications of Psychiatry, the Study of Interpersonal Relations, for Investigations in the Social Sciences," and "The Data of Psychiatry." [Both articles appear earlier in this book.]

particular group relationship. Durable associations in the general interest of beauty, truth, or humanity—security, love, lust, income, deference—may readily be mistaken one for another by the investigator. The subject-individual, if the relationship to the psychiatrist is not explicit, may also "mislead himself" almost endlessly.

It is clear that the study of interpersonal relations in contrast to the study of persons and group has validity. The demarcation of the field is made difficult by the conventions of speech and thought and by other aspects of the controlling culture. The new type of orientation that can be obtained by this type of approach is quite certain to be fruitful both in social theory and practice. It has some fundamental implications for the field of education.

6

Commentary

WHILE THE FOLLOWING article, originally published as an editorial, was undoubtedly evoked by the actions of the Nazis in Germany, Sullivan has only made passing reference to the fact that "hatred of the Jews has been made a national creed by at least one state." Instead he traces the etiology of this hatred in any person trained in the Christian tradition and posits the necessity for extreme introspection, even by the psychiatrist, if this irrational prejudice is to be overcome. While Sullivan compares anti-Semitism to other prejudices against minorities, he states that it is the most general of all prejudices. All Jews have one characteristic: "they have been taught to expect at least covert anti-Semitism. . . . this characteristic is inevitable as long as Christian teaching distinguishes the Jews and makes them hatefully different."

It is clear that Sullivan sees some connection between the intensity of the prejudice and the presence of resentment at parental authority: "All too many children have come along paths that make them cruel. In these, often the products of unwitting punitive influences wholly beyond their capacity for rationalizing, the torture of Jesus may strike a peculiarly responsive chord. A displacement of resentment at absolutistic parental authority on to the persecuting Jews is convenient. . . ." In this particular, he anticipates, of course, some of the findings from later studies of prejudice. At the same time, he again generalizes the presence of the prejudice, in varying degrees, in all those of the Christian tradition, and makes anti-Semitism a *process* in which all those of the Christian tradition participate.

In this editorial, Sullivan makes an autobiographical reference of some interest: "Up to some two decades ago, persons reared in certain

Protestant communities had profound—early emergent—hatred of Catholics that approached, apparently exceeded, the intensity of their anti-Semitic attitudes." In a footnote at this juncture, he refers to an anti-Catholic weekly called *The Menace*, which "had good circulation in some areas as recently as 1912." He is obviously referring to the fact that in 1912 it circulated widely in both his home area, Chenango County, New York, and in Chicago, where he was then a medical student. Actually *The Menace*, published in Missouri, flourished until 1915—when it was at least temporarily stopped through legal action—rising to a circulation of a million and a half in the United States alone. The acclaim with which the crudities of *The Menace* were greeted in various communities throughout the United States seems almost unbelievable in terms of present-day attitudes.[1] It is obvious that Sullivan recognized in this paper attitudes that were a viable part of his early experience, for the area in which he grew up was mainly Old Yankee and somewhat less than friendly to the only Irish Catholic family, the Sullivans, in the immediate neighborhood. Thus when anti-Semitism began to appear in Germany, Sullivan was clear on its meaning and saw the Nazi publication, the *Stürmer*, as a part of the same pattern as *The Menace*.

[1] In 1913, it claimed a circulation of 24,000 in New York State alone and that figure doubled within a year. A typical headline is taken from the issue of August 30, 1913: "NOTICE is Served HERE and NOW That No Compromise Shall Be Made: No Cessation of Attack Permitted Until Every Convent and House of Good Shepherd is Open for Inspection and Rome Taught Her Proper Place in the Scheme of American Government. We are Determined that Every Human Being Shall Enjoy Perfect Freedom."

Anti-Semitism†

HATRED is an attitude of a person involved in interpersonal relations. Unpersonalized objects and abstractions are not hated. Collectivities of people are hated only in so far as they are embodied in concrete personalizations or personifications. These you-patterns implicit in the act of hating rarely approach a coincidence with the objectively verifiable characteristics of any real person. They may be entirely fantastic, with no validity whatever outside of the person who has elaborated them. They always include characteristics of this person himself, and they are always real and significant in explaining some phases of his activity. They are, however, complex entities that are relatively uncommunicable, quite beyond consensual validation, and therefore unsuited to rationalize the basis of any collaborative interpersonal action. Two people who have discovered that each 'hates greed' are not nearly so ready for mutually satisfactory performance as are two people who discover that each hates a particular third person. The more seriously the first two discuss their alleged common antipathy the more they become puzzled at each other. The more the second two discuss their hated third person, the more detestable he becomes to each, and the greater is the facilitation of hostile and destructive activities towards him, by either one or both of them.

The most widespread hatred of a collectivity in the Western world today is anti-Semitism. Hatred of the Jews has been made a national creed by at least one state. A trend in this direction is

† Reprinted from *Psychiatry* (1938) 1:593–598.

being manifested by the other totalitarian powers, and there is a disturbing responsiveness to the formula in many of the citizens of more democratic countries. Hatred under any circumstances can scarcely be constructive. It is essentially a destructive motivation. Irrational hatred may be assumed to be detrimental to the hater and the hated, and to others among whom the hatred is manifested. Widespread hatred of a group of citizens who make up an important minority in a democracy is a contravention of the philosophy of the state which stultifies the haters and diminishes their feeling of security in the governmental system under which they are living. Confidence derives from one's interpersonal relations, and, when rational and dependable, is not based on demonstrations of personal power but rather on prevailingly favorable, friendly, or positive, attitudes towards one. The presence of enemies, real or imagined, is nugatory to untroubled progression. It calls out tension states that reduce interpersonal efficiency and diminish the pleasure of living; that are in fact expressions of biological insecurity, fear. Democratic systems are expanding emergents of recent origin that require for their functional success confidence, self-respect and respect for others, on the part of the electors, the people. The more widespread these conditions prevail, the better the system works and the greater is the good that it confers on its citizens. Any pervasive enmity within a democracy is dangerous. It increases the proportion of people who feel insecure. It intensifies feelings of individual difference. It undermines that general respect for other people which is the real basis for dependable self-respect. Anti-Semitism is this very sort of a pervasive enmity. It is also an enmity peculiarly difficult to combat because of its particular irrational basis. These considerations make the genesis and meaning of anti-Semitism a current major problem of psychiatry and our democratic state.

The people of the Western world, wittingly or unwittingly, are almost universally anti-Semitic.[1] The more cultivated one is,

---

[1] The hostile sentiments of a Jew towards other Jews is not germane to the nuclear formula of this presentation. It is a complex reaction of the individual who has suffered from submersive identification with the unpleasant personalizations of the minority of which he is a member, and who fears further injury of this sort.

the more probably one adheres to the ideal of tolerance, especially in abstract fields of behavior and belief. This ideal makes conscious hatred of a Jew *qua* Jew unwelcome, unless some formula is found that removes the Jews from the realm of the fully human. Ideals of tolerance in this sense in fact have had their most dynamic role in this very matter of anti-Semitism; it has for many years been less shameful to admit a hatred of Catholics, of Irish, of Negroes or the like, than to be confessedly a hater of the Jews. This specific focus of the mores of tolerance points in itself towards the universality of a tendency towards anti-Semitic prejudice, and to a need to exclude it from consciousness.

The psychiatrist has learned that each of one's personalizations is understandable. In any collaborative effort towards formulating the more private world of factors that manifest in one's interpersonal actions and beliefs, many of these unique personifications of objects, abstractions and collectivities have to be resolved into personal insight. Social intercourse depends primarily on a rough consensus of personalized abstractions; a person who can achieve this cannot escape doing so; a creature who cannot can scarcely become human. In a stable phase of culture when social change is of low velocity, the factors that make for high individuation of personalizations are unimportant and even the poorly-equipped can grasp enough of "what everyone knows" to live comfortably. In the modern world of swiftly but unevenly expanding horizons, of enormous inequality of economic, political, socio-geographical, and skill opportunities, it is quite otherwise. Individuation to the extent of actual psychosis is frequent. The biologically handicapped are increasingly disadvantaged. Everyone comes to have some personalizations that are so impractical, socially, that they give rise to definite maladjustment in living. The psychiatrist cannot guide his patient towards greater success around these unique artifacts. They have to be converted into forms that are more nearly valid approximations to the equivalent personalizations of the other people who are necessary to the patient. This process is said to result in insight, more valid information about one's personality as it manifests itself in one's interpersonal relations.

In the study of personality, there appear for investigation the more troublesome of one's me-you patterns, including some of those that personify objects, institutions, abstractions, or collectivities. Each one of them unfolds itself as a dynamism that was evolved in an inevitable fashion in the individual's concrete life experience. The origin of each personalization is seen to have been *historically necessary* for the adequate functional development of the personality concerned. From its origin in concrete experience and a real interpersonal situation, each personalization has itself had a developmental history which is in turn completely understandable in terms of the functional adequacy of the person in the series of interpersonal situations through which he has had to live. The personalizations concerned in anyone's hatred of the Jews are dynamisms that emerged at some specific time in his life and that thereafter evolved in strict accordance with his personal experience and the adaptive necessities that inhered in the series of his subsequent life situations. The presenting content of one's personalizations of the hated Jewish collectivity may show little obvious relationship to the content of one's original anti-Jewish dynamism. Their manifestations, however, are explicable only on the basis of its evolution. The person may say that he hates Jews, Catholics, and Negroes with equal intensity. Superficial inquiry, however, will reveal significant differentials in his beliefs and his actions towards persons whom he identifies with each of the hated collectivities. In general, his anti-Semitic attitudes will be the most primitive, the most diffusely universal. This is subject to individual exception where known injury has been sustained from a representative of the hated group. Moreover, it has not been equally true at all times in all parts of the Western world. Up to some two decades ago, persons reared in certain Protestant communities had profound—early emergent—hatred of Catholics that approached, apparently exceeded, the intensity of their anti-Semitic attitudes.[2] ·The content of most anti-Catholic sentiments

[2] The reservation of "tolerance" in this case sheds much light on the psychopathology of irrational prejudice towards a collectivity, and the facilitation of pseudo-collaborative behavior by propaganda techniques. The contemporary "Stürmer" was a weekly called "The Menace." It had good circulation in some areas as recently as 1912.

differed widely from the general patterns of anti-Semitism; in fact, at least in the period of anti-Catholic decadence, approximated some major formulae current in anti-Negro prejudices. There were also conspicuous individual exceptions to a regional universality of the conscious or unwitting hatred of Catholics, as there have always been more abundantly in areas of strong anti-Negroism. Exceptions to a general anti-Semitism are quite another matter.

These three instances of hated collectivities are especially revealing for comparative psychiatric study, because the personal origins of these particular hostile dynamisms are not intimately related to the influence of economic, political, or socio-geographical factors. In hatred of Jews or Catholics, the origin is much too early; in hatred of Negroes there is often found to have been a pro-Negro dynamism which has been warped into a subsequently enforced hostility—with peculiarly wide discrepancy between conscious and unwitting behavior and remarkable inconsistency of beliefs, in many denizens of the region of general hatred.

The roots of any hatred of a collectivity are to be sought in influences as widespread as are its manifestations. The roots of anti-Semitism must be influences coterminous with the Western world. There is but one group of these influences. It is the Christian ideology itself, as it is presented to and inculcated in the personality of almost every child.

Religions are structures of transcendental beliefs and rituals that serve certain great necessities of the persons making up the adherents or communicants of the particular faith. These structures are not static, but they are among the most stable of all cultural entities. They tend to be systematized but, being essentially additional to the world that can be treated logically, their systematizations have to include some irrational, magical, factors.[3]

[3] The term *magical* is used to refer to that body of phenomena that includes incomprehensible relationships, to "effects" having no necessary relationship to "causes," to events held to be other than inevitable sequents of preceding events. It is a great mistake to regard "magical" as derogatory: science rises from the investigation of the magical, often with magic as a tool. Science tends to convert magic into rigorous formulation; this is exceedingly practical, whenever it can be achieved. Natural science has been very successful; biological, far less so; the science of personality is only beginning its enormous task.

From the standpoint of psychiatry as the study of interpersonal relations, the most significant difference between a religion, as held by a person, and a state of systematized delusion resides in the element of social participation. Some people necessary to the particular person have incorporated in their several personalities approximately the same structure of transcendental beliefs and rituals. Actions and foresights of actions in situations integrated with these people therefore prove valid. One "knows what to expect," not because one has a correct view of inevitable inter-personal relations, but because there is a community of assumptions as to the inevitability of certain courses of personal events. The achievement of such a community of assumption, especially in this relatively boundless universe of things and relationships that can be imagined, is usually the result of a rather methodical education. It is not necessary to set up a special teaching situation in order to inculcate in the young the most consistent and constantly manifested traits of the family culture-complex. Very special educative situations indeed are needed if one is to eradicate the effects of this most facile sort of acculturation. It is safe to assume that the nucleus of one's personal religion has been acquired in this automatic way, in the great majority of cases. With this assumption, one may then consider the more formal religious education of the Christian young. Everything that is not self-evident from the previous experience of the young has to be "explained" or learned as a verbal formula imposed by authority. The more formal Christian training provides the child with impressions closely approximating the following: There are at least two Gods, one the Son of the Other. The Son was made man, became a person like other people, and lived as a person among others. He was a truly godly person, the ideal kind of person one should strive to be. He was the only person who did no wrong whatsoever. . . . He was crucified, killed by torture, by some people who regarded themselves as the most favored peoples of God the Father, who is of course God of all peoples although some heathens refuse to accept Him. These Jews, the people who killed by torture Jesus, Son of the God of whom they believed themselves to be the Chosen People, were among the people to whom Jesus did nothing whatsoever but good. He was Himself, in so far as he was a man, a Jew. He was betrayed by another Jew, Judas Iscariot. He forgave Judas, He forgave the Jews; by His death as a man, He redeemed all those who believed in Him. Jews who believed in Him ceased to be Jews and became Christians. This happened a long time ago. There are still Jews.[4]

The stress laid on the various steps in the story of Jesus is in part a function of the past experience of the teacher. The emotional coloring of these steps, as they are incorporated in the personality of each Christian child, is a function of the past experience of that particular child. All too many children have come along paths that make them cruel. In these, often the products of unwitting punitive influences wholly beyond their capacity for rationalizing, the torture of Jesus may strike a peculiarly responsive chord. A displacement of resentment at absolutistic parental authority on to the persecuting Jews is convenient, all the more in that it carries with it a shadowy feeling of personal godliness, the Christ-identification that can grow into a classical psychotic state, one of the forms of catatonic parergasia. In any case, the Jews stand out as the archetype of the enemy of God, the Savior —epitomes of ingratitude and cruelty, the people whom even God could not turn from sin and corruption. This is the nucleus of anti-Semitism, the original configuration which gives directional characteristics to a dynamism which can be released by propaganda to channel brutality astonishing even to some of those who are manifesting it. It is silly to suppose that adult reasoning will eradicate this ingredient of Christian personality. It is dangerously self-deceptive to fancy that one has "outgrown" it. It is absurd to argue that one "never had" it, unless one grew up under circumstances very exceptional indeed.

Ubiquitous Christian anti-Semitism exists. It is a definite menace to Democracy, for the reasons already stated. It is all the more a menace because in cultivated people and in cruder public figures

[4] This outline, based on children's accounts, makes no mention of certain of the Mysteries such as the Trinity, the Virgin Birth, and the Communion. It does not refer to the themes of omnipotence, omniscience, and omnipresence; the first two are very important indeed to psychiatry. It does not touch on many of the Miracles that interest the young and become fixed in personality. It does not refer to some of the striking statements; e.g., "Forgive . . . as we forgive," "Lead us not into temptation."

who have acquired at least a veneer of civilization, it is ignored, excluded from awareness, and thus freed to act in dissociation without any feeling of personal responsibility inhering in the "accidental" or "misunderstood" acts to which it gives rise.

The psychiatrist of all people feels constrained to a realistic course towards the remedy of perceived mental illness. The psychiatrist of Christian tradition must confront his inevitable anti-Semitism, as just such an illness. In dealing with himself alone, the psychiatrist cannot use his special techniques, for psychiatry is the study of the interpersonal relations in which one integrates oneself as a participant observer. He is but human, here; but he is unusual in that he has learned the futility of "trying to make himself" do or be this or that that would be "better." His advantage lies in the fact that he is trained in alertness as to what is actually transpiring in his dealing with others. Knowing from experience that childhood is a very significant period in personality development, he has but to recall the more accessible details of his Christian training to see the inhering probability of a nuclear anti-Semitism. To become certain of its presence, he has to observe his actions and reveries in situations which might be expected to stir the dynamism. Calmly convinced of its presence among the motivational systems that characterize him, he has taken the first great step towards its remedy. Most of the chronic maladjustment that we encounter has been perpetuated by selective inattention and wonderfully facile forgetting. A person for example may entertain hostile fantasies in many of his spare moments every day of his life. A noticed instance of this preoccupation causes him astonishment. He can go on surprising himself this way for years. It makes each incident of hostile rumination a novel, discrete, unprecedented peculiarity of his "mind at the moment." It is only when he has come to accept quite as a matter of fact that he habitually entertains hostile fantasies, that he has arrived at an observational position from which he can study the factors really concerned.

The psychiatrist knows that a deeply rooted irrational prejudice of this nature impairs his objective independence. It renders him relatively helpless to avoid manipulation by others who adapt their procedures to appeal to the dynamism. Anti-Semitic propaganda *must* appeal to him, if only to the end of calling out powerful inhibitory processes to cancel the automatic response of interest and hatred, but at the cost of visceral tensions that weary him and tend to discourage him in meeting the problems of life. He knows too that the radical remedy is at the end of a long road of retrospective examination of experience, a path open to the more fortunate, only. Like many of his patients, he is apt to have to choose the still less prompt and more uncertain road of diligent scrutiny of those of his acts and reveries which show the stereotypy of the hostile dynamism that he acquired in the course of his education to love his neighbor as he loves himself.

At very least, he ceases to be complacent in reacting automatically on the basis of a person's inclusion in the vague and variegated congeries, Jew. He quickly comes to see that there is but one fairly consistent characteristic of almost all Jews: that they have been taught to expect at least covert anti-Semitism. He will know that this characteristic is inevitable as long as Christian teaching distinguishes the Jews and makes them hatefully different. He may hope that the influence of those who love democracy will quickly alter this; whereon, perhaps, the Jews who are citizens of democracies may be emancipated from the ancient burden of an even more primitive faith that somewhat protects them from the blind enmity in which they have existed for centuries.

7

Commentary

THE NEXT TWO brief selections are the only published record of
Sullivan's formal research on Negro youth, although some of his
Selective Service writings afford additional insights, in passing, on the
same subject; undoubtedly Sullivan's research in this area was cut
short by his work on Selective Service beginning in 1940. His formal
research began sometime in 1937 or 1938, when the Negro sociologist,
Charles S. Johnson, asked Sullivan to participate with him in a study
of the personality problems of the Southern rural Negro youth (for
Johnson's account of this, see the prefatory piece to this book);
shortly thereafter Sullivan went to Nashville, Tennessee, to work
with Johnson for a brief period. The book emerging from this study
was titled *Growing Up in the Black Belt;* [1] and an appendix written
by Sullivan forms the next paper in this book. Johnson's study was
one of four sponsored by the American Council on Education as
part of their American Youth Commission; these studies should
be seen, of course, as part of a broader research interest among
American social scientists, which eventuated in Gunnar Myrdahl's
An American Dilemma, contracted for by the Carnegie Corporation
of New York in 1937.

After Sullivan completed his work with Johnson, another Negro
sociologist, E. Franklin Frazier, asked for Sullivan's collaboration on
another American Youth Commission study of Negro youth in the
Middle, or Border States; Sullivan's contribution to Frazier's study
(*Negro Youth at the Crossways*) forms the second of these two
selections on the Negro. In both instances, Sullivan himself felt that

[1] Charles S. Johnson, *Growing Up in the Black Belt: Negro Youth in
the Rural South;* Washington, D.C.: American Council on Education, 1941.

his participation in the studies was too slight to warrant a formal statement in the books; but both Johnson and Frazier insisted that his insights were important and should be included. In this manner, some record of Sullivan's work with Negro youth survives, however fragmentary. In summarizing the two experiences, Sullivan writes: "The border Negro struggles with rage where the Southern Negro suffers from fear." In the twenty years or more since that was written, the southern Negro has achieved some rage of his own, but the shift of emotion from fear to rage was clearly seen by Sullivan as a natural outcome of a developing ability in conflict with a restricted —or at best retarded—social opportunity.

Sullivan's collaboration with Johnson and Frazier belonged to a pattern of collaboration between Negro and white social scientists and educators that extended back for several decades and that can be seen as an important prologue to Myrdahl's study. As early as 1910, for instance, the Chicago sociologist, Robert E. Park, had significantly collaborated with Booker T. Washington; [2] this collaboration was viewed by Park as a rare opportunity to study the intricate social system by which the Negro's relationship with the white folk was defined: "I think I probably learned more about human nature and society in the South under Booker Washington," Park has said, "than I learned elsewhere in all my previous studies." [3] Subsequently Johnson had found his way, after considerable hardship, to the University of Chicago and had come under the influence of Park. Frazier also was trained at the University of Chicago, obtaining a Ph.D. in sociology in 1931. That both Johnson and Frazier should have sought out Sullivan was no accident; and Sullivan, like Park earlier, saw these encounters as rare opportunities in the quest for knowledge on "man as man," and the search for avenues of remedial action in the areas of social and personal distortion.

[2] See Booker T. Washington, *The Man Farthest Down: A Record of Observation and Study in Europe* [with the collaboration of Robert E. Park]; Garden City, N. Y.: Doubleday, Page & Co., 1912. Traveling in Europe together, Washington and Park had observed the plight of the man farthest down in Europe—the dispossessed and the lowliest peasant—in order to get some perspective on the plight of the American Negro. In general they both felt that the American Negro in many ways had more hopefulness in his situation, over time, than the European peasant.

[3] See Charles S. Johnson, "Dr. Robert E. Park, 1864-1944" [obituary notice], *Psychiatry* (1944) 7:107–109.

The first of the two papers, "Memorandum on a Psychiatric Reconnaissance," forms an appendix to Johnson's book. In introducing this statement, Johnson notes that Sullivan's impressions "reveal interesting insights and contain a considerable measure of confirmation of this study's findings regarding the effects of minority status upon the personality of Negro youth."

Sullivan's use of the word "reconnaissance" in the title evokes his general perspective on psychiatric interviewing. This is his term for the second step in psychiatric interviewing in which the psychiatrist obtains a rough outline of the social or personal history of the patient; at the end of the reconnaissance, the psychiatrist should attempt a summary statement with the patient.[4] Here Sullivan has attempted a summary statement on the reconnaissance of several Negro youth and leaders; it is in fact a psychiatric reconnaissance of a *sociological grouping* rather than of a single patient.

Sullivan's comment on Negro leadership in this memorandum is a reminder of how far this leadership and its organization have developed since the end of the thirties. He notes that the outstanding leader he found at the time "suffered so vividly . . . from rage at the whites that one of the elements of distrust expressed [by other Negroes in the community] to me about him seemed all too well founded." These informants told Sullivan that they feared that this leader would get into serious trouble through his expression of hatred. As for other Negro leaders, Sullivan found them as unreliable as did his informants. The responsible leadership among Negroes at present, as exemplified by Martin Luther King, is an index of an historic change in both the organization of the Negro community and its leadership. At the same time, the prototype of the Negro leader who "suffered so vividly . . . from rage at the whites . . ." as reported by Sullivan, continues to exert dangerous influence today.

The Memorandum comments on the phenomenon of nonreciprocal first-naming between whites and Negroes, and this, too, is interesting historically. Sullivan reports that his inadvertent calling of a Negro by the name of Mr. _____, for instance, would arouse so much anxiety that he could not use that particular person as an informant thereafter. It is doubtful that the use of formal address by a white

[4] See Sullivan, *The Psychiatric Interview* (Norton, 1954) index entry for Reconnaissance.

man speaking to a Negro today would arouse such extreme anxiety; although the advance is painfully slow, the Negro has gradually become more accustomed to being treated as a *person*.

In one of the most important passages in the Memorandum, Sullivan notes the great—often derogatory—generalizations that white men hold about Negroes—beliefs that persist in the face of *contrary evidence* from individual encounters between the white man and the Negro. With characteristic awareness and in the best tradition of the participant observer, Sullivan notes in the later study for Frazier that "unhappily, when my role has been commonplace instead of that of an investigator, or a friend and colleague, I have had experiences [with Negroes] that could readily be rationalized in accord with these 'typical characteristics.'" Negroes "deserve to be observed as they are," Sullivan concludes, "and the blot of an American interracial problem may thus gradually be dissipated."

One last comment on the Memorandum: In speaking of Jews in the editorial "Anti-Semitism," Sullivan notes that the one general characteristic of the Jew is that he has been taught to expect "at least covert anti-Semitism." Sounding the same over-all note, Sullivan points out here that "it is impossible to find much of anything that is unique or general in American Negro personality, excepting only an almost, if not quite, ubiquitous fear of white people." Both of these are powerful statements on the rigidity of the interaction pattern rather than the uniqueness of the 'individual.'

Memorandum on a Psychiatric Reconnaissance[†]

AN INTENSIVE psychiatric study of a few American Negroes of northern urban habitat having inspired in the writer an intense interest in the possibilities of obtaining significant data on inter-personal relations, he was persuaded to undertake a visit of exploration in the deep South. Nothing of optimistic expectation as to results was developed, despite the encouragement offered by Hortense Powdermaker and Charles S. Johnson. Such preliminary formulations as came of the experiment are largely to be credited to the group of graduate students at Fisk University, who were most cooperative in supplying personal data, to the assistance of the white and the Negro leaders in the area chosen, and to that of two clergymen who superintended a school there.

Throughout my work with marginal individuals, I have heard a variety of all-inclusive generalizations about the Negro group. In work with persons representative of more privileged American society, I have observed the coexistence of these generalized beliefs with contradictory individualized thinking and behavior towards members of this group. The "logic-tight compartment" principle is conspicuous here. It appears that the generalized (often derogatory) belief is an essential part of one's emotional make-up, whereas the more valid individual formulations are much less emotionally significant.

In a few words, it was easy to discover not one general type

† Reprinted from Charles S. Johnson, *Growing Up in the Black Belt: Negro Youth in the Rural South;* Washington, D.C.: American Council on Education, 1941; pp. 328–333.

but very wide differences of personality among Negro youth in the Southern area. It is impossible to find much of anything that is unique or general in American Negro personality, excepting only an almost, if not quite, ubiquitous fear of white people. These interracial attitudes always came to the front; one of my three best informants in this area shocked himself by realizing belatedly that he was telling me how deeply he hated all whites. Here, too, we seem to have a generalization essential to the self; again, one that is no barrier to quite contradictory specific beliefs and behavior. This particular young man was quick and accurate in perceiving the nuances of our relationship, and, aside from this one instance of painful embarrassment, expressed himself with rather astonishing freedom from restraints.

The personnel studied included highly talented people, rather mediocre individuals, and at least one amiable imbecile. They made themselves available for a variety of reasons, rather generally with some vague hope that an improvement of their individual lot might perhaps come from the interviews. The spread of this general hope varied from a wide consciousness of the need of the whole colored population to a narrow, sometimes very shrewd, self-seeking. The formulation of the hope varied extremely—sometimes approximating the surmised eternal diffuse optimism of the Negro, sometimes reaching no further than an anticipation of a little money. In a few, it was formulated in terms of the distant future, with realism and excellent logic. In one, whom unforeseen accident had but recently thrown out of a vassalage [1] relationship with a white plantation supervisor, it rapidly focused on the re-creation of such a situation with me. [The formulation began] as a fleeting fantasy that he expressed among several "thoughts" about the immediate future; I was able to observe its progression to a resolve to break with everything familiar to him and trust his fate to me—all this with no expression of emotion. At one stage, however, he showed a transient disturbance of personality, a period of troubled sleep followed by the dream-like detachment which the psychiatrist associates with

[1] See "A Note on Formulating the Relationship of the Individual and the Group." [The article is included in this book, and Sullivan's definition of the term can be located through the index entry for Vassalage. H.S.P.]

the schizophrenic forms of mental disorder.

An abortive experiment in more intensive psychiatric study was undertaken with this individual. He was removed to New York City and supposedly headed towards a more independent career. He showed good capacity for controlling the anxieties that the actual translation included, but he was felled by his almost complete illiteracy and came to suffer such nostalgia that he returned home—at once to become a vessel of regrets and of urgency to return to the North.[2]

Everyone was encouraged to talk of the Negro community. Everyone commented more or less directly on its lack of organization, and of the inability of Negroes to cooperate in long-term projects. Almost everyone spoke of the unreliability of Negro leaders. I saw one of the prominent Negro clergymen and came to feel that distrust of his integrity was not in any sense abnormal. The outstanding Negro leader of the community, on the other hand, impressed me favorably. He suffered so vividly, however, from rage at the whites that one of the elements of distrust expressed to me about him seemed all too well founded. One of the young men remarked that this leader was going to "get himself in trouble"; another said that it would not be long before he "gets killed resisting arrest"—the local improvement on lynching. I think that this leader—though he came to express himself with great freedom about some topics—progressed in our acquaintanceship only from a distrust of my motives, through a distrust of my judgment, to a vague wondering if I might actually be a detached observer without blinding preconceptions and group loyalties hostile to him and his people. He seemed to me one of the

[2] It is to be noted that this young man is not included among the three most useful informants above mentioned. One of them was in fourth-year high school, one—nearly incredibly—was a student of aviation, and the third, while of but lower grammar school education, had kept closely in touch with events and was quite unusually well informed. The boy of the experiment had an effective formal education amounting to a good second grade, an intelligence that would have carried him through at least junior high school. His career had encouraged him to but little curiosity about events external to his narrow personal horizon. He had, however, rather firm ideals as to working for a living which, too, suffered in the debacle of the northern translation, in no small part, doubtless, because of my inability to assume a useful role in the transitional phase. I was away most of the time on the study in a border area.

loneliest of men; a well-trained professional man of rather keen sensitivity, isolated in the nexus of several fields of hostility, so driven by some complex of motives (which proved mostly inaccessible to me) that it seemed wholly unpredictable how long his remarkable judgment of people would suffice to insure him from retaliation for the anxieties and fears that he tends to focus.

The Negro's hostile attitudes toward whites are partly a reaction to discriminatory custom, an important example of which is the "Mr.—Mrs." taboo. No Negro is to be addressed as Mr. or Mrs. In general, they are to be called by their given name and not by their surname. I three times made the mistake of using the formal address; once from ignorance, with the result that the laborer concerned became highly suspicious of my *bona fides*, twice from preoccupation in seeking out a particular one in a group. In all cases, I created a disturbance such that the individual concerned was of no further use as an informant.

Besides these measures to "keep the nigger in his place," there are incidents of violence, some of them official in character in that they are initiated by the police. I learned that lynching, which had long since ceased in this particular area, was practiced recently in a neighboring town. The poor whites have a good deal to do with lynching parties. This may be determined in part by economic factors, as the Negro is often preferred as tenant or as laborer; it is partly determined, I surmise, by the need of a thrill, for these whites suffer almost as great a dearth of recreational activities as do the Negroes. There are, however, some middle-class lynching enthusiasts, some of whom are reputed to be unusually kind to "their niggers" when things are going well.

The occasions of great violence towards the Negro arise chiefly in connection with the master taboo of the society, the prohibition of any intimacy between a Negro male and a white woman. The force and importance of this taboo can scarcely be exaggerated. I have been told that the integrity of the whole social system rests on its inviolability. I know that mere unsubstantiated rumor of its violation has necessitated the prompt evacuation of the accused youth to a Northern city, in the interest of civic quiet. Several of the young men interviewed remarked on the unwisdom of looking at a white girl if there were any "peckawoods" (poor whites) around. One of them had been beaten for staring at a girl whom he insists he had not even seen. It must be understood also that this taboo is absolute; nothing declasses a white woman and nothing exempts a Negro man. A white prostitute's pursuit of a Negro taxi driver culminated in her calling him from the yard which serves as cab stand, showing him $50, and remarking that he would take the money and come home with her, or she would tell the police he had made advances to her. He refused, repeating his oft stated "I don't want to mess around with no white woman." The protector of the civil peace had shortly thereafter to provide him with means for leaving town for good. Mongolians may or may not be "white" for taboo purposes—it varies in different states—but certain Eurasian immigrants who are darker than light Negroes, *are* white for taboo purposes and woe betide the Negro male who proves attractive to one of these women.

Knowing the channels of rebellious attitudes, one might expect covert violations of this taboo to occur. They are probably much less frequent than many people surmise. I make this statement on the strength of observations of a probable instance, with persistent severe anxiety, and on reports of dreams. There are indications that in many Negro personalities in this area this taboo carries with it a large component of awe. The sophisticate of the border and the Northern areas should not be taken to be a characteristic denizen of the Negro population in America.

The sanctions which restrict Negro personality and which fix Negro men as inferior to the most degraded white woman are probably the prime factors in determining the ubiquitous hatred of the white. The unwavering performance of the rituals which emphasize these sanctions is an index of the meaning of the Negro patterns incorporated in the white personalities concerned. I must pause here to mention the occasional phenomenon of the "nigger-lover"—a white who fraternizes with the Negro in preference to the white. Such a person is ostracized, if possible; he is regarded with a more complex attitude than mere contempt. The suggestion that one may be a nigger-lover usually suffices to cure any tendency to diverge from the white pattern. Northerners who settle in this region find it expedient to become "meaner" than the native Southern families.

I have gone to some length to indicate the factors in the inter-racial situation that must have extraordinary effects on personality development. There are equally interesting factors in the Negro family patterns which still reflect economically conditioned practices of the slavery period. There are factors inhering in the single-crop agriculture of the plantation. There are factors in the disenfranchisement of the Negro and the more recent fall of the plantation owners from political power and the ascendancy of the poor whites.

The Negro of the deep South seldom escapes serious warping influences and a large proportion of them doubtless come to be measurably close to the reality underlying the prevailing white views of the Negro. I did not succeed in establishing contact with any of those who were described by my informants as "just average niggers." I learned in the first few days that I could not bridge the cultural gap with most of the plantation workers. The Negro seems to have a notably great capacity for sensing by intuition interpersonal reality. This faculty led to a good many pseudo conversations, early in my stay. It may be worth mentioning that one informant carried on in some eight hours of conversation an account of the consequences of a highly improbable experience—later found by collateral channels to be almost certainly mythical—without showing any of the phenomena by which I am customarily warned that an account is becoming wishful rather than valid. The one other detail of my provisional hypothesis which may merit mention bears on the *amiability* of the Negro as compared with whites and Chinese with whom I have worked. A timeless, formless optimism about life in general seemed to be remarkably widespread—even in obsessional personalities that I encountered. Something of this attitude also persisted in two thoroughly disillusioned and rather definitely embittered intellectuals who assisted me in various ways. I could not help but conclude that the Negro had escaped in some way those cultural-personal necessities which had compelled the Western Europeans to look to another world. Religious practices have importance in life in the deep South, but the effective religious beliefs, attitudes, and behavior [of the Negro] do not seem to be functional counterparts of the circumambient white culture.

In conclusion, it may be said that psychiatry as the study of interpersonal relations has a difficult but a most rewarding field in the American Negro, that the Negro of the deep South seems in many respects the most promising for a beginning, and that he and his social situation, with its chronologically well-separated variations from the influx of new elements, constitute one of the most significant social science research fields.

8

Commentary

SULLIVAN's brief collaboration with Charles S. Johnson on the problems of the Negro youth in the rural South, as reported in the last paper, was followed by a somewhat similar collaboration with E. Franklin Frazier, for many years head of the Department of Sociology at Howard University in Washington, D. C., and trained at the University of Chicago. Frazier's task was to find out something of the personality development of Negro youth in the Middle (or Border) States; in all, Frazier and his staff interviewed 268 girls and boys living in Washington, D. C., and Louisville, Kentucky. As a part of this larger study, Sullivan interviewed 20 boys living in Washington, D. C.; but the major collaboration between Frazier and Sullivan came to focus on one respondent—Warren Wall, a member of a Negro family of middle-class status living in the Southwest section of Washington. The next paper is a report of Sullivan's work with Warren Wall; as background, I have included at the beginning of the paper some excerpts from Frazier's chapter on Warren Wall from *Negro Youth at the Crossways*.[1]

Sullivan's role in the project has been described by Frazier as follows:

We [members of the project] have attempted to analyze the organization of [the subjects'] earliest impulses and wishes and to discover whatever traits were apparent at different periods in the development of their personalities. The greater attention has, however, been focused upon their present behavior—both overt and covert. In attempting this we were naturally faced with the difficult problem of probing beneath what they said or even did. Fortunately, we were aided in this difficult task by a psychiatrist who possessed the special-

[1] E. Franklin Frazier, *Negro Youth at the Crossways: Their Personality Development in the Middle States;* Washington, D.C.: American Council on Education, 1940.

ized competence required for depth analysis of personality. This does not mean that we were able to ferret out all the hidden motivations or that the psychiatrist himself felt that he had solved the problem in hand. In fact, because of the extreme limitations within which he worked, the psychiatrist hesitated to present his tentative findings. However, since the psychiatrist as well as the writer viewed the whole undertaking as an exploratory and a pioneer study of the personality of the Negro, the psychiatrist agreed to supplement our analysis with a discussion of the problem.[2]

Sullivan had a series of rather intense interviews with Warren Wall; after each of these interviews, he would meet with Frazier in the evenings at Frazier's home, and they would discuss at length the meaning of the material they had collected.[3] While neither Sullivan nor Frazier considered Warren Wall typical in any way, they seemed to agree that this respondent could avoid many of the usual pitfalls found in an interview between a white man and a Negro youth: "The particular factor that focused my principal effort on Warren was the success of his discriminating me as a person from 'the white man' as a generalized object of hostility," Sullivan writes.

Interviewing across race lines, particularly when the respondents are adolescents, raises so many problems that one often wonders about the validity of the data obtained. Frazier reports a number of comments made about Sullivan by his respondents, talking among themselves or with a Negro interviewer, and these provide an insight into Sullivan's capacity to achieve meaningful communication with these adolescents. Warren Wall notes that a paper route had helped him learn something about white people and that he had even learned to like some of them. Frazier goes on to say that "although such contacts helped to remove some of his suspicion of white people, Warren was influenced in his attitudes toward white people more decidedly through contacts with a white professional man [Sullivan] who became interested in him. His change in attitude was due partly to the fact that the colored interviewer told him that the white man was 'all right.'" Warren's comment on Sullivan follows:

I learned to like and trust Dr. X . . . [though] I didn't feel as friendly toward him as I wanted to at first. And when he asked questions about racial matters and how I felt going to white places where

[2] *Ibid.*, p. 198.
[3] Personal communication, E. Franklin Frazier.

Negroes weren't wanted, I did feel funny and uncomfortable. I don't know whether it was because he was a white man and I a Negro or just that the subjects were touchy ones anyway. I think he's sincere and will do all he can to help me as he promised and till he proves otherwise I intend to be honest with him and trust him, too. I usually get suspicious when white people get all solicitous but after you told me he was all right I was willing to take the chance. I've never known another white man like him. In fact, he was so kind and friendly like I thought he was a Negro until you told me he was white. I then got sort of scared and felt quite embarrassed for I was afraid that I might have said things I shouldn't have—things I certainly wouldn't say ordinarily to a white person.[4]

In the Introduction to Frazier's book, there is a recorded conversation between several boys who participated in the study, and they too mention Sullivan in passing. The conversation was recorded by a settlement worker who had the boys' confidence, and it would seem to be spontaneous and real:

CHARLIE—That white fellow, Dr. Y [5] is a funny old coot. He asked so many damn fool questions that I got sick of him for a while. Then I heard about the money he gave Bill and Henry and how he treated the fellows who went up to see him at Howard [University]—I took a new interest in him. I could stand a lot of questioning for $5.00.

FREDDIE—I liked him all right, I thought he was one of the nicest white men I'd ever met. I didn't understand a lot of his questions or what he was driving at. It is unusual to have a white man really interested in Negroes. At first, I didn't trust him and even when I'd seen him a number of times I was suspicious. I just couldn't help feeling uncomfortable around that white man. Those I've known were either hard-boiled employers or white men who want to push Negroes around. You just can't learn to trust white people by one nice one. I guess there are others but I'll bet they're far between.

DICK—I liked him from the start. I thought he was a very funny guy. I was all right with him till he started asking questions about girls and my relations with them—how I found out I was a Negro and all that; I felt very uncomfortable. I don't like to talk to white people about what Negroes do like that. They sort of expect it anyway and it just makes us all look that much worse. I can talk to Mr. X or some other Negro I like or trust about such things—but it just seems out of place to tell such things to white people. You know in the first place that you wouldn't be expected to ask the same questions of

---

[4] *Negro Youth at the Crossways*, p. 224.
[5] "Dr. Y" and "Dr. X" are both references to Sullivan.

them and, second, you just about know what they're expecting for answers. But he was smart, though, and when he got on the army and athletics we got along swell. I didn't hear about all that money that he passed around or I'd been there, too.[6]

This interchange seems to me to be high praise from three adolescents —Charlie was 19, Freddie was 15, and Dick was 17. At the same time it is clear that Warren was more experienced—perhaps through his paper route—in seeing the white man as a person.

[6] *Negro Youth at the Crossways,* p. xix.

Discussion of the Case
of Warren Wall†

[BACKGROUND for Sullivan's discussion of the case of Warren Wall, excerpted, as noted, from Frazier's chapter on Warren Wall:]

The Wall family, consisting of father and mother and nine children, occupies a large, red brick, six-room house in a run-down section of Southwest Washington which is gradually being rehabilitated to serve white people. A large vacant lot has already been converted into a playground for whites, notwithstanding the fact that there are no white children in the immediate neighborhood. Although the house occupied by Warren's family is poorly furnished and the wallpaper and floors are in need of repair, it is not so bad as the dilapidated structures which surround it. . . .

Although the Wall family lives in a section of the city occupied largely by lower-class families, the family is really of middle-class status. Mr. Wall, who has a highly skilled and responsible position, is a veteran of fifteen years' service in the employ of the municipal government. . . . In maintaining discipline in his family, he has not lost the confidence or respect of his children . . . [p. 200].

† Reprinted from E. Franklin Frazier, *Negro Youth at the Crossways: Their Personality Development in the Middle States;* Washington, D.C.: American Council on Education, 1940; pp. 228–234. [Sullivan's discussion of the case of Warren Wall appeared in Frazier's book as a supplement to Frazier's analysis of the case. H.S.P.]

The central fact in Warren's life is that as a first child who had been the center of attention and secured what he wanted, he has lost this privileged position and has been denied many things because of the large number of brothers and sisters. He places the blame upon his father and mother because he believes that they should have known better. . . . Though his home provides a certain amount of security and emotional satisfaction, yet it is distasteful to him because it is shabby, crowded, and noisy. He cannot have privacy and the exclusive enjoyment of his possessions. All of this, of course, could happen to a white boy as well as a colored.

There is one factor in this situation which involves Warren's racial status. Warren feels that his father is intelligent and could advance in his work were it not for the fact that he is a Negro. . . .

His hostility toward whites has been nurtured by certain contacts which he has had with them. . . . He has . . . been impressed by the way Negro children are excluded from a near-by playground which is reserved for a few white children. . . . For though Warren is a race conscious youth and believes that Negroes can compete successfully with whites when given an equal chance, he admits that if he could be born again he would rather be white in order to escape the disadvantages of being colored.

This leads to a final observation concerning Warren and his status as a Negro. He spends most of his life in the relatively isolated world of the Negro and his outlook on life as well as his hopes and ambitions are largely oriented within this world. He has seen Negro men and women rise within this world despite the handicap of race. Warren believes that if he is not completely submerged by his family, he can do the same. If he cannot obtain the highest rungs, he can at least escape the fate of his parents [pp. 227–228].

After a hurried inspection of an area in the deep South, I came as a white psychiatrist to discover what I could of the Negro in a city of the middle or border area. Some twenty contacts were made with young men from sixteen to twenty-five years of age, and of these three or four proved readily accessible and informative. "Warren Wall" of this chapter received the most attention. This was not by reason of his eminent suitability to represent the average Negro youth. Quite the contrary, he impressed one as definitely unusual. Certainly, he was the most simply communicative. This seemed to result from a personally fortunate combination of traits themselves of wide distribution, but usually organized into more secretive or otherwise inaccessible patterns. Some of the young men knew more about life in their area; some of them had far more striking personality problems that would have provided useful levers. The particular factor that focused my principal effort on Warren was the success of his discriminating me as a person from "the white man" as a generalized object of hostility. While this did not make me by any means an object of unmixed affection, it reduced the number of illusory people concerned in our conferences.[1] Warren took me to be a probably transient phenomenon in his life, as did most of the subjects. This, in his case, however, did not mean that I was to be treated with amiable superficiality and inconsequence. He took himself, his past, and the problematic future with considerable and rather realistic seriousness. He regarded white people as both more powerful and less irresponsible "friends"—and he was very clear in his realization that, to achieve any of the objectives that he contemplated with pleasure, he would need assistance on which he could depend. His generalizations (thinking patterns) of the Negro represented them as low in capacity for durable friendship, greatly handicapped economically, and much given to envious ill-wishing. This is doubly interesting because Warren is one of the few subjects of this study who had unquestionably durable friendships with Negro compeers, and because envy of the economic and other advantages of the whites did not seem to be a great factor in his hostility. There was less of simple projection of personally undesirable traits and more of personal experience in his generalizations.

The Negro of this city would appear to be significantly dif-

[1] See, in this connection, Harry Stack Sullivan, "A Note on the Implication of Psychiatry, the Study of Interpersonal Relations, for Investigations in the Social Sciences," and "The Data of Psychiatry." [Both articles appear earlier in this book.]

ferent from the Negro of the deep South. I cannot vouch for the universality of the difference throughout the middle or border area, but I can say positively that I encountered no exception to the difference—among upper-class, middle-class, or lower-class youth. I saw no upper-class youth in the South, where a Negro upper class is clearly delineable. Here, I saw the only child of a family which would unquestionably be upper class among Southern Negroes. The stratification is somewhat confused in this city of the middle area as a result of several factors—freedman ancestry and skin color, among others. It seems to be peculiarly difficult for a really dark-complexioned Negro to elevate himself by intellectual or financial success and rigid sexual morality. Contrariwise, some of the older free-born families do not seem to be troubled by the mid-Victorianism which characterizes the upper class in the South.[2]

Warren is dark-brown; his father and his two most intimate friends are very dark. Both the latter are middle class, and both are quite certain to amount to something. Warren and one of his friends—the other is quite a "lady's man"—are unusually continent, have "steadies" who are sisters, and have solved the "masculinity problem" of their prevailingly lower-class environment. Most boys in the neighborhood became sexually experienced at an early age. The girls feel quite free to pursue whom they desire, and a failure to respond is interpreted—and widely—as evidence of one's being "sissy" or "queer."

The significant difference does not appear in this sexual freedom of the lower-class Negroes, so far as I could determine. I believe that in this respect middle-class life also parallels the South. Heterosexual activity seems to be one of the few unrestricted recreational outlets. I judge that there are many definitely promiscuous people and that this laxity arises from factors of personality development as well as from a permissive culture. Vividly outstanding factors in the structure of many Negro family groups are superficially identical with those which in whites eventuate in arrest of heterosexual development and thus to obligate homosexual or bisexual patterns of behavior. While homosexuality is by no means unknown in the Southern com-

2 Hortense Powdermaker, *After Freedom;* New York: Viking Press, 1939.

munity and is apparently fairly frequent in this sophisticated border city, it would require careful, intensive personality study of a number of Negroes to convert one of my surmises in this connection into fact.

It has seemed that a remarkable number of the subjects studied —including some people in their thirties—have definitely immature personalities. In particular, their affections seem shallow, if not also fugitive. This applied with as much force to friendship (isophilic) tendencies as to their relations with the other sex.[3] At the same time, some facts were to be observed in their interpersonal relations which in white subjects would be explained on the basis of persisting isophilic preferences, the handling of which entailed very little anxiety. These observations led finally to the surmise that the "promiscuity" in sexual relations and the "superficiality" in friendship relations arise from a complex of traits that we would refer to a frustration in elaborating the *good-mother preconcept*.[4] This implies a general very early distortion of personality, presumably by almost ubiquitous interracial factors. In this connection, certainty—and sound remedial formulation based thereon—would require comparative psychiatric exploration in the United States and, say, the Brazilian culture-areas.

Appeals to vague racial mythopsychologies seem to be the "intellectual" equivalent to those self-protecting rationalizations to which reference has already been made. I hope that it will be

[3] I refer to their relations with other Negroes; the relationships with white people are far too complex to be relevant in this connection.

[4] The theory of personality development concerned here has been evolved over a period of years. See, for the original statement, "Erogenous Maturation," *Psychoanalytic Rev.* (1926) 8:1–15. It was developed extensively in the manuscript *Personal Psychopathology*, which was used as collateral reading in the Yale Seminar on the Impact of Culture and Personality (1932–33). . . . See also the articles "Mental Disorders," and "Psychiatry," in *Encyclopaedia of the Social Sciences* (New York: Macmillan, 1933–34), 10:313–319, and 12:578–580.

[A revision of the first part of *Personal Psychopathology* appears in this book under the title "The Data of Psychiatry," and an excerpt from the same manuscript appears in *Schizophrenia as a Human Process*, under the title "Cultural Stress and Adolescent Crisis." The article "Mental Disorders" may also be found in *Schizophrenia as a Human Process*. The article "Psychiatry" is reprinted as the first selection in the present book. H.S.P.]

clear that psychiatry proceeds by the elucidation of differences in the patterns of interpersonal relations among people immersed in approximately uniform cultural matrices. Our particular subject, Warren Wall, while showing peculiarly distinctive patterns, showed clearly the interracial attitudes which I surmise to be quite general in the United States, but which I also surmise to show specific regional differences that are important data for science. I refer here to the elaborations of antagonism toward the whites.

The striking and perhaps most significant difference of the Negro of the deep South and of the border area shows itself in the surface adaptation to the white. The Southern Negro tends to be friendly, either diffident or elusive, and emotionally responsive. The border Negro tends to be unfriendly, antagonistic, or morose. The discrimination against the border Negro seems to be much more haphazard than in the South. There is nothing like the general etiquette derogatory to self-esteem. There are abundant educational opportunities. My informants showed a consensus of opinion to the effect that, while the physical equipment, schoolhouses, laboratory apparatus, and so forth, were "second-hand," one could secure adequate instruction in practically anything one could learn. But they all agreed also that occupational opportunities were waning. One Negro said:

In my father's time a gifted Negro could compete with mediocre whites. That is not the case any more. It's getting to be very difficult to get a position as clerk. They want us to be laborers. I don't think it even comes from discrimination against us because we are colored. As the jobs get scarcer, they look more and more after their own people. There wouldn't be pick-and-shovel work for Negroes except that they work better than whites, and are willing to take less pay.

Rather than being at least subconsciously made to be chronically afraid, the border Negro is ignored and treated with indifference or frank contempt. I believe that the commonplace Negroes fare more ill in personality in this atmosphere than do they under the distance-fixing etiquette and caste-distinguishing system of taboos of the Southern regions. I believe that there are far more contented Negroes there, despite the lower basic scale of living, the seasonal hardships, and other undesirable conditions.

Gifted youth in the South come early to suffer the limitations in educational opportunities. Gifted Negroes in both areas come all too soon to recognize the limitation in opportunity to exercise their talents. Neither area is conducive to mental health for those well above the average in endowment.

The border Negro struggles with rage where the Southern Negro suffers from fear. The unconstructive wish-fulfilling fantasies that are evoked by these states are respectively malevolent and escapist. The diffuse optimism which seems ingrained in the Negro also manifests itself in somewhat different forms. The border Negro—and in this Warren is not an exception—seems to fix on goals of superiority to the whites in terms of the whites' pyramid of income and deference, in so far as it is comprehended. Reality is anything but encouraging to such ambitions; the result is anxiety, and protections against anxiety, compensatory and substitutive behavior.[5]

The tragedy of the Negro in America seems to be chiefly a matter of culturally determined attitudes in the whites, by the manifestations of which the Negro is generally distorted into a pattern of interracial behavior which permits the continuance of the attitudes without much change. This is a vicious circle, the interruption of which is an undertaking of great difficulty. In serious discussion of this problem with highly intelligent and ordinarily resourceful confreres, I have been told in essence that there doubtless are unusual Negroes, but that it takes a psychiatrist interested in the problem to find them. I have heard much about "typical Negro characteristics" and, unhappily, when my role has been commonplace instead of that of an investigator, or a friend and colleague, I have had experiences that could readily be rationalized in accord with these "typical characteristics." Even here, however, when the role is shifted and the techniques of intensive study of interpersonal relations have been substituted for those of a detached and generally preoccupied professional

[5] A certain loud boastfulness in the presence of white bystanders belongs in the last mentioned category—and is perhaps the most unfortunate in its effect on white attitudes toward improving interracial relations. More subtle but similarly unfortunate dynamisms are seen in preoccupations which minimize the interest free for investment in activities important to white employers.

man, the presumptively "typically Negro" performances have been resolved into particular instances of the "typically human." On the one hand, the social distance of the Negro and the white ordinarily conceals the personal facts; also, the Negro, well-trained in the almost infrahuman role, finds certain utilities in playing it out.

It is evident that, if we are to develop a real approximation to national solidarity, we must find and cultivate a humanistic rather than a paternalistic, and exploiting, or an indifferent attitude to these numerous citizens of our commonwealth. As a psychiatrist, I have to speak particularly against using them as scapegoats for our unacceptable impulses; the fact that they are dark-skinned and poorly adapted to our historic puritanism is really too naive a basis for projecting most of our privately condemned faults upon them. They deserve to be observed as they are, and the blot of an American interracial problem may thus gradually be dissipated.

9

Commentary

IN THE initial statement of the aims of the William Alanson White Psychiatric Foundation, the founders gave a prominent place to the development of a "political psychiatry." In a world ridden with "collective discontents" that might eventuate at any time in "hostile political action," research into socio-political phenomena seemed obviously an appropriate area for the Foundation's interest. The collaboration of Harold D. Lasswell in the early activities of the Journal and the School was, of course, of crucial importance in this whole development. Before the Journal had been in publication a year, the members of the Foundation's Board of Trustees had decided on the necessity for turning this socio-political interest in the direction of international crisis. From 1938 onward, until Sullivan's death in 1949, the Journal devoted a great many of its pages, first, to Selective Service, then to problems of morale in a country and world at war, and throughout to postwar problems. In all of this, there were many instances of clear and impressive foresight. Thus before the United States was at war, Sullivan was already worrying about the realistic problems of a postwar world. By 1940, this interest had been formalized into a series of memoranda on urgent current political matters, issued officially by the William Alanson White Psychiatric Foundation; one of these early memoranda is included as the next selection.

As a preamble to this 1940 Memorandum, I would like to quote from a formal statement of the Publications Committee in 1939:

Some readers have kindly assisted the Publications Committee by expressing their various opinions of the journal. There have been statements both of praise and of criticism. The praise has charm;

the criticism, utility. Some people have found the journal too elementary; this would seem inevitable if it is to perform usefully as an integrating agency. . . .

Another type of criticism hinges on the opinion that it is not within the province of the scientist to deal with general values and valuational judgments. The psychiatrist has to recognize the role of values in every personal situation. No science of interpersonal relations can ignore such dynamic factors as strivings towards truth, beauty, and humanity. Neither can any psychiatrist avoid manifesting valuing judgments in his participant observation of his patients. His effort in this connection is to be aware of his valuational processes, and of the factors that operate in them. He strives towards objective evaluating, as contrasted with the conventional unnoticed acting out of irrational prejudice.

A few readers object to some specific policy formulated by the Publications Committee. Thus the journal is said to be engaged in propaganda or to have mixed politics and psychiatry. Dr. William Alanson White believed that psychiatry has to serve in order to study. He came to recognize diffidence and detachment as frequent masks for fantasies of omnipotence and omniscience. Propaganda is a powerful force in modern life; all the more powerful because people are so generally ignorant of its techniques. The psychiatrist has to avoid the influence of pervasive propaganda and to remedy its more pernicious effects on his patients. He must therefor understand propaganda processes. Also, in so far as the psychiatrist is interested in hygienic reform, he must know how to make effective benevolent propaganda as a necessary preliminary to the spread of national enlightenment. If he cannot do this, he is impotent to deal with intrenched prejudice.[1]

This is an early and succinct statement of the Publications Committee's intent to shift the knowledge gained from the psychiatrist's participant observation of the patient over to the larger social and political scene, with the firm belief that *political psychiatry, as well as clinical psychiatry, has to serve in order to study*. It is interesting to see how this intent was used in the next paper, "Propaganda and Censorship," to try to make some sense out of the confusion between propaganda and education, social forces and pressure groups, censorship and sensitivity toward the "ill-defined levels" of social status or class in the United States.

[1] First page of February 1939 issue of *Psychiatry*, untitled, unsigned, and unnumbered. While the statement is indirectly attributed to the Publications Committee, the quoted part seems to have been written mainly by Sullivan.

The reader should bear in mind that Sullivan is attempting in "Propaganda and Censorship" a precise and inclusive statement of a complex subject. As such, the selection is closer to a summary statement for a book, rather than an article per se. Yet the Memorandum becomes useful in and of itself as soon as one begins to illuminate it with examples from the political scene. In brief, it outlines the difficulties involved in reaching a public consensus for the benefit of all citizens, particularly in a nation such as ours in which the self-esteem of so many social and ethnic groupings are involved. It applies, for instance, to the problem of racism in the United States and sheds light on the mistakes made over the years in this particular area of national opinion leadership.

Propaganda and Censorship†

IN ITS most definite sense, propaganda is the sometimes wholly unwitting utilization of presumptively informative action to promote more or less irrational changes in the valuational attitudes of those subjected to it. Advertising is mostly deliberate propaganda. Political speeches are often a blend of deliberate and unwitting propaganda. Advice about handling personal problems is frequently propaganda of the entirely unwitting kind.

In a less definite sense, propaganda includes the similar use of impressive rather than informative action, of demonstrations of prestige and privilege, of spectacles, parades, and rituals, and of carefully timed acts of mercy, preferment, repudiation, or violence.

There is also the propagandistic use of prevailingly aesthetic symbols—posters, cartoons, drama, music, and fiction.

Censorship is deliberate interference with communication. Because value attitudes can be influenced by all the forms of propagandistic activity just mentioned, censorship may apply to any and all of them.

To distinguish propaganda and censorship from those ubiquitous activities which are called education, we introduce the conception of achieving conformity to conventional values as contrasted with attempts by a minority to control mass valuational

† Reprinted from *Psychiatry* (1940) 3:628–632. [This was originally published as a Memorandum of the William Alanson White Psychiatric Foundation, with no authorship given. But Sullivan lists himself as the author in a 1947 bibliography. H.S.P.]

attitudes. All the propagandistic and censoring activities which tend to universalize conventional standards of value are education —manifestations of "the social forces." The rest are "social pressures" exercised by "pressure groups."

Propaganda works through a complex of leadership patterns, reaching most of its objectives through unnumbered face-to-face conversations in which direct interpersonal factors are effective in giving currency to the views concerned. Most people, even when deeply troubled, spare themselves the effort of analyzing situations and seeking out the personal implications of events. They "talk about" what is troubling them, and accept as correct or probable the views that are consonant with their aspirations and unsatisfied desires. They then repeat as their views excerpts from the statements of people who stand in the relation of conversational leadership to them, or who are respected for other causes.

The aspirations and wishes that determine the currency of views are in greater part very widely disseminated in the population. These are the products in personality structure of the early education in the home and the primary grades of school. Verbal symbols invested by empathy and by sympathy with high positive (pleasure, approval—and thus an expanded feeling of personal security) and negative (pain, discomfort, disapproval— and the feeling of personal insecurity) emotional tones have a great role in the socialization of everyone. These symbols, for the most part, continue indefinitely to exercise their power of evoking positive or negative feeling. A few may be analyzed; a few may be disintegrated by more powerfully evocative symbols which are acquired in later life—perhaps in adolescence. This, however, is decidedly the lesser part of the emotionally freighted vocabulary that each of us uses—and to which we are blindly responsive.

Besides the aspirations and desires and related evocative vocabulary that are almost universal among our people, there are subordinate aspirations, desires, and vocabularies that are almost universal among the people who were reared in homes of a particular social status or class. In any society which has open vertical classes, in which the individual is taught to conceive the possibility of his rising or falling, invidious factors contribute generally perduring color to the personalities socialized at each of the, in the U. S. A., ill-defined levels. The child of an unskilled laborer, be he now a successful physician, still responds emotionally to certain words and concepts that are impotent to move many another physician whose career-line has been parallel, say, from the second year in high school.

The aspects of personality that are products of "social forces" which bear on the individual from birth into adolescence are the relative uniformities to which education and propaganda are addressed. Most people develop but a modicum of insight into the underlying events and relations that validly explain the blend of facts and highly elaborated rumor that make up "news" and the conversational exchange of opinion. People by and large have long since abandoned the embarrassing and otherwise difficult and disconcerting pursuit of information as to their own reality and that of others. They read and listen not to be informed but to be reassured and entertained; moreover, this has usually been increasingly the case since early in the adolescent phase of personality development.

Personality is primarily the result of cultural influences superposed on the remarkably plastic human animal. The Western civilization and each of its national subcultures are heterogeneous and include many inconsistent and contradictory elements. Personality can scarcely be more than a rough approximation to a unitary system of relatively durable tendencies to integrate particular types of interpersonal situations—in turn, to be resolved with satisfaction, a feeling of personal security, or both. Few career-lines show an uninterrupted unidirectional course; many show complex patterns of now progression, now regression, or finally a rather consistently downward path. The self-consciousness of the individual, on the other hand, almost always reflects his personality as a unitary, consistent, and noncontradictory system. He thinks of and talks about *himself* in this simple way, untroubled today by recollection of yesterday's behavior which cannot be assimilated to today's rationalizations. If his attention is called to the incongruities, he is discomposed and has to 'do something' to relieve the threat to self-esteem which he experiences.

No particular propaganda can be perfectly adapted to more than one of the personality systems exposed to it. Most propaganda collides with important integrating tendencies in some few at least of the personalities on which it bears. The most gratifying result that the propagandist can achieve in this latter case is the provocation of a conflict of tendencies so severe that the person concerned is rendered ineffectual. From this consideration, it comes about that propagandistic efforts in areas of deep-rooted disagreements have to include elaborate preparatory phases. Significantly different personalities among the subjects to be influenced have to be "interested" by different—and often apparently unrelated—approaches. The several divergent phases of the propaganda are addressed to reducing critical awareness of the personal tendencies that conflict with the purpose of the main effort. And, to be effective, propaganda must always be subtle enough to avoid offense to its subject's self-respect as an "intelligent person capable of dispassionate judgment."

Subject to these and related reservations, propaganda best follows the patterns of the myths and fables which are a part of the common background above mentioned—with due regard to any special class hostility that may have attached to a particular few of these myths and fables, from our second group of background factors, above [that is, the ill-defined levels of social status or class in the United States].

A glance at the history of the Nazi success in securing leadership of the German peoples will illustrate the principle just mentioned. The "still-unmixed Nordic-Germanic human beings, the noblest surviving element of our nationality, indeed of all mankind," is the fair, pure, and noble lady in the thraldom of sundry evil genii—the Jews, the Socialists, and the Communists, and now the English—whose power over her derives chiefly from the talisman, the Treaty of Versailles. Once she shall have invoked the leader, the hero, Hitler, he shall rescue her and they together will live happily ever after, and will do great and good things without end.

The myths and fables in the culture-heritage of a people are essentially dreams of a particular type. The particularity lies both in the fitness of the symbols to represent dynamic patterns that are very widely distributed and persistently unresolved, and in the effectiveness of the symbol operations—the action portrayed—to mean satisfaction without guilt, remorse, or other depreciation of self-esteem. The dream, individually, and the myth and fable, for a great many people, are fantastic supplements to interpersonal relations, to fill in the voids caused by prohibitions and inhibitions, and to minimize tensions connected with ideological absurdities. These supplements depend for continued usefulness on their obscuring the crude interpersonal reality. As long as the dream suffices, it is not given very much attention—one leaves well enough alone. If dreams are not adequate to discharge certain interpersonal tendencies, and the crude desires come to be experienced in clear conflict with other tendencies that one has learned to consider indispensable to his personal security, a mental disorder has occurred.

The dream serves the necessities of the dreamer, only. It exists and is functionally effective in the wholly fantastic interpersonal relations that make up the social situation of the sleeper—which, however, reflects a significant aspect of his waking life. The myths and fables, while they have no meaningful existence by and of themselves, are held in closely approximate forms by the many people in whose interpersonal relations they are functionally effective. They may serve as valid ingredients of one's more private fantasy, or they may directly implement real interpersonal adjustments, facilitating or impeding particular motives called out by a social situation—as witness arguments by parables and proverbs, the whole panoply of socially effective rationalizations, and the fictions that serve as firm foundation for various institutionalized elements of our social order.

As has been indicated, the functional utility of dream or myth depends on its capacity for dealing with tendencies that would be unwelcome if clearly recognized. The successful avoiding of conflict by these instrumentalities is, however, not quite as simple as it seems. If, for example, a person has a tendency that would achieve satisfaction if he could find someone with whom he might engage in mutual embracing—a 'need for physical intimacy'—which performance would destroy his conviction that he is fully qualified for his particular life-work by being emotionally cold and self-sufficient, he will *not only* reduce the tension from this need by dreaming, remembered or not, *but also*, will add to his waking behavior some obscurely motivated performance that marks an avoidance or reaffirms a taboo.

In a parallel way, propaganda concerning powerfully conflictful situations can succeed only when it both avoids attracting attention to the crude interpersonal realities to which it is addressed, and offers a path of action which includes some obscure token act that propitiates the principal tendency system that it is thwarting. To the extent that it succeeds in this, it increases the feeling of security of those who are influenced by it. If, however, in a given situation, the propaganda proves inadequate to channel the comfortable discharge of unwelcome social necessities, morale and social solidarity are destroyed, the panicky attitudes and morbid suspiciousness become widespread.

Also, along this fundamental parallel from the wide personal validity of sundry myths and fables, there is no magic in propaganda. Its power comes from utility in avoiding conflicts of motives and the attending feeling of insecurity. If and when there is no such conflict involving the feeling of personal security, propaganda is without effect.

Again, as the number of impulses and tendency-systems that are chronically thwarted by motives in the service of personal security is great, the stability of propagandistically achieved effects may be slight. Counterpropaganda derives chiefly from this situation. "News" following the pattern of either a more fundamental or a more acutely revelant myth dissolves the original attitude and recrystallizes a new and contradictory one, without much awareness of the change on the part of the person influenced.

Finally, since motives to achieve or protect the feeling of personal security are, as it were, artifacts built into personality in the educational process, and they refer primarily to one's relations with others—including, in varied degree, one's personal ideals, etc.—they are much more evident in public behavior than in interpersonal relations in one's accustomed, congenial group.

Propaganda is, therefore, chiefly effective in the control of public behavior.

Everyone has a great deal of personal experience with censoring. However bitterly one may feel about governmental censorship, however elaborately one may rationalize one's deep-rooted objection to it, one censors one's own thoughts before giving them utterance; nay, most people censor their fantasies before according them clear awareness.

The effectiveness of more subtle forms of censorship as an instrument of social control can be very great. They are effective over a wider field of behavior than is propaganda in that they affect convivial and "purely personal" behavior.

The principle is that certain verbal formulae shall not be stated, in print or in conversation; from this the restriction extends to the discussion of certain topics. A perhaps quite rationally formulated taboo is imposed; it becomes a quasi-religious factor for the members of the group who subscribe to it. If they are a majority, and the taboo does not affect some master-symbol of an influential minority, it is apt to become quite universal in its effect. A great number of taboos—to expressive and to other acts—are embodied in the *mores* of any people. The sanction behind each taboo largely determines its durability—in the sense of resistance opposed to the development of contradictory *countermores*, or of simple disintegration from failure to give returns in personal security. If it is to succeed for a long time, there must be recurrent reaffirmations of the taboo in connection with the sanctioning power.

The occasional circulation of stories about a breach of the taboo and the evil consequences that flowed from this to the offender *and* to the public cause (the sanctioning power) well serves this purpose. Censorship of this sort has the color of voluntary acceptance of a ritualistic avoidance, in behalf of oneself and the higher power. A violation, after the primitive patterns to which we have all been exposed, strikes at both the sinner and his god.

The suppressions of behavior to which everyone was subjected in early childhood leave in most people some unresolved hostility to the authorities. This is apt to break cover whenever one's presumed "rights" are openly infringed. The rebellious behavior that ensues is often of a remarkably immature type, perhaps quite as disastrous for the person as to anyone else. It follows that, wherever possible, gross censorship should be restricted to such manifestations as errors and carelessness with respect to utterances previously tabooed. Otherwise, particularly in an ill-disciplined people, the censorship is apt to imperil morale and solidarity.

Attempts to protect solidarity and morale by gross censorship of the channels of public information are very dubious ventures, particularly in the case of our people. On the positive side, we retain a great deal of idealism and enthusiasm for under-dogs and lost causes, so that we are not readily discouraged. On the negative side, we are remarkably lacking in self-discipline and a sense of civic responsibility, so that it is easy to swing from extravagant patriotic zeal to rather paranoid suspiciousness of the Government. A superficially polite, but generally shy and socially distant people, we suffer little—however much we may hurt—from extravagant enthusiasm, but find it relatively difficult to regain balance after our suspicions have been aroused. A person can trust others only in the measure of his own trustworthiness, as he appraises it. Because one can project disagreeable aspects of oneself upon others, anything that disturbs trust in another is apt to be considerably reinforced by this process.

In the present international situation, it is almost impossible to escape the influence of some propaganda. The first indication for a public policy in this connection would seem to be caution in formulating plans for our protection. When one is not being told about the "good sense of the average American" which will penetrate infallibly to the gist of things, one is hearing about our need for counterpropaganda. Both of these notions are beside the point. Under pressure, the proponent of the 'good sense' view will add "if he is given the facts"—as if there were some source whence these facts could be obtained. The proponent of counterpropaganda comes nearer to a practical recommendation. Something must be done. It cannot take the form of an instantaneous education of the public to all the social realities that give current events their present meaning and portent. It cannot be a magic information service that will give the public facts that the Government itself is unable to secure. It certainly should not take a form that will increase public uncertainty and individual indecision, one of the effects the enemy desires to achieve by his psychiatric strategy, and precisely the result that is to be expected from indiscriminate counterpropaganda.

Psychiatry teaches that a person's ability to adjust is a function of his awareness of the situation in which he is involved. If he is alert to all significant factors, his adaptive capacities are generally adequate. He cannot be alert and understanding about events wholly foreign to his experience, but he will encounter few events that are wholly without precedent. The principal handicap to alertness is that peculiar misidentification of events which arises from unresolved situations in the person's chronological past. These emotionally toned remnants of earlier difficulties complicate the present situation and befog the field of observation. It follows that anything which increases these emotional concomitants aggravates the maladjustment while anything which increases clarity is helpful. Even though we cannot hope at this juncture immediately to do much to reduce the emotional warp of most people, we can have these factors clearly in mind when we are organizing information that is to be communicated to the public, and when we are engaged in communicating it.

10

Commentary

THE NEXT PAPER, "Psychiatry and the National Defense" (1941), is a partial record of a central area of Sullivan's contribution to the Government during World War II—planning for Selective Service. It seems cogent to see this activity of Sullivan's in terms of the title of this book. In the national emergency occasioned by the approach of World War II, Sullivan was, in a sense, forced back into his own discipline. That is, he indicates in this paper that psychiatrists, of all social scientists, are the only ones that have a useful contribution to make to many of the problems arising from the international crisis: selection of the armed forces, the maintenance of civilian morale, the mobilization of industry, and so on. In reality, this highlights the dilemma envisioned for some time by Sullivan and by those social scientists who had collaborated significantly with him: *It was the psychiatrist, and not the social scientist, who had access to the important clinical data and who had, however reluctantly at times, been forced to experiment with intervention in crisis situations; the social scientist for the most part lacked this action-research experience.* However unskilled a psychiatrist might be in reporting on his work within a scientific framework, he was a member of the only group in the behavioral sciences, generally, who had opportunity to learn by doing—excluding, of course, the service professions, particularly the nurse and the social worker, who have historically often lacked the autonomy and prestige to communicate, even informally, their significant insights. As a result, the psychiatrist, in terms of the national emergency, was a member of the only professional group that had practical experience in gross prediction of areas of human trouble.

Some such dilemma still persists today. The research psychiatrist often finds himself moving away from his historical area of competency; he sometimes attempts to solve his self-styled dilemma of not being scientifically "objective enough" by trying to be "hard-boiled" about the patient and by separating his research function from his clinical duties. But characteristically he often finds that his humanistic action-research manner of functioning—that is, of studying how his interaction with the patient affects positively and negatively the patient's progress—eventually reasserts itself, even if he has difficulty in admitting it.[1] On the other side of the same coin, the 'responsible' social psychologist, sociologist, and so on, often denies that he ever intervenes with the values of his interviewee, no matter how desperately the interviewee seeks such intervention in the process of the interview. Nor is the social scientist, of whatever profession, usually willing to report on ongoing research in an institution (so that he might intervene with, for instance, administrative problems and then be able to observe whether he had made a contribution that was useful), since this would "ruin" his data.

At the end of the First World War, there was a clear understanding among many psychiatrists that the draftee program had been wasteful in human and material terms; the Foundation generally, and Sullivan particularly, wanted if possible to profit from this experience in preparing for the new Selective Service program.

With no official mandate from the Government, the Foundation issued a "Memorandum on the Utilization of Psychiatry in the Promotion of National Security," dated June 17, 1940. This Memorandum came to the attention of Clarence Dykstra, then Director of the Selective Service System, and a plan was instigated by him for the general and specific use of Sullivan and the Foundation in selective service programming. With the support of Carnegie and Rockefeller funds, Sullivan was appointed consultant to Dykstra. The next article reports on the kind of progress made in the mutual shaping of psychiatric technique and the military program, during the period when Sullivan was being productively utilized by Selective Service.

[1] For a clarification of this dilemma, see Stewart E. Perry, "Social Processes in Psychiatric Research: A Study in the Sociology of Science," unpublished Ph.D. dissertation, Harvard University, 1963.

But Dykstra was only briefly on leave from Columbia University, and he was soon succeeded by his deputy, General Lewis B. Hershey. Hershey's attitude toward Sullivan's ideas was negative, as reported by Albert Deutsch in the newspaper *PM*, for August 13, 1942: "Sullivan was stopped in his tracks. . . . Hershey, who takes pride in being an amateur psychologist, did little to disguise his distaste for the ideas of Sullivan and other psychiatrists." Within a few months after Hershey became Director of Selective Service, Sullivan had resigned; by January, 1942, the Selective Service System had given up the attempt to sift out even the most obviously psychiatrically disabled registrants, including those on parole from mental hospitals. It was several months before the Army itself finally stepped in and commissioned a psychiatrist (Roy D. Halloran) to deal with Army psychiatry; at that time, a *two-minute* psychiatric examination—administered by a psychiatrist or other physician—was budgeted for each draftee. Sullivan himself had felt that *fifteen minutes* was minimal in his earlier evaluation of the situation; and he left Selective Service feeling that he had failed to achieve any useful, durable result.[2]

Perhaps one of the significant unintended results of psychiatry in this emergency was the development of the "high-speed" screening interview. Despite Sullivan's sense of failure in establishing what he considered adequate pre-induction psychiatric screening, he did formulate some significant and communicable procedures for adapting psychiatry to the screening situation. During Sullivan's connection with Selective Service, he organized seminars in various national regions to acquaint the general practitioner (and the psychiatrist) with procedures for using competently the brief time available for the pre-induction interview. A report of one of these seminars, not included here, illustrates Sullivan's capacity to put clinical sensitivity to didactic use for meeting a broader social problem. Psychiatry, he emphasized, had to be practiced differently in the high-speed examination, but it must still be practiced competently and rationally. The good psychiatrist would have an opportunity through Selective Service to organize his techniques into words in the process of arriv-

[2] See "Psychiatry, the Army, and the War," *Psychiatry* (1942) 5:435–442. This is an excerpt from the President's Report to the Board of Trustees, William Alanson White Psychiatric Foundation. The President was, of course, Sullivan.

ing at a replicable procedure with his colleagues, and this would "lift his work from a perhaps quite varying degree of efficiency and validity to scientific psychiatric diagnosis." [3]

[3] See Selective Service System, "A Seminar on Practical Psychiatric Diagnosis," *Psychiatry* (1941) 4:265–283 *passim*.

Psychiatry and the National Defense†

IT IS only proper to start my somewhat discursive comments with an historical reference to how it happens that it is I who am talking about this subject. The William Alanson White Psychiatric Foundation, created during Dr. White's lifetime as a memorial to him and to continue some of his major interests, felt in the fall of 1938 that things were moving rather toward an international crisis which would involve us, and at that time the Board bestirred itself to focus psychiatric attention on the possibilities in the crisis. The first conspicuous evidence of this was a contribution by Captain Dallas G. Sutton,* of the Navy, one of our Trustees, which seemed particularly timely, because it set forth very lucidly the peculiar problems created by the environment of the Navy. You know that the Navy is more or less centered on the battle fleet in action. Everything is focused on that; plans are made with that as the final reference point, and on a battleship, everybody including the cook and the scullery boy have battle positions; and when they are not engaged in battle, they have to live in remarkably crowded quarters, in a very highly

† Reprinted from *Psychiatry* (1941) 4:201–212. [This is a transcript of an address given at the annual meeting of the New York Society of Clinical Psychiatry, the Academy of Medicine, New York City, January 9, 1941.]
[* One of Sutton's writings on military psychiatry had earlier been published in the journal Sullivan edited. Dallas G. Sutton, "The Utilization of Psychiatry in the Armed Forces," *Psychiatry* (1939) 2:1–9. H.S.P.]

organized life. Human contact is at a maximum, and the Navy is confronted, as a result, with the necessity of having people who show no material abnormalities of adjustment to their fellows. There is probably no service concerned in the present crisis that imposes such rigid demands on its personnel as does the Navy.

We started out with the problem of the Navy, and went on from that, gradually elaborating the general problem of the utilization of psychiatry in the national defense. Characteristically, many things went wrong. For example, in the fall of 1939, the Southern Psychiatric Association, perhaps under the provocation of the Foundation, [sent a memorandum to] the Government asking for a survey of psychiatric necessities and nothing came of it. Finally, the Foundation organized a committee to go to England to study actual experience; and at that time Assistant Secretary of State Long seemed to be feeling very keenly about the Neutrality Act and refused to waive its prohibition against travel on vessels of a belligerent power, which meant there was no way to get back, except by swimming. As a documentation of the project, the Foundation got out a rather hurried and extremely condensed memorandum [1] which is the basis of a good many of the things that have happened.

From the failure of the study—that is, the expedition to make a study of actual combat experience—the next problem that came up was the jittery state, as someone put it, of the country, which led to our considering how psychiatry might apply itself to relieving panicky movements in the general population,* and then came conscription.

The program as it was elaborated started out with the place of psychiatry in a democratic, capitalistic world in general, and in the defense of such a world; second, the particular psychiatric attack now being made by the totalitarian powers, their strategy of terror, and economic penetration; third, psychiatry and the

[1] "Memorandum from the William Alanson White Psychiatric Foundation on the Utilization of Psychiatry in the Promotion of National Security," Psychiatry (1940) 3:483–492 [unsigned].

[* Sullivan soon published two analyses of civilian morale and panic. The first appeared as "Psychiatric Aspects of Morale," American J. Sociology (1941–42) 47:277–301. The other is reprinted in this book as "Psychiatry and Morale." H.S.P.]

building up of armed forces, which came to be the first thing that we actually went hard to work at; fourth, psychiatry and the building up of machines, munitions, and other defense materials, that is, the psychiatry of wartime industry; fifth, psychiatry and the problem of basic solidarity and morale on which the armed forces and industry depend during a crisis; sixth, the psychiatric therapy of public disturbances, paranoid reactions; and finally, the extremely difficult field of a counterstrategy that would actually neutralize the psychological warfare, strategy of terror, war of nerves, whatever it pleases you to call it, that has been invented in part by Dr. Goebbels, and in part by his staff.

The first real call came from Selective Service. I think I had best give a little history here, because it is an enormous going concern in which you may all have practical interest. The plans for Selective Service were worked out by a joint committee of the general staff—that is, the general staff of the Army, and what corresponds to it in the Navy. The plans were fairly complete in 1933. They were rather in abeyance for a good many years after that, and were suddenly stirred up as this crisis really came to our shores.

The medical function, as it had been established in 1933, had undergone some changes in the years between, and it was in what I would describe as a distinctly amorphous condition, when the organization of the bureau was actually undertaken on a grant from the President's emergency funds. A medical corps officer attached to the general staff joined the Selective Service organization and rapidly whipped the medical division into order. He worked very much against time, and achieved a minor miracle in organization. In doing this, he worked from standard specifications of the Army in regard to manpower.

About this time the Veterans Administration exerted pressure to focus the attention of Selective Service on the stupendous burden from neuropsychiatric problems which resulted from the last conscription. The Federal Board of Hospitalization was asked to prepare a memorandum, and this was done. It reached the President a few days before the representative of the William Alanson White Foundation reached Selective Service. As a result of the President's interest, his civilian Advisory Committee on

Selective Service became concerned about the neglect of psychiatric aspects in conscription, and just as this began to gain attention around Selective Service, I happened in as the emissary of the William Alanson White Psychiatric Foundation with a statement of the minimum psychiatric considerations for examining physicians which had been worked out by a committee of about fifteen people who had been studying it for several weeks. One might say that it had become official because it came at the right moment, but I assure you it was not that simple, because it was taken under consideration immediately, and ten more people went to work on it. After a number of revisions, it was finally published as Medical Circular No. 1 of the Selective Service System. It is a child's guide to psychiatric diagnosis—in other words, it is something which is supposed to be within the grasp of the intelligent physician who is making examinations of people called under the Selective Service Act.

Now, there are at least 6,401 of those physicians; actually there are many more, but there are 6,401 local boards, and each has at least one medical examiner, and he frequently has the good sense to have several assistants or associates. The structure is as follows: every person who is not exempted for dependency, or other statutory reason, is called for physical examination. If the local board examiner becomes suspicious of a registrant's mental state, or is puzzled about his heart or any other condition, he is authorized to send this person to the appropriate specialist on the Medical Advisory Board. There are 548 Medical Advisory Boards throughout the United States, and each is required to have a psychiatrist. Actually, their location is such that quite a number of them do not have psychiatrists in the true sense of the word, or even a rough approximation thereto. Most of them by now have experienced physicians who have shown some sensitivity to personality factors, where they do not have psychiatrists or alleged psychiatrists. We trust that they will all come to have people who are really sensitive to personality factors.

You will notice that this provision of the Selective Service System does not guarantee that each registrant or even each disturbed registrant will be seen by a psychiatrist; very far from it. The only people seen by the psychiatrists are those about whom the examining physician is worried, puzzled, or doubtful. We try to impress upon the examining physician when to be worried, puzzled, or doubtful, and what to do; namely, to refer the patient to the Advisory Board's psychiatrist.

Let me give you an example of what happens, to illustrate to you how well that works. I dropped in with a colleague at a local board one evening where there was a team of three people, two surgeons, I believe, by specialty, and one general practitioner. We were known to be psychiatrists, and there was some vague surmise that one or the other of us had something to do with Selective Service, and, sure enough, we were sent three people to see, three registrants. One of them never got to us; he became worn out waiting and disappeared. The other two impressed me very greatly. One of them was a low-grade moron, or high-grade imbecile, pretty weak in thinking abilities.

The other was a very interesting person whom I would call a pre-schizophrenic. Depending on one's peculiar interest, you might say that he was a case of neurocirculatory asthenia, a schizoid personality, even possibly, you might say, a compulsive character; but, at any rate, he was a person doing fairly well as a bank clerk, and I would not trust him to last very long in a training camp.

That was amazing. Here were three people. We see two, and both of them are the sorts of people that a psychiatrist should see. This was interesting enough; so I went out and discovered that the good old general practitioner was responsible for all of these references. "Why in the world did you send these people to us?" I asked him.

He was embarrassed, and replied, "Why? Wasn't anything the matter with them?"

I said, "Well, before we go into that, tell me why you sent them to us."

He said, "As I was going over them, I got the impression there was something odd about them."

I then asked, "If we hadn't dropped in this evening, what would you have done?"

"Well, we would have sent them on to the induction board. Nothing ailed them. They are perfectly good material for soldiers."

That is a tragically true story. Here is a good physician who recognizes the presence of personality warp, but in common with, I fear, 4,962 of the 6,401 local board examiners, he has not the vaguest notion of what he should do when he hits something that does not seem to be quite usual. In the end, not knowing what to do, he sends them on for duty.

I am afraid I will be a bore on this thing, but still I will say a little bit more about it. In the first place, such a situation will not do, because we have spent—the taxpayers of the United States have spent—on neuropsychiatric disabilities related to the conscription and war of 1917–1918, 946-odd million dollars. The cost is still going up. Everything else has gone down. Tuberculosis maintained a level for years, and is slowly dropping, but the neuropsychiatric load goes up steadily, in its magnitude, year by year, and a billion dollars of taxpayers' money has already been spent. . . .

Further than that, the disorder, inefficiency, and grave risk which these patients caused in combat units were very sharply impressed on everyone serving in combat troops in the last war; and we have every reason to believe that the fundamental stability of American youth has diminished and that many of the strains of warfare have increased.

In the last war two per cent of all registrants examined by physicians were rejected by local boards and another two and one-half per cent by the camp boards; they then innocently thought that if they got such people out of the service in a few weeks they would be no expense to the taxpayers.

Now, whereas that is four and one-half per cent from the 1917–1918 experience, I believe we should multiply that by two, and look to about eight per cent of the total registrants otherwise eligible for service in this conscription. There is some reason for this, also some indices that may or may not seem to you to point at all in that direction, such as the fact that of volunteers accepted by the Army in the year of 1938, 1.75 per cent became neuropsychiatric disabilities. Army examinations are in general fully as good as those that are being given by the local boards today, and the volunteers who went into the service at that time are a representative cross section of those who are being called in now.

You may agree that this is an appalling problem, but you may also be extremely skeptical as to whether anything can be done. There are people who have gone to great pains—fortunately for their purpose, omitting certain methodological controls—to show that the incidence of psychosis is identical in people who were involved in the last unpleasantness and in the general population. Now I have no doubt from their figures that the per capita rate is fairly approximate, but they have not taken the trouble to notice the characteristics of these psychoses and various features about their course, which are distinctly different.

I believe there are some evidences that something can be done which are not open to argument at all. Dr. Hall, Dr. Simon, and Miss Hagan, the Red Cross Social Worker, made a hurried study of all service cases received at St. Elizabeths Hospital, from the Army, Navy, the Marine Corps, and the Coast Guard—there being four of the latter—in the period from 1 October 1939, to 30 September 1940; of course, all volunteer enlistment material. The total was 183 patients.*

[* Sullivan's report is apparently based on a preliminary and personal communication with one of the participants in the study, probably with Roscoe W. Hall, an associate of the William Alanson White Foundation and a member of the senior staff at St. Elizabeths. The final study was formally published soon after Sullivan's article, although Sullivan had obviously not seen it as yet: Alexander Simon, Margaret Hagan, and Roscoe W. Hall, "A Study of Specific Data in the Lives of One Hundred and Eighty-Three Veterans Admitted to St. Elizabeths Hospital," *War Medicine* (1941) 1:387–391. The formal statistical results are somewhat different from those reported by Sullivan, as the result perhaps of a later stage in analysis; also some information that Sullivan reports does not appear in the *War Medicine* article. The figures from the latter study indicate that of the 183 veterans examined (all those admitted directly from the armed services during the years before the draft began), 20.9 per cent had been previously hospitalized for mental illness; 8.3 per cent had shown anti-social behavior; 19.4 per cent had shown excessive alcoholism; 6.6 per cent were intellectually retarded (moron level); 37.3 per cent had come from a "broken home"; and 33.9 per cent had immediate family members who had been mentally ill. In summary, the authors report that 46 per cent, or 84 of the 183 enlistees, had at least one gross social characteristic that was an indication for psychiatric examination before induction; but for 54 per cent "no social data or observations could have been made at the time of enlistment which would have indicated that subsequent mental trouble would develop" (p. 390). H.S.P.]

Ten per cent had had the onset of the psychosis for which they were sent to St. Elizabeths on the first day at their station. In other words, they were psychotic in all likelihood long before they reached their station. I believe that all of you will be inclined to agree that psychiatrists can recognize psychotic people, so ten per cent of this outfit could have been prevented by good psychiatric examination, unquestionably. Fifty per cent had onset within the first year of service. That looks strongly suspicious, does it not?

[However,] according to this study, fifty-four per cent showed, in all the documents—and in some cases these were careful social histories—no evidence which a fair-minded psychiatrist could claim indicated the probability of psychosis. Depressing as this may sound, it does suggest that forty-six per cent showed, at least by psychiatric hindsight, historical factors in their performance which suggested the possibility of psychosis. When this was broken down—and this I toss in just for your information rather than to convince you that something can be done—more than ten per cent of all these people had had mental hospital residence before enlistment. Over twenty per cent had had arrests directly referable to their being drunk and disorderly; thirty-four per cent had psychotic relatives in the immediate group, that is, excluding all cousins, and thirty-seven per cent came from homes that had been broken by death, divorce, or something of that kind before they had reached the age of thirteen.

Now, the fact that ten per cent had been psychotic before enlistment—that is, ten per cent were discovered to be psychotic when they reached their training station—suggests that everything else being equal, we could still reduce this potential burden of about one billion dollars twenty-two or twenty-three years after this conscription by at least fifteen per cent, and as a taxpayer you might be interested in that. . . .

When people are passed by the local board with or without the benefit of advice from the Medical Advisory Board, they are sent to an Army Induction Board. There are seventy-five Army Induction Boards at the present time, as against about 550 Medical Advisory Boards. The Personnel Branch of the General Staff has very wisely instructed that on these Army Induction

Boards a psychiatrist will be provided for each fifty candidates to be examined per day.

After a lot of thought on the part of our trustees and others, the conclusion was reached that it is impossible to figure on competent psychiatry at the rate of more than thirty or thirty-five people per day. The General Staff made it fifty, which I think, for the Government, is an incredible approximation. That really is the best news in the war so far.

From these seventy-five Induction Boards, the candidates . . . will go to some one of twenty-five Reception Centers where they will be open to rather intensive study. It is the present intention that the Army will pay quite a lot of attention to psychiatry, and that the reception centers will have really competent psychiatric officers. At that point, there will be a chance to do some real study of behavior under Army circumstances.

You understand that once the person is accepted by the Army Induction Board, he is yours so far as taxes are concerned. In other words, he is entitled to all sorts of benefits, and there is very little probability that he will be denied many in the future. But from the standpoint of military efficiency, the present strong inclination to give psychiatry a hand and see what it can do suggests that we will eliminate a lot of the potentially bad material.

It may be well to point out that the mission of psychiatry in Selective Service is twofold, the two being necessary concomitants of each other. First, it is the exclusion of unsuitable candidates from among those sent to the Army Induction Board. These unsuitable candidates are of three categories: there are those people who are now useful members of the community, whose capability for self-support and utility would be destroyed or gravely reduced by the circumstances they encountered in the service; second, there are those who would definitely break down as psychotic or seriously psychoneurotic disabilities with bad effects on the morale, solidarity, and discipline of the units; third, a group that you might not immediately think of, a group of people who will do well under the circumstances of military training, in fact, in some cases do better than they have done previously in civil life, but who cannot be discharged back into civil life without serious disturbance of personality. We saw quite a bit of that at demobilization last time, people who had been distinguishing themselves, but who have been veteran patients ever since. These are people who find the particular characteristics of the military situation so well suited to them that to give it up is not a welcome prospect. Social pressure, boredom, and so on, move them to getting released as soon as they can, but they rapidly develop disabling personality disorders.

The job is first to exclude these three [categories of registrants], if possible, but the second and absolutely necessary concomitant of this task of psychiatry is that of protecting both those who are rejected and the general solidarity and morale of the country—civilian morale—from the evil effects that can inhere in this extraordinary development of psychiatric classification, which is without parallel and has many by-products which I will touch upon shortly.

To accomplish the first of these tasks—namely, the exclusion of those not properly suited to the military vocation—Selective Service has found itself confronted with the initial problem of mobilizing psychiatric ability, psychiatric competence, if you please, which is slightly different from mobilizing psychiatrists. . . . This is the reason for a very elaborate consideration of [psychiatric] training: in contradistinction to every other medical specialty involved in this mobilization, psychiatry is a medical specialty which takes on a novel task when it turns to the Selective Service.

[Ordinarily] almost every psychiatrist sees only people who have been recognized to be problems of one kind and another. Many psychiatrists see patients who are psychotic or such extremely troublesome psychopaths that it is too bad they are not psychotic, so that they could be retained in hospitals. But in Selective Service the psychiatrist sees the human race as it exists in the U.S. in the age group of 21 to 35, without specification. Now, if he is on the Medical Advisory Board . . . then he sees only those that some doctor thinks he ought to see, but still far from typical clinical cases. He is called upon to recognize potentialities for serious mental disturbance under the military circumstance, or in discharge from the military circumstance, or (and this is something you might overlook) in what would in all likelihood occur in the next eleven years of the person's life—because this training project [Selective Service Act of 1940] keeps a man in training a year, and in the reserve force for ten years thereafter.

I think, if I have made myself at all clear, you will see that this is quite a different task from that in which most psychiatrists have been engaged. For that reason, when we speak of mobilizing psychiatric competence, we mean that we feel we have to set before psychiatrists the characteristics of the Army environment as it is today and will be in case of combat on the total war pattern as it has recently been revealed—with its mechanized side, for example. Along with that, we have to invite psychiatrists to notice what they know about potentialities, which is a great deal; and finally, we have to invite their attention to how they do their diagnostic work. Most of them have become very skilled at that, and the more skillful they become, the less inclined they are to observe and formulate the steps by which they achieve their good results. When you are to move from working with psychotics, for example, to the business of looking over comparatively normal people, and making good guesses about a bad future for them, you must go through certain operations of formulating and reorienting your skills to this job.

That is what I mean by the mobilization of psychiatric competence [as the first problem]. . . . There is an enormous amount of competence among psychiatrists, but to make it readily available for this particular task requires some expenditure of effort at organization.

Second, we have to unify the diagnostic viewpoints and practices. Supposing that every one of you does have the authentic blown-in-the-bottle, correct psychiatry, anything as massive as mobilizing the manpower of America cannot make sense if one of the most essential techniques applied to the personnel problem is of as many varieties as there are workers in that field. I do not know how soon this will cease to be the case—I surmise privately it will be the case for some time to come. Be that as it may, psychiatry has been boiled down, in the local examiners' circular, to the identification of five gross types of peculiarities, of which mental defect and deficiency is one; the second is psychopathic personalities; the third, mood disorders; the fourth, the psychosomatic and psychoneurotic conditions; and the fifth, the pre- and post-psychotic personalities. A revision that will appear presently adds chronic inebriety, neurosyphilis, and organic nerve disease.

This is the outcome of elaborate and sustained effort on the part of about fifteen people to discover what everybody could agree to and what the intelligent and interested physician could probably notice. I think that will tend to be the diagnostic viewpoint that matters in the Selective Service for some time to come. It eliminates many of the refinements that we are interested in, but I think their elimination may be useful, because this is the job of selecting personnel for a place in total defense; and refinements beyond this would probably pay very small dividends, either in procurement of manpower for the military service or in the industrial mobilization.

The third big problem—and it is a big problem—in this business of eliminating the unfit is, of course, the education of the local board physician. When the Medical Advisory Board psychiatrists have had a little time to see the special aspect of their problem, we shall have to look to them to do an amount of professional post-graduate educating among their colleagues in the community. This is really a very considerable addition to their already overburdened life, but without the active, interested and somewhat unified teaching by Medical Advisory Board psychiatrists, it is scarcely possible to get the local board examiners to utilize psychiatry as psychiatry needs to be utilized. . . . I will come back to this after I have taken up some other aspects of the topic.

You recall that I said the mission for Selective Service was not only eliminating the unfit but also shielding those who were rejected and protecting the general public from evil effects of this classification. Forgive me if I touch upon points which are probably painfully apparent to you. Lest somebody is not following me, bear with me while I present two or three examples.

Take, as an example, a small factory town. Johnny Jones and Tom Brown are two men who are working on lathes in the same factory, earning the same money. Each, let us say, has a mother and father living, and both of the mothers are fairly social, given to communication with other members of the neighborhood. Johnny Jones is accepted and Tom Brown is rejected by the Selective Service System. They were doing the same work, receiving like wages, and neither had been sick; their community life was quite parallel. We can picture Mrs. Jones, if she has a little paranoid tendency, or perhaps is Republican in politics, feeling that there is something very funny indeed in the Selective Service. If she is also a very energetic and outspoken woman, she will probably drop in on the local board and present them with an ultimatum that either they will explain how this came about, or she will know that this thing is crooked. Suppose they say Tom Brown was nuts, or neuropsychiatrically disabled, or something to this effect. Well, let us be charitable about Mrs. Jones. This is still news, which is very interesting indeed; and what it does to Tom Brown in the course of the next six weeks or so, may be quite tragic indeed—that is, if Mrs. Jones even accepts this explanation. At present I think she would say that the board was nuts instead of Tom Brown. So you can see that we must do a lot in order to maintain the feeling of public confidence and to protect the people who are rejected from the evils of gossip and archaic ideas about mental disorder; otherwise we will be doing a great deal of harm while we are doing some good by the armed forces and the taxpayer.

To do [something constructive about] this, we literally have to organize and collaborate and maintain liaison with social agencies, churches, educational bodies, and other groups. Way beyond that, however, we as psychiatrists must take up the burden of public education and attempt to accomplish in the next six to nine months much that the National Committee [for Mental Hygiene] has not been able to accomplish in the past twenty years.

That may seem a very steep order, but let me suggest to you that there has never been such a setting as the psychiatric classification service will provide. There is nothing that has brought psychiatry so emphatically and openly to the attention of the public as this will when it begins to work, and, therefore, the soil will be riper for public education than it ever has been before. Selective Service, so far as I can predict, will do what it can to carry the torch through the press and magazines and other channels, but it is the psychiatrists who have the facts and the prestige and position in the community, and I am afraid they must take up the cudgel. There again I believe that as a sort of by-product of this attempt on our part to educate the local board examiner, we will perhaps actually be useful in the work of public education, because the sort of simple psychiatry that we need to have is perhaps also quite acceptable to the general public. In so far as it is based on extremely practical considerations, it is probably rather sound and not apt to get one into a cul-de-sac of explanation.

I have spoken thus far of the actual problem of the Selective Service. Some of you will know from personal experience that the Medical Advisory Board psychiatrist does not have many persons sent to him, and, therefore, has time to make a study of them. The Army Induction Board psychiatrist, on the other hand, will have at least fifty people a day whenever he is working. His problem is precisely and exactly the same as our Medical Advisory Board psychiatrists'—the same standards. You know the standards are identical for the Army and Selective Service: the same difficulties of prediction of potentialities—rather than diagnosis of gross maladies for the most part; the same problem of trying to get the history of whether the person has been in a mental hospital; the same necessity for access to such social records as may be made available to him. But all [of this must be done] with much greater haste.

I believe I have already suggested that in my opinion—and I have never suspected myself of being an optimistic idealist, [although] maybe some of you will before I am through—a great many psychiatrists are capable of doing remarkably well on an average of fifteen minutes per stranger. To do that, needless to say, the first moment of contact is utilized as well as all the succeeding moments of the fifteen minutes. You do not greet people in a state of abstraction and talk nonsense about the weather, or whatever, for five or six minutes, with no idea of what you said or what the patient has done. You simply must utilize every single thing that happens.

I am wondering whether I can go into a few details of this problem, because unhappily I still have several hours of things to discuss.

The way an interview can be given fairly successfully, is this: be very alert. I do not care what you say or how you greet a person, but be very alert to what happens; notice any clue to the first impression the patient has of you. You get the patient into the room and have him sit down while you look at the paper, and you can see quite a wide range outside the paper while you are looking at it. Even if you do not see anything on the paper, notice what the patient does, how he sits in the chair, studies you, looks at your papers, stares at the floor, studies the office furniture, or becomes fixed on something, all of which can be observed while you are looking over the very scant medical records that come with him. Then perhaps one has him undress. While he undresses, you can talk to him about all sorts of things, and of course he stops undressing every time you ask him a question, until you point out to him that he can undress while talking. That in itself is an interesting difference in people; quite a number of them seem to feel that answering a doctor's question is much too important to do anything else at the same time.

What one talks about is something that seems natural to the patient, always trying to avoid some complex reaction which cannot be interpreted, because we have not the time to explore it. Assume that human personality shows itself however slightly in almost everything that a patient does. In a particular instance that leaps to my mind, the examinee happened to be very lightweight for his height.* My first comment to him was, "Have you always been thin?" He said, "Yes." Shortly after that, however, it developed that not only had he always been thin, but he had gone to tremendous effort to gain weight, in fact, never smoking, drinking, or being up late at night. He had no lady friends, and had joined a religious cult strong on vegetarianism and other physical 'hygiene.' In other words, this business was a tremendous problem to him.

Well, such luck, of course, comes once in a lifetime, but one proceeds, if possible, from the commonplace in fairly obvious

[* I have rewritten this sentence somewhat for readability. H.S.P.]

lines of thought, so that the patient will have some idea of what you are driving at, and, incidentally, you will have some idea of what he is replying to. Certain of the crude categories [of disability], I believe, can be determined with reasonable probability in more than fifty per cent of the cases. This is not apt to be the case with the psychopathic personality, who can be detected by brief examination only under the most fortunate circumstances. That is almost entirely . . . a matter of [having a] history, not now provided; but we hope that will be remedied very soon. [The brief examination] will not ordinarily pick out the hysterics, because the hysteric is keyed to meet any novel situation with such enthusiasm and interest that unless you are very sensitive to his key as a few people are, he will go through with flying colors; in fact, it is only after four weeks at camp that they begin to be themselves. And it will not pick out the mood swing cases. The only times they can be detected without history are either when they are going up or coming down, which it is not apt to be our good fortune to encounter.

Those three groups I feel are beyond this technique, except by very fortunate accident. I believe a psychiatrist will have far more than fifty per cent of successes with the rest of them if he utilizes every moment and all the alertness that he can marshal and all the insight—perhaps never formulated—which he possesses, for determining how the interview progresses between himself and the patient.

Now, what else about psychiatry and the national defense? I have said a lot about the Selective Service; it is very much the going thing. Both the Selective Service and the Induction Board are going to run very much faster after the first of April [1941] than they have thus far. They are going to make heavier demands on the psychiatrists concerned—regrettable, and I fear unavoidable—but as the [men] are inducted into the service, a novel aspect of [military] service psychiatry is going to appear. The fact that they are to go from training to a ten-year period on the reserve means that the ordinary mission of the military psychiatrist—namely, to identify and discharge as quickly as possible all mental casualties—can give place to some mental hygiene work.

In other words, there are men with eccentricities of personality that will not take much time in correcting; [these men] will improve and benefit from military training and increase in probability of mental health throughout the period of the reserve.

This is rather unpleasant news to the Army and its Medical Corps at present, for medical officers at the rate of 6.5 per thousand do not provide many psychiatrists for their regular work, but it seems to me to be a quite inevitable development. Certain aspects of the service, such as the highly technical branches, air service, and the mechanized troops, are emphasizing the need for this, and I believe it will spread fairly rapidly: Instead of being merely diagnosticians to expel casualties, I think the military psychiatrists will have some peacetime therapeutic work to do. Therapy is not so novel a matter in actual military operations, for certain of the acute psychoneurotic cases, unless they are treated very wisely and immediately, become foci of menace to the morale of the whole outfit and, of course, [become] permanent total disabilities, when all that they really should require is to be removed from combat duty to the line of communications duty.

Industrial Psychiatry

But beyond all this business of the combat troops, what about the rest of the problems that I have touched upon? You know industries are rapidly expanding, there is an enormous amount of re-employment, and the people who are being employed have, in many cases, been without employment or on WPA and similar projects for years, during which time the general level of faith and conviction about democracy and capital and labor have undergone a good many changes, perhaps all for the worse. When these people go back to work, there is a rather shocking amount of absenteeism, sickness, time lost, accidents, and trouble in the sense of altercations, disagreeableness, morose attitudes, and the like, as is already demonstrated in many places.

Every one of these things, when looked at closely, is a well-known psychiatric problem. The psychiatrist has a lot to offer in industry, but again he can not be the psychiatrist he has been before the war. In other words, no industrial organization can afford three hundred analytic hours for most of its workers. Again we have one of these high-speed performances, and again we have nowhere near the number of psychiatrists necessary to do the work. Just as in Selective Service, we must then turn to the local physician, in this case, the industrial physician, the plant physician and surgeon, and they, just as our local examiners in Selective Service, have to be sensitized to some comparatively understandable rudiments of psychiatric diagnosis of the problems encountered in industry. They have to be educated to refer the problems that require expert handling to psychiatrists in some fashion made available for this purpose, perhaps in the end something similar to our Advisory Boards. These psychiatrists will have to utilize all the time they have with the industrial patient, not alone for diagnostic, but in this case for therapeutic results. Here again I am sure I am not an optimistic idealist. The psychiatrist, once he looks the problem quite squarely in the face, will find he can do quite a lot more than he might offhand surmise, if he goes at it in a fashion that offers a reasonable probability of working.

Some people have said to me, "But, Doctor, think what happens in our outpatient clinics. Here these people come in; my Lord, you listen to them and they haven't time and you haven't time, and they come again and again, and they get worse before your eyes, and you become completely discouraged."

I think that this tragic picture is often true. I am not quite certain that it is solely the defect of the economic and dispensary system. I am afraid that a number of the psychiatrists who have made this sort of complaint to me have never paid any attention to the difference in the job they had as a dispensary psychiatrist from their job as an office practitioner, and, therefore, they were not really coming halfway to meet the problem of dispensary psychiatry. Of course, it is more like industrial psychiatry, as I envisage it, than is one's office practice; and needless to say the whole problem of industrial psychiatry, except possibly five per cent of it, is quite different from dealing with major psychoses. It is nearer the Selective Service diagnostic level, plus some practical, not very "deep" therapy, which will do an amazing amount of good.

You see in Selective Service we expect to miss somewhere around fifty per cent of the neuropsychiatric disabilities that will appear before these people are through with the government service; but we figure we are saving perhaps half a billion per quarter century by saving half. And in industrial psychiatry we figure there are a good many things we will not be able to solve, but we will be effecting an enormous economy of manpower by doing what we can do. Again it will be a matter of securing a wholly trustworthy body of techniques and conceptions.

Public Morale

Then we come to the relationship of psychiatry to the more general national situation, the business of psychiatry as it bears on the general public. You see we have touched on the fighting arms and on the industrial mobilization. Now, what of the people in general? I am afraid that psychiatry cannot close its eyes to this problem. I hope that you are not going to get the impression that I suggest psychiatry has all the answers in any of these fields. In this field, however, if it does not have anything to offer, then I am terribly afraid that there is nothing to offer. In other words, while psychiatry should have something to offer, it is yet to be discovered whether it is sufficiently well organized to make the grade at this time. We know that in total warfare now the civilian population stands to suffer far more assault and privations than the armed combatants, and, of course, we do everything we can to protect the industrial arm, so that the civilian population in general is in a pretty exposed position, while the morale in the fighting arm and the industrial arm depends to an extraordinary extent on the morale of the general public.

[There is a general consensus] that the keynote in the morale of combat troops is the command—in other words, the line of authority that bears on the people—but that the basis [of their morale] is the contact with the people at home who make the self-abnegation and devotion to military objectives meaningful and worthwhile; and if everything is happening to [the people at home] that is disagreeable and demoralizing, the best command on earth will not maintain very high morale in the particular troops affected. So in modern warfare, the civilian community must be maintained in a reasonable degree of solidarity and with a reasonably high morale, if possible.

There are two aspects to this: one is the combating of the personality problems, peculiarities, and the like, in ingredients of the general public which are disastrous in their effects on others. [People undergoing] certain paranoid states, which appear whenever depressing news strikes 'near home,' are extraordinarily disturbing to lots of [other] people. They develop suspicions of their neighbors, and their best friends, and the Italian newsboy at the corner, to mention a few. The Federal Bureau of Investigation for a long time received three thousand letters per day, turning in all sorts of people as spies, or probable spies, from people who had been pushed over toward definite paranoid conditions. Beyond that there are quite a number of these disturbed people, subpsychotic and postpsychotic, who literally are public enemies, in part from their mental disorder, and in part because there are other clever people who are glad to use them for what they are worth in causing a general feeling of uncertainty, suspicion, doubt, or insecurity.

The psychiatrist knows a good deal about these disturbing people in the community and can perhaps evolve some really practical and worthwhile attack on that aspect of the morale problem.

Then there is the other, the most difficult thing that I have had thrown at me on which I can say very little more than to name it. The psychiatric strategy, or psychological strategy—some people call it strategy of terror—which the propaganda ministry of Germany has worked out is pretty clever. Some of this work is, I believe, highly dangerous, particularly to the kind of highly individualistic and not very friendly—although very polite—sort of people that we are.

If there is anybody who has anything to offer in digging up the principles on which might be based a counterstrategy to this sort of attack, I think perhaps he is in the psychiatric group. I do want to say that the ordinary kind of wisecracks which are offered as solutions for attack by psychiatric strategy may be very reassuring to the wisecracker, but are not very helpful. For example, almost anybody will tell you, "Well, if they use propaganda, we will just have to use better propaganda."

Many [of you as psychiatrists] know that by exposing a person to plenty of contradictory propaganda, you can reduce him to a state of complete indecision and helplessness, so [that] he closes his ears as best he can and is out of touch and a prey to his own pessimistic or optimistic reveries. You have not cured anything; you have created a special disorder, which certainly does not improve solidarity or morale in the general public.

There is also the misplaced enthusiasm about American penetration, about which I have suffered a good deal from my friends, on how citizens can see through things. Well, now, can they? For heaven's sake, let's not depend on defeating Germany by virtue of the unemotional analytic abilities of our citizens, generally.

I believe that the strategy of personality factors which I call psychiatric strategy is quite a serious problem and one for which there is at present very little in the way of remedy, but for which I believe we have to look to psychiatrists.

The gist of what I have said means that as I see the patterns of the future, psychiatrists, a singularly small number of people among us, are called upon to carry weighty responsibilities which will be hard indeed to delegate. Many of the performances simply require years of practical training in order that one shall be at all expert and useful at them. If these are valuable functions, then these functions have to be performed by this small number of people, plus such increments as come along year after year through our training facilities. If we are to do the job, we must do a very good job, first, of organizing our competence and skills. The people who cannot, because of physical difficulties or other reasons, do military work, should be occupying themselves in filling the needs of the civilian community and in becoming expert at certain new functions in that connection, new functions in public mental health, if you please. Those who are particularly skilled at diagnosis should be at these many diagnostic tasks. The women who are excluded traditionally from certain fields of psychiatry should be taking up certain other positions which will be made vacant by the mobilization.

Every psychiatrist will have much more to do than he is now doing, and it is a national responsibility one way or another to discover the energy to work two or three hours a day for the United States. That I believe is but a mere statement of fact. If psychiatry is to carry its burden, then every psychiatrist must do more work, however overworked he may be already.

11

Commentary

DURING World War II, Sullivan wrote many lengthy editorials in *Psychiatry*. These were for him a means of stating, in a less scientifically restrictive format, the immediate social and political implications of his own ongoing research and developing theory. Sometimes themes from such editorials were developed later in systematic research by himself or others; but some themes, despite their cogency, never came to scientific and theoretical fruition.

The following selection is a particularly significant illustration of Sullivan's thinking as he combines his scientific and social commentary functions as a journal editor. I have deleted certain topical passages from this selection in order to sharpen the central area of interest in this editorial—*opinion leadership in the primary group*. The primary group is of course the small group that has frequent face-to-face interaction at work, at home, at play, and so on; and social scientists have considerably expanded this whole concept since the time of Sullivan's article.

Sullivan himself later developed some of the ideas that appear in this paper, especially the concept of the "conference of self-respecting people," which he tried to apply in the postwar period for assessing and utilizing psychiatry in the international scene.[1] Strictly speaking, however, he did not further develop specifically the idea of informal opinion leadership ("conversational leadership") in his own published work. In later research by social scientists, such as Lazarsfeld and others,[2] the idea was developed extensively; but prior to 1942, it

[1] See "Remobilization for Enduring Peace and Social Progress" in this book.

[2] The work on mass communications and its filtering through local opinion leaders probably began, in the area of voting studies, in the Erie

had been a long time since social scientists had gone through the periodic process of "rediscovery" of the significance of the primary group in opinion formation.[3] Certainly the idea must have been in the air when Sullivan wrote this editorial. By 1942, there were a number of social scientists in Washington who had given their disciplined attention to problems of rumor, propaganda, and information transmission in the public mind, and Sullivan had been in especially close contact with some of these workers, like Harold D. Lasswell. But the phrases "opinion leadership" and "conversational leadership" may have been first enunciated by Sullivan; certainly he was one of the first to search out their wider meanings in terms of psychiatric insights—a matter not recognized in the historical treatment of the topic in social science literature. The primacy of the term is not the important consideration here, however. What is arresting is the fact that a psychiatrist was able at this early period to single out this particular concept, so cogent for the emergent national and international crisis, from the relatively unformulated and unpublished conversation of social scientists and see its relation to his own clinical data. Certainly this is one of the early instances of psychiatry and social science *fused and applied to the social scene* in a historically current manner.

On another level, it is not surprising that Sullivan was able to see public opinion in terms of primary group relations. As early as 1927, he had felt that it was not necessary to study "aggregations larger in number than four because one found in aggregations of people living intimately together or working on one project reactions which seem in no way more distinguished or more complex than the reactions that had appeared in the experimental society of two or three or four." [4]

County study of the election of 1940, an analysis of which was not published, however, until 1944. See Paul F. Lazarsfeld, Bernard Berelson, and Hazel Gaudet, *The People's Choice;* New York: Duell, Sloan & Pearce, 1944; second edition, 1948. For a review of the emergence of opinion leadership as an area for study, see Elihu Katz and Paul F. Lazarsfeld, *Personal Influence;* Glencoe, Ill.: Free Press, 1955. In the latter book, the only reference to Sullivan is to a posthumous book, published in 1954, so it is obvious that the authors were unaware of this early work by Sullivan.

[3] Actually Sullivan referred to "conversational leadership" in his 1940 Memorandum included in this book, "Propaganda and Censorship," but he did not develop the concept at that time. See index entry in this book for Leadership, conversational.

[4] See *Schizophrenia as a Human Process,* p. 184.

In this book, the second and fifth selections also document Sullivan's growing awareness of the primary group in the forming of opinion, and his hypothesis that society is held together with the overlapping memberships of such small groups. While some sociologists may be reluctant to concede that all essential social process is clearly observable or even present in groups of two or three or four, nevertheless Sullivan's conceptual apparatus here was doubtless the bridge to the formulation of the concept of opinion leadership within the tradition of American social psychology.[5]

[5] Sullivan's contribution here is another illustration of his theoretical continuity with the tradition of Chicago social science. The concept of the primary group came from Charles H. Cooley to Sullivan, as mediated, in part, by the thinking of George Herbert Mead. And Harold D. Lasswell has suggested to me that Robert Park's doctoral dissertation, *Masse und Publikum* (Buchdruckerei Lack & Granau, 1904), probably contained the first statement of the importance of public opinion by an American sociologist.

Leadership, Mobilization, and Postwar Change†

MOBILIZATION for total war must be understood to mean fundamental changes in the circumstances of everyone's life. All the manpower and the other resources of a people have to be coordinated in a stupendous tripartite effort: to defeat and destroy their enemy; to protect and encourage the growth of positive values in their society; and in all ways possible to make certain of a better postwar world. It is clear that we in these United States are far from mobilized in this sense. . . . [and that] we must complete our mobilization. This is inescapably necessary, required for any conceivably desirable future. We have a great and unavoidable part to play in the postwar reconstruction. Unless we previously shall have completed mobilization, we shall prove unequal to our part in this task. We will be inadequate not only in power and production, but in vision and understanding, and the war will have wasted an infinity of lives and hopes and treasure to very little purpose, and will have sown the seeds of the perhaps ultimate war. "Victory" will not bring peace but, instead, an era of social disorganization and upheaval. It is doubtful if democratic forms of government would survive long here or elsewhere

† Reprinted from *Psychiatry* (1942) 5:263–282. [This was originally titled "Completing Our Mobilization," and published as an unsigned editorial, although Sullivan lists himself as the author in a 1947 bibliography. I have shortened the original article by about five book pages here; the new title and subtitles have been supplied by me, although the actual words are taken from text. H.S.P.]

—longest, perhaps, in the already somewhat regenerated United Kingdom.

The values of the Western world, the aspirations and realizations which have made life worth living, and ours a country in which one could be content to rear one's family, have been endangered for a long time, and are now in dire peril. It was perhaps beyond human wisdom to draft wise policy to guide us in meeting conditions which are now seen to be nothing less than world-revolutionary change. The awesome complexity of the pattern may well have been too great for any mind to grasp and realize the certain future. It may be that an indeterminate course with wide freedom of action in meeting emergency is the best that any one could have achieved. Certainly, many of the instrumentalities created by the Government have been well designed to meet critical aspects of world events. That they have sometimes become useless and new instrumentalities have been called for almost before the old were completed is no reflection on the caliber of the plans.

It is profoundly disturbing, however, to encounter recurrently a fear that, what with human limitations both of initiative and of vision, no great good is being sought as an outcome of the war; that no moving conviction of the universal worth and dignity of man exists; and that utterances on these subjects are but facets of "psychological warfare," potent to unnerve the enemy and inspire us in a struggle that will restore something like the past. . . .

There are plenty of unmobilized and partly mobilized citizens who continue to be indifferent to the portents of the world scene. Whatever they may now leave unsaid, they feel that we will return to an isolated national life in which the ancient "rights" of capital and labor, of property and prestige, of income and profits, of lobbies and tariffs and monopolies and cartels, will be guaranteed firmly. They hope to survive this time of stress and limitation, moving cautiously like a mariner in a fog, and to be ready to go into high gear and alert participation in current events when the nightmare of war and revolutionary change presently departs.

This detached nonparticipation which still characterizes many significant people and groups at this stage of our mobilization to wage total war is simply antithetic to the solidarity and morale that are required to undergo and win such total war. It imperils the rest of us. Whether we recognize this, merely sense it, or enforce an anxious obliviousness to its existence, those of us who are concentrated on our phase of waging total war are made insecure by this morbid automatism in the social organism. Some of us remember vividly the reactionary minority, the tongue-in-the-cheek participants in the First World War, who gradually dominated that postwar scene and made a mockery of the widespread conviction that we had won through to a better world.

Today, it appears that of all the United Nations * it is these United States that might be doomed by a precipitate victory to be the reactionary element in a world elsewhere more or less fully awake to the necessity for new values and new principles of living. . . .

Integrative Factors

Psychiatric consideration of total mobilization has to distinguish the positive integrating factors which make for collaboration and the achievement of successful outcome, from the negative, disintegrative factors that interfere with the war effort, endanger social values, and render improbable the ultimate achievement of a better world. In both cases, it is useful to separate these factors on a tripartite basis—that of the person, the community, and the central administrative function.

At the personal level the positive integrating factors appear as motives (values, purposes understood and approved, and more or less entirely unconscious drives attached to socially useful ends); as participation in social institutions; and as experience of the influences of administrative control.

The community is the aggregation, or more or less organized group, of significant fellow-beings in one's proximity through which most of the characteristics of the social order are realized and by which the force of social institutions and the central administrative control are exercised.

It is primarily at the community level that solidarity and morale

[* Sullivan is writing this in 1942 and is of course referring primarily to the nations united for war against Germany and Japan. H.S.P.]

are meaningful; that information is interpreted or misinterpreted; and that collaboration is achieved.

The central administration is necessarily a prepotent factor in the adequate integration and coordination of practically all people and communities. Among its prime integrative responsibilities are the taking of actions to achieve adequate effort; the providing of instrumentalities to distribute the burdens equitably; and the carrying out of measures to protect effectiveness—chiefly the health and security of the citizen—from unnecessary risks.

Wise and foresightful policy implemented with decisiveness, clarity, and dispatch of action is the citizen's ideal of a central administration. The central administration is, however, made up of people. Our wartime administration is composed of literally a horde of people who make up a whole congeries of more or less separate communities. Hence, the ideal of leadership in the central administration that the citizen is able to maintain is an important factor in determining the personal effects of administrative control.

It is a truism that judgments arise out of experience and that communicable reasoning is the product of operations with materials accessible to awareness. Any idealization of the leadership in Washington must be based on one's recognized experience of leadership or it will be fantastic and, as such, subject to great, and generally irrational, changes. It is not certain that we of these United States tend toward clarity in formulating our experience with leadership and it would perhaps be timely to attempt to alter this in a positive fashion.

There is no group in which the phenomenon called *conversational leadership* [opinion leadership] is lacking. Few of our fellowmen express much of anything except views that they have more or less unwittingly acquired from such leaders. Their opinions and their changes of opinion are rather simply related to events at this level of leadership.

This does not mean that an influential person can easily remedy the personality warp derived from unfortunate early influences. The conspicuous effects of conversational leadership are manifested at the level of verbal formulation and expression and in the associated ratiocinative and rationalizing processes which are so significant a part of social life—in contradistinction to the levels of more intimate interpersonal relations at which the signs of personality warp may be all the more conspicuous because the relatively impersonal community life and adjustment to accepted standards are causing strain.

It is unfortunate that conversational leaders are not better equipped to realize their responsibility in the national effort, and better organized for use in integrating their communities—both as communities, as centers for mentally hygienic activities and the development of high and durable morale, and as units in the higher integration, the solidarity of our people—nay, of all peoples who are struggling or waiting for their chance to struggle for the emancipation of human beings from fear of their fellows, from want and disease and suffering, and from archaic institutions and practices that delay for them, and delay for all of us (inasmuch as we are one world) progress towards an ever better life.

SEEKING AND ENCOURAGING CHANGE

It is good doctrine that man is essentially benevolent, not malevolent; that, given opportunity, he moves towards mutual understanding and helpfulness, not towards defrauding and exploiting the less fortunate. Perhaps the psychiatrist alone, and by no means every psychiatrist, knows a strong argument for this altruistic view of man, although its ultimate correctness is probably intuited by everyone who can still look forward to an enrichment of his relations with other people.

In any case, it has been given to some psychiatrists to discover by systematic observation how greatly their patients are impelled towards mental health, once some fatal blockage of personal development has been removed. It is clear that man is a stupendously capable creature. Even the not-too-human imbecile is capable of most of the performances done by the average peacetime citizen, were he but fortunately—and very patiently—trained. Most of the more superior equipment of the average man gets little or no use from adolescence onward and it is doubtful if even Leonardo da Vinci came anywhere near finding his full metier. The range from the lowest imbecile to the greatest genius is perhaps richer in differences of relevant factors than is the range from the beginnings of life on Earth to the highest non-anthropoid creature of today. The millennia of recorded history, on the other hand, while they are but a moment in the flow even of biological time, seem incredibly impoverished in signs and wonders wrought by man for the perduring good of his fellows. Wherefore, even if we should believe that man is in his essence—in the ultimate limiting pattern of the events in which he may have part—prevailingly benevolent to others, how can anyone find room for hope that progress towards more fully human living may be accelerated, and greatly accelerated, in the very next few years? Is it not simply inevitable that the numerous puny souls who by accident of birth and their particular course of experience have come to accept the recent past as better than any different future shall outweigh in their certainty and narrowness of goal all the rest of us?

There is one case in which this grim, reactionary course is by no means inevitable. The puny are at one with the more capable in seeking and encouraging change when, and only when, they are certain that things are going from thoroughly bad to much worse. The almost uninterrupted history of sadly truncated steps in social progress no more disproves this than it shows that only a little progress can be made on any one historic occasion. Reaction always threatens, nearly always destroys the possibility of a great forward step. Is this because the great mass of the people is preponderatingly reactionary?

The great mass of the people *have to follow* and the brake on social progress is to be found not in their reactionary tendencies but in the irresponsible and incompetent leadership to which they have thus far been subject.

The failures of man reflect the limitations of the men who have exercised the function of leadership—often unwittingly, therefore quite irresponsibly; generally emotionally, therefore with less than good judgment; almost uniformly without simple clarity about the situation in which leadership has been thrust upon them.

Man has needed no supermen to lead him. Of all things, he has needed leaders who did not share his vanity and revel with him in the pomp and circumstance of elaborate voluntaristic myths. The course of human affairs may now be reaching the end of this long phase of necessary self-deception. It is quite possible that events will now reshape a path to take us out of the twilight world of wordy dreaming about not-quite-happening marvels performed by not-quite-life-sized magicians, into the sufficiently wonderful, and also dependable and satisfying, world of interpersonal reality.

The Western world is a profoundly sick society in which each denizen, each person, is sick to the extent that he is *of it*, of its blended vitality and debility, of its chances of dissolution or reorganization and recovering after a dangerous crisis. Those who are relatively untouched by the critical reorganizing processes will continue sick, ineffective, foci of disorganization in the world of culture which is as necessarily a part of the human milieu as are air and food and water. If they are an effective majority, the outcome will inevitably be continued sickness, not only for them—who will enjoy the conceit of being 'normal' and 'regular' —but for everyone, in the measure of his humanity, his socialization. All this is biologically axiomatic. Only our traditional confusion in the current dream world of myths about godlike Selves obscures this from any fairly intelligent person.

In these United States, we have the world's most elaborate— extensive and intensive—mechanisms for education, both formal and incidental. The average citizen's access to the sensory—the distance-receptor zones of interaction with circumambient reality —has never been any greater in the history of man's progress from the tribal family. [Because of this], a modern version of the time of Pericles is wholly feasible: those who find themselves for the time being leading others could be really informed and wise; those who follow could be intelligently secure and comfortable. Are there those who can use these mechanisms effectively to dissolve the shackles of ignorance necessarily applied to all of us in our early development, promptly enough to permit us the great role that we should play in world reconstruction, and wisely enough so that human society will progress to robust health? If so, who are they? Where are they to be sought? How are they to be insured opportunity to save us, the people of the West, and to spare the rest of the world the dark age that would follow extinction of the West?

It has often been said that this is all quite obviously hopeless, for we cannot have these leaders without skipping a generation, without their having grown from birth in a society free from our ubiquitous distortions that make up and perpetuate in every one of us the very sickness which these master-physicians must understand objectively and radically cure. This is the pessimistic view which sees in man no quintessential striving upward, but makes him the indifferent outcome of "tropisms" and pure chance, or else a feeble tool in transcendental hands—which the psychiatrist has to assume are motivated, if at all, by a transcendent wisdom amounting to utter human madness.

Neither in cynicism nor in pessimism—nor, certainly, in complacent optimism—is the dynamism of human salvation to be sought. What light there is to guide us in the quest is shed by humble reverence for human possibilities and an unremitting alertness in scrutinizing plans and actions as they are reflected to us in collaborating with others of goodwill.

MOBILIZING OPINION LEADERSHIP

The integration of practically complete national solidarity and collaboration is very difficult but not impossible. It depends primarily on good leadership in every community and this, in turn, depends on leaders who are aware of leading, who are inspired by high responsibility in exercising influence, and who are adequately informed both about people and interpersonal relations and about the current and immediately prospective necessities which have to be met. The filling of these requirements can scarcely be left to chance. Many influential people are opposing the efforts of the Government, wittingly or quite without realizing it, and influencing others in ways that make for skepticism and indifference towards the war effort, if not for frank disunity.

A nationwide effort to discover the particular people who are now constructively influential in guiding public opinion and community action would prove extremely useful. Response to the emergency of war has leavened an actual deterioration which was settling upon us. Many potentially forward-looking people had been drifting in almost apathetic acceptance of things as they were. There seemed no point in questioning the leadership of the times. Most influential people had demonstrated their ability to do well in the social system. If they seemed overconservative, this perhaps only accentuated one's own unrecognized limitations.

The coming of the New Deal stirred hopes in many liberal-minded people, but again as in making the world safe for democracy, things settled back to much the same as they had been before. The only reasonably certain reward for "sticking one's neck out" in the public interest was getting oneself labeled a screwball, a starry-eyed theorist, or a communist. There was no such risk attached to being reactionary, and one could scarcely expect much sound progress to come from the sick overzealousness that characterized many radicals.

Nothing very profound in the way of favorable change followed the outbreak of war 'in Europe.' We went about our more or less consistent efforts to help the forces opposed to the Axis, but what we did for ourselves in forefending the increasing menace was in general pretty conservative—like LaGuardia's activation of the State Councils of Defense.

The shock of attack in the Pacific changed this. The mass of the people were stirred. The isolationist poison became nauseating. People who made sense in plans and action for national, for community, or even for personal security and cooperation stood out clearly as the ones who had been in better touch with reality. The demand for practical leadership swept them into positions of importance and influence. People saw that the activities and interests of civilian defense and cooperation in war activities often call for somewhat different types of competence than those which had brought eminence and influence in times of peace. There was a shift from the more conservative to a dynamic type of leader—not without perturbations when a socially quite myopic person was agile enough to retain his prestige in an outwardly altered role. But the great thing was the emergence of socially responsible citizens to whom others are glad to turn for guidance of thought and organization of effort, from the mass of our almost unknown neighbors.

Our nation of vast population, great regional differences, and innumerable minority groups and special interests needs the integrating influence that these new leaders could exercise. None of them should be overlooked in the development of our war effort, and every effective one of them should be mobilized for service for national solidarity and community morale.

A definite, practical mobilization of leadership would be no more difficult than is the responsible mobilization of men for the armed forces, or for industry and other supporting activities.

It would call for the same sort of foresightful regulations to establish procedure, a regional organization of functions, *and supervision* to see that people incapable of teamwork are elimi-nated from the system, and that other sources of misunderstand-ings and controversy are promptly explored and remedied. It would call for the same acquiescent attitude on the part of the public, generally, which would have to be brought about by the same process of demonstrating the reasonable and necessary character of the mobilization of leaders. Perhaps this may seem to be the impossible feature of the plan: the public will not ac-knowledge its dependence on leaders and would not follow leaders whom it knew to be coordinated in the national effort. In this argument we hear again the cynical, pessimistic view of man: he has to deceive himself about the independence of his judgment and opinions, and becomes suspicious of any leader whom he knows is himself led.

This misanthropic view might take as its slogan, "Every man his own leader," and make everyone look for leader-leading to one peerless figure, who could reach them all. Overlooking the blatant fraud in such an appeal to popular credulity, ignoring the widespread popular demand for much more and better leadership than is now evident, one might conceivably deceive himself into believing that there is something in this idea, what with the wonderful channel for communication which the radio provides. The notion is self-evidently antidemocratic—however one exactly conceives of government of the people, by the people, for (we hope) the people—and, to the psychiatrist who knows something about interpersonal relations, almost completely chimerical. It might on occasion be made to work in some relatively narrow field of behavior to the extent of producing a numerical majority of assenting citizens. This has very little to do with mobilizing the personal resources of the country to meet the vicissitudes of total war, to save our social values, and to reconstruct the world after military defeat of the enemy.

If people could not be led to observe the cruder facts of interpersonal relations, and thus prepared to remedy the more unfortunate of their chronic misapprehensions about living, then there would be no great future before us, in any case. Fortunately for the doubtful, this capacity so to be led to observe is already reasonably well demonstrated in Great Britain. It is now clear that the mould of a century of cultural trend can be broken, and that new and more adequately human ways of behavior and thought can be developed rapidly even by people mature in years and habits. It remains to be seen whether the favorable changes, the new direction of culture-growth and the new values, will survive the emergency that gave them a chance to appear, will escape the nibbling and gnawing of the sick reactionaries who will have escaped the salutary influences. This pernicious element will have the advantage of operating with anciently familiar tools in their efforts to "perpetuate the mistakes of their grandfathers" for the peoples of the world.

To return to our fellow-citizens and their probable response to a plan for mobilizing leadership: let it be said at once that there would be much less of disturbing shock than of blessed relief to almost any of us to learn by guided observation how little he understands thoroughly and how wonderfully capable he is of understanding—once he is free of the necessity for knowing all about everything about which he happens to talk. The mighty reassurance that comes from discovering that one's mental operations are slightly more apt to prove adequate than otherwise whenever they are given something tangible to work on is ever so much more valuable and durable than anything that belonging to the right group of phonograph records can ever provide. Once the never-quite-believable myth of personal infallibility has been brushed aside, one can see—and be happy about the fact of—the wide range of differences in human ability, in background experience and acquaintance with data, and in freedom from personality warp which prevents adequate observation and analysis of events and the relatively simple and natural elaboration of information about them. The series of gods and demigods that one has always been quoting and striving to emulate—and worrying about—then fade into place in the history of one's personal development, and correspondingly one's possibilities and limitations for human collaboration begin to become apparent and real.

The discovery of our constructively influential people and the organizing of those who are demonstrably useful in integrating national solidarity and collaboration in the war effort into an agency of popular government may seem revolutionary and dangerous to the future of the democratic system. The need which calls out the suggestion is simple. No one can expect to be fully informed and always correct in the long series of urgent situations that will confront us over the next several years. An enlightened government, however, will strive to extend the popular base of its operations by providing all citizens with the best information that it can safely release, and by promptly correcting any dangerous misapprehensions that may arise in any group of its relatively loyal supporters. These objectives are the more certainly accomplished, the more immediate and face-to-face—the less mediate, remote, and myth-wrapped—is the contact with relevant agents of the government, by the people concerned in this effort.

The organizing of leadership would begin with a wide dissemination of the nuclear facts of opinion, or conversational, leadership. These facts are essentially: that we automatically look to some well-informed, presumptively relatively disinterested people from whose known experience and consistent clarity of formulation we gain an impression of superior competence to deal with the data of some field significant to us; and that these folk in turn respond more or less readily with expressions of judgment and opinion couched in language and other action that more or less helpfully and congruously augment our fund of ideas about ourself and others and about the course of events. Other factors being constant, this relationship tends to recur, and communication between the leader and the led to improve, unless or until the field of the leader's competence ceases to be significant, or his leadership relation has otherwise come to an end. In the first case, the person who was the leader also becomes relatively insignificant, excepting in retrospect. In the latter, he may retain high significance in some other interpersonal category; for example, that of a friend or a friendly collaborator. It ceases also and is replaced by hostility and negative suggestibility or negativism when the leader is believed to have violated the interpersonal implication of the situation, and to have "taken advantage of one"—the hostility being mobilized as a protective measure to cope with the insecurity inspired by relative incompetence in the significant field.

This analysis is relevant in the great field of living in which leadership phenomena are not associated with "external" compulsion, whether by material rewards—income or deference, or both—from being led, or by punishments for rebellion or the showing of independence towards the "leader." The quasi leadership implemented with rewards and punishments manipulated by the "leader" to maintain his authority—the most astonishing development of which is seen in German National Socialism but plenty of examples of which occur around us, for example, in "society" and in "politics"—is quite another and a more complex interpersonal relationship, and one anything but helpful in the promotion of national solidarity.

The overlapping of the two fields of leadership and "leadership"—or at least the difficulties attendant on an attempt to distinguish the two in some given cases—might seem to offer a serious, if not a fatal, difficulty to the mobilization of true leadership which we are urging. Collaterally, this is indeed worthy of consideration. There is always, in operations pertaining to personal influence and influential people, the danger of creating a bureaucracy instead of an integrating system. A "leader" may reach a key position in the initial organization, or weak central leadership may later expose the organization to bureaucratic domination. On the other hand, "leaders" do not fit readily into a system of opinion leadership—unless, as sometimes happens, one there finds his true metier and, responding on the basis of previously neglected personal abilities to the opportunity to achieve genuine worth among his fellows, abandons the principle of *quid pro quo* and manifests true leadership.

There is danger of overlooking leaders who are gradually finding their place in a community still outwardly dominated by people of the prewar period who have taken on new roles but are incapable of performing the necessary function. Conversely, there will be tendencies to turn aside from capable people accustomed to the responsibility of leadership, merely because they have been leading, and a little change always seems attractive. This corrects itself ultimately by very force of circumstance, but should not be encouraged by central or regional administrative influence. The maladroitness of capable but relatively unsocialized people is sometimes a serious strain on community morale.

The *system* of opinion leadership which we hold to be urgently needed would provide all the collaborating community leaders with timely *statements of fact or policy* on all matters of critical significance and would furnish its central executive agency with data on public opinion and subjects of doubt, controversy, and discontent which came to the attention of local and regional leaders. Its work, as reflected in the information which it disseminated, would be oriented to promoting the dynamic unity of our people as an effective social organization for improving their own conditions of life and contributing positively to an emerging benevolent organization of all peoples, and concomitantly with both, winning the war.

This information, the statements of fact or policy, would never be any one man's views nor subject to the final approval of any one person. Everyone knows from experience that no man is always competent and wise, and the organization would disintegrate—or change character into an essentially ethico-religious system—as soon as responsible community leaders discovered that they themselves were following anyone so irresponsible that he would willingly carry the awful burden of final decisions about the future of everyone.

There are some occasions—in wartimes, many—on which the decision of one man must be final and utterly effective in determining the course of exceedingly important events. No psychiatrist would wish this otherwise. The psychiatrist would hope that any man who from the nature of his position has to make these decisions will be able to make an adequate analysis of relevant factors in the situation, to accurately foresee at least alternative courses of events, and then to come to his judgment without doubts and scruples, with clarity and dispatch, and with a sufficient understanding of the people who must grasp and execute his intentions. In the realm of action, we can sympathize with the comment credited to Lieutenant General [William] Knudsen about the first solo Atlantic flight, "It would have been much more of a feat if he had done it with a committee."

In the organization of community leadership, however, we are not primarily concerned with action to achieve a given objective but with supplying the information and foresight on the basis of which more and more of our people can automatically reach decision about necessary action, and escape from the doubts, uncertainties, obscure conflicts of motive, blind impulse and extravagant self-deception which now characterize so many of our attempts to live and work together. To have lasting effect, this, shall we say, Office of War Information * —for its great contribution would have to be made while we are still at war— must inspire *well-founded*, therefore enduring, confidence. More and more people must be taught to observe and from observation must be able to learn that this governmental agency is well-informed, sound, and farsighted in judgment, and free from any influence that runs counter to the welfare of the people primarily significant to the person concerned.

The discriminating of fact and the formulation of communicable knowledge are two aspects of the group of processes which are called *consensual validation*. In principle, that which "appears in one's mind" is subjected to comparison with past experience in which others have agreed as to what was the case. One's thoughts are evolved from a much more general type of process technically called revery by recasting the operation in verbal statements, formed *for*, or *as if for*, expression to another. The *as if* hearer who functions in thinking may be adequate or

[* Interestingly enough, Sullivan uses here the name of the organization established on June 13, 1942, by Presidential Executive Order, although the editorial (published in the May, 1942, issue of *Psychiatry*) was obviously written at least a month before the Order. Whether or not Sullivan was aware of this impending reorganization of the Office of War Information under Elmer Davis is not apparent from the editorial, but certainly all those concerned with civilian morale had been dismayed by the inadequate attention paid to coordinating domestic information programs up to that time. H.S.P.]

inadequate from the standpoint of objective success in communication. He has been a failure in the case, for example, when one discovers that one is making an unconvincing statement. Cues from the listener may be in point in making this discovery; on the other hand, one's 'own listener' may have improved in judgment in the interval, recovered from fatigue and preoccupation, or otherwise be more on his mettle.

The more highly intelligent and more widely experienced a man is, other factors remaining constant, the better he is at this 'internal' consensual validation. An infinity of fools in conference could not assess the truth about a novel, complex situation because they could not distinguish and formulate the relevant factors. Yet a genius, in explaining something, may "come upon" a formula of superlative clarity, the merit of which is so great that it astonishes its author and shows him a new perspective on a subject about which he had previously considered himself well-informed. Just as certainly as unnoted revery processes have contributed to this occurrence, so also has the hearer played a part in evoking the event, this new, more adequate, insight into the way the world hangs together.

The roles of experience, intelligence, the inner consensual validation, and the processes of communicative verification are never more apt to succeed than in the context of a conference of self-respecting people. The factor of self-respect of all participants is crucially important, for a person who does not genuinely respect himself cannot simply respect others, and, therefore, always introduces troublesome complexities and nuisance values into interpersonal relations. Moreover, because of peculiarities of personal experience, not all self-respecting people can work with particular others, be the latter however healthily secure in self-esteem.

From consideration of these and other factors, it becomes evident that the special work of our Office of War Information will have to be a product of conference of persons both justly eminent in their respective fields and secure in themselves, and of demonstrable capacity for an extraordinary degree of collaboration. Not otherwise could we trust the Office to be reasonably successful in performing its task; nor will a mere combination of such rare people suffice. They must be given free access to all relevant information which they may require, and they must be so constituted as a council that considerations of expediency will have but a rightful place in their deliberations, and the possibility of political rewards and punishments becomes an insignificant factor.

With such an office to correct, amplify, or repudiate indiscrete, erroneous, or misleading utterances of other government officials, we could expect a rapid change for the better with respect to consistency and responsibility in the news from Washington. The Office of War Information could be one place where fatigue and its pernicious effect on foresight—and flaming ambition, with its incurable astigmatism for consequences—would not show themselves.

Total mobilization includes the revision and closer coordination of civilian supplies to meet the basic needs for food, shelter, clothing, warmth. It calls for reorganization of the health services of the nation so that medical care and the benefits of sanitation may reach all the people despite the call to the colors of a great many physicians and related personnel. It puts a new premium on the work of public education. It demands new attention to recreational activities. It calls for intensive efforts at social rehabilitation of underprivileged groups. It requires new devices of reward and punishment with which to implement some emergency measures of an interim character.

It requires practically complete mobilization of manpower for agriculture, mining, and the like, for the basic industries, for commerce and communication, for the armed forces, and for special technical purposes such as the maintenance of health. It requires the mobilization of all our nonpersonal resources, and rigid control of income, credit, and the cost of living. Why, then, do we lay such special emphasis on the supplying of war information in the broad sense here implied?

The reasons for this stress on the structure of leadership, the supply of information, and the wise formulation of statements of policy are to be found in the negative side of the current national situation, in the disintegrative factors that interfere with the war effort, endanger vital social values, and make improbable the achievement of a better postwar world. These, again, can be divided into personal, community, and central administrative factors. Some of them have already concerned us; some are too recondite to have yet appeared clearly.

Disintegrative Factors

The negative, disintegrative personal factors can usefully be separated into primarily cultural elements pertaining to sundry class-conscious groups and occupations, and personal elements pertaining in essence to mentally defective and disordered citizens. The farmer, for example—and merely for example, because he is one with every other group with clearly distinguished functions and at least fairly clearly formulated demands, including the psychiatrist and, certainly, organized medicine—as a part of the voting public is of peculiar interest to sundry elective officers of the Government. His support as a class can be secured by manipulations designed to give encouragement to his particular utopian hopes, in this case high income for produce, an easy market for farm labor, and a low cost of living. In the present state of society, it is much easier to tinker up a series of political expedients that seem to be well directed than it is to plan and carry out measures that attack the farmer's problems at their source. The expedients are often patterned in terms of protecting the farmer from predatory interests, saving him from other elements of the social organization which at best are indifferent to his interests, and at worst are definitely hostile to them. This does not make for national solidarity nor does it improve the morale of farming communities. That it is easy to find color for almost any discriminative ideas is in itself a symptom of our ubiquitous social illness.

MENTAL DEFICIENCY AS A BRAKE ON SOCIAL CHANGE

Mental deficiency has to be distinguished from mere ignorance, including illiteracy. Mental defect arises primarily from failure of the central nervous system to develop some of its parts. This may be a result of genetic factors or of damage in the earlier stages of growth, as by birth injury or infectious disease in infancy. The potentialities of central nervous system function set limits to the possibilities of skill learning and the detection of differences in the sensory basis of experience. The degree of mental defect or deficiency, crudely reflected in the rubrics of idiot, imbecile, moron, and borderline intellect, are of profound significance in understanding the limitation of life possibilities that they entail. An idiot is a quasi-human creature so deficient in central integrating dynamism that it cannot acquire the use of language. As becoming human entails acculturation, and as the culture heritage which the young must assimilate is to a very great extent a matter of inhibitions and facilitations inextricably bound up with words and verbal propositions, the idiot cannot become human and does not develop any interpersonal relations in a fully meaningful sense.

The imbecile can and does assimilate and come to manifest language habits of a simple kind. A vast area of civilization is beyond his discovery or comprehension, and most of the generally significant complexities of life escape him entirely. His performances in interpersonal relations, however difficult, are uncomplicated by the maze of discriminative judgments and considerations that characterize the life of the mentally mature. His religious, ethical, exact, social, and political ideas and principles all remain at an elementary level of elaboration otherwise left in early childhood. His proficiency in uncommunicable "grasp" of some limited area of human interest, and dexterity in behavior connected with it, may in rare instances be simply uncanny, giving the impression of true genius. The extreme limitation of social intelligence which is shown even in this field of extraordinary competence is most painfully apparent.

The moronic and particularly those of borderline intellect are much more difficult to discover. They often, when well-reared and spared the development of intrinsically absurd expectations and ambitions, pass as commonplace, 'normal,' good citizens and contribute quite as much as the average person to the general welfare. To the extent that our formal education system discourages curiosity and communicates a veneer of manners with which to conceal one's failure to understand another, it tends to reduce everyone to a superficial resemblance to morons, and complicates greatly the problem of quickly identifying which of one's personal contacts is merely uninformed in contrast to those who cannot be taught to grasp the higher complexities of a situation. The uneven, high development of some particular human ability, mentioned in connection with an occasional imbecile, is much more generally—but much less spectacularly— the case with the moron; and this, too, giving much the same superficial impression as do either mere situational limitations of experience or sharp circumscription of interests, makes the casual diagnosis of instances of these higher levels of mental deficiency impossible.

The poignancy of the question of mental defect in total mobilization and all the problems of the war lies in the fact that, other things being equal, one's *general intelligence* determines the complexity of the world with which one can deal. In a representative, democratic system of government, then, there must be a series of social worlds expressing themselves in the political behavior of the citizens; and the considerations that are most relevant to persons living in the simpler and in the more complex of these worlds, which at least rationalize their political behavior and make up all that can be communicated about it, are widely different from the considerations of force with the person of median general intelligence.

Practically, there is no chance of meeting the precise needs of the most or of the least competent person among us, and the level of needs met tends to be established on the basis of distribution in the population of *effective social intelligence*, a somewhat complex homologue of general intelligence, in that it includes the element of past educational opportunity. The best informed and the most skillful among us can seldom comprehend why social change takes so long or proceeds so clumsily. The ignorant and the mentally deficient citizen, meanwhile, lives in a world that moves too fast for him, proceeding on its quite inscrutable way by a series of minor social miracles. There is thus an inherent difference and lack of community—oneness—in the population on the basis of effective social intelligence, to the development of which mental defect sets almost absolute limits.

MENTAL DISORDER AND THE SICK SOCIETY

Mental disorder, in contradistinction to defect, has little direct relationship to the quantity and quality of the central nervous system refinements, or to any other part of the animal organization of the human being. It, like general social intelligence, is a product of opportunity and experience, of acculturation and past interpersonal relations; and, like social intelligence, it manifests itself in one's adaptation in the community, and in related thinking and behavior about the larger world. A person who had been taught as a child and come fully to believe that he is entirely benevolent in attitude towards his fellowman, all of whom will be uniformly benevolent in their dealings with him, is a victim of a grave personality warp—manifesting as mental disorder—which might easily get itself called hereditary because only parents who were themselves gravely disordered could give rise to so eccentric a product of acculturation. This particular hypothetical mental disorder is now infrequent if not nonexistent.

Mental disorders manifesting personality warp—distortion of personal development—of the opposite type, the established belief that people are almost entirely malevolent in attitude towards one, so that one is never too sure of one's personal safety or "rights" or property in dealing with them, is by no means uncommon. A profound insecurity in interpersonal relations might, in fact, be taken to be the rule, the 'normal,' at some levels of relative privilege in our social organization.

The relevant points about personality warp—and its manifestation, mental disorder—in this consideration of general mobilization are principally two. While minor differences in personality are as numerous as are the cultural patterns of the homes from which people have come, the structure of society and the character of human potentialities combine to limit the conspicuous manifestations of mental disorder to a reasonably small number of patterns which can be discriminated, at least by the psychiatrist, and which carry implications of high probability about the future course of the victim's interpersonal relations—given an unchanged social order and no material alteration in his functional capacity for living.

A digression on this last parenthetical clause may help to make the whole psychiatric conception of man and society somewhat clearer. A person gravely disordered "in mind" often requires removal from his home and community to the strict confinement of a hospital for the mentally disordered because "his mental state makes him a menace to himself or others." He may have manifested a relatively uninhibited impulse to kill himself for some reason, the expression of which does not inspire in others a conviction of adequate justification. He may say, for example, that he is no good, has never been any good, and has caused everyone else a great deal of trouble which can only be ended by destroying himself. This depressively grandiose notion can scarcely occur to the occasional social pariah in whose case it would be roughly appropriate. Experience teaches that this sort of all-embracing negative self-appraisal—any rich documentation of which by quoting from experience is utterly beyond the psychotic person—appears in association with active suicidal impulses only in a group of people characterized by marked swings of mood, so that their intimates know them as people apt to be at least mildly elated or somewhat "blue"—with, almost invariably, an associated manifest tendency to physical overactivity in the 'up' phase, and strikingly reduced physical activity in the 'down.'

Once the 'up' phase has gone out of bounds to the point that the man's judgment is seriously impaired by his physical distractability and "flight of ideas," or the 'down' phase has made him incapable of actions necessary to his survival, in combination with a "poverty of ideas" (because his thinking has been reduced to slowly and repetitiously going over some such depressive formula as that given above), then the man has ceased to be able to look after himself *and others* in ordinary life and he and society have to be protected until he has "recovered." This sort of person does usually so "recover" in the course of a residence in the extraordinary social system called the Hospital for the Mentally Disordered, returns to his community, and at least for some time carries on his usual round of socially acceptable performances.

Treatment in a hospital for the mentally disordered may not impress one as an adequate instance of undergoing a change in the social order. A sojourn as patient, physician, nurse, or attendant in such a hospital will teach the observant sociologist that any institution that provides good treatment for gravely disordered persons must be *very significantly different* from the society in which we are living.

The other part of the digression will first refer to a [so-called] recent addition to the ways of quick treatment of the victims of grave mental disorder. Following the vogue which sundry "convulsive therapies" were enjoying or had recently enjoyed—"insulin shock," "metrazol shock," camphor "treatment"—it was recalled or rediscovered that the electric current, applied appropriately to the brain, will also cause convulsions. We thus came to have the "electroshock" treatment of mental disorders—quite a refinement.* Now the fact in point is this: some mentally disordered people get promptly "better" and some proceed quickly to "recovery" as a result of these various "shock treatments"— just as some are "greatly improved" as sequel to a surgical operation which *destroys* the functional activity of part of the central nervous system. And presumably [the "improvement" occurs] for the same general reason; namely, that [the patients] are *reduced in human capabilities* and drop back from a world the complexities of which provoked some insoluble conflict of adaptive impulses to one simpler and within the range of their surviving human abilities. Mental disorder is thus rectified by acquiring a mental defect, a material alteration in functional capacity for living.

Fortunately, besides this ablative or reductive type of alteration, we can, in some instances, bring about very material change in the direction of increased functional capacity for living, with resulting favorable effect on the future course of the person's interpersonal relations. Everyone is familiar with some of the effects of *fatigue* and some have learned the way to avoid it. Also, most of us have at times reached the mental state of *exhaustion* and know how a good night's sleep restores capability. The change which follows an adequate diet in those who are suffering serious nutritional deficiency is a spectacular increase in functional capacity. This is equally true of thyroid feeding in those with deficiency of the hormone internally secreted by this gland. There are some potent drugs which alter metabolism more selectively, with equally

[* Sullivan is being sarcastic here. H.S.P.]

noticeable results. Moreover, the specific reductive effect on more complex interpersonal capabilities brought about transiently by ingesting ethyl alcohol has been observed for centuries—and, in 1923, turned to excellent use in starting the recovery of some gravely psychotic patients.* Some more potent agents that work in much the same way have also proven useful in giving the patient and the psychiatrist a chance to collaborate towards rectifying personality warp, and the more commendable way of using insulin in psychiatry belongs in this category.

To resume the theme, it must be evident from this bare sketch of some elementary facts that persons suffering a grave mental disorder are not susceptible to remedial change by mere argument or opportunity for ordinarily impressive experience. The same is well known by the psychiatrist to be the case with the milder manifestations of personality warp called the *psychoneuroses*—or even more unsatisfactorily labeled neurotic disorders or neuroses. These, too, however numerous are the minor differences in the people who suffer them, tend to eventuate in some one of a small number of patterns of troublesome interpersonal relations which have high probability of continuing to be conspicuous features of the victim's living.

Without repeating the text of Selective Service System *Medical Circular Number One—Revised 5/19/41*,** let it suffice to say that there is a degree of intensity of each type or group of mental disorder patterns the manifestation of which indicates that the sufferer is incapable of adapting in the military environment. If he is inducted into the armed service, he may be or may rapidly become far worse than useless, because he will require types of attention that the military establishment is not designed to supply; or, if this perhaps less unfortunate eventuality is delayed, he may presently fail in a crucial task and actually endanger the efficiency or even the lives of many of his fellows. The section of the Army General Staff charged with shaping policy with regard to per-

[* Sullivan is referring to his own work with psychotic patients. See, for instance, *Schizophrenia as a Human Process*, p. 287. H.S.P.]

[** This contains the instructions to Selective Service physicians on criteria for psychiatric evaluation, based upon a memorandum drafted by Sullivan and others at the William Alanson White Psychiatric Foundation. H.S.P.]

sonnel is keenly aware of these risks.* The Bureau of Medicine and Surgery, Navy Department, is making great efforts to eliminate unsuitable recruits at their receiving stations. In time, with continued encouragement from those who recognize the problem, the psychiatry of military selection may become quite adequate.

The first principle of psychiatry in mobilization is the selection of manpower on the basis of personal suitability, appropriateness of personality, to meet the characterizing stresses of the war work concerned. From the standpoint of stress as primarily interpersonal, the armed forces are at one extreme of a rank order in which farming is at the other, and industrial employment is higher than transportation and communication. [If one ignores the counterbalancing] element of interpersonal support, morale, in resisting demoralization,[1] the work of merchant seamen on an oil tanker would top all others [in stress], and, considering the relative public inattention which these men's heroic contribution is receiving, we cannot but wonder, gratefully, that they carry on. The points, however, are that men who are suited in personality neither to the armed forces nor to administrative responsibility in wartime Washington are not necessarily or even probably disqualified for an equally significant role elsewhere in the national effort; that their potential utility should neither be overlooked nor recklessly imperiled; and that these considerations require a better understanding of the subject by all concerned, including the general public—for their employers and their neighbors have sometimes made it very difficult for men rejected for psychiatric reasons by Selective Service or Army examiners.

This touches on the second basic principle of psychiatry in mobilization, the protection of manpower from unnecessary damage by precipitating or aggravating mental disorder in persons previously able to look after themselves adequately. This is both an outrageous misuse of the citizen and an unnecessary increase in the total cost of the war. As has been stated repeatedly, each

[* Sullivan appended here a long footnote in which in typically indirect style he reported that in contradistinction to the Army General Staff, the Army Surgeon General's Office was not acting on an awareness of the risks of inducting unsuitable recruits. H.S.P.]

[1] See "Psychiatric Aspects of Morale," *Amer. J. Sociology* (1941–42) 47: 277–301.

veteran of the last war who finally became a charge of the U. S. Veterans Administration because of "neuropsychiatric" disability will have cost the taxpayer some thirty thousand dollars before it is over, and this figure includes nothing for economic waste, distress and disorganization of families, and impairment of community morale. . . .

With one out of four of our citizens either significantly deficient in intelligence or so distorted from an optimum development of personality that the vicissitudes of life are a considerable risk for him, the social system certainly comes very near being impeached, the protection of what positive social values there are becomes imperative, and the emergence of a better postwar world cries loudly indeed for realization. Equally obviously, for him who can read the signs—the sickness of our society being as serious as these findings indicate—the dynamism of remedy will be no simple matter to be compounded of enthusiasm and hope.

The personal elements which render many of us inept or actually antagonistic to the waging of total war are now seen to be outcomes of acculturation, eventualities of the very social system that grew through the era of sovereign states, of U. S. imperialism and post [World War I] U. S. isolationism, of unregulated industrialism holding over into a period of shrinking economy, with as personal manifestations a whole congeries of security motives —the pursuit of prestige and profits regardless, and the cultivation of group and individual hostilities, along with the inevitable encouragement of survival of alien loyalties in groups of more recent immigrants—even a reaching out for something alien among some of our more anciently subordinate minorities.

We see something of the ingrained preconceptions that still lead to misunderstanding, the perpetuation of ignorance, and the spread of misinformation. We begin to realize the extent to which *unwitting* misdirection of effort can give aid and comfort to the enemy by way of noncooperation, obstruction, sedition, and sabotage. The continuance of institutions and groups serving objectives dissonant with the total effort is more understandable, and the "neutral" and pacifist folk—those devoted to ideals of appeasement and compromise, the doubters of our allied United Nations, all or a particular one, even the people who are quietly pro-Nazi in sympathy—all these disintegrative phenomena become less outrageously but more disturbingly evil. Anti-social "groups," whether they be international cartels, unhappy circles of anarchists, or merely a couple of psychopaths solving everything in a barroom, loose their inspiration by Satan, and become highlights on the times. We are—and one hopes that we are beginning to realize that we are—a very sick society confronted with an opportunity, if an exceedingly risky opportunity, to recover by crisis.

This perspective may serve to check the righteous indignation all too readily called out by skillful emphasis on disintegrative factors in the central administrative function. We may be less blindly intolerant of incompetent, ignorant, and irresponsible public officials, of their seeming preoccupation with "politics as usual," of their sensitivity to pressure groups with short-sighted if not utterly blind propaganda. We may realize that some contradictions, conflict, and confusion of leadership are inevitable in this stage of reorganizing the national life, and that the coordination of administrative functions can only emerge gradually. We may even become unemotionally effective in insisting that self-seeking at our risk be discontinued, that discriminative treatment of persons or groups be recognized as dangerous to national solidarity, that hoarding and profiteering and the misuse of any and all war resources be recognized as symptoms of mental disorder requiring a special type of custodial care.

The most crucial remaining problem of our mobilization is then the organization of responsible community leadership and the coordination of such leaders to the end that we may achieve solidarity as a nation and the measure of knowledge and understanding collaboration of which each in his personal measure is capable, to win the war, to save the social values that have already been gained, and resolutely and wisely to achieve a better postwar world.

The central administration of this organized community leadership needs to be something vastly more important than an information bureau, an office of propaganda, or even a service for political or psychiatric warfare. It has to combine all these functions in a much more inclusive and fundamental adult educational activity adjusted to the particular needs of the variety of personalities enmeshed in sundry types of communities which make up the people of these United States.

The peculiar mission of the proposed Office of War Information and its representatives everywhere among us is to teach practically everyone that world freedom is necessary if one and one's children are long to enjoy personal freedom, that the welfare of all peoples of the globe determines the final measure of one's own and one's children's welfare, and that the great tangible value on earth—the general pursuit of which would solve all employment problems, provide unlimited opportunities for personal development and happiness, and give immediate and ultimate security to all—is an ever more benevolent social order in which the dignity and worth of human beings may gradually expand towards horizons of now inconceivable greatness.

This mission is the part of winning the war that will lift it from the category of world catastrophes and national disaster and make its hideous costs wise contributions to the future.

12

___

Commentary

DURING the general period of this book, Sullivan wrote two articles on the explicit subject of psychiatry and morale—"Psychiatric Aspects of Morale," given as an address before the Society for Social Research at the University of Chicago, in August, 1941,[1] and "Psychiatry and Morale," presented at a Conference on Psychiatry at the University of Michigan, in October, 1942. Only the second paper, which represents a somewhat later development in Sullivan's thinking on the subject, has been included here; but a reading of both papers is essential for a full exposure to Sullivan's contribution in this area.

In this second paper, which follows, Sullivan emphasizes the importance of the primary group in the study of morale. In time of crisis, the event may shape the composition of the primary group, so that it is situationally determined. Sullivan warns that one cannot ordinarily speak of the "morale" of a large group of people; in general, "the larger the group the less meaningful the remark [about the morale of the group]." Only in case of an extreme situation, could one talk about the morale of a large group: "Only at the disastrous end of a decisive battle could a whole field army be subject to gross demoralization. Even then, I surmise, there would be companies who would fight to the death if they were not trodden on by their retreating companions." Ordinarily one could not speak of the morale of the French peasant, without specifying a certain small geographic area and/or a particular agricultural crop, for instance. Yet at the time of the blitzkrieg during World War II, the French peasant in the path of the German ad-

[1] The text of this address can be found in *Amer. J. Sociology* (1941–42) 47:277–301. It has also been reprinted in *Personality and Political Crisis*, edited by Alfred H. Stanton and Stewart E. Perry; Glencoe, Ill.: The Free Press, 1951.

vance—regardless of locale or crop—exhibited a generalized group despair, comparable to the despair seen in a particular psychiatric patient.

Sullivan points out that a Navy ship in a time of national disaster offers a rare opportunity for research into the functioning of a self-contained community, in which there is "an intense realization that in a crisis the life of everyone may depend on the life of anyone." For this reason, Sullivan suggests, naval units may constitute one of "the world's best laboratories for the study of morale." It is not enough for the psychiatrist to study demoralized people; Sullivan states that he must also study "people who survive really desolating experiences with unimpaired drive, coherence, coordination, and collaborative abilities." The morale of the Merchant Marine during World War II is another important area for study, Sullivan notes; there are obviously different group values here than with an Army or Navy combat group.

Sullivan ends the paper on what seems to be a note of personal despair, stating briefly that there is a group of communities in the United States in which "problems of morale are literally gravely pressing. I refer to most of the Negro communities." In the midst of war, as I have noted earlier, the subject seems too "complex" for discussion.

Psychiatry and Morale†

THERE is a reason for psychiatrists having to deal with many relatively interesting and important topics other than patients suffering mental disorders, and I think I am justified in taking a moment to discuss this reason. The study of man and of all things cultural, man-made, has in the science and art of medicine fallen to the lot of psychiatry, as in the field of social sciences it has fallen to the lot of social psychology. The chance of anyone's making an adequate discrimination between social psychology on the one hand and modern psychiatry on the other seems to me to be rather small. The most one can say is that they sound very different and they do not like each other very warmly—perhaps chiefly because the social scientist comes along an academic path which seldom touches the biological disciplines closely, whereas the psychiatrist comes along the path of medical education which is rather strikingly biological in its roots, and, at least until recently, sadly lacking in any attention to social-scientific data. The facts are that the two disciplines are very closely related in subject matter and as the years pass will quite certainly become more and more closely related in the type of theory, experiment and conclusion with which they are occupied, and in the formulations and advisory statements about important matters occasionally de-

† Reprinted from *Psychiatry and the War: A Survey of the Significance of Psychiatry and its Relation to Disturbances in Human Behavior to help provide for the Present War Effort and for Post War Needs*, edited by Frank J. Sladen, M.D.; Springfield, Ill. and Baltimore, Md.: Charles C Thomas, 1943; pp. 327–340. [A Record of the Conference on Psychiatry held at Ann Arbor, Michigan, October 22, 23, and 24, 1942, at the invitation of the University of Michigan and the McGregor Fund.]

manded, as, for example, that asked of the psychiatrist now addressing you.

Of course, morale, whatever it means to you—and I shall spend no time on that—is important. We had a profoundly shocking instance of its importance in our recent conversion from a country wonderfully wishful in the belief that we could get other people to fight our war into a people frantically at the business of preparing to defend itself against the most dangerous enemy which has appeared in the history of the Western world.

It would be a waste of time to struggle with a definition. Let me content myself simply with discussing how the psychiatrist attacks the problem of morale. As a number of the essays in this remarkable Conference on Psychiatry have indicated, psychiatrists tackle a good many problems because there is no one else to tackle them and because they do in their way fall rather clearly in the broad and fundamental field of interpersonal relations. This means the way in which people live together, deal with each other, and come to have the beliefs, convictions, and attitudes, real or imaginary, which they are constantly manifesting to friends and enemies, neighbors and distant correspondents. Just because psychiatry includes the only body of scientists who are clearly aware of a primary concern with the field of interpersonal relations, which has only quite recently been recognized as the really proper field of social psychology—in so far as this is the science of personal interaction—psychiatry is called on to deal with a good many things far indeed from the alienism in which it perhaps had its birth in this phase of culture.

Psychiatry, when it tackles a problem, distinguishes itself from its sister discipline of social psychology by looking for the most aberrant types of interpersonal relations which have some bearing on the problem, while social psychology, traditionally social-scientific, is apt to seek the great middle ground for its data. In the problem of morale, I think that the psychiatric approach seems the fortunate one. When one looks for major aberrations in the field of morale, they stand out clearly. Demoralized people, on the one hand, and the people who survive really desolating experiences with unimpaired drive, coherence, coordination, and collaborative abilities—those are the aberrant poles that the psychiatrist has to study in attempting to make sense of morale. He studies the abnormal, and gradually expanding the field to the less abnormal, discovers that he has crossed the normal without noticing it and has covered the ground.

The study of demoralized people as a way of approaching the problem of morale is somewhat illuminating. We and you—because you must remember that psychiatrists and others have much the same experience—certainly know people who have been acutely demoralized and probably know people who are chronically demoralized.

A degree of acute demoralization which is practically beyond the true meaning of demoralization—which is related to it as lightning is to any other celestial illumination—is panic. Now "panic" is unhappily both a technical term and a word which appears in the newspapers. So let me say that the panic I speak of is an exceedingly ghastly experience which usually passes over and into the kind of blind terror the newspapers mean by the term. When one is in panic one does nothing. In blind terror, one rather blindly seeks a scheme for action, for escape. Below this intensity, the degree of fear which we call blind terror, there are various levels of fear to be observed in states of acute demoralization in which one is horribly afraid and tries to escape, more or less purposively and effectively. Still lower in intensity in this same series, and a part of the picture of acute demoralization, is the fear and anxiety from which arise what we may call the psychoneurotic disablements. In these, a person who is acutely demoralized, neither panic-stricken nor a victim of blind terror, but very much afraid, rather abruptly is relieved of a large measure of that fear by the occurrence of some apparently organic disease. Some of the war neuroses are striking instances of this, the threadbare example being the boy with none too good a background for mental health who had been drafted and sent overseas. He had been delayed a terribly long time on his way to the front and had finally been there about two weeks when word came that his battalion was to go "over the top" that night. While he had the usual symptoms of very real fear, the first barrage came and ended and he was still among those present and ready to go over the top. But a little before the zero hour he had a painful seizure

in his right arm and it was found that his index finger was paralyzed. That unfortunately reduces the usefulness of a marksman
to zero. In other words, being right-handed and depending largely
for effectiveness on using a gun and having lost the use of his
trigger finger, he suddenly became what the services call "ineffectual."

There are some people, I suppose, even in such an intelligent
audience as this, who are impressed by the singularly purposeful
character of this disablement and are inclined to look down the
nose at this soldier and say, "Huh, not a very honorable performance." Let me assure you that psychoneurotic disablements which
relieve the fear and anxiety that would otherwise drive one to
perhaps most disastrous attempts at escape are no more the voluntary choice of the person who suffers them than is your eye color
an instance of your deliberate selection. They are not psychoneurotic disablements if you select them and cook them up and
stage them as a dramatic performance; then they are usually rather
transparent fraud. They are psychoneurotic disablements when
they come without calling, notwithstanding the fact that they
come very conveniently.

A thing much more commonly encountered in acute demoralization of mild degree is what is meant when one speaks of getting
rattled. A famous example I remember from the days when I
practiced in New York City was the case of a gentleman who had
just acquired his first automobile, who, while driving, spotted a
dear friend in a car going the other way, reached for his hat to
greet her and drove his car straight into the other. He was rattled.

Then there is the mild stage of demoralization which we do
not ordinarily recognize as such (but the appearances of which the
psychiatrist sees through, realizing this is the most probable explanation)—that is, an occasion when one flies into a rage. Often
in mere anger one is angry because something has tended to de-
moralize him. So much for acute demoralization.

The picture of chronic demoralization is quite different from
that of acute demoralization. The time factor in acute and in
chronic demoralization is important, perhaps unusually important.
Acute demoralization is always a brief affair. There are some
acute conditions which are sustained or which recur—and de-

moralization can recur, but it does not ordinarily go on. It is almost always sharply time-limited; and what follows is something else. Thus, our psychoneurotic soldier has his finger paralyzed while he is demoralized, but then, after the paralysis, suffers a psychoneurosis, a so-called war neurosis, without any particular demoralization. *Chronic demoralization*, in contrast, can go on for months or years. There are two great polar manifestations of these conditions. One is *discouragement*. By discouragement I do not mean that you decide you really are not interested in something and give it up, but I mean being discouraged to the point that a psychiatrist might mistake you for a regression: You do not do much of anything; you do not think of much of anything. But you are not depressed, chiefly because the victim of a depression does think of something, a circling of the same thought: [for example,] "I have committed the unpardonable sin. God will never forgive me. I am lost," and this goes on. A discouraged person thinks as little as possible, but such thinking as he does is *progressive* or *retrogressive* preoccupation, with gloomy evidence of failure and not merely circling. Now and then there may be a moment of spontaneity, and he thinks of attacking the thing again; then comes a flow of gloomy recollections of when he tried that before and it failed and how many other things have failed, and so on.

The other polar contrast in chronic demoralization, still not so different, is *despair*. Now "despair" may seem to some of you just a beautifully dramatic word which should appear in romantic literature. When it is renamed *disorganization apathy*, it sounds pretty impressive. If I remind you that the inculcation of mass despair was the great success of the German psychiatric strategy in the early days of the blitzkrieg and that it was the widespread dissemination of this mental state that contributed most vividly to the sudden collapse of France, then you may take despair as something more than a dramatic word. The person in despair is reduced to a vestigial state of humanness. What goes on in the mind is almost entirely accidental and goes on to no particular purpose; and what goes on as behavior is a matter merely of what has been begun. If a person in despair were standing at the top of the aisle here and someone gave him a firm push he would walk at a fairly steady rate, probably stumble around the corners, come down here and I suppose wind up looking blankly at the curtain behind me. They keep going, not anywhere in particular and with no evidence of enthusiasm or purpose; they have very little in mind. They are quite incapable of grasping anything which requires concentration or immediate, alert response. The blitzkrieg succeeded in filling most of the roads any good for the transport of troops, tank supplies, and so on, in France with hordes of peasants, demoralized—already chronically demoralized—to the point of despair. They wandered blindly along these roads, making little or no effort to get out of the way of troops, getting hit or run over—and the troops could not stand it and did not go ahead.

This is something of what the psychiatrist finds when he attacks the problem of morale. He sees the picture of demoralization and having realized this and having filled in many more details than I can do here, he comes to the problem of what the circumstances are under which people become demoralized, and what the circumstances are under which some people avoid demoralization when the average person would logically be demoralized. Study shows that demoralization in various degrees follows when some implicitly trusted and very significant aspect of one's universe suddenly collapses. Your universe and my universe are not the same. I am not talking about the physical universe but about the universe in which you live. To some of you, the greatest of all values and certainties in your universe is the certainty of divine law and ultimate justice. If that part of your universe suddenly fails rather dramatically, under circumstances which bring its failure to you quite abruptly, you will pass into acute demoralization. The principle is so true that it holds for all sorts of situations. If you were used to walking on a certain sidewalk, which you crossed twice a day, and it suddenly sank under you, you would be acutely demoralized—how gravely, depending on your past experience. I mention these two examples to suggest to you that if something always trusted, never doubted, is swiftly wiped out, if it suddenly proves wholly inadequate to support you in some way or other, then demoralization follows immediately. The state as it is experienced, in so far as one experiences anything, is of suddenly becoming a prey to utter insecurity. No feeling of security remains, whether it is trust in the ultimate character of divine law or trust in the sidewalk. When one is demoralized all one's security has disappeared.

Next to this in the causing of acute demoralization are any grave threats of insecurity. In other words, any rapidly appearing, pretty convincing suggestion that you will be made deeply insecure in any field is quite apt to provoke acute demoralization. In some cases where you suddenly find that you are in a position where all your major satisfactions can be cut off, then, too, you can become acutely demoralized. These threats fail under one circumstance to be demoralizing and this is very illuminating. If the threat to your security, or in the rarer case the threat to all your important satisfactions, appears gradually enough and under circumstances when you are in fit condition so that you can engage in what is called rational analysis of the threat and achieve an understanding of how it has come upon you—I need not tell you how far from logically perfect your analysis may be or how relatively empty your understanding may be—then acute demoralization does not follow. But if you are tired, or at a great disadvantage from some social reason when the threat impinges on you, you are reduced to a state of acute demoralization. These are the outstanding illuminating instances of the occurrence or nonoccurrence of acute demoralization.

The psychiatrist is used to seeing certain acute mental disorders progressing into chronicity. My distinction between acute and chronic demoralization is somewhat different. Chronic demoralization does not necessarily or even usually begin as acute demoralization, but gradually grows under circumstances different from the ones which are acutely demoralizing. The striking instance is where one rather [un]expectedly fails to perform something while sure that he knows just how to do it; he checks on his technique and goes on trying and trying and trying, and it does not happen. In other words, what—according to the best information he can get—should work, does not work. Gradually one slips into the state of discouragement and under certain circumstances, if the goal is important enough, becomes desolate and beyond any constructive effort.

Again, if one encounters any devastating experience and discovers by experimentation, by effort, that he cannot improve his situation, that he can do nothing about it, he becomes demoralized. And if one discovers that this is the result of the enmity or the lack of affection of others—in other words, if one just does not have any friends or if one has enemies who stand firmly in one's way—and one finds one can do nothing about it, yet one's security depends on these people's performance, then one demoralizes as rapidly as one's self-deceptive fantasies about the situation are broken down. A special case which does not pertain particularly to the war is when you find out that a person entirely necessary to your satisfaction or security actually has no respect or affection for you, is just being polite or something of that kind. Under those circumstances demoralization is apt to occur and to become rather profound.

I have given you a sketch of the type of interpersonal situation in which demoralization happens. You will see that other people have a good deal to do with it, but it would be unfortunate if you took this to be the whole story. There are other important factors, sometimes no more complex than mere physical matters; physical conditions which impose great strains on our bodily organism can and do facilitate the occurrences of demoralization. Moreover, there are certain types of stress which are, you might almost say, directly demoralizing; to a great many people, shrill noises are an example. That is the reason for shrieking bombs and so on. There are people who will probably—through the very long war—be somewhat demoralized whenever the air raid siren goes off. A shrill progression of sound increasing in pitch is apparently directly demoralizing. I do not know how much this is the case because it preoccupies the hearing apparatus and thereby closes off one of our contacts with the world.

I am going to suggest the next factor by mentioning that obscure states of the organism which we call fatigue and exhaustion have a place in explaining the occurrence of particular instances of demoralization. The onset of so grave a thing as *schizophrenia*, the more modern name for what was called *dementia praecox*, can be delayed for a day or two by giving the person a good night's sleep, which is simply a matter of attacking the element of exhaustion. Other physiological aspects of the organism and demoralization could be dealt with, but I must pass on to my current topic.

Let us consider the person who in an ordinarily demoralizing situation is not demoralized. This is the other extreme in the interest of psychiatry. What do we find about him? In general, we find that he maintains an unusually alert attention to the situation which might ordinarily be demoralizing and that when he encounters one of the generally demoralizing interpersonal situations to which I have referred, he reassures himself by quickly demonstrating his ability to do something about the situation. A variant of this is seen in children who might be demoralized by an unsympathetic adult. While the boy or girl is not able to do anything directly to ward off the demoralizing onslaught, he immediately makes himself a nuisance in some way. He becomes thoroughly unpleasant. While this does not remedy the situation that is causing him distress, still he is showing that he can do something; he can be somebody, even if merely a nuisance. This saves him from being demoralized. From instances of this kind it is easy to demonstrate that, along with alert attention to the situation, there must go a constructive preoccupation. The strange thing is it does not matter much with what one is constructively preoccupied. It may be something highly irrelevant to the situation. Sometimes hopeless situations are survived merely because one plunges into an irrelevant but constructive preoccupation.

These are the general statements of instances when one could become demoralized but does not. I might add that in all these operations the real menace that hangs over the person who escapes or avoids demoralization is still fatigue. If the alertness to the actual course of events, which is essential to an understanding of what is going on, has to be continued very long, or if efforts to keep oneself reassured that one can do something about something have gone too long, then we see these phenomena which are almost as definite as particular types of poisoning, in that one's attention shrinks in spite of anything. One's ability to maintain a perspective on the situation dies out. Fatigue, boredom, or a state of exhaustion set in. Under the circumstances, the protections that these people have against demoralization fail them and they become demoralized—incidental to the fatigue.

Now what does all this teach us? I have attempted elsewhere to demonstrate how these considerations underlie a good deal of what we call psychiatric or psychological strategy, which Germany has developed to an extraordinarily high degree and which I surmise Russia has carried even further.[1] From these principles and from our analysis of the enemy's psychiatric strategy, we can work out certain measures of counterstrategy. One of the things that stands out, which seems necessary to implement my recommendations, is the production of a national community or solidarity. I cannot give much attention to the methods. So I will refer to an editorial entitled "Completing Our Mobilization"[2] where I have indicated the major operation necessary for the production of a community or national solidarity, namely, the mobilization of leadership. I must refer the interested to these two articles because I wish now to talk on what may be called the morbid in discussing morale.

We hear a good deal about the national morale. I am unable to find any meaning in that expression. I know it points in a general direction, but indices do not always mean that there is reality at the other end of the arrow. If a psychiatrist has to do anything about morale, I am sure he will be barking up the right tree instead of getting lost in a largely imaginative forest if he realizes that he must deal with persons and discoverable groups of people instead of with great generalized entities which are supposed to represent some curious kind of addition to all these people and groups. We do find some very large groups of people in the United States about whose morale we can perhaps make meaningful remarks. I assure you, however, that, in general, the larger the group the less meaningful the remarks. If I were to talk about the morale of our Army, I would come so near to talking about nothing, that I am not going to say anything about it now. I am very much more than interested in any discussion about the morale of the 86th Division of our Army, or of a particular company or a

[1] Harry Stack Sullivan, "Psychiatric Aspects of Morale," *Amer. J. Sociology* (1941–42) 47:277–301.

[2] "Completing Our Mobilization," [unsigned editorial], *Psychiatry* (1942) 5:263–282. [An extract from this editorial appears in this book under the title, "Leadership, Mobilization, and Postwar Change." H.S.P.]

particular installation. Why? Because the people concerned in these units show morale and demoralization in the face of concrete events which the large entity can scarcely be conceived to experience. Only at the disastrous end of a decisive battle could a whole field army be subject to gross demoralization. Even then, I surmise, there would be companies who would fight to the death if they were not trodden on by their retreating companions.

The Navy is somewhat different, but to talk about the morale of the Navy in general is a little bit beyond the limits of reason. The significant difference between the Army and Navy lies in the fact that many of the Navy units are almost incredibly self-contained. The organization of a battleship, for example, is not only a strikingly isolated community but an intensely compact and intimately interdependent community with very highly differentiated duties and highly cultivated sense of personal responsibilities and, over all, an intense realization that in a crisis the life of everyone may depend on the life of anyone. The utter closeness and (recognized) interwoven, mutual security in many of the naval units make them among the world's best laboratories for the study of morale.

I wish I could add something about the morale of another body of people who are waging this war, of which I was so happy to hear Assistant Surgeon General Kolb speak this afternoon; I refer to the Merchant Marine.* Unhappily, if I did, I would be even more absurd than in talking about morale in the Army and the Navy, because the Merchant Marine is not a highly organized national arm, with highly developed public relations. They are scarcely mentioned in the press. They are a lot of people who expose themselves, often with reckless abandon, to the most

[* See Lawrence Kolb, "Post-War Psychiatric Perspectives," in: *Psychiatry and the War,* work cited. Kolb says, in part: "The type of casualty of which the public hears very little is that occurring daily among our merchant seamen. These seamen without benefit of uniform or the title of fighting men keep the supplies moving to our forces, our allies and to ourselves through exceedingly troubled waters. Twenty-three hundred of them have lost their lives since the war started. Hundreds have been shipwrecked and have arrived on land in great need of medical and hospital care. . . . They have suffered from shock similar to that so common among soldiers at the front, shock due to harrowing experiences, exposure to wet and cold for days in open life boats, and to deprivation of food" (p. 301). H.S.P.]

appalling risks in performing an absolutely necessary war work of transport and supply. The way that these people come through the experience of having a ship torpedoed under them, getting out of it into a sea of burning oil, having a few pot shots taken at them, drifting perhaps days before being rescued, and then, after they rest for a little while, taking on another ship which is apt to undergo the selfsame experience—that is something for the student of morale.

Now let us come to what I conceive I am supposed to talk about. The communities which make up the United States are the places where morale or its absence, its height or its lowness, is to be studied and, if possible, improved. These communities are many and interpenetrating. For example, the morale of American psychiatry has occasionally demonstrated itself to the profound amazement and great satisfaction of everyone in the last two years. The very attendance at this Conference on Psychiatry of people who are harassed with twice as many responsibilities and important duties as they had a year ago is a measure of the incredible responsibility and public-spiritedness developed by these essentially very individualistic physicians. They have been showing this, to my personal knowledge, for the past two years, whereas the morale of medicine in general has by no manner of means been so uniformly and unswervingly very high over that period. This is interesting, quite aside from their being psychiatrists, because here is one profession, a community within a much larger community, and in many ways very closely related, identical in many aspects of training. As I said, morale in regard to national objectives among psychiatrists is extraordinarily high, even though there is one region—and that not in the great middle country—where it is not yet perfect.

What of the morale of agricultural communities? I do not know "the agricultural community." I know only of communities in such and such counties where they grow so and so. Almost uniformly their morale is remarkably high. They are frightfully distressed at the present labor shortage not because their crops are going to waste and they are suffering monetary loss, but because they grew these crops to feed the Army and the United States and they hate to see crops rotting. That is what is distressing people in many agricultural communities around the country. That is impairing their morale. But in general their morale is excellent, because the government has seen that the agricultural communities should have organization of leadership. To the extent that this program has succeeded, they have become most exceptional among American communities.

In industry, unhappily, morale is widely varied from one plant to another and the nearest we have come to organizing leadership is something about which a psychiatrist, I believe, is entitled to feel bored. When a factory seems to be doing badly, somebody in Washington sends out a cheer leader who beats the drums and tells the workmen how utterly essential to winning the war their production in this particular factory may be, and so forth.

Finally, I wish to mention a group of communities in the United States in which morale is in general anything but satisfactory, where problems of morale are literally gravely pressing. I refer to most of the Negro communities. The present state of our long neglected brown brethren is a source of very great distress to some of the thoughtful. Time permits no discussion of this complex field of problems. Perhaps I have given you a notion of how the psychiatrist is confronted by the problem of morale and have shown you why he must always get to something reasonably concrete in terms of interpersonal relations in his recommendations for alleviating low, and protecting uncertain, morale.

13

Commentary

IN ADDITION TO Sullivan's intensive work with Selective Service during the early 40's and his writings in political psychiatry, he managed to find time during the same period to formulate a major theoretical statement on psychiatry as an orienting discipline for the social sciences. The first complete theoretical statement—and the only one published during his life span—appeared as a monograph in the February, 1940, issue of *Psychiatry*, "Conceptions of Modern Psychiatry." [1] After Sullivan's disappointment with his work in Selective Service, he turned with new vigor toward the task of teaching an orienting course in the Washington School of Psychiatry, with the same title as the monograph, in which he began a major revision of his thinking. Each year of teaching after 1944 encompassed some further revision, expansion, modification of this theory. The last full year of this lecture series was published posthumously as *The Interpersonal Theory of Psychiatry* (1953). While this remains a fairly final and complete theoretical statement, there is at least one major lacuna in this book. The next two selections ("The Illusion of Personal Individuality" and "The Meaning of Anxiety in Psychiatry and in Life"), both given as individual lectures for special occasions, help to fill this gap. Although the theoretical point made in each paper is couched in separate, almost disparate, frames of reference,

[1] In 1947, this was reprinted by the Foundation, with a new Foreword by Sullivan. See *Conceptions of Modern Psychiatry*; Washington, D. C.: The William Alanson White Psychiatric Foundation, 1947. [New edition: Norton, 1953.]

both are actually concerned with the same problem—*how to find a way to make sense of operationism in the behavioral sciences.*

  The first of these two papers, "The Illusion of Personal Individuality," was given before the Society on the Theory of Personality, New York Academy of Medicine, on May 3, 1944. The presentation was probably, by Sullivan's standards, more or less extemporaneous, and it was taped at the time. But in the five intervening years before his death, he never attempted to rework the transcription, as far as I know; it was finally published posthumously, with very little change, in 1950.[2] By Sullivan's own standards, the formulation as stated in the title was very close to the heart of his theory; but this particular formulation was rejected by many of Sullivan's colleagues in both psychiatry and social science; and I think that he was reluctant to publish the paper as such and engage with his colleagues in unrewarding argument. The second of these two papers, "The Meaning of Anxiety in Psychiatry and in Life," presented before the same Society four years later, represents an attempt to make the same theoretical point but with new theoretical tools, in order to avoid argument. Yet the 1944 presentation makes several important points not made elsewhere as far as I know, and it is a necessary introduction to Sullivan's operational thinking.

  It seems to me that a good deal of confusion has arisen around Sullivan's stand on the "illusion of personal individuality." Various social scientists have expressed some concern that Sullivan is talking about cultural relativism, or is attacking the dignity of the person, or is advocating conformity. I do not think that any of these charges is accurate. It would require a long essay to discuss the various attitudes developed by Sullivan on this subject; I shall confine myself here to only a few suggestions as to how a more accurate picture of his thinking might be obtained.

[2] The reader should bear in mind that this paper is probably the closest to Sullivan's spoken word of all of his published writings. That is, Sullivan did a lot of reworking and rewriting on papers published before his death; and my co-editors have collaborated with me in considerably modifying the language in the posthumous books. But this paper is very close to the taped version. While some of the sentences are difficult to understand—and I would do considerably more changing if I were editing it now—there is some merit in leaving it essentially as it was delivered, for it communicates some of Sullivan's platform manner.

To begin with, one must differentiate sharply between the individual career line, as conceptualized by Sullivan and others, and the notion of absolute human uniqueness. Sullivan certainly recognized that he had an individual career line, but he used this experience as a tool for clarifying all human experience. That is, the individuality of one's career line emphasizes one's similarity to other human beings to the extent that one is engaged in communication with others. A skilled observer can often infer many aspects of another person's individual career line sometimes by relatively limited ongoing interpersonal data, as Sullivan noted. One's humanness is limited by one's experience; at the same time, one's humanness is created by that same unique line of experience. This is basically related to what Mead describes as the discontinuity in the determination of the self; but the discontinuity is determined by the continuity, and over time the discontinuity may become part of a new continuity.

This problem of the fierce loneliness and the feeling of isolation in the American, which tend to make him feel unique, is an old one. The loneliness and the isolation are realities in the American experience; but the uniqueness is an American myth, according to Sullivan. One of the early statements of this dilemma in the American scene is found in Bronson Alcott's writings; while the entire statement is less sophisticated than Sullivan's, it seems to emerge from the same experience:

Excellent people wonder why they cannot meet and converse. . . . One is individual, the other is individual no less. Individuals repel. Persons meet. And only as one's personality is sufficiently overpowering to dissolve the other's individualism, can the parties flow together and become one. But individuals have no power of the sort. They are two, not one, perhaps many. Prisoned within themselves by reason of their egotism, like animals, they stand aloof, are separate even when they touch; are solitary in any company, having none in themselves. But the freed personal mind meets all, is apprehended by all, by the least cultivated, the most gifted; magnetizes all; is the spell-binder, the liberator of every one. We speak of sympathies, antipathies, fascinations, fates for this reason.[3]

Sullivan's more immediate intellectual antecedents for an operational approach probably came from two directions: first, it was essentially within the tradition of Cooley and Mead, particularly

[3] See A. Bronson Alcott, *Tablets;* Boston: Roberts Bros., 1868; pp. 77–78.

their theory of the genesis of the self; and second, it was informed by modern physics, in particular by P. W. Bridgman. "Simple observation shows that I act in two modes," Bridgman observes. "In my public mode I have an image of myself in the community of my neighbors, all similar to myself and all of us equivalent parts of a single all-embracing whole. In the private mode I feel my inviolable isolation from my fellows and may say, 'My thoughts are my own, and I will be damned if I let you know what I am thinking about.'" [4]

In essence Bridgman and Sullivan seem to agree that as the inviolably isolated mode of interaction is defined and brought into awareness, science and human patterns of living will improve. Within Sullivan's definition of the clinical experience, the psychiatrist is concerned with moving the immutably private of the patient out into the area of human experience; for when a patient is engaged exclusively with the immutably private, he is in fact hopelessly ill. While there is a part of the immutably private that can never become a part of general human experience and consensually validated, both science and civilization must move toward the goal of restricting more and more the area of the immutably private. Neither the clinician nor the scientist can deal with the immutably private, Sullivan states: "That there are particular human lives, each with a unique career line, I no more deny than do I the fact that I am a particular person who has a particular dog. . . . [But] the immutably private in my dog and in me escapes and will always escape the methods of science, however absorbing I may once have found the latter." [5]

Paradoxical as it may seem at first blush, Sullivan as Editor of the journal *Psychiatry* insisted that its contributors define the pronoun "we," or avoid it. Did the author mean "we" in this society? or the members of a particular organization? or the author and the reader? and so on. This might seem to be at variance with his theory of "the illusion of personal individuality," but it again fits the opera-

[4] See "Symposium on Operationism," *Psychological Review* (1945) 52: 241–294; particularly p. 283. Sullivan first cited Bridgman's work in his unpublished book manuscript, *Personal Psychopathology* (1929 version); here he stated that Bridgman's *The Logic of Modern Physics* "includes a clear argument as to the inutility of other than 'operational concepts' in scientific descriptions of reality."

[5] See p. xii of *Conceptions of Modern Psychiatry* (Norton edition).

tional approach: the individual bias or distortion of the observer must be defined, at least for the observer himself. Again this is very close to Bridgman's approach: "There should be two words in science —'my-science' and 'your-science,' " Bridgman insists. In the same article, he states, "If I want to express what obviously occurs, I have got to use the first person." [6] In the context of the entire article, Bridgman means the first person *singular*.

A final measure of Sullivan's emphasis on the importance of operationism is found in his 1947 decision to change the subtitle of the journal *Psychiatry* from *Journal of the Biology and Pathology of Interpersonal Relations* to *Journal for the Operational Statement of Interpersonal Relations.*[7]

Perhaps Sullivan's actual expression—"the illusion of personal individuality"—is unfortunate. And certainly the word "operational" is somewhat formidable in the social sciences and has sometimes been used as a façade for pseudo science. But the conceptual usefulness of what Sullivan is talking about remains; and the difficulty of finding 'acceptable' words to spell out a major change in a new model for thought is not easily solved. Undoubtedly, interpersonal processes as the unit for study in the behavioral sciences has had some of the conceptual usefulness of the concept of sub-atomic structures in physics. The physicist is not concerned with whether the "particles" "exist" or not: this is a philosophical question. Sullivan implies that the existence of the individual personality is a philosophical question, irrelevant to the scientific study of personality.

As a young man, Sullivan had seriously considered the possibility of becoming a physicist, and it is not surprising that he was able to use the thinking of modern physics as a tool for making psychiatry a more precise science. In fact, Bridgman's 1927 statement is a fairly accurate formulation of Sullivan's own hope for the utility of operationism in the social sciences generally:

[6] See P. W. Bridgman, "Science: Public or Private?" *Phil. Sci.* (1940) 7: 36–48; esp. p. 46 *ff*.

[7] See "Ten Years of Psychiatry: A Statement by the Editor," *Psychiatry* (1947) 10:433–435; esp. p. 435. Incidentally, this subtitle of the Journal existed for only two years; after Sullivan's death, the new editor changed the subtitle to *Journal for the Study of Interpersonal Processes*—a more felicitous description, although I now tend to believe that some important meaning was lost in this last change.

Operational thinking will at first prove to be an unsocial virtue; one will find oneself perpetually unable to understand the simplest conversation of one's friends, and will make oneself universally unpopular by demanding the meaning of apparently the simplest terms of every argument. Possibly after everyone has schooled himself to this better way, there will remain a permanent unsocial tendency, because doubtless much of our present conversation will then become unnecessary. The socially optimistic may venture to hope, however, that the ultimate effect will be to release one's energies for more stimulating and interesting interchange of ideas.

Not only will operational thinking reform the social art of conversation, but all our social relations will be liable to reform. Let any one examine in operational terms any popular present-day discussion of religious or moral questions to realize the magnitude of the reformation awaiting us. Wherever we temporize or compromise in applying our theories of conduct to practical life we may suspect a failure of operational thinking.[8]

[8] P. W. Bridgman, *The Logic of Modern Physics;* New York: Macmillan, 1927; see p. 32.

The Illusion of Personal

Individuality†

WHEN ONE has the notion of studying personality before him, the ideas of maturation, growth, and development ought certainly never to be too far from consciousness. And if you will have those ideas in mind at the beginning, I will avoid talking about them for some time.

A word that is much more common in all discussions of personality is adjustment, and I would like to state the idea of this paper as a special use of the term adjustment; namely, the adjustment of potentialities to necessities—just as, for example, each person who is going to be a full-fledged person very early adjusts his potentialities for learning to do tricks with his speech apparatus to the overweening necessity of learning the mother tongue of his family. Now the learning of language, which is terribly important in any approach to the study of personality on a general scale, is the classical and perhaps the most important single instance of adjustment in the sense of an immensely capable organism—the vast potentialities of which have perhaps never been adequately

† Reprinted from *Psychiatry* (1950) 13:317–332. This paper was first presented before the Society on the Theory of Personality, New York Academy of Medicine in New York City, May 3, 1944. [After Sullivan's death, the William Alanson White Psychiatric Foundation established an *ad hoc* committee charged with the responsibility for editing the numerous unpublished papers of Sullivan, and this paper was the only one issued by that committee. The actual work was done collaboratively by Stewart E. Perry and myself, with the consultation of James I. Sullivan. H.S.P.]

envisaged, much less explored—adjusting itself to the necessity for verbal communication with significant people.

Another great word in thinking about personality is experience, and I have never found any better definition of experience than that which is, I believe, embalmed as the first meaning of the term in all good English dictionaries: experience is anything lived, undergone, or the like. But to add slightly to this very general notion, let me say that experience can usefully be considered as of two kinds: *direct* experience, in which you are directly undergoing, living, or the like; and *mediate* experience, in which that which has been previously undergone or lived is passed in review. Another form of the mediate experience occurs when we take select excerpts from the past and string them together on the basis of probability, in which case we are engaged in prospective experience, commonly called foresight. Now, experience is quite clearly susceptible of consideration from another standpoint; namely, what happens in awareness, consciousness, or in what we like to term our mental life. And from this standpoint, experience is either noted or unnoticed or, in the first case, formulated. In other words, we note many things which we do not formulate; that is, about which we do not develop clear ideas of what happened to us. And there is also experience which we do not notice but which can be demonstrated to have occurred in explaining subsequent events.

All of us have developed some view of the world, and in general the routes over which we have moved in developing these views of the world are capable of being put under three rubrics. These rubrics that I shall use are terms with pretty definite meaning in certain biological fields, and I am using these terms in a much more general sense; but I think you will see that they have some justification. They are viewpoints. We develop our views of the world from the viewpoint of *morphology*, of our understanding of the way that material is organized; and from *physiology*, in which we gradually come to understand how functional activity, the working of things, is organized; and *ecology*, in which we finally begin to see that materials interpenetrate and that materials and activity are related in some more or less enduring way. So, from these three standpoints—the organization of material things, the way that activity is or the pattern that activities tend to follow, and the interpretation and interrelation of the whole—we gradually develop our views of the world. I should say that these views are, in their currently best form, either notions of a pluralist universe or notions along the line of the doctrine of organism, which is, while it sounds monistic, very different indeed from any monistic philosophy. Now a pluralist universe is probably not unassimilable to the doctrine of organism; but be that as it may, wherever we have a great deal of data assembled and free ourselves from prejudices that obscure our study of that data, we discover that there are the three aspects that I have already mentioned, including very importantly the interrelation, the interdependence of this and that.

A classical instance of this interdependence is the organism's relation with oxygen. Every seventh-grade grammar school boy, I am sure, knows that oxygen is a gas which is an ingredient of the atmosphere and that this gas is in some fashion vital to life. It is a very clever seventh-grade boy who knows that the oxygen gets out of the atmosphere into the body and is presently returned to the atmosphere in the shape of carbon dioxide; but what very few seventh-grade pupils know, and some fourth-grade medical students have not yet quite captured, is the notion that there is very little storage of oxygen and that life is dependent on the continual, almost uninterrupted, exchange between the oxygen of the atmosphere, the oxygen in the body, the carbon dioxide in the body and in the atmosphere. They interpenetrate through marvelously capable cells in the lungs, and the balance of the oxygen in the body is very delicately adjusted by a most elaborate apparatus. But life without an atmosphere including oxygen is not possible for man, and, similarly, an atmosphere which could not receive or would not take the oxygen which we have processed would rapidly prove fatal. There is a continuous interchange which can be called communal existence, if you please, of the organism and its necessary environment.

In this development of a world view, nearly all of us start—not because it is the first thing that intrudes itself upon us but it is the first thing that we can grasp—with some element of the physicochemical world, the world of the nonliving objects and their relations. And then we go from that to the idea of the biological world, the world of the living, living objects and their relations, realizing, as I say, certainly from the seventh grade onward, that the biological world requires some part of the physicochemical world to live. And only as we get well along, do we contemplate the world of people, although they are the first things that impress themselves upon us; and it is at this point —the field of the psychiatrist's interest, the social scientist's interest, the educator's, the lawyer's, and so on—that views of the world are most poignantly deficient in breadth, or depth, or both. All these worlds are encountered through their significant relation with us in our roles of experiencers and formulators. It is probably true that we can experience almost anything for an indefinite length of time; and if we do not fortunately run it through the process which we call formulating, we don't really know what we are doing—although we may get more and more clever at eluding unpleasantness, and so on—and we certainly can't tell our children about it. So the double role of undergoing or living through things and having more or less descriptive and defining thoughts or formulae is the common route by which these various aspects of the universe—the various worlds, if you please—come to be encountered. Because we know of the universe by way of our experience and according to the skill of our formulating faculties, it becomes clear to the thoughtful that whatever the perduring, the long-continuing entities of the universe may be, and however curious their relations may be, in some respects these will forever be unknown to us because we have no channels for experiencing these things and therefore nothing to formulate. And more in keeping with what I intend to talk about in this paper, the current views which are entertained about any of these worlds and their relations are almost inevitably going to undergo change, the rapidity of change in these views probably being greatest in the world of people—and slowest in the physicochemical world with which serious people have been seriously concerned for the longest time.

Now, there is a word which is not particularly an ingredient of common speech but has long since delighted me—it pleased

Whitehead * also, so at least I am in good company for the moment. I believe that the word in its parental Greek tongue meant "knot"; the world I mean is *nexus*, the place where things get together and are snarled up or tangled. The nexus of all this experience by which we form views of the world, the universe, our place in it, and so on, is always in the experience of me-and-my-mind, or you-and-your-mind if you feel very separate from me. And in this you-and-your-mind there are some things which are fairly clearly capable of being named which go on in experiencing and formulating. We analyze and understand the past, and to understand means that we see certain relations in certain parts of it with the still earlier past, which has gradually taken on personal meaning. We symbolize and formulate the present—and by symbolize I mean we relate it to things, thought forms, words, and so on, which will stand for it. With this conversion of something—which for all I know may be unique—into more or less familiar things that stand for it, one becomes able to throw it into statements and conclusions, to deduce relationships which may not have been clear in the experience, and so on and so forth. And as I said before, we project the future by juggling with past symbolizations, understandings, and present formulations in terms of probable future events. To the extent that we project well —that is, we are careful in deciding the probabilities of certain courses of events—we sometimes exercise foresight and are prepared for what happens.

The mind—you know I am now talking about me-and-my-mind or you-and-your-mind—the mind is phenomenologically coterminous with consciousness; that is, so far as anything that you can observe or can get anyone else to observe about your mind or his mind, anything that can be sensed and perceived, will be of the same extent as the state of mind called consciousness; and the various ingredients, the contents of consciousness, which cover a wonderful bunch of alleged or real entities, are what one ordinarily means when he talks about his "mental life." In this we find

[* Many of Sullivan's words, phrases, and actual concepts are of course reminiscent of Whitehead's; in particular, nexus, prehension, pattern and enduring pattern, and so on, seem to have been particularly useful to Sullivan. See, for instance, Alfred North Whitehead, *Science and the Modern World*; New York: The Macmillan Company, 1925. H.S.P.]

a marvelous congeries of things, some things being just terms invented by psychologists, and others being such anciently associated labels that we may assume that they pertain to things: sensations; perceptions; feelings of pleasantness and unpleasantness; sundry wishes, desires, and personal needs; beliefs and ideas, of various orders of abstraction—some that refer to very concrete entities, some that refer to classes of entities, some that refer to some totality of all entities, such as the idea of the universe; thoughts and reveries; and even recollected dreams. Besides these, we find rather less clear, less easily communicable, less easily describable ingredients, such as "the exercise of choice," the manifestation of volition, the state of having intention—always good if you are anything like fully human—and the manifestation of decision; and occasionally, of course, indecision, perplexity, and that peculiarly unpleasant experience which is properly called anxiety—about which, if I am lucky, I will have quite a bit to say presently. And most exciting of all the things that one finds in one's mind is the feeling of power and effectiveness which is connected with objectifying "the mental life," which is ordinarily done by thoughts or remarks about I-and-myself.

Now perhaps all of you or most of you are so familiar with thinking about I-and-myself that you don't realize how delightfully powerful you feel many times when the time comes to say, "I believe so and so." That reaches out and changes things, and only disagreeable people fail to be swayed by the power that you are experiencing and indicating, so that while you-and-your-mind are, so far as phenomena are concerned, coterminous with consciousness, I-and-myself are rather more powerful, more forceful entities, you see, which are in fact somewhat slower in appearing in life than is me-and-myself. The way the "myself" part—you know, that sort of Old Dog Tray that follows along—fits into life gets to be obscure when a patient tells you, "Well, I shall hold myself to doing it." Now I have often tried to picture this process and usually experience a mild tail spin. But it is certainly very reassuring to the patient to announce that he is going to hold himself to something or other, or force himself to do something or other; it's really the most safe and therefore the most sane field in which to exercise power when you don't have it.

In this audience it is scarcely necessary to stress the fact that the content of consciousness, the mental life to which people are really referring when they talk about their minds, is entirely inadequate to account for events, or to exercise very powerful influence directly on the course of events, or even actually to control the contents of consciousness. And for a very long time the science of mind, psychology, was in rather a rum position because its events—in contradistinction to those of the respectable, natural scientific world and even in rather inferior contrast to the growing world of biological knowledge—were discrete and didn't follow each other with due proper copulae and connections but instead were erratic and unpredictable. It is hard to build a science where things have gaps between them. Who knows what's in the gap? And so, as I say, psychology wasn't doing very well with the conscious life as a subject matter for scientific formulation. But things changed a great deal when, through Freud's and Breuer's careful observations and Freud's brilliant thinking, it became possible to postulate the unconscious. The unconscious, from the way I have actually presented the thing, is quite clearly that which cannot be experienced directly, which fills all the gaps in the mental life. In that rather broad sense, the postulate of the unconscious has, so far as I know, nothing in the world the matter with it. As soon as you begin to arrange the furniture in something that cannot be directly experienced, you are engaged in a work that requires more than parlor magic and you are apt to be embarrassed by some skeptic. And so I say, the postulate of the unconscious as that which fills the gaps explains the discontinuity in the conscious life; that's bully, but don't be tempted to tell the world all about the unconscious because someone is almost certain to ask you how you found out.

One reason why people were not content to realize that the unconscious was a hypothesis which was immensely useful is that in this Western world of ours, with its vast success from technology, it has become extremely important for one's feeling of personal prestige that he shall discriminate the reasonable and rational; and in case he finds himself doing anything in which he might be thought to be unreasonable or irrational, he just devotes, oh, almost any necessary portion of the rest of his life to demonstrating that he was both reasonable and rational. So, as I say, since it is one of the great and specious values of this Western world of ours to look upon the reasonable and the rational as very dignified compared with all the rest of the things that can be said about behavior, it isn't enough to have hit upon a splendid hypothesis and arranged a great many experiments and observations to demonstrate that the hypothesis is not just an intellectual convenience but actually gives a sort of common explanatory pattern for many things which can be observed once there is something postulated to fill the discontinuity. Instead of that, one proceeds to make the unconscious—that not susceptible to direct experience—full of reasonable irrationalities and irrational reasonablenesses, and so on, and thereby, I believe, makes oneself magnificently and completely a clown.

Even in the comparatively simple realm of the nonliving some people have long since learned to avoid explanations that offer no possibility of any operational validation, explanations that cannot be converted into any type of act or experiment that will prove whether they are right or wrong, or whether they are to some extent right or to some extent wrong. Physics, for example, has found that it could get itself into wonderful entanglements as long as there was no way of discovering quite what it was talking about. But if, on the other hand, before giving voice, it thought, "Well, now how could one do something to demonstrate whether this term is empty or, at least likely, full of reference to the world" —as soon as that attitude was developed, physics began to make remarkable sense in its newly expanded world of atomic physics, in which the good old rules did not apply; rules on which we were educated and on which most technology, other than electronics, is based. As I say, once this new world of the quantum had been discovered, a great deal of abstruse nonsense was taught and finally compelled physicists to realize that if they couldn't devise some operation that had a bearing on their concept, they had best be quiet. That is really quite a good rule, I think, in our very much more complicated, much more treacherous field in which prejudice and wisdom are almost indistinguishable—unless of course the wisdom is in you and the prejudice in someone else.

In the world of people, explanations are very easily obtained for almost any act of any person. All you have to do is say, "And why did you do that?" and he rattles like a machine gun with great streams of words, verbal statements; and if you go away, he is apt to use streams of words in a letter to complete the demonstration of how unutterably easily he deceives himself into feeling that he knows what he is doing, which is apparently all that most people need in order to feel comfortable. But for the study either of the actions of groups of people or of the inter-relation of groups of people—or even of what I will ultimately say is as purely hypothetical as the unconscious, the individual personality, if you can guess how to study it—it just doesn't do to ignore this fabulous world of verbal statements which seem to do so much and have actually done so much harm to human life and human thinking, although inexplicably mixed in with being the basis of the great evolution which is human civilization and all the sciences and technologies that there are.

There would be none of all this without this particular potenti-ality for making articulate noises and for recognizing phonemal areas in those noises, in other words learning very early in life to discriminate when a certain part of a continuously varying frequency passes from the "ah" to the "à" [*a* as in *a*dd] phoneme so that you catch the word even though some people's frequencies for "à" are within a few cycles per second of other people's frequencies for "ah." These we call phonemal stations in sound, and they characterize each language. There are phonemal stations covering the whole range of audible frequencies, I guess, and each language has only a comparatively small number of them—which is why you have to work so hard to make some of the Chinese noises and even some of the German noises, if you weren't educated to them in childhood. This potentiality for learning these exquisite discriminations of a really very complex field, the field of audible sound, and for reproducing them with dependable accuracy; and the potentiality for learning a vast number of combinations of these things which make up words, and for learning a fairly complicated system of rules for sticking them together so as to give the impression of past, present, future, action or rest, order, and so on—these potentialities and the evolution of language have underlaid a great deal of the exceedingly distinguished part of human performance.

So I want to have a good deal to say in the course of time on words. I want to invite your attention to the common experience that you have all undergone and that you are imposing on your children—and know that everybody else is imposing on his children—and to the efforts which not only parents impose on their children but are very anxious indeed to have certain surrogates, in the shape of school teachers, and so on, impose on their children: the education of the young to competent use of the language so that, as the parent often says, you can say what you mean, more generally so that what you say can be understood by people of comparable education who happen to speak the same tongue. Now this takes the learning of not only those things I have mentioned but also of a very large vocabulary, and quite a precise grasp of the principles of grammar; some at least of the rudiments of rhetoric; and, if you expect to move in polite society, speech etiquette—a thing commonly ignored by scientists. Even on back wards in mental hospitals there is a kind of etiquette: there are people who do not speak to each other but who nonetheless stay silent until the other fellow is through speaking, whereupon they talk to themselves for awhile. Moreover, if you are going to be smart, you must also be able to keep up with speech fashions or even, in the case of some slang, speech fads. Now, this is a big job, as each of you can remember when you think how much of your schooling was devoted to English and its various divisions and what not.

I don't suppose anyone in the audience is a deaf-mute, and so I have to ask you to realize that in talking about speech I am using speech—or at least verbal behavior—a fact which is terribly important not only in its own right, but also because a good grasp on the ideas which I am attempting to express about verbal behavior in its role in the development of personality is applicable to many other aspects of the acculturation, or of the socialization of the young. It is easy to see it in speech. It is easy to talk about it in speech. It is notoriously easy to talk about talk. It is somewhat more difficult to talk about toilet habits, and so on, particularly to mixed audiences.

So I will have to leave to you the throwing of inferential bridges from the general consideration that I give to verbal behavior to all the other things which are necessary in order that you will be respected by the people that you want to respect you. And I will ask you to realize that what I have said about getting the child to talk so that he will be understood is a pressing necessity on all parents, with respect to this whole gamut of socialized performances. Their child must be acceptable to some other children. He must be regarded as a decent person, must grow into a decent person. He must be able to get his just deserts because he knows how to go after them, and so on, and so forth. It is an imperative necessity which parents cannot escape feeling, however wretchedly they and others may discharge the responsibility. It is this urgent pressure to try to get your offspring something like a fair chance in the world as it is realized to be, that makes the acculturation or socialization of the human young—almost from the cradle way into the twentieth year—a more or less continuous task, interrupted only when they are safely tucked in bed, or supposed to be safely tucked in bed. And the amount of things that go on during this period can be explored at your leisure the rest of your life, with illumination on the problem of interpersonal relations every time you see a new aspect of the process of socializing the young.

This is a function of the complexity of the social order in which we live. So far as I know, there is no reason to believe that anywhere at any time thus far has there appeared a system of institutions, emphatically right ways of doing things, traditions, prevailing prejudices, fashions, and so on, which have been, from the standpoint of reason, unitary; that is, explicable as a series of deductions and inferences from a central proposition, or internally consistent and congruent. Always the systems of social organization, civilizations, cultures, whatever you wish to call them, have grown in an erratic fashion, in sporadically emerging directions, and under disparate and often conflicting influences, so that they become a wonderful congeries having anything but a common central principle. And the outcome of that is that even if a child were born with the mature genius of Einstein, or of any of the other great figures of human history, he would still have to learn the culture, because it is not capable of being understood; that is, you cannot develop insight into it, you cannot see how it necessarily hangs together because it doesn't necessarily hang together—it falls apart.

So the child is subjected to a simply tremendous amount of rote learning, and rote learning—which is one of the beloved terms, I believe, of the educator—is another term for *sublimation*, a conception that is beloved at least of a few psychiatrists, and I really want to get it beloved by many more of you before the evening is over because the poor term has fallen into some disrepute. Its origin was peculiar. It, I believe, was borrowed from chemistry in which it referred to how sulphur gets from one place to the other under the influence of heat. You know, it doesn't go through all the performances that water does, but you begin to see it disappearing from one place and crystallizing somewhere else. This is called sublimation. Well, sublimation was gathered from chemistry as so many words are and applied to a somewhat obscure process by which low and unworthy human motives sort of move mysteriously to a higher level. Once one saw that there was something in this queer notion and began to look at it, it wasn't necessary to raid chemistry or even to feel mysterious about it. The thing is essentially quite easy to state, and may I assure you that the definition that I give is subject to operational control: If a person is possessed of a motive which, as the parents feel and therefore presently he himself feels, endangers his acceptance by the society to which he should be welcome; then if in some way or other he can be led to find a partial satisfaction for this motive by some worthy type of activity—play or what-have-you—and if this happens without his noticing it, he has sublimated the unworthy motive. And this works beautifully unless the motive demands something so strongly that so charming a solution won't work. And so this vast rote learning of culture is the general instance of which sublimation as seen in psychiatry is a special instance by which the victim without knowing it finds a socially acceptable, more complicated way of living; and that is how rote memory comes to work. It satisfies, more or less, something given, but it follows socially approved patterns [in doing so].

And so actually, the thing which distinguishes the human being from the human animal is the incorporation in the poor human animal of vast amounts of culture, of socially meaningful, rather than biologically meaningful, entities, which exert very powerful influence on all subsequent performances of the creature. This process begins in practically identical shape with a rather cute sort of solution that some people find for some problems; namely, they just without noticing it find something estimable to do which gives them considerable satisfaction. Now the operational attack on sublimation—this is a digression—is that if you tell people how they can sublimate, they can't sublimate. In other words, the unwitting part of it—the fact that it is not run through consciousness—is what makes it work and gives a very strong hint of what a vast bunch of abilities we have which do not manifest as such if the contents of consciousness are involved; that doesn't prove anything about the unconscious but it does prove something about the capabilities of the human being. Well, I tell you that human beings are human animals that have been filled with culture—socialized, if you like the word—in which process they move from the biological realm into the world of people. Do not permit yourself to think that because they started as animals, clearly members of the biological realm no matter how immature, and although their bodies and their abilities mature at a more or less specified rate, and although there is parallel development through the shape of experience, trial-and-error learning, and this and that—all of which can be seen in a dog, a horse, or various other animals—don't permit yourself to think that the animal can be discovered after it has been modified by the incorporation of culture: it is no longer there. It is not a business of a social personality being pinned on or spread over a human animal. It is an initially animal human developing into what the term human properly applies to—a person.

And this statement implies one thing which I have to state specifically, although the implication is reached by several steps which I have no time to get into: *While the many aspects of the physicochemical world are necessary environment for every animal—oxygen being one—culture, social organization, such things as language, formulated ideas, and so on, are an indispensable and equally absolutely necessary part of the environment of the human being, of the person.* It is for that reason that we can see and can easily document in many cases the deterioration of the outstandingly human, of the more highly socialized aspects of the person, when he is subjected to isolation and does not have in him the capacity to provide a very active cultural interchange because he is dealing with imaginary or ideal persons. Even in the case of the person well equipped with these possibilities for supplying a great deal out of the richness of his past, nonetheless his end-state after a year or so of separation from the channels of mediate communication, the radio, and so on, is by no means as estimable as was his state at the beginning; so the absolutely necessary element of a cultural world with which active interchange is maintained and in which functional activity is carried on is just as necessary to the person as is oxygen, water, foodstuffs. And this business of becoming a human being, which is the great preoccupation of one's parents and teachers and the more or less full-time job of each one of us over a good many years, is an exceedingly important part of each of us, and has an enormous amount to do with civilization and the intricate systems of institutions which are always associated everywhere in history with the appearance of performances of human size, of life size, you might say. Throughout all of this process, a very great part of the refinements of the social order is presented through systems of verbal reference, vocal behavior, graphic behavior, and so on, pertaining to words.

Now, let me run over briefly this particular aspect of the general process of becoming a human being, which is manifested in the early years of life: The transfer from the manifestations of potentialities to learn phonemes and words, and even rough grammatical structures, to the capacity to use language to communicate information and misinformation. All children and for that matter, I believe, all the young of all the species on the face of the earth enjoy, whatever that means, playing with their abilities. As the young mature, these abilities become manifest in play-activities and are obviously pleasant to manifest in that way. And so, before it is possible for a child to articulate syllables, there is a playing with the phonemal stations which the child has finally been able to hit on in the babbling and cooing business. There follows the picking up of some syllables, and sooner or later every child falls upon the syllable "ma." If there is a slight tendency to perseveration so that it becomes "ma-ma," then truly the child discovers that there is something that he had not previously suspected: namely, magic in this noise-making apparatus of his, because very significant people begin to rally around and do things, and they don't hurt—quite the contrary, they are pleasant. I suppose that that little experience is the beginning of what to most people seems to be a lifelong feeling that there is nothing about them that is as powerful as the noises they make with their mouths. But anyway, it will not be very long before this child has a whole flock of articulate noises more or less strung together as words; and those words, which will be the delight of grandma and the satisfaction of mama, and perhaps even a source of mild satisfaction to papa, will have very little to do indeed with those words as they will be in that person ten years later. The words as they originally come along are happy accidents of maturation and combination of hearing and motor impulse—and vast bunches of potentialities that I couldn't name if I had time to. Especially we see in the case of "ma-ma"—where almost anything might have been said but that happened to be and it causes commotion among the great significant environment —that this obviously represents some personal power. This is one of the most remarkable performances thus far observed. And so "ma-ma" is of course not the name of a creature that runs around offering breasts and rattles: "ma-ma" pertains much more to the general feeling of force, magic, and so on. And I suppose it comes to everyone as a little bit of a letdown to discover that "ma-ma" is the thing that this creature [the mother] feels is its proper appellation, and it is only because the creature responds to that name that all this wonderful appearance of magic was called out.

The transfer from the feeling of power in this combination of noise to the realization that it is a pet name for the maternal relative is a transfer from the realm of the autistic or wholly personal, almost animal meaning, to the impersonal, social, conventional, or, as we like to say, *consensually validated* meaning of the word, and to the realm of scientific discourse, and I hope often to the realm of common speech. One's experience in using words has been observed with such care that one has finally learned how to create in the hearer's mind something remotely resembling what one hoped he would think of. Now, that takes a lot of experimenting, a great deal of observation, many corrections, solemn exhortations, rewards and punishments, and, as can be demonstrated in the case of almost everyone, applies only to a large working vocabulary. In addition to that, there is perhaps twice as large a collection of words in an additional vocabulary that isn't used very much, the meanings of which would come as a mild shock to a lexicographer, and a few words in a very personal vocabulary which are definitely retained in an autistic state—they are a secret language which will be expressed only obscurely in a very intimate relationship. Now, so far as there remain autistic words, those words would be fragments of the culture, torn from it, and kept as magic possessions of, let us say, an animal, and that is not what I am dealing with. In so far as a great deal of consensual validation has gone on and one can make noises which are more or less exactly communicative to a hearer who knows the language, the words have been stripped of as much as possible of the accidents of their personal history in you, and it is by that process that they come to be so peculiarly impersonal, just as if, you see, you hadn't learned them with the greatest care, having a wealth of meaning to your original words, and gradually sorting out that which was relevant from that which was irrelevant to the purposes of verbal communication.

A great deal of life runs through this process. It starts out defined by the more or less accidental occurrence of something. One experiences, observes, formulates—after perhaps naming, symbolizing—and subsequently thinks about, that is, analyzes, and perhaps finally gets insight into or thoroughly understands the relationship of various parts of this complex experience, has information about it; but it is more or less a unique performance. And then, because of the way we live, the equipment we have, the tendencies we mature, and so on, and perhaps the necessities to which we are subjected by others, we want to talk about this; and as we first discuss anything new in our experience—as you may be able to observe from day to day, however mature you are—we don't make awfully good sense; and now and then we have the unpleasant experience in the act of telling somebody about it of discovering that we don't know what we are talking about, even though it is our experience.

The point is that the process of consensual validation running here before our eyes calls in an illusion, an illusory person, in the sense of a critic, more or less like what we think the hearer is. We observe what goes on in him when we make this string of words or say this sentence, and it isn't satisfactory; and so, we feel that it is an inadequate statement, and therefore, of course, it doesn't communicate, even to us as hearers, what we are trying to say. So we look again at our experience, and we consider, from the standpoint of illusory critics, and so on: How can the thing be made to communicate? How can I tell somebody about this? And we finally, if we are fairly clever, get the answer. Once we have got that, the unique individuality of the experience begins to shrink, it becomes part of the general structure of life, we forget how strikingly novel the experience was and how peculiarly it had fringes which apply only to us—we lose all that in the process of validation.

You might feel that we were impoverished of much of the original richness of life in the process; maybe we are, but we get great richness from social intercourse, the sharing of experience, the growth of understanding, and the benefits of other people's more or less parallel experience, and so on. In fact, the whole richness of civilization is largely due to this very sort of thing. We can't be alone in things and be very clear on what happened *to* us, and we, as I have said already, can't be alone and be very clear even on what is happening *in* us very long—excepting that it gets simpler and simpler, and more primitive and more primitive, and less and less socially acceptable.

In all this process of being socialized and particularly of developing the ability to communicate by verbal behavior, quite a time after little Willie has gotten to talk about "me wanting" bread and jam, little Willie begins to talk about "I"; and when little Willie gets to talking about "I," just the same as when you hear other people talking about "I," you will notice that something is going on that wasn't there when it was "me" that wanted bread; and it is really much more important than when he finally gets around to saying that he is Willie Brown, or something like that. The coming of "I," as a term, is great stuff.

I have now to refer to a type of experience which may or may not exist—I wouldn't know. I believe it exists, but no one seems to have any time to make many observations; and so since it is more or less important from my way of explaining things and since I know that no one can now controvert the idea, I will present it to you for what it is worth. Some way or other—and the less said about that the better—there is a certain direct contagion of disagreeable experience from significant adults to very young children; in fact this continues in some cases far into life and is part of the paraphernalia that is so puzzling about certain mediumistic and certain hypnotic performances. A simple way of referring to this is *empathy*.* Whether empathy exists or not—as I say, take it or leave it—it is demonstrable that there are feeding difficulties when mother is made apprehensive by a telegram, and that it is not communicated by the tone of her voice; so since it occurs and is often noticed by pediatricians, I guess maybe I am in a moderately defensible position. And, the encouragement of the sublimation by the rote learning of a vast part of the social heritage in the very young is by way of approval and disapproval. Approval, so far as I know, very early in life has almost no effect, but in that case no effect is very welcome. You know that a very young child sleeps as much as possible, and so if there is no disturbance, well, I think it is doing what it wants to do. Disapproval, on the other hand, insofar as there is empathic linkage between the young and significant older people, is unpleasant, lowers the euphoria, the sense of well-being, interferes with the ease of falling asleep, the ease of taking nourishment, and so forth.

[* Since Sullivan's paper was first presented, empathy has become a field for research. See, for instance, Leonard S. Cottrell, Jr. and Rosalind F. Dymond, "The Empathic Responses: A Neglected Field for Research," *Psychiatry* (1949) 12:355–359. The authors note in this article that Mead accepted empathic reactions as given, which was essentially Sullivan's position; neither of course found a way to 'prove' it. H.S.P.]

All this type of interference is originally profoundly unconscious in that it is in no sense a pure content of consciousness
made up of sensations, conceptions, deductions, and inferences;
but it does come ultimately to be clearly connected with
disapproving attitudes on the part of others, with other people
not being pleased with what we are doing, or not being satisfied
with our performances. This early experience is the beginning
of what goes on through life as a uniquely significant emotional
experience, called by the name of a profoundly important concept
in social study and psychiatry—the conception of *anxiety*. Anxiety
begins that way—it is always that way, the product of a great
many people who have disapproved. It comes to be represented
by abstractions—by imaginary people that one carries around
with one, some of them in the shape of ideal statements, some of
them actually as almost phenomenologically evident people who
disapprove. The disapproval and its effect get to be so subtly
effective that a great deal of anxiety which shoos us this way and
that, from this and that feeling, emotion, impulse, comes finally
to be so smooth-running that very few people have the foggiest
notion of what a vast part of their life is influenced by anxiety.

Anxiety is what keeps us from noticing things which would
lead us to correct our faults. Anxiety is the thing that makes us
hesitate before we spoil our standing with the stranger. Anxiety
when it does not work so suavely becomes a psychiatric problem,
because then it hashes our most polite utterances to the prospective
boss, and causes us to tremble at the most inopportune times. So
you see it is only reasonable and very much in keeping with an
enormously capable organization, such as the human being, that
anxiety becomes a problem only when it doesn't work smoothly,
and that the anxiety which has had to be grasped as a fundamental
factor in understanding interpersonal relations is by no means
an anxiety attack, a hollow feeling in the stomach, and so on.
Much, much more frequently it manifests as what I have called
selective inattention, by which I mean you just miss all sorts of
things which would cause you embarrassment, or in many cases,
great profit to notice. It is the means by which you stay as you
are, in spite of the efforts of worthy psychiatrists, clergymen, and
others to help you mend your ways. You don't hear, you don't

see, you don't feel, you don't observe, you don't think, you don't
this, and you don't that, all by the very suave manipulation of the
contents of consciousness by anxiety—or, if you must, . . . by
the threat of anxiety, which still is anxiety. This very great extent
of the effects of disapproval and the disturbance of euphoria by
the significant people in early life—the people who are tremen-
dously interested in getting you socialized—is what makes the
concept of anxiety so crucially important in understanding all sorts
of things.

The part of the personality [1] which is central in the experience
of anxiety we call the "self." It is concerned with avoiding the
supposedly distressing—which is often illuminating—with the exclusion from awareness of certain types of very humiliating
recollections, and correspondingly the failure of the development
of insight from experience. It maintains selective inattention.

Now the "self" is not coterminous with the ego of the old
ego-psychologist, or the ego of Freud, or the superego of Freud,
or anything except what I will say it is—which incidentally I
believe is a very simple statement of practically universal experience: *The self is the content of consciousness at all times when
one is thoroughly comfortable about one's self-respect, the prestige
that one enjoys among one's fellows, and the respect and deference
which they pay one.* Under those estimable circumstances there
is no anxiety; the self is the whole works; everything else in life
runs smoothly without disturbing us the least bit. And it is when
any of these things begin to go a little haywire, when we tend to
remember a humiliating experience which would disturb our
self-esteem, when somebody says something derogatory about
us in our hearing or to our face, when somebody snubs us,
showing the very antithesis of deference, and when somebody
shows up our stupidities, thereby impairing our prestige—it is at

---

[1] When I speak of "parts of personality," it must be understood that
"personality" is a hypothesis, so this is a hypothetical part of a hypothesis.

[The importance of the explicit recognition of the pyramiding of
hypotheses was continually emphasized by Sullivan. In writing about personality, it is particularly easy—and common—to conceal the pyramiding of
hypotheses by the facile use of terms of common speech, the ambiguity or
hypothetical nature of which is not obvious because of their familiarity.
H.S.P.]

those times that anxiety is very apt to manifest itself; but, again, it is apt to be overlooked because it is so generally followed by anger. Anger is much more comfortable to experience than anxiety and, in fact, has much the relation of "I" to "me"; anger is much more powerful and reassuring than anxiety, which is the antithesis of power, which is threat and danger. Anger, however, is supposed to intimidate the other fellow, and at least it obscures the damage to our self-esteem, at least temporarily. And so we say that the self is a system within a personality, built up from innumerable experiences from early life, the central notion of which is that we satisfy the people that matter to us and therefore satisfy ourselves, and are spared the experience of anxiety.

We can say that the operations by which all these things are done—in contradistinction to taking food, getting sexual satisfaction, and sleep, and other delightful things—the operations which maintain our prestige and self-respect, which are dependent upon the respect of others for us and the deference they pay us, are *security operations*. Security operations are things which we might say are herded down a narrow path by selective inattention. In other words, we don't learn them as fast as we might; we never seem to learn how unimportant they are in many circumstances and where they get in our way. They are the things that always have the inside track with denizens of this best of possible variants on the Western culture, the most insecure culture I know—our American people. Well, security operations are the things that don't change much, that have the focus of attention, in and out of season, if there is the least chance of feeling anxious. And the security operations are in many cases assertive, starting out with "I"—and "I" in its most powerful fashion. Sometimes the security operations are more subtle—in fact there are always quite subtle security operations in a person of [at least] ordinary abilities— but they interfere with all sorts of grasps on the universe, grasps which would in essence show that the regard in which a person holds us is defined by the past experience of that person and his actual capacity to know what we were doing, which in some cases is very low. [We often fail to grasp] that the prestige we did or did not get had little bearing on the prestige which we might get for this particular act six weeks later; that all this vast to-do which in early childhood and the juvenile era is practically necessary to survive the distress of the parents is mostly ancient baggage that could very well be replaced with a few streamlined pieces that make a great deal of sense in the interpersonal world in which we have our being.

As I say, the self does not "learn" very readily because anxiety is just so busy and so effective at choking off inquiries where there is any little risk of loss of face with one's self or others. And the operations to maintain this prestige and feeling of security, freedom from anxiety, are of such crucial importance from the cradle on—I mean actually from the very early months of childhood, somewhere around two months onward—that the content of consciousness pertaining to the pursuit of satisfaction and the enjoyment of life is at best marginal. It is one's prestige, one's status, the importance which people feel one is entitled to, the respect that one can expect from people—and even their envy, which becomes precious in that it gives a certain illusion that one has prestige—that dominate awareness. *These things are so focal in interpersonal relations of our day and age that the almost unassailable conviction develops, partly based on the lack of information of our parents and others, that each of us, as defined by the animal organism that we were at birth, are unique, isolated individuals in the human world*, as our bodies are—very figuratively—unique and individual in the biological world.

Now I started out by suggesting that the interrelations, interdependence, interpenetration, and so on, of the biological world are very striking. Yet, no one will quarrel with the separation as an instrument for study, for thought, and so on, of organism and environment. And if you are human biologists, I am perfectly willing for you to talk about individual specimens of man. And in so far as you see material objects, I am perfectly willing to agree that you see people walking around individually, moving from hither to yon in geography, and even persisting from now to then in duration; but that does not explain much of anything about the distinctively human. It doesn't even explain very much about the performance of my thoroughly domesticated cocker spaniels. What the biological organism does is interesting and wonderful. What the personality does, which can be observed and studied only in relations between personalities or among personalities, is truly and terribly marvelous, and is human, and is the function of creatures living in indissoluble contact with the world of culture and of people. In that field it is preposterous to talk about individuals and to go on deceiving oneself with the idea of uniqueness, of single entity, of simple, central being.

So it has come about that there has developed this conception of interpersonal relations as the field of study of those parts of the social sciences concerned with the behavior of people and as the field of study of psychiatry. In so far as difficulties in living are the subject of psychiatry, we must study the processes of living in which the difficulties are manifested, since otherwise we can't really sort out what is "difficulty" and what is perhaps novel genius; we really do have to study interpersonal relations to know what we are talking about when we talk about difficulties in living. As I say, the conceptual system has grown up which finds its subject matter not in the study of personality, which is beyond reach, but in the study of that which can be observed; namely, interpersonal relations. And when that viewpoint is applied, then one of the greatest difficulties encountered in bringing about favorable change is this almost inescapable illusion that there is a perduring, unique, simple existent self, called variously "me" or "I," and in some strange fashion, the patient's, or the subject person's, private property.

Progress begins, life unfolds, and interpersonal relations improve —life can become simple and delightful only at the expense of this deeply ingrained illusion and the parallel conviction that that which has sensations must under all conceivable circumstances be the "same" as that which has tenderness and love—tenderness and love being as obviously communal, involving two personalities, as anything known to man can be.

And so let me say very simply that in so far as you will care to check over these various incomplete sketches that I have made on a vast field and will not dismiss what you heard me say as a misunderstanding, you will find that it makes no sense to think of ourselves as "individual," "separate," capable of anything like definitive description in isolation, that the notion is just beside the point. No great progress in this field of study can be made until it is realized that the field of observation is what people do with each other, what they can communicate to each other about what they do with each other. When that is done, no such thing as the durable, unique, individual personality is ever clearly justified. For all I know every human being has as many personalities as he has interpersonal relations; and as a great many of our interpersonal relations are actual operations with imaginary people—that is, in-no-sense-materially-embodied people—and as they may have the same or greater validity and importance in life as have our operations with many materially-embodied people like the clerks in the corner store, you can see that even though "the illusion of personal individuality" sounds quite lunatic when first heard, there is at least food for thought in it.

Discussion *

(*In answer to a question regarding the concept of the unconscious:*)

I tried to say nothing about the unconscious except to suggest that it was not phenomenologically describable. I don't use the conception particularly, certainly didn't in this paper, never do in work with patients or in teaching because so far as I know it is very useful for theory, but there are some other expressions that are perhaps more communicative to other people. But I might say what I could imagine to be true of that which is perhaps properly called the conceptual unconscious, because it fills the discontinuities present in conscious life: I would say that it includes much that has been conscious but is pre-verbal, sub-verbal, if you please; a great deal that has never been attended to and therefore may have been or may not have been on the margins of awareness; and certainly some experience of the person which has not received any representation within what we call his consciousness or his awareness, including a great development of process which has simply been sidetracked in the process of socialization but which manifests, in various ways, as remnants of previous endowment, previous experience, and previous behavior.

[* In the recordings from which this lecture was taken, there are gaps in which questions from the audience can be faintly heard. I have tried to indicate the nature of these questions. H.S.P.]

In dealing with patients and in attempting to follow the course of psychotherapeutic endeavor by others, the big problem seems to be to elude the interventions of what I have called the self-system—which is not coterminous with awareness but which is certainly the most emphatic and conspicuous and troublesome influence *on* awareness. You might contrast the self-system with the rest of the personality system, always realizing that I am talking about a hypothesis to explain what happens. I don't know that I have any use for anything except what can be observed. But what can be observed by an acute observer in his relations with another person is something quite different from what that other person, at least initially, can observe; and much of it can be accounted for by reference to processes which are not ordinarily noted, some of them so glaringly obvious that one literally is justified in positing a process like *selective inattention* by which I mean that we always overlook certain obvious things which would be awkward if we noticed them.

(In answer to a question asking, in effect, Can we not say that there is a justifiably characterizable self in each person we deal with, which might be called the "real" self?)

It is, I believe, a statistically demonstrable fact that the interpersonal relations of any person, even though he feels very full of the conviction of his individuality, are under ordinary circumstances rather strikingly restricted in variety, freedom you might say. Such a person is very much more apt to do the same sort of thing with a number of people than to do very different things with each one of that number. Furthermore, even more striking are the observable performances in which he will persistently misfunction with certain people in characterizable ways, despite the most incongruous objective data—of which, of course, *he* is unaware. It is a notorious fact about personality problems that people act *as if* someone else were present when he is not—as the result of interpersonal configurations which are irrelevant to the other person's concern—and do this in a recurrent fashion without any great difference in pattern. These various factors are so striking, in interpersonal relations, that it is perfectly easy and for many purposes very practical to speak of the structure of the character of the person.

All these are, I believe, correct statements of observable data. But when it comes to attempting to form a general theory on which to approach explanations of everything that happens to one in one's intercourse with others, and all the variety of things that occur in particularly-purposed interpersonal relations such as the psychotherapeutic situation, then it is just as easy to notice that the person maintains quite as many of what you ordinarily call imaginary relationships as he does of those that have the peculiar virtue of objective reference. A person, for example, may be said, with considerable justification, to act towards his wife as he did towards his mother. Now it is true that there are many differences in detail, but the general patterns of emotional relationship of conscious versus unnoticed motivation, of intended versus experienced acts, are very much those that the person first developed in manifest behavior with his mother; and it is quite useful to think of his experience of that mother as interpenetrating the experience of the wife and, in fact, frequently completely suppressing any individualization of or any attention to the characterization of the wife. That is the more difficult part of this conception, but it is quite useful in the sense that it can be made to make sense in many of the maneuvers of interpersonal relations that have effect; whereas operations on any other set of assumptions that explains the same phenomena raise very considerable theoretical difficulties. In other words, it is a matter of what is most generally useful as a theoretical point of departure.

And now to come to the more specific question: Are we not entirely justified—however much we have respect for the fictions which masquerade as human individuals—in realizing that there is a justifiably characterizable self in each person that we deal with?

I, myself, have come gradually to find that unnecessary, whether that be some serious misunderstanding of mine or an insight remains, of course, for others to determine. You know that is true of the evolution of most hypotheses.

One listens, for example, in psychotherapy to a great number of revealing communications, hoping and generally finding finally that the thing has been reviewed very simply in a very small context; and then you run up the flag of hope, and so on, and go hammer and tongs to seeing what can be made of this very simple series of statements which the other fellow won't forget while you are trying to make your point clear. Now, it is decidedly easier to explain this great difficulty on the, you might say, individual-less type of hypothesis than on any other that I have yet dealt with.

(*In answer to a question regarding the lability of behavior in the human being and in animals, posing whether humanness—a quality produced by the effect of the cultural, interpersonal environment upon the lability of the human animal—can exist outside of a culture and therefore whether a sense of self within the person is possible apart from the culture:*)

You raise a wonderful field of comparative study. Contrary to what would be nice and simple to say at this point, we have pretty convincing evidence of the lability of patterns of behavior in characterizable environments, down as low as certain of the rats; for example, it is known that one of the Florida species of rats can be moved from the state of full-fledged wildness to complete domestication in five generations. This is a very interesting observation of a quite remarkably primitive mammal taking on adjustive habits to utterly novel sets of necessity.

But man is the only animal, if you will understand the locution, that ceases to be an animal in the most significant respect when he becomes a person, and to be a person it is necessary that one live in the world of persons and personal entities, and personal organization, and so on, which we ordinarily call the social order or the world of culture. And insofar as a person is separated from the world of culture, he begins to deteriorate in his attributes as a person. His interpersonal relations, after a period of isolation, are distinctly degenerated from the development of refinement and elaboration which they showed at the start, and while it doesn't work quite as rapidly as separation from the physicochemical universe and oxygen, still it is a move in the same direction, explicable on the same basis. Human potentialities are suited to the building up of the person; and when the person is built, he is something else than was implied or given in the human animal at birth. How would you describe that in terms of the Florida rat? You might say that the potentialities of man—in contrast to those of the rat—are almost infinitely labile, even though there is a very rigid, or a pretty rigid, system of maturation. Even that system of maturation gets less and less rigid the further one goes from birth; thus puberty, the appearance of lust in the human, the furthest very dramatic maturation from birth, is much more susceptible of disturbance in its timing than other maturation of things that come earlier. Even internists recognize the condition of delayed puberty; it happens to coincide statistically very closely with what I as a psychiatrist describe as a schizoid type of interpersonal relations. Both the latter and the former, I believe, are explicable as the result of what are ordinarily called strongly repressive influences applied much earlier in life to operations and thought pertaining to the genital regions and genital acts. So here what would certainly be described as purely interpersonal influences, interpersonal manifestations of cultural views, and so on, have a marked effect on the maturation rate of what is much more inherently of the animal than of the person.

(*In answer to a question regarding the permissibility of thinking in terms of the individual:*)

We have, thus far, I believe, thought in terms of the individual, which is certainly a demonstration of the possibility. The point, rather, I think, is on the utility. I have been at some pains not to deny you the privilege of going on in your convictions, but to suggest to you that there is another view that may—well, if nothing else—permit considerable technological advance, or technical advance as we call it in psychiatry, and may even be useful as a new orientation for certain types of social investigation. I also tried to say at the beginning that for certain purposes it is certainly very useful to separate organism and environment, particularly for example if one is talking about colonies of paramecia, but I think that perhaps there are biologists who think of the paramecium as a particular part of the world showing certain remarkable features of organization in functional activity, but ceasing very suddenly to manifest those if separated from certain parts of the universe which do not manifest those peculiarities of organization in functional activity. It is all perfectly well, if you wish, to limit your personality to the skin over your bones and adnexa, but my notion is not what can be done or what should be done; it is rather a suggestion of a system of reference which seems to eliminate a great many terms, conceptions, perplexities, and to provide some fairly simple operations that seem to bear up pretty well—and which also is extraordinarily unwelcome from the standpoint of our educational training.

My son has to be to many a mother or father something thoroughly unique, almost pricelessly different from anyone else; and with that background it is not difficult to realize that when everything else fails one, membership in that family, which makes one unique and distinguishes one on the basis of the very early valuation, would be a treasured possession. I am talking not so much as to what we are to deny our fellowmen or our colleagues, but only in favor of a conceptual system which I believe is defensible and useful.

14

Commentary

THE NEXT PAPER, "The Meaning of Anxiety in Psychiatry and in Life," represents Sullivan's attempt at a matured restatement of his thinking in the last article (see Commentary 13). Essentially, he is addressing the same audience here as the one he addressed four years before in "The Illusion of Personal Individuality." Since there were many psychiatrists present, the paper is couched in clinical terms. But the theory—particularly as illustrated in the diagrams—was designed for a wider audience in the social sciences generally. Sullivan considered this one of his most important papers, although he was dissatisfied with the diagrams; he had planned, particularly, to revise these diagrams, but his death intervened.

Here again, as in the last article, Sullivan is dealing with "the illusion of personal individuality," although now he is using a device for indicating operationism rather than any exhortation. Anxiety is now the explanatory concept, for it is anxiety that is the great disjunctive force "in psychiatry and in life." And it is this disjunction—particularly as it manifests itself in Western society—that results in "the illusion of personal individuality" (although this phrase per se does not appear in this second paper).

The diagrams in the paper picture a relationship between Johnnie Jones and Richard Roe. Jones is obviously a less developed person than Roe. In the beginning encounter between the two, conjunctive forces, tending to improve the relationship, are depicted. This is, in part, made possible by the fact that Roe is relatively less anxiety-ridden than Jones. In a series of mishaps, the conjunctive forces disappear almost completely, and Jones is left further crippled by the encounter with Roe.

When this paper was first published, many readers were intimidated by the diagrams. Yet they are clarifying for Sullivan's theory, once the reader has gotten past their apparent complexity. I have inserted a Key that I hope will be of some help. Also, I have identified certain parts of the diagrams for ease in reading the text. And finally, I have made some corrections in Fig. 5.[1]

It is useful to remember in reading this paper that Sullivan is "inventing" a device to describe interpersonal relations as he understands them. Such devices have, of course, certain implicit dangers; they are oversimplifications and, at best, only temporary measures to 'explain' phenomena as they are currently understood. Yet mathematics is also such an expedient; and it, too, changes its devices or models from time to time. As Bridgman notes, "The concepts of mathematics are inventions made by us in an attempt to describe nature."[2]

In this paper, Sullivan is using Whitehead's concept of time; the shaded area above the lower drawing in Fig. 1, for instance, is very close to Whitehead's concept of prehension. In both Whitehead's and Sullivan's theories, the so-called present is interpenetrated with both the past and the prehended future by a series of interpersonal processes.[3]

A student of Whitehead's at Harvard, the Negro philosopher Albert Millard Dunham, Jr., is responsible for Sullivan's concept of tension as it is used in this paper; in other writings, Sullivan explicitly credits as his main source Dunham's paper, "The Concept of Tension in Philosophy."[4] Dunham, too, belonged to the network of influence coming out of the Chicago tradition, as reported in the Introduction to this book, for he had done his undergraduate work at the University of Chicago while George Herbert Mead was still an important influence there.

[1] Since I helped in the preparation of the original Figures, I was aware that some error had crept in in the process of transposing the designated shading devices from slides to the printed page.

[2] Bridgman, *The Logic of Modern Physics*, see p. 62.

[3] See, for instance, Alfred North Whitehead, *Adventures of Ideas*; New York: Macmillan, 1933; particularly the index entry for Prehension.

[4] *Psychiatry* (1938) 1:79–120.

The Meaning of Anxiety
in Psychiatry and in Life †

TWENTY-FIVE YEARS AGO, when I was working on my first venture
into theoretical psychiatry, I had opportunity to study a patient
who seemed to be having a rather good time in the Sheppard and
Enoch Pratt Hospital except for an occasional abrupt attack of
severe anxiety. We knew that he was married to a most remarkably domineering woman; there did not seem to have been anything else obviously troublesome in his life situation for a long
time before the onset of the attacks, and he was as certain as could
be that there had been nothing about his domestic life which
bothered him in any way. All data on recent or remote events
which could be thought to have direct bearing on his symptoms
were inaccessible. He made a few starts at significant communication in the interviews held soon after an attack, but these rapidly
came to nothing.

The attacks themselves were of remarkable severity, approaching in 'content' a terror of immediate death, with arrest of all
gross motor activity including speech, and striking superficial re-

† Reprinted from *Psychiatry* (1948) 11:1–13. Presented to the joint meeting of the Society on the Theory of Personality and the William Alanson
White Institute of Psychiatry of New York City, on the occasion of the
presentation of the first William Alanson White Memorial Award, for
distinguished contribution to psychiatry, by the Institute, at the Academy
of Medicine, New York City, February 2, 1948. [The first award was made
to Sullivan, and this was his acceptance address. H.S.P.]

semblance to the appearance of a person in incipient schizophrenic panic. I believe that he simply stated the facts when he said that he could not recall anything that had been going on 'in his mind' just before the intense emotion appeared. I failed to uncover a clue to anything by most detailed inquiry into the social context surrounding the one episode which occurred in my, I believe, unnoticed presence one evening while the patient was playing cards and conversing with others.

It was all too convenient to see in this patient an instance of a quasi-physiological "actual neurosis," in contrast with the dynamically explicable psychoneuroses; but, as the equally convenient idea of *narcissistic neurosis* in schizophrenic states was becoming more than suspect to me, I had to consider him simply a person whose trouble I did not understand at all.

By this time, I had noticed that circumstances surrounding the first instance of a to-be-recurring pattern of difficulty are often much more suggestive of its dynamics than are those which are to be observed on later occasions. This patient's account of his first attack was so vague that it helped nowise.

My next clinical encounter in this field of the so-called "anxiety neurosis" was a young man who had recently suffered the first of several attacks of "paroxysmal tachycardia [sudden, painful heart attack]." Only the first of these attacks had ended in syncope [swooning]; he did not lose consciousness in the others. He had a wealth of information about the days and the hours preceding the attack; knew all about his activity right up to the minute when his heart suddenly accelerated. I found no clue to the event, nor could I connect it with anything in his developmental history with any impressive probability.

There came presently other patients who suffered relatively pure attacks of anxiety, as the jargon has it—one of them a mysteriously timed episodic sweating "with no emotion." Some of these patients could supply many details about the circumstances of the first attack. Some of them revealed gross, perhaps "secondary," usefulness of their trouble for dealing with a life situation. None of the latter would entertain the idea that their attacks served any interpersonal end, even if accidentally. None of them undertook intensive psychotherapy with me.

If I had had to rely on this particular category of patients, I would have learned nothing, except that I consistently failed of useful contact with them. It was reasonably certain that "the anxiety neurosis" was something for the adequate exploration of which I had either very little facility or great handicap.

This was in distressing contrast to having participated—as, fortunately, did my successor—in the restoration of a very high percentage of young males with acute schizophrenic disturbances, through the instrumentality of an organized interpersonal set-up.* I need scarcely add that a considerable proportion of these young people had arrived in, or subsequently underwent, approaches to *panic*, as psychiatrically defined; that they were often beyond perchance anxious; and that our psychotherapeutic efforts were not by any miracle divorced from dealing with, and sometimes acutely aggravating, the patients' anxiety.

Let me make three marginal comments at this point. Thus far in my remarks, any psychiatrist's unsophisticated idea of anxiety is what I mean. I hope to sharpen the meaning of the term, presently. Second, once my formulation of anxiety had been established, I was able to escape some of the handicap in being useful to "anxiety neurotics," at least by proxy. Third, and this is a real digression, some recent work—particularly the investigation of a patient by Dr. Mabel G. Wilkin, now of Houston, Texas **— has suggested an unsuspected relationship between the inaccessibility of the "anxiety neurotic" and the *uncanny emotion* which I shall presently discuss as peculiarly related to the schizophrenic way of living.

To resume the historic account, work with schizophrenic states had presently made me realize that obsessional ways of life would have to be investigated before more headway could be made. The first research had presented three genera of questions. In what way

[* Sullivan is referring here, of course, to his work with schizophrenic patients at Sheppard-Pratt; his successor at Sheppard was William V. Silverberg, M.D. See *Schizophrenia as a Human Process* (Norton, 1962). H.S.P.]

[** Shortly before this paper was presented, Dr. Wilkin was living and practicing in Washington, D.C., and she consulted with Sullivan there on several patients who fell into the same general pattern of illness; she is not certain as to which patient he had in mind. None of her work with patients has been reported in the literature. (Personal communication.) H.S.P.]

is the schizophrenic sort of interpersonal relations significantly different from any other way of living? Second, what developmental eventualities are found invariably associated in the prepsychotic life-course? And, third, what sort of events bring about further change so that a schizophrenic way of living may pass over into more adequate and appropriate interpersonal relations?

I wish now to talk about the second of these questions.

There were a number of instances in which a definitely obsessional overcomplication of living had antedated the schizophrenic episode; showed itself in the more accessible intervals of the disorder; and remained after psychotic 'content' had disappeared. There were instances in which severe "obsessive-compulsive" disorder of long duration had passed rather rapidly into schizophrenic disorder which progressed unfavorably.

On the to me safe assumption that the schizophrenic and the obsessive-compulsive complications of life now under discussion are primarily an outcome of developmental eventualities, these observations show that the two can have significant elements of personal history in common. The question of whether there are also significant differences, such that only *some* of the people who are prevailingly obsessional are at all apt to pass on to schizophrenic disorders, is in no sense answered. Every psychiatrist knows that such a sequence is relatively infrequent; most of the strikingly obsessional people remain that way, perhaps with some amelioration in later life, and, may I add, all too frequently tend to remain that way in seeming despite of prolonged psychoanalytic or other treatment.

To make a long story unreasonably short, the obsessional-schizophrenic instances and a few instances of unquestionable alternation in these disorders threw doubt on all provisional answers to the first and the third of our generic questions; and I had to conclude that nothing of high probability could be asserted in the way of a definition of the schizophrenic way of life, or about the essential pattern of therapeutic events, until I knew more from participant observation in the obsessional-compulsive disorders. Another seven and one-half years went into this; * and I bring you

[* Sullivan is referring here to his private practice in New York City (see Introduction to this book). H.S.P.]

tonight some of the results from prolonged collaborative working over of the data of the two inquiries.

A theory of personality which would organize the data of the two studies did not seem to be available, although there were many distinguished approaches, mostly in the psychoanalytic formulations of Sigmund Freud. His 1923 revision of the theory of anxiety* had been a great improvement on the earlier quasi-physiological statement, but it too left much of the data of observation unexplained or too variously explicable. My first fairly clear formulation of psychiatry as the study of interpersonal relations[1] left a great deal unclear about difficulties in dealing with strikingly obsessional people. Some of this inadequacy had been remedied by the time of the first White Memorial Lectures,[2] in the last year of the inquiry into obsessive-compulsive states. The problem of anxiety still continued to be in an unsatisfactory condition, *although what was presently to be found to be an adequate statement* had long since been reached.[3]

Only by dint of intensive collaboration with numerous colleagues in exploring practical problems of therapy and training in the light of the interpersonal theory, with increasing conviction that the theory actually accounted for all the data, was I relieved of anxiety lest fatal errors had vitiated the work of some seventeen years, and enabled to "see" some logically inevitable implications which had previously eluded me. Do not, I beg you, assume

[* See Freud's *The Problem of Anxiety* (Henry Alden Bunker, tr.); New York: The Psychoanalytic Quarterly Press & W. W. Norton & Co., Inc., 1936. The German edition was published in 1926, and this is obviously what Sullivan is referring to here. H.S.P.]

[1] Foreshadowed in the 1930 report to the American Psychiatric Association [see "Socio-Psychiatric Research," in *Schizophrenia as a Human Process*, pp. 256–270]; stated positively at the Toronto meeting of the American Psychoanalytic Association the next year [see "The Modified Psychoanalytic Treatment of Schizophrenia," in *Schizophrenia as a Human Process*, pp. 272–294]; and the extended development of which [the unpublished book *Personal Psychopathology*] was used as one of the texts in the Yale Seminar on the Impact of Culture on Personality, 1932.

[2] *Conceptions of Modern Psychiatry* [see Norton edition, 1953].

[3] This in itself constitutes one of my choicest instances of the role of anxiety in the life of a psychiatrist, a psychiatrist not too erroneously considered by his training psychoanalyst to be an outstanding example of the relatively "anxiety-proof personality." [Sullivan's training analyst, Clara Thompson, M.D., acted as chairman for this particular meeting. H.S.P.]

from this statement that you are about to hear "the last word," the solution of everything. I am bringing you nothing but a theory; a theory which, like every other theory, will doubtless undergo marked improvements as the years pass.

In extreme abstract, the theory holds that we come into being as persons as a consequence of unnumbered interpersonal fields of force, and that we manifest intelligible human processes only in such interpersonal fields. Like any mammalian creature, man is endowed with the potentialities for undergoing *fear*, but in almost complete contradistinction to infrahuman creatures, man in the process of becoming a person always develops a great variety of processes directly related to the undergoing of *anxiety*.

As felt experience, marked fear and uncomplicated anxiety are identical; that is, there is nothing in one's awareness of the discomfort which distinguishes the one from the other. Fear, as a significant factor in any situation, is often unequivocal. Anxiety, on the other hand, in anything like the accustomed circumstances of one's life, is seldom clearly represented as such in awareness. Instances of fear in the course of accustomed peacetime living are not numerous, while instances of—generally unrecognized—anxiety are very frequent in the waking life of a great many people.

The significant pattern of situations characterized by the tension of fear is not recondite and is roughly the same for all people, excepting for the effects of habituation. The significant pattern of situations which arouse anxiety is generally obscure; can be almost infinitely varied among people; and shows much less, and very much less obvious, effects of habituation.

Habituation is a function of observation and analysis, of information and understanding, of recall and foresight. While fear may impede these processes, anxiety invariably interferes with their effective application to the current situation. The felt component of any 'emotion,' if sufficiently intense, will interfere with the application of these abilities to the immediate situation, and action in discharge of the tension will become correspondingly undifferentiated and imprecise. Up to the point at which this interference appears, the tension is attended by increasing alertness to factors in the situation which are immediately relevant to the relief of the tension, however great the inattention to other factors may become. In the case of anxiety, the diametrically opposite is the case. Anxiety from its mildest to its most extreme manifestation interferes with effective alertness to the factors in the current situation that are immediately relevant to its occurrence, and thus with the refinement and precision of action related to its relief or reduction.

In the case of every other tension the relief of which is sought by overt and covert activity, excepting only the tension of anxiety and its complex derivatives, energy is transformed in ways that can be said to achieve, approach, compromise, or suppress action towards the objective. Thus the tension of fear is commonly manifested in activity which removes (destroys) the provocative situational factors, escapes them, neutralizes their importance, or defers being afraid to the near future. The tension of anxiety and its congeries, on the other hand, does not ensue in energy transformations directed to its relief by the removal of the situational factors obviously concerned in its provocation. Actions towards avoiding or minimizing anxiety certainly occur, but anxiety combines with other tensions only in opposition. In vector terms the tension of anxiety is always at 180° to any other tension with which it coincides. Moreover, other tensions cannot suppress or defer activity resulting from anxiety.

This series of contrasts should suffice to indicate that anxiety cannot be conceptualized in the terms which cover many other 'gross human motivations.' Let me now show in summary form [see Table I on the next page] some of the conceptual structure which has been constructed to account for anxiety and its many obscure manifestations.

Table II carries us somewhat further [than Table I]. The term, *euphoria*, refers to a polar construct, an abstract ideal, in which there is *no* tension, therefore no action—tantamount in fact perhaps to something like an empty state of bliss. The level of euphoria and the level of tension are inversely related. There is no zero or utter degree of either. Terror is perhaps the most extreme degree of tension ordinarily observable; the deepest levels of sleep, perhaps the nearest approach to euphoria.

TABLE I

Experience is of $\begin{cases} \text{tensions} \\ \text{energy transformations} \end{cases}$

occurs in 3 modes $\begin{cases} \text{prototaxic} \\ \text{parataxic} \\ \text{syntaxic} \end{cases}$

Tensions are those of $\begin{cases} \text{needs} \\ \text{anxiety} \end{cases} \begin{cases} \text{general} \\ \text{zonal} \end{cases}$

Energy transformations are $\begin{cases} \text{overt} \\ \text{covert} \end{cases}$

TABLE II

EXPERIENCE

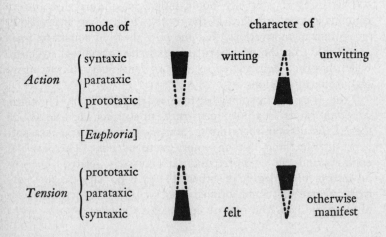

mode of   character of

Action $\begin{cases} \text{syntaxic} \\ \text{parataxic} \\ \text{prototaxic} \end{cases}$ witting   unwitting

[*Euphoria*]

Tension $\begin{cases} \text{prototaxic} \\ \text{parataxic} \\ \text{syntaxic} \end{cases}$ felt   otherwise manifest

TABLE III

Personality: the relatively enduring pattern of recurring interpersonal situations which characterize a human life.

Pattern: the envelope of all insignificant differences.

TABLE IV

Stages in the development of potentialities which may be manifested in interpersonal fields (from mostly West European data):

1. *Infancy* to the maturation of the capacity for language behavior.

2. *Childhood* to the maturation of the capacity for living with compeers.

3. *Juvenile Era* to the maturation of the capacity for isophilic intimacy.

4. *Preadolescence* to the maturation of the genital lust dynamism.

5. *Early Adolescence* to the patterning of lustful behavior.

6. *Late Adolescence* to maturity.

Table III shows the basic formulation of personality to which this particular theory has come. And Table IV reflects the developmental framework on which our further consideration of anxiety will be spread.

Anxiety as a factor in behavior is first manifested early in infancy. Let us pause to consider what a positive statement of this kind can mean. It cannot be based on anyone's alleged recall of having been 'anxious' at age four months. It cannot be based on observations of infants' play of facial expression—for even adults' facial expression of anxiety is unreliable and at best undistinguishable from the appearance of fear. It cannot be based on detecting physiological changes in the infant, for measurable physiological changes, too, are not that specific. The statement is in fact an inference derived from the observation of *something* which occurs in infants—which something is in one-to-one correspondence with phenomena observed in later life when anxiety is certainly present, and something which is seen to develop into these presently to be observed phenomena without any break in the series.

Perhaps you may wonder if there is any sufficient justification for pushing inference about "mental states" as far back as the early months of postnatal life. No one would question the influence of *some* past experience in shaping present performances. Moreover, no one who has had much experience in studying personality would question the *occasional* recall and approximate reproduction of "mental states" from the relatively distant past. A psychiatrist who seeks to exhaust simpler hypotheses before he turns to more complicated ideas about myths, dreams, and schizophrenic phenomena is bound to explore the inferentially probable about very early stages of personality development; and it is in this area that he finds a great deal of confirmatory data for the particular pattern of inference about anxiety which sets its beginning so early.

Very young infants show grossly identical patterns of behavior when they are subjected to 'frightening' situations and when they are in contact with the person who mothers them *and that person is anxious, angry, or otherwise disquieted*. Something which develops without a break into the tension state which we have discriminated on the basis of its specific differences from fear can be *induced* in the infant by *interpersonal influence*, in contrast to the evocation of primitive fear by sundry violent influences from 'outside' or 'inside' the infant's body.

This *interpersonal induction* of anxiety, and the exclusively interpersonal origin of every instance of its manifestations, is the unique characteristic of anxiety and of the congeries of more complex tensions in later life to which it contributes. I would have to present a good deal of evidence before I convinced some of you that this statement, so glaringly in superficial variance with a large body of data, is the simplest hypothesis that will cover the facts. If I succeeded, I should have shown you the probable explanation for such incidents as the "anxiety attacks" undergone by my first-mentioned patient, as well as for a great many instances of inappropriate and inadequate performances of one person with another to be seen around us in patients, in friends, and "in ourselves."

The circumstances of this single lecture are scarcely suited to the adumbration of such proof. I must content myself with a few hints to the more open-minded. Let me now take the risk of

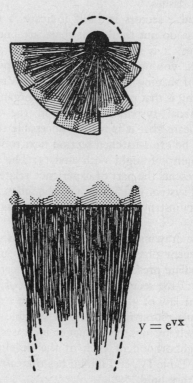

$$y = e^{vx}$$

Fig. 1—Schematic of 'Personality'

hopelessly misleading many of you by using a perhaps ill-conceived visual aid to indicate how the "purely personal" can actually be very really the interpersonal. In Fig. 1, I show a way of depicting "a personality," the hypothetical entity which we posit to account for interpersonal fields.

Looking first at the upper figure, note that there is a complete central disc—representing the serially matured inborn capabilities, half of which have been developed by experience as shown in the sectors, and half of which, in this instance, have not been realized because no related experience has occurred, as indicated by the semicircle of dashes.

Each of these sectors in itself indicates a major motivational system. Please do not think that there are but six major motivational systems; it is convenient to draw six sectors. In each of these sectors, you will note that in their periphery, there are three types of shading [see also Key to the Visual Analogy]. The dotted shading is that part of experience organized in the particular motivational system which is in the *self-system*—which ordinarily means that it is readily accessible to awareness, recall, and so on. The cross-hatched section next to it represents the experience which is fraught with anxiety. The single-hatched area beyond represents the part of experience related to that particular motivational system which is not in the self-system and, under all ordinary circumstances, is quite difficult or impossible of access to awareness.

The lower drawing in Fig. 1 represents an extension in time of the more recent phases of the personality under discussion up to the immediate present. The formula indicates that the boundaries of each of the sectors will be instances of the so-called snowball law,* the law of growth—$y = e^x$; the v [inserted in Fig. 1] in the formula represents a complex variable about which I will content myself by observing that it increases rapidly in the immediate neighborhood of each of the developmental thresholds indicated in Table IV, and diminishes thereafter to the proximity of the next threshold.**

Now, the other thing about this lower figure to which I invite attention is the projection of the shading above the surface of the immediate present, by which I wish to communicate an idea never

[* By "snowball law," Sullivan is referring to the law of geometric progression (see Oxford English Dictionary). H.S.P.]

[** Sullivan emphasized in his theory that one has a special capacity for change near the thresholds of each of the developmental stages. See *The Interpersonal Theory of Psychiatry*, particularly pp. 227–228. H.S.P.]

KEY TO THE VISUAL ANALOGY †

SHADING DEVICE	USED FOR:	
	A. *Sectors of Personality* (Durable Personality Organizations; i.e., major motivational systems, such as fear or heterosexual interest)	B. *Shifting Field Forces in a Relationship*
	Experience fraught with anxiety.	Disjunctive force—anxiety, for example.
	Experience not incorporated in the self-system—quite difficult or impossible of access to awareness.	Sudden severe anxiety—uncanny emotion—a disjunctive force associated with outcropping of schizophrenic processes.
	Experience within the self-system—accessible to awareness or recall.	Conjunctive force—tending to improve the relationship.

[† This key has been prepared by me, but the words have all emerged from Sullivan's two papers—this one and the 1947 lectures, entitled "The Study of Psychiatry." H.S.P.]

to be overlooked in considering human life; namely, that time as the present never exists merely in the clock sense but always with an element of the near or neighboring future. This [projection of the shading], you might say, represents expectation and foresight in connection with the active components of any motivational system.

I shall next run through Figs. 2 to 5 from the discussion of 'a schizophrenic episode' which appears in "The Study of Psychiatry," [4] which may well be read as a supplement to this lecture. Be warned that the same devices of shading are used in depicting durable personality organizations and in indicating shifting field forces.

[In the most relevant part of "The Study of Psychiatry" (1947), Sullivan elaborates on the background of a particular patient's illness:]

Let us take, first, the concept of the patient, say Johnnie Jones, who comes to you [the psychiatrist] "because," he says, "someone is trying to poison me" . . . You say "So! what makes you think so?" The ejaculation, "So," we shall assume conveys to him a hint of astonishment and chagrin. Mr. Jones then pours out to you a rambling account somewhat as follows: He had noticed that he was having headaches and a feeling of profound weariness every day that he went to work. He finally noticed that this happened to him at a certain time of the day; and at last saw that this was shortly after he had eaten his lunch, which was prepared for him by his landlady. The lunch always included coffee, and he began to suspect the coffee and investigated. He found that she, the landlady, often left the thermos bottle on the kitchen sink, after filling it after breakfast, until she had time to put the rest of the lunch together.

Now, there was another man living at the boarding house who had treated Mr. Jones very peculiarly, who had a chance to get at this thermos bottle, while the landlady was busy with other things. So on and so forth.

You remark "Who is this other man? Tell me a little about him." You learn that he is a Richard Roe who is something of a figure of mystery, even though supplementary inquiry leaves you in the dark about just what is mysterious about him. About all that you can confirm is that Mr. Roe seems to have been moved to be friendly with your patient and that it miscarried.

You then ask, somewhat abruptly, "Tell me; when did you begin to suspect the coffee?" You learn that it was the afternoon after your patient saw Mr. Roe go into the kitchen after breakfast, at a time the landlady was upstairs. You ask if he often did this and learn that it is the only time that the patient can remember having *known* that it happened. You add "But you *assume* that he did it secretly on many occasions?" The patient looks puzzled, and before he can get in an unhappy 'yes,' you continue "I wonder if there is not some other explanation of your symptoms." The patient seems

[4] *Psychiatry* (1947) 10:355–371. [On p. 365 of this article, the fifth line of the second column should read Fig. 3 (instead of Fig. 2). On the same page, the diagram, Fig. 5, contains errors that have been corrected in Fig. 5 as it appears in this book. H.S.P.]

relieved and pleased in a mild way, but also still somewhat anxious.

You then proceed with an outline inquiry to discover how he has come to be the person that he seems to be; why the Richard Roe's of the world seem to have significance to him; and why he cannot deal with this significance in a straightforward, factual, fashion. The time comes when he says "Do you think that that is why I had those funny ideas about Richard Roe?" and you perhaps say "Looks so, doesn't it; but let's see what comes to the mind." And so forth.*

In Fig. 2 we are no longer concerned with the representation of a hypothetical personality but with depicting an instance of an

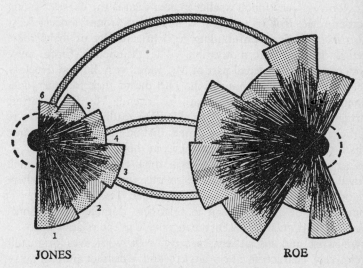

JONES   ROE

Fig. 2—Early in Relationship

interpersonal situation, the sort of thing that can be studied by a psychiatrist. I attempt to show a simplification of the early stage in a relatively durable relationship of two people, one of whom

[* Excerpted from "The Study of Psychiatry" (1947) *ibid.*, pp. 359–360. H.S.P.]

you will observe is more nearly a 'well-rounded' or more developed personality than the other. Let me for brevity call the six-sectored representation, Johnnie Jones, and the other, Richard Roe.

You will note that the uppermost line representing a field force is cross-hatched. This is intended to represent force which tends to keep these two people from growing more intimate, what may be called disjunctive force, and *the* great disjunctive force in interpersonal relations is anxiety. Below that there are shown two dotted lines of force which represent conjunctive forces, forces tending to improve the relationship or, in ordinary discourse, to draw the two people closer together.

Let us notice that the uppermost sector of the left-hand figure, Mr. Jones, is very much smaller in area than is the corresponding sector in Mr. Roe to which it is linked by "Jones' anxiety." At the risk of adding confounding to confusion, let us make these sectors 'heterosexual motivation.' The disjunctive force arises from the anxiety-ladened part of Mr. Jones' very limited development of heterosexual motivation. This means that Johnnie Jones cannot discuss comfortably with his friend, Mr. Roe, matters pertaining to this phase of living. Mr. Roe readily becomes aware of the embarrassment and avoidances that ensue after any remarks which touch upon Jones' deficiencies in this area.

Fig. 3 represents a later stage in their relationship in which notice, with particular reference to this same sector, that there are both disjunctive and conjunctive forces. This reflects a development not at all infrequent in relatively durable interpersonal relations, particularly in a fortunate course in the relationship of a psychiatrist and his patient; namely, that what was originally exclusively characterized by anxiety and a distinct pulling away from any contact comes gradually to be susceptible to a certain amount of somewhat 'risky' discussion.

Observe that another conjunctive force has appeared, reflected in the dotted line immediately below the double one, which force is shown as arising exclusively from the extra-self areas in the sectors concerned. This also reflects a situation often to be observed in interpersonal relationship; namely, that powerful conjunctive force can arise from congruent motivational systems and exert influence in the interpersonal field wholly exterior to the awareness of the persons concerned. And this can be quite all right; it is by no means "abnormal." Fig. 3 represents a definite improvement of the situation over the stage depicted in Fig. 2. In ordinary language these people are getting to be better and better friends. The more experienced one is coming to be more and more helpful to the less experienced one. The situation is

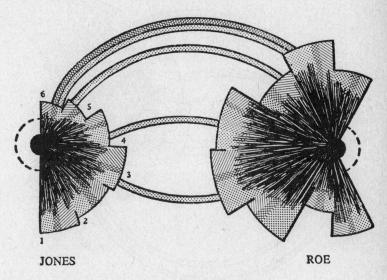

JONES   ROE

Fig. 3—Later Stage of Relationship

contributing to the growth of the respective personalities, particularly that of Mr. Jones.

Looking again, however, at the origin of this uppermost simply conjunctive force, note that, in the symbolism here used, it reaches to the very edge of the anxiety-fraught part of the relevant sector in Mr. Jones. Were it to become more powerful, which would mean that it were broader, Jones' anxiety would be involved, and, as it were, [involved] in the sense suggested by the phrase "anxiety arising from unrecognized motivation."

We will assume that this development has occurred in the interval before the situation reflected in the next diagram.

The great change in the pattern of the field forces shown in Fig. 4 is intended to reflect an approach to an equilibrium situation which has come into being as a result of a 'schizophrenic episode' in the relationship of Jones with his friend. By referring to

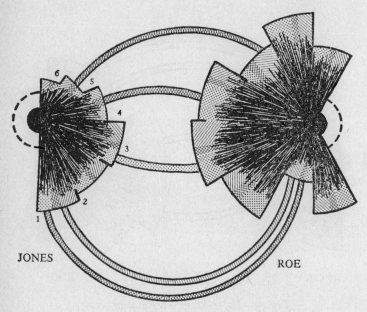

JONES

ROE

Fig. 4—'As If' Relationship After 'Episode'

equilibrium, I wish to suggest that no further approach or separation is to be noticed but that contact with Mr. Roe is now of the relatively fixed character shown by an *eidetic* personification forcibly shutting off further development of acquaintance with Mr. Roe. One may say that from now on it is not with Mr. Roe as he has been experienced in the course of the development of the friendship but with Mr. Roe as the disastrous outcome of Jones' relationship with him that Jones continues in a relatively durable field relationship.

The amazing change in the pattern of field forces such that all but one has become disjunctive and a new kind of disjunctive force—the second lowest, single-hatched line, representing *uncanny* emotion—has appeared, reflects an important aspect of

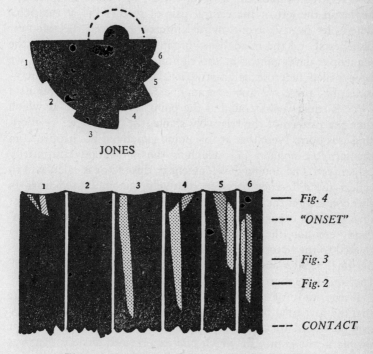

Fig. 5—'Surface' Pattern of the Experience

personality development; namely, the interlocking connection of past experience not only in, as it were, the sub-sectors of personality currently manifested, but also throughout the historic past of personality. All anxiety-fraught experience can be thought to be related to—perhaps better, can, if necessary, be made to lead in the direction of recall of—the earliest experience of anxiety which, according to this theory, has been involved in one of the first pair of personifications in the history of any one, the personification of the *evil mother* which is formed in later infancy.

In Fig. 5, there is shown the 'surface' pattern of all of Mr. Jones' experience from his initial meaningful contact with Mr. Roe to the present in which actual contact with Mr. Roe has yielded to a relative equilibrium with an eidetic Mr. Roe. This "story" begins in the left of the central pair of sectors [3] at the point where, let us say, strong mutual interest between the two was discovered and the relationship began to grow. Notice next the sequential development in the rightmost sector [6], which we have called heterosexual motivation, where first only anxiety-toned but presently also conjunctive force appeared. This field force is entirely obliterated at the point marked 'onset' at which time the pattern of the relatively stable, the 'psychotic,' relationship was born. Note that at this point something has happened in the leftmost column [1] which is the motivation customarily called *fear*. The double development in this sector is calculated to reflect the difference between relatively uncomplicated fear—in this connection the fear of the effects of poison—and the aspect of a person's capacity 'to feel' that which is experienced as uncanny emotion, the outcropping of which 'emotion' is peculiarly related to the outcropping of schizophrenic processes in an interpersonal relationship, and the displacement of a relatively 'real' [person] by a more or less wholly eidetic "other person."

In the study of any anxiety-fraught experience, one discovers that the particular pattern of the situation which provokes anxiety can be traced to a past relationship with particular significant people in the course of which one experienced anxiety that was more or less clearly observed to relate to particular interaction with them.

The complement of eidetic people which each of us carries with us and lives with reaches back in every instance to the first pair of our personifications: the *good mother* associated with the relaxation of the tensions of recurrent needs, and the bad or *evil mother* associated with the undergoing of anxiety.

The next link in the inevitable developmental chain is the triple personifications of *good-me, bad-me,* and the always rather shadowy but dreadful *not-me*. Bad-me is constructed from experience with anxiety-fraught situations *in which the anxiety was not severe enough to preclude observation and analysis*. Not-me grows out of mostly retrospective analysis of observed precursors to the paralysis of referential processes which is always associated with sudden severe anxiety.

Anxiety as a *functionally effective* element in interpersonal relations has to be mild in degree or gradual in its increasing severity. Sudden severe anxiety, or anxiety which increases very swiftly in severity is undergone in later life as what I call *uncanny emotion*, chilly crawling sensations, and the like, often meant by the words 'awe,' 'dread,' 'loathing,' and 'horror.' Uncanny emotion is an all but *functionally ineffective* element in interpersonal relations; it arrests useful transformations of energy other than (1) certain obscure covert processes which, if they occur, may be called "adjustment to the uncanny" with escape into more refined and less paralyzing anxious states, (2) those which make up the schizophrenic disturbance of awareness with its varying influence of the not-me components, or (3) apathy—which I shall not here discuss.

I shall conclude my remarks with a consideration of the dynamic role of milder, often vestigial, tensions of anxiety. It is in this area that the concept of anxiety makes its great contribution to understanding the difficulties in living, and to developing the technology of therapy—procedures useful in inducing favorable change in interpersonal relations. Let me suggest that the concept of anxiety as here suggested is useful in explaining, for example: a great many instances of irritation, anger, and unpleasant misunderstanding; all more or less enduring hateful relationships; the welter of belittling, disparaging performances which seem to be almost a national—at least, a national psychiatric—characteristic; a world of unreasoning prejudices and preferences; the time-destroying more or less obsessional preoccupations which so frequently characterize the gifted; the sad way of the pathologically alcoholic; and a startlingly great proportion of the so-called sexual problems of our times. The self-system, in its control over one's awareness of resentment which would entail anxiety, is central in understanding the ever more widespread vicissitude of peptic—and, probably, duodenal—ulcer, and the symptom picture related to it, as well as I know not what others of the so-called psychosomatic disorders.

I hope, though I know from experience that I hope forlornly, that these statements will not be taken to show that I am making anxiety the "explanation of everything" in difficulties in living. There are many other factors that are important—loneliness, envy, the effects of conventional prejudices about lustful sports, and doctrines of sin and atonement, to mention a few. I am committed tonight to discussing anxiety, and, even if anxiety is far from an adequate explanation of all our troubles with other people, there can be no doubt about its being an ever important and ever recurring complication in all efforts to help people out of their difficulties in living. The self-system, from its beginnings and throughout its historic development, tends always to resist significant change in the direction of living. The meaning of anxiety in day-to-day life is to be found by study of the self-system interventions which tend to keep us living in our accustomed way.

The felt tension and activity known as rage, usually called out by any grave or rapidly developing threat to our survival—the pattern of which is foreshadowed by the fury of the cornered rat—is not a commonplace experience of many of us. But the lesser manifestation of a very close relative of this tension, the emotion of anger, is for many people a very common experience—as is its complex relative, resentment, a common experience of others. Yet in the peacetime phases of our society, corresponding threats to our survival are not very numerous, and occasions for fear, as I have said before, are comparatively infrequent. The welter of irritation, bad temper, and frank anger that we live in is not the outcome of "real" dangers to our physical organism, but comes from threats to our prestige, to our conviction that we are worth while and respected.

The observed failure of someone to treat us with the deference which we had expected him to show calls out anxiety. Very few of us notice the initial anxiety, but most of us can be led to see that the person annoys or irritates us. We can propound more or less impressive verbalisms to "explain" his offensive effect on us. These verbalisms help to keep us vulnerable to such people, because they help us to overlook the initial anxiety by "justifying" our anger. It is only when we have been led to see that we expected—needed—the other fellow's deference, and suffered anxiety when it failed to materialize, that we are looking at the right place to find something in our interpersonal relations that would benefit by favorable change.

To be angered by the patterned rudeness of a shop girl reflects unfavorably on the stability of one's self-esteem. Servants of the public are not apt to show delicate discrimination of their customers' relative worth, if only because they themselves are seldom treated like fully human beings but instead are abused as if they were insensate embodiments of shortcomings in the store, the traffic, the administration, or whatever. A good many of these people have come to *hate* "the public" for the same reason that anyone hates someone else: namely, they are recurrently made anxious by people whom they cannot escape.

Time and again in the practice of any psychiatrist, one hears of a couple, married or "lovers," whose every act one to another seems to be calculated to hurt. We say, correctly, that this couple is held together not by love but by hate. If we are to help one of them to escape, or to improve the relationship, we have to help him see wherein he is vulnerable to anxiety from acts of the partner, and how he is entrapped in a futile effort to destroy the other by the tedious method of "causing" anxiety.

Not but that anxiety and its congeries of complex derivatives can undermine health or actually hasten the death of a person. The mounting rate of cardiac deaths probably correlates rather exactly—once rheumatic heart disease has been eliminated—with the rising level of general insecurity. A startling number of coronary occlusions have followed on relief from a chronic rather severe anxiety, not because the relief was harmful, but because the long-continued anxiety had reduced the vital reserves of the cardiac circulation.

I said years ago that if one swallows much resentment it will ruin one's belly; there are few better established hypotheses than that which sees in unrecognized recurring resentment the prime factor in troubles from the stomach onward in the alimentary canal. Resentment itself often if not always includes anxiety in its composition. If one cannot admit the fact of resenting into awareness, that means that a knowledge of the situation resented which would be felt as the tension of resentment becomes, because it cannot 'be known,' increased tension in the belly, and with this there generally goes the experience of weariness. Many a person who is chronically tired at home, though often lively elsewhere, is "exhausted" by unacceptable resentment about the way he is treated by his mate—who may suffer in turn because he is too tired to do anything pleasant.

By dubious transition I come next to tense people, and to the people who "work themselves to death." Persistent high tone in the skeletal muscles is often expressive of anxiety about becoming anxious, or about being discovered to be anxious. Feverish over-activity in work or in play may be a substitute activity to keep one from being aware of a serious anxiety-provoking situation.

The classical substitutive activities, the obsessional preoccu-pations, are obscurely but very intimately related to anxiety. It is not far wrong to say that obsessional people are very rarely notably anxious, but are rarely free from hints of anxiety. The intensity of their preoccupation varies directly with the risk of anxiety in the particular interpersonal situation confronting them.

I here touch upon—and it is the last instance that I shall touch upon—the enormous contribution of anxiety to inefficiency in work, play, and the pursuit of happiness. It is only when one realizes the relation to anxiety of the obsessional substitutions, the compulsive rituals, and the like—which waste so much energy not only of the person who suffers them as a patient, you might say, but also of all those who suffer him as a contact—that one is adequately oriented towards these pervasive interferences with human progress. It is only when one comes to see wherein self-system operations of the nature of anxiety are the hints, the barely detectable hints, which call out or increase the degree of practi-cally useless preoccupation and ritual that one is able to make moderately rapid favorable change in these obsessional ways of life. If there were no other reason for holding for the time being quite firmly to this theory of personality and of anxiety, it would be well justified by the fact that it presents a therapeutic attack for the obsessional-compulsive situations which is unparalleled in its time-saving effectiveness.

The great purpose of all psychiatry in this day and age, how-ever, has, I believe, to be something other than therapy. As a matter of fact, many of the noninstitutional psychiatrists of the United States, certainly of those in the larger centers of popu-lation, are now chiefly engaged in the training of psychiatrists. We must have ever better theory to teach, and we must find ways of teaching such alien conceptions as interpersonal fields, inter-personal relations, interpersonal difficulties to medical men so that they can finally come to think as easily about living as they now think about statements about symptoms. The nonmedical layman consulting a doctor about a 'physical' ailment, tells some symp-toms, some of them irrelevant, some of them seriously misleading in the way that they are expressed. The doctor has a pattern of disease that begins to work in his mind—a frame of reference—so he asks a few questions and thinks to himself "Oh, yes, now I know what this is about." But when you go to any one of a good many medical men and tell him about the difficulty you seem to be having in getting up in the morning to get your husband's break-fast, or something of that kind, he has no frames of reference for organizing this kind of data, he understands nothing; and if you are troublesome, he sends you to a psychiatrist. Then you can find no psychiatrist who has any time available, which makes it all very helpful.

With the world situation as it is and is apt to be for some considerable time to come, it is quite certain that we cannot depend on any however augmented supply of psychiatrists to handle the rapidly mounting evil consequences of a steadily mounting level of general insecurity which, as it were, kicks the pins from under a great many feebly going concerns of the recent past.

For that reason, it becomes of much more than merely personal interest to me to discover if there is a way of greatly augmenting the utility of psychiatric conceptions and approaches, and of preventive psychiatry—competent interventions at the time when it doesn't take a long time, or a great deal of experience, to be extremely useful.

This is the enormous responsibility which must be met by the development of psychiatric theory and methodic psychiatric teaching if we or any other people of the world are to carry many more of our citizens to actual personality maturity; that is, to the reasonable development of ability to participate adequately, appropriately, and constructively in interpersonal relations, which is imperatively necessary, I believe, if the world is to be held together much longer.

15

Commentary

THE NEXT PAPER, "Beliefs Versus a Rational Psychiatry," was originally designed for psychiatrists in training in the Washington School of Psychiatry. In both 1947 and 1948, Sullivan gave three orienting lectures for physicians only, at the beginning of the academic year. They were directed "towards remedying unreasonable preconceptions and impracticable expectations brought to the study of psychiatry and towards guiding candidates in assessment of their progress," as described in the School catalogue. With a minor omission, this is the second of the three lectures given in 1948.

Here again Sullivan is striving to establish the idea of an operational statement for psychiatry. The psychiatrist must develop a critical attitude about what he says: "Do I know what I mean by this statement? Is there any way of checking the meaning of this statement as I suppose it exists, or is it actually some conventional aspect of the doctrines in which I have been trained?"

Unless psychiatry begins to define human behavior cross-culturally, the psychiatrist is merely operating in a new cult; and psychiatry is no better than any other belief. "Man is a simply terrifically gifted creature, and the most profound of imbecilities . . . seem to me well within the possibility of man's profiting from them if, and only if, the people concerned can be cut off from the perturbations of people around them." But the Washington School of Psychiatry strives toward a psychiatry "formulated in terms that are meaningful to an intelligent denizen of a quite alien area."

In the primitive culture described in this paper, there is much reliance on what Sullivan calls the "doctrine of the will." This is one of the clearest statements Sullivan made on his exception to this doctrine.

Beliefs Versus a Rational
Psychiatry†

. . . MERE ACCIDENT of my life has given me a rather good text;
and at the risk of doing a very distinguished social scientist an
injury, I am going to give my impression of an anthropologist's
discovery now being applied as a psychotherapeutic principle,
all of my acquaintance with which is based on a 45-minute
conversation. I hope you understand that this may be grossly
unfair, but I am nonetheless telling you something that interested
me intensely and that, as I turned it over in the succeeding twenty
hours, I realized was too priceless an instance of something to be
omitted from this evening's talk.

There is a certain notable anthropologist who after very good
training at the London School of Economics took himself to the
Negrito area to study the peoples there. The Philippines and the
Malay Peninsula were his last areas of study; and from there he
went to look into a very isolated community well up in the Malay
Peninsula which was in some ways reputed to be truly astounding.

Among the reputedly astounding features, which he seemed to
validate in a considerable study among them, was that in rumor
and memory there had been no capital crime, no homicide, no

† Reprinted from "The Study of Psychiatry: 1948 Orienting Lectures,"
Psychiatry (1949) 12:325–337; pp. 325–331 only. [This paper is taken from
the second of three orienting lectures given in the Washington School of
Psychiatry, on October 22, 1948. This lecture, published after Sullivan's
death, has been edited only slightly; the title has been supplied by me from
the text of the lecture. H.S.P.]

rape, and things of that kind, in this community for about a century and that the types of violations which we regard as felonies, and so on, were extremely rare. To find any fragment of the human race of which such a statement could be made is in itself astounding. He spent a good deal of time with these people. He found that a very elaborate course of education, as I would call it, was applied from early childhood along the lines of what he calls, rather correctly I believe, the transformation of dreams.

As he laid the account before me, a child who has stubbed his toe on a rock is, for reasons which a student of personality might guess, apt to dream in the near future that the spirit of this rock appears to him and, to put it succinctly, plays hell with the child, whereupon the child's parent points out to the child the errors of his ways: that it is to some extent his fault that the spirit of this rock was so unpleasant, that he must cultivate an ability to attract, encourage the cooperation of or otherwise to circumvent, neutralize, or remedy the hostility of the spirit of this rock. Later on, perhaps at the time of adolescence, someone may dream of being attacked by a tiger and be very badly frightened—that is, he has a nightmare or anxiety dream; and by that time he is entitled to the attention of the shaman, the medical man, who indicates that this is an occasion on which he must vanquish the tiger, kill him in essence. And presently he does dream of killing the tiger, and the shaman then wants to know whether he observed the spirit of the tiger leave the animal and enter into him, and so on. In other words, this seems to be a very curious cult in which one is taught to vanquish all the symbols in one's dream life marked with intense anxiety or uncanny emotion.

I asked how this community was isolated from the rest of the world and learned that there was valid basis for that. We then discussed the psychotherapeutic system that this gifted anthropologist has developed from his experience in this community which has been very successful in dealing with delinquents in England, and is undoubtedly being very successful in dealing with certain people in Manhattan now.

We then discoursed together, and it was finally brought out that from childhood on, the mandate of this culture was: "Thou shalt bear no ill will." Ill will to another human being or to the denizens of the spirit world presumably is forbidden as one of the basic principles of this culture.

Forty-five minutes is a rather short time for investigating so amazing a matter, so there are unnumbered things about this psychotherapeutic system derived from an upper Malay, not truly Malay, culture island. [Nevertheless this] seemed to me a marvelous text for laying before you: *I know no reason other than one's fellow man which would interfere with the success of such a psychotherapeutic system.*

I said to this gentleman at the end of our discourse that curious vicissitudes had brought him to the one psychiatrist in the world who was probably least inclined to encourage the development of the psychotherapeutic system which he had very cleverly invented and tested for some seven years. Not being a psychiatrist but an anthropologist, he immediately felt that there was a mistake somewhere and urged upon me the truly astounding results that had been achieved by this therapeutic system. They are astounding.

As you grow old in this game, you will discover that every system which has got any following among our fellow men has achieved astounding results. Many of them, so far as I am concerned, are too preposterous to be taken seriously, such as the Jungian system with its racial unconscious, according to which you are a sort of bud on a great reservoir of God knows quite what—but it is extremely successful for those that it succeeds with. They are far more zealous than most religionists, and they go about the world distributing good—so do many other people who, as I say, bore me too much by the nature of their speculation to be taken seriously; not so at all this anthropologist.

Why is this of such interest to me in introducing you to the study of psychiatry? Because it seems to me the purest culture —now I am using "culture" in the sense that you use in bacteriology and not in anthropology—of two very important things: the doctrine of the will in a startlingly different form from what is ordinarily offered you in the Christian West; and the importance of dream processes.

I know no reason in the world if you get the right formula in connection with the indwelling power of man and fit it to a technique of suggestion and minor and major hypnosis—that is, suggestion under great prestige—why one cannot actually produce in the group over which you have control a workable system of interpersonal relations. There is actually no reason why operations in the syntaxic mode—that is, energy transformations that can be made clearly and succinctly communicable to others of good will and of proper background—should be required for marked improvement in the state of general citizens of a particular area. Were it not for the fact that this is so, the progress of the human race until the era of science would have been impossible.

So understand me clearly as saying that almost anything you have in your mind as to what is psychotherapy and what can be done with it may be within the simple and easily demonstrable realms of the possible. Man is a simply terrifically gifted creature, and the most profound of imbecilities—just so they are woven into a consistent system of beliefs, however imbecile—seem to me well within the possibility of man's profiting from them if, and only if, the people concerned can be cut off from the perturbations of people around them.

We have today in certain places in the United States and elsewhere what are called by some people eccentric religious cults and what by some other people in some cases are called schools of psychiatry, in which what seem to me incredibly irrational basic premises have been woven into techniques that work as long as the community is isolated.

The special purpose of the Washington School of Psychiatry is quite different. It is to present a system for studying, with a view to influencing, interpersonal relations in such fashion that the results which mean the change from a previous situation to a present situation tending toward a future situation can be formulated in terms that are meaningful to an intelligent denizen of a quite alien area. In other words, the claim to distinction of the psychiatry that we attempt to teach here is that it is capable of communication and of performance in the sense of improved living, regardless of the impinging of alien systems of thought, and so forth; that is, it seeks to be rational, to be capable of relatively definitive formulation in words which will be statements that can be grasped by persons of different backgrounds—though not without effort, it is true.

In the latter part of the summer, I had a paper,* which had been characterized by some of my colleagues as the clearest thing I had ever written, translated into the French. I had very great distrust as to what an excellent translator would make of a psychiatric paper which was somewhat out of his experience, and so I referred it to a very distinguished psychiatrist colleague of mine in Switzerland. . . . After struggling for weeks with the translator's translation of my best article, he wrote back asking me if he were going schizophrenic or if he would have to look forward to three years in America in order to understand the nuances of the American language; he said that the translation was literally excellent but meaningless, that when he attempted to outline my views, to summarize my views to guide him in translation, he found that they became incomprehensible. That was what happened, you see, to my best paper when it ran through the hands of a very gifted French Swiss.

So that when I say that the Washington School attempts to teach a psychiatry that can be translated and can be seized by people of good will of alien cultures, that does not mean that it can be seized instantly, because people of all cultures have a large number of preconceptions, views of things, and so on, which interfere with the simplicity—that is, appreciating the simplicity— of that which we are sure is communicable about interpersonal relations.

And one of the most profound and overwhelming barriers encountered in many but not, I am glad to say, all climes is the notion of powerful will. When a culture like this isolated Malayan culture ordains as the first principle, Thou shalt not entertain ill will toward a fellow being, do you see that that implies that you have the power to not entertain ill will; and they, because they are wonderfully isolated and because they operate in the parataxic mode, are able really to produce people who for all practical purposes in that culture manifest that power.

Now we are trying here not to work out something that will

[* This undoubtedly refers to "Towards a Psychiatry of Peoples," originally published in *Psychiatry* (1948) 11:105–116. Much of this paper is included as part of the article "Tensions Interpersonal and International," which appears in this book as the last paper. H.S.P.]

work in American Christianity 1948 but something that, insofar as it can gradually be translated, will work in the world sine die; needless to say not in the condition in which we hand it out in 1948, but in the condition in which a scientific statement will be at the particular date when the people concerned are considering it.

To do anything of that kind requires that one shall, as fast as possible, strip off more or less antiquated and indefensible views with which you are thoroughly acquainted but which are functionally impotent at the level of communication, excepting in what I will describe as the society of the faithful. If you believe that you meet the gods after you have smoked hashish, all that is required for you to be content in that belief is that you discuss the matter only with those who meet the gods when they smoke hashish. It will work fine under those circumstances. But it will not be psychiatry that can be communicated on a world scale if and when numerous interfering preconceptions have been brushed aside. You see, I cannot possibly deal therapeutically with the extraordinary superiorities conferred on the smoker of hashish by his contact with the gods until I have been able to intrigue him in the possibility of other less select interpretations of his experience. It is sometimes really surprisingly easy to make contacts across such barriers as that which separate the hashish smoker of the creed that I have mentioned from the atheist. Crossing these barriers is more feasible than most of you can dream. But to cross them, you must cross them without equally nebulous baggage which contradicts the most cherished possessions of the denizen in that realm. In other words, the great struggle of the religions, and so on, rests in large part on the fact that no person concerned in these struggles can afford to look to see what his position might mean. He is defending his faith.

If someone shows up who is merely scientifically curious, who has no faith to defend, who is not attacking to destroy but to resolve perplexity—in other words, someone who applies the best scientific technique of attempting to observe dispassionately the data on which beliefs rest, and having done that to inquire what is wrong with his provisional hypothesis, and so on—that sort of person is far more effective than you might dream in bringing about movements toward a unification and sanification of other-wise singularly contradictory and irrational systems of belief.

Well, that is what we strive for in psychiatry of the Washington School: a rational system as to what can be done about anyone anywhere who is not living as well as he seems capable of living with his fellow man.

Needless to say, we do not have to gallop out and try this every-where and anywhere at once. First, it is impossible and, secondly, it would be preposterous beyond words because only some ten or twenty years have been expended in an effort to be sure that we have not included a large number of irrational elements from our own home land—that is, from the peculiar people who become psychiatrists. Recently there have been some faint movements to see whether certain rudiments of this system of thought were acceptable in western Europe.

What I wish to get across to you tonight is that the very first principle which has to be cultivated in you is the acquisition of a critical attitude which starts out something like this: Do I know what I mean by this statement? Is there any way of checking the meaning of this statement as I suppose it exists, or is it actually some conventional aspect of the doctrines in which I have been trained?

Returning to the upper Malay culture, I have no disparagement of the truth of their having achieved a way of life that is without major crime or of the rumors of success in adapting something borrowed from them to the treatment of certain pathological conditions in the Western world. Regardless of all that, it is in no sense psychotherapy as we mean it, any more than is the doctrine that "love conquers all"—which as it is ordinarily exemplified in psychotherapy means a person entirely incapable of love gives the patient love and cures him. Nor is it a refinement of "what seriously ill people need is tenderness"—as a result of which a very insecure psychiatrist quite blind to his bitter hostilities, and so on, to his fellow man pours out from a magical vessel tenderness upon the patient. These techniques often singularly miscarry. That is often mentioned in reports nowadays—successful treat-ment which failed. The reports invariably leave mysterious gaps to account for the miscarriage of what is presumed to be technique. Any failure is invaluable for the development of psychiatric therapy, but it must not be a failure based on a lunatic doctrine, the evidence of which lunacy is concealed in the report.

The psychiatry we attempt to deal with here rests on a basic assumption: namely, that man is, while not uniquely, at least exceedingly, conspicuously characterized by vulnerability to anxiety; that anxiety is a relative, if you please, of fear; but that it arises, from one's relations with others, in the later stages of life * and manifests itself fairly readily under provocation as a rationalization pertaining to the ill-esteem of another. This rationalization has extraordinary power to interfere with and complicate any of the manifestations outside of itself which might be called direct action in human living. What you think about anxiety and what we mean by anxiety are startlingly different for the most part, and the manifestations of anxiety as they are ordinarily experienced in life and in psychotherapy have little directly to do with anxiety. The extraordinary truth is that the experience of anxiety is so unpleasant that most of the things one encounters in life, among anything like an adult population and in the practice of psychiatry, are characterized by very fugitive manifestations of anxiety and very extended manifestations of processes for the control of a minimizing of anxiety. All of these are in a very meaningful sense the problems of psychiatry, this meaningful sense being that they are the things you are eternally falling over, getting stuck up with, mixed up with, frustrated by, and so on, in your work of psychotherapy. But they are not the central problem of psychiatry.

Some of you who like myself may have an agricultural background realize that much of the heartache of the farm is the weeds; but the weeds are not that which is essential on the farm. The crop is essential, but the weeds are the trouble. And so it is in psychotherapy: Anxiety is the problem, but the unnumbered operations which human skill has devised—your patient's skill and experience have devised—to avoid and minimize anxiety, are what you have to struggle with in getting to the problem. But very much like the farmer's experience—after he has killed some

[* That is, the juvenile era, or the preadolescent era, rather than infancy, for instance. H.S.P.]

weeds, other weeds will appear—in this work concentration on the unnumbered security operations, the protective performances, and so on, called out by hints of anxiety can go on forever. You can make a good living doing that. The only thing you can't do is make very marked change in the patient, aside from the process of aging.

So that a rational psychiatry—a psychiatry that can be put into words which with reasonable precautions will communicate to a gentleman in Malay as well as to someone in this room—is based on the theory that, not the unnumbered things that people do which get in their way, but the vulnerabilities based on their past experience which lead them to do them—all of which vulnerabilities are manifested by at least fleeting evidences of anxiety in select situations—are the things you are trying to deal with. When you have become fairly clear on the specific and particular vulnerabilities to anxiety which are irrational from the standpoint of the broader culture or the particular world in which a person is living or is to live, you have come to that which can be cured, that to which psychotherapeutic technique can apply.

In conclusion, I have tried to tell you, first, of a psychotherapeutic system based on a very brilliant anthropological study of a most significantly unique culture, very many remnants of which exist today. I tried to show you how unutterably far that was from the sort of psychiatry that we are trying to teach here. In the process I hope that I have let you see that this system not only worked incredibly well in upper Malay—a crimeless community in the world today is truly a miracle of something—but I also conveyed to you that under particular circumstances this, like unnumbered other systems of healing, seems to work in metropolitan London and metropolitan Manhattan.

And I stress all this to contrast this something that would work and which would pay your living, until the depression at least, with the thought of psychiatry and psychotherapy which we are struggling to communicate here. The point I make is that we have, I believe without loss, stripped off a great many of the dearest elements of your cultural heritage and many another cultural heritage in the pursuit of that which might be universal, originally under the hope that man was more simply man than different one from another, and on the gradual realization that no data strikingly to the contrary appeared.

So that now I think there are quite a number of us who are fairly firmly convinced that anyone, barring the idiot who cannot possibly be called a human being except by poetic license, is more distinguished from every thing else in the world than he is from any other instance of human being. Whether it be with Chinese, Malays, American, or African Negro, [northwestern] European, Greek, or Italian, there are certain phenomena which are universal and intimately related to the so-called difficult performance of the person. These universal phenomena are not the difficult performances per se, for the latter are patterned by the particular culture and by the particular successes and failures in the person's personal history. Nevertheless, these universal phenomena are exceedingly closely related to any particular instance of the manifestation of these difficulties. The difficulties themselves are in turn to be understood as the result of critical limitations of experience which have occurred in connection with the phase of development in which such limitations could be significant. The phases of development are to be found in the series of years from birth until at least ten, but almost invariably fifteen or more, years—and in our variant of the [northwestern European] culture, a startling variant in some ways, probably fifteen to eighteen or nineteen years. These particular limitations or excesses of critical experience in connection with development of interpersonal relations or the capacity for interpersonal relations are each and every one of them often significant. The idea that the story is ended at four or seven or ten is actually found on careful exploration to be far more often false than true.

People who have had permanently devastating experience very early in life are usually so crippled that they do not come to the attention of the ordinary practicing psychiatrist. People who have been very seriously deprived of necessary interpersonal experience in infancy are seen only in very special institutions where they are often mistaken for idiots. So devastating can very serious warp in infancy be that a person with perfectly good germinal equipment can be made practically incapable of growing to the estate of a person. And people with very serious warp in childhood are seen in general only by those who work with the gravely ill.

Only minor distortions in the very early years of life are to be expected in the instances of patients that you see outside of institutions; but, far more important than that, unfortunate experience at any developmental phase may do great damage to one's possibilities of future interpersonal relations and—curiously enough, equally true—very fortunate experience at any developmental stage may do much to remedy the limitations already introduced by previous developmental misfortunes.

16

Commentary

THE LAST TWO articles in this book represent Sullivan's consuming interest in the issues of war and peace during the period from the end of World War II until his death early in 1949. In particular, he came to focus on the meaning of the new international organizations charged with responsibility for finding a way to an ordered world, and on seeking ways for psychiatry as a discipline to expedite the work of the World Health Organization and UNESCO. The importance of this work in his estimation can be gauged by the fact that in the last full year of his life (1948), he devoted one-fifth of the pages of the journal *Psychiatry* to articles and communications on international conferences, on methods for collaboration towards peace, and so on. It is impossible to adequately cover in this compass the outpourings of this three-and-a-half-year period; only a careful reading and rereading of all of the articles and editorials in *Psychiatry* on the subject of war and peace would suggest to the reader the enormous activity carried on by Sullivan personally. In these last two commentaries, I shall confine myself to mentioning a few landmarks.

The Chisholm Lectures (1945).—In October, 1945, only a few weeks after Hiroshima and the end of World War II, Sullivan arranged for his friend, G. B. Chisholm, M.D., to give two lectures, one in Washington and the other in New York City, under the auspices of the William Alanson White Psychiatric Foundation. These lectures, later published in a monograph entitled "The Psychiatry of Enduring Peace and Social Progress," [1] dramatically stated

[1] G. B. Chisholm, "The Reëstablishment of Peacetime Society" (including discussion), *Psychiatry* (1946) 9:1–35; 81–87. Also republished as a monograph by the Foundation, under the title, "The Psychiatry of Enduring Peace and Social Progress."

the task for psychiatry in the postwar world. Essentially Sullivan and Chisholm were in agreement on the nature of the task. In the early years of the war, Chisholm had been concerned with the same kinds of problems in recruitment of personnel for the armed forces in Canada that Sullivan had tackled in the United States. As the war progressed, each saw that "the soldier's return," as they termed it, would constitute a new crisis in a world unable to return to the old order. The old fixed values of right and wrong must give way to a new maturity that implied qualities of adaptability and compromise, Chisholm stated.

The responsibility of training society in new directions belonged to psychiatry, Chisholm thought:

If the race is to be freed from its crippling burden of good and evil it must be psychiatrists who take the original responsibility. This is a challenge which must be met. If psychiatrists decide to do nothing about it but continue in the futility of psychotherapy only, that too is a decision and the responsibility for the results is still theirs. What the world needs from psychiatry is honest, simple and clear thinking, talking and writing. It needs the same from psychology, sociology, economics and politics . . . words which are understandable by the people who matter in a democracy . . . the teachers, the young mothers and fathers, the parent-teachers associations, youth groups. . . . Can we psychiatrists give up our protective device of hiding behind a specific, difficult and variable vocabulary to avoid our obvious responsibility? [2]

One can find in Chisholm's lectures many of Sullivan's ideas and hopes, although they had been developed independently. The fact that Sullivan had a new and powerful ally in this period was a sustaining force for him in the unpopular role he assumed in the postwar years among his own psychiatric colleagues in the United States. In an editorial entitled "The Cultural Revolution to End War," Sullivan commented on the significance of Chisholm's lectures and noted that the psychiatrist must begin to "make public sense instead of private marvel." Communities are awakening from their trance and they will expect to find leadership; a logical source for leadership is to be found among psychiatrists. There has been a change in the affairs of men, Sullivan thought:

The bomb that fell on Hiroshima punctuated history. The man

[2] Chisholm, *op. cit.*, p. 9.

whose wisdom and foresight in large measure made that bomb had dealt with human destiny with fully human competence.

The gods of local certainties, of local moralities, of local loyalty, of personal salvation, of hate and prejudice and the intolerance of others passed into history.

As mundane distance shriveled into insignificance in the eddies of radioactive matter which swept space around the earth, so also did the swathings of immaterial fictions and habitual evasions with which everyone had been methodically enwrapped.

The peoples of the world, wherever language reaches, caught a glimpse of Reality, felt with whatever terror a moment of insight into alike the minuscule and the magnificent in Human Being.[3]

The World Health Organization.—By early in 1947, the Constitution of the World Health Organization had been drawn up and signed by sixty-one nations; Chisholm had been appointed Executive Secretary of the Interim Commission of WHO and was slated to be its first Director General. To Sullivan this seemed to open up a whole new method for the collaboration of the several social sciences, particularly psychology and psychiatry. The preamble to the Constitution put great stress on health as "a state of complete physical, mental and social well-being and not merely the absence of disease or infirmity." International organizations concerned with the prevention of various physical diseases—tuberculosis, cancer, venereal disease, and so on—were in 1947 already actively preparing to cooperate in the work of the World Health Organization. *But there was no truly international and representative psychiatric organization.* There were only the mental hygiene societies or committees in the various countries; and these organizations were often more moralistic than scientific. Sullivan called for an organization of psychologists and psychiatrists to make recommendations on real preventive work in mental health:

It is clear that the World Health Organization will need to be advised as to programs designed to ensure healthy mental and social development of children.

It is also clear that psychologists and psychiatrists will be expected to take up this responsibility. If they themselves can cooperate sufficiently to set up a common international organization which can speak with one voice, their recommendations can hardly be ignored by the World Health Organization or its member govern-

[3] "The Cultural Revolution to End War," *Psychiatry* (1946) 9:81–87; p. 85.

ments. . . . Surely the very many psychiatrists and psychologists who have seen and examined vast numbers of neurotics could agree on some of the most consistently found destructive or limiting factors in the early histories of their patients, and also on some of the consistently constructive factors tending to be found in people with well-integrated mature personalities. . . . What about the ages at which children should be helped to look at various things, sex, religion, and so on? Should they commonly see their parents naked, both parents or only the one of the same sex? Should they be told about the local customs of the natives only, or about other ways of living which happen to be in vogue in other parts of the world? Should such other experiments in living be presented as equal or less valid? What are the emotional needs of children at various ages and how can these be satisfied? What attitudes in the environment of children lead to prejudices, intolerance, hate, inability to compromise or live harmoniously with other kinds of people? What points of view in parents and teachers tend to lead to the development of responsible, tolerant mature people who will be capable of avoiding war in the future? [4]

Sullivan did not at the time offer any solution as to what organization would take the initiative in drafting some tentative answers to such questions, although he ended his editorial by asking: "Shall we look to the American Psychiatric Association or to some other body to take the initiative?"

The International Congress on Mental Health (London, 1948).—By the summer of 1947, both Sullivan and Chisholm felt that they had found a partial answer to the question of some beginning international organization in the field of mental health. The next paper, "Remobilization for Enduring Peace and Social Progress" (1947), proposes that local groups, intradisciplinary at first, begin to get together and attempt to pool their knowledge in a beginning toward world-wide collaboration. The immediate task for such local groups would look toward the International Congress on Mental Health to be held a year hence: "It is proposed," Sullivan reports, "that no facts or opinion be considered by the Congress unless the facts and opinions be the established consensus of a group of collaborators, and preferably of an interdisciplinary group." But the interdisciplinary group would grow out of the beginning work of intradisciplinary groups at the local level. In ever widening circles, these local groups

[4] "The World Health Organization" (unsigned editorial), *Psychiatry* (1947) 10:99–103; pp. 102–103.

would send questions and suggestions through representatives to various area interdisciplinary groups. Out of these area groups would come recommendations for what came to be called the International Preparatory Commission—a group of specialists from all over the world who would meet just before the London Conference and pool these recommendations. Hopefully out of the London Conference would emerge a new international organization which would continue to be advised and informed by a network of area and local groups throughout the world. In some such manner, the World Federation for Mental Health did indeed emerge from the London Conference.

Before presenting the next paper, I should like to take note of the fact that Sullivan is now moving into a new pattern for the "fusion of social science and psychiatry." As I have already pointed out, Sullivan was largely dependent on his own profession, psychiatry, in his work with Selective Service at the beginning of the war, simply because it was the only profession that had the necessary training and experience for the task. In his work after the war on problems of international tensions, he is also more concerned with his own discipline, psychiatry. But the rationale for this is quite different. He is now dealing in an operational way with the problem of collaboration—and he invokes Bridgman's concepts in the course of the article—particularly as it concerns communication. A psychiatrist can learn the lingo of the sociologist; and certainly the sociologist, like the layman generally, has long been infatuated with psychiatric terminology. But learning the lingo of another discipline does not imply anything about communication; in fact learning the lingo of another profession can simply be used as a camouflage for everyone's feeling quite comfortable and talking inanities indefinitely at interdisciplinary conferences. This Sullivan hoped to avoid. Psychiatrists, he felt, must first learn to define their own terms and talk to each other about what they knew in the simplest language that they were capable of. Is there any consensus, for instance, among psychiatrists as to what is meant by the term *envy?* Until there is such consensus, the psychiatrist has little to contribute to the cultural anthropologist for his observation of different cultures. Only a few psychiatrists, or social scientists generally, as Sullivan points out, are in any position to effect any interdisciplinary collaboration at this stage in the behavioral sciences, simply because they have seldom effected any true communication with their own colleagues. It seems to me that the pattern for this kind of thinking came from Sullivan's clinical theory about the meaning of preadolescence in the developing personality; in that stage of personality development, the person has an opportunity to collaborate with someone like himself, to establish trust, as a prelude to a harmonious relationship with someone different from himself, in adolescence.

In the light of more recent happenings, it is noteworthy that whatever collaboration has emerged in the 1960's towards lessening international tensions has indeed been largely centered within discrete professions—the physicians, the social workers, and so on, with some beginning collaboration among small groups of social scientists more generally. While most of this collaboration has been somewhat short of what Sullivan hoped for, since it has been largely directed towards rather simple political pressure, it is nonetheless significant that at this level of our development consensus within profession, or among colleagues working closely together, is vastly more likely than any real, broad, interdisciplinary consensus. At the same time, significant interdisciplinary collaboration, certainly to meet the needs of science, remains as a desideratum—the ultimate goal in a maturing social science, as Sullivan saw it.

Remobilization for Enduring Peace and Social Progress†

THE CALL for a world-wide mobilization of psychiatry implicit in General Chisholm's 1945 memorial to William Alanson White is now made explicit.*

We have something to do that is greatly important; something that we cannot delegate to a committee, or leave to the few who are intensely interested.

We have to make sense; we, every one of us. We have to make sense not about everything, but about principles that are important in promoting harmonious human relations.

Few indeed are the psychiatrists who have nothing to offer to such an effort, and each and every one of us is called upon to further the achievement of this objective in full measure of his capacity.

Some of us have learnt that a psychiatrist can matter in the complex effort of actual war. All of us can now learn that psychiatry matters crucially in the more complex effort to insure enduring peace and social progress.

† Reprinted from *Psychiatry* (1947) 10:239–252. [Certain topical material has been omitted in this printing, as indicated at the appropriate junctures. Also a section headed "Whence the Urgency" has been previously reprinted in the posthumous papers, and is not included here; see *The Interpersonal Theory of Psychiatry* (Norton, 1953), pp. 382–384. H.S.P.]

[* G. B. Chisholm, "The Reëstablishment of Peacetime Society," with Foreword and Discussion, *Psychiatry* (1946) 9:1–35; 81–87. Also published as a monograph by the William Alanson White Psychiatric Foundation under the title, "The Psychiatry of Enduring Peace and Social Progress." H.S.P.]

Much that was wasteful of psychiatrists' value had to characterize the war effort. Nothing at all wasteful need characterize the present mobilization. There are certain to be good returns to psychiatrists and to psychiatry in exact measure of effort expended. The objective to be achieved, moreover, is the salvage of the very aims for which at least some of us feel the war may have been fought in vain.

I think that nearly everyone did his stint gladly in the national war effort, whether in the service or in the civilian home front. I think that many of us found too little to do, and too little that we could do certainly. There need be none of this in the new mobilization.

There is a place for everyone and a plan that should put everyone in the place where he can function adequately.

What is chiefly lacking is time. . . .*

Why Now?

What is the pattern of the times that calls for instant action by every psychiatrist? Is it of overweening importance to you and to those whom you serve professionally?

By the time that this paper reaches your attention, eleven States, members of the United Nations, and six others will have ratified their membership in the World Health Organization, in recommending which action to the Congress of the United States Secretary of State Marshall stated: "I would like to emphasize that the World Health Organization is intended to provide the international machinery for bringing about conditions of health essential not only to the welfare of the United States but to a stable world order."

This United Nations subsidiary, the WHO, with UNESCO, can be accepted as the administrative agencies for world peace towards the success of the work of which psychiatrists and the other students of living can make invaluable contribution immediately.

The WHO defines health as "a state of complete physical, mental, and social well-being and not merely the absence of dis-

[* At this point, the actual detailed plan for the collaboration of psychiatrists and other social scientists has been omitted. H.S.P.]

ease or infirmity" and has committed itself specifically to fostering activities in the field of mental health, "especially those affecting the harmony of human relations."

General Chisholm, now Executive Secretary of the Interim Commission of the WHO, said in his address to the 103rd annual meeting of the American Psychiatric Association: ". . . the period covered by the next two years is the crucial time. There is a coincidence of responsibility and opportunity now which has never occurred before and may never occur again. Firstly, there is now a highly important world-wide anxiety which is thoroughly justified . . . [which] provides fertile soil for the planting and development of seeds which could be of the kind that Hitler and his like have planted or could be of new scientifically developed kinds which will produce fruits valuable to the whole world. . . .

"Secondly, it happens, largely as a result of this widespread anxiety, that the United Nations is in process of developing a great variety of contacts across international boundaries. One of the most important of these groups of contacts will be the WHO. . . .

"The WHO, to fulfill the obligations in the field of mental and social health which have been laid on it by the nations of the world, must develop plans which will reach far into the future and will be world-wide in scope. Where will these plans come from? Who will initiate them? From what body will their technical authority derive? Who will bring together the experience of all the nations in this field and advise the World Health Organization?"

He looks with hope to the International Congress on Mental Health called to assemble in London in August 1948. From this Congress there may develop a permanent advisory organization. "Perhaps never before in history has there been a more important meeting of any kind than that Congress can be, if all the people qualified . . . by a free pooling of their knowledge and experience, offer even a little, but concrete, hope for a frightened world."

The plan of this International Congress on Mental Health is in one respect exemplary indeed. It is proposed that no facts or opinion be considered by the Congress unless the facts and opinions be the established consensus of a group of collaborators, and preferably of an interdisciplinary group.

Whether this International Congress shall succeed greatly or indifferently is primarily dependent on the thoroughness with which its work reflects the constructive counsel of the world's psychiatrists, social scientists, educators, social workers, and others concerned.

Were there nothing more at stake than the great success of this one Congress, there would be good reason for geat effort to pool our knowledge and experience. Beyond the direct benefits of informed discussion, we have the prospect of sustained activity by the WHO.

I think that there is a very great deal more at stake than that.

The WHO will function for some time at the level of political entities approaching or maintaining full sovereignty. While its charter empowers it "to assist in developing an informed public opinion among all peoples on matters of health," public opinion on mental health in the sense of harmonious human relations is truly a field in which, again to quote Secretary Marshall, "we must have the facts about the truth and the truth about the facts," and facts and important truths derived from them are lamentably scarce in this field.

When we have sought to develop an informed public opinion on matters of mental health in our own U.S.A., we have, I fear, all too blandly overlooked some of the truth reflected, for example, in Kingsley Davis' "Mental Hygiene and the Class Structure." * We have not been very bright in analyzing our implied position, nor at all thoughtful in foreseeing quite what to the achievement of which we were futilely committing ourselves.

There is a great need for facts, stripped of the inhering prejudice that affects their perception, which derives from the culture and the seeming social necessities involved in their interpretation.

[* See *Psychiatry* (1938) 1:55–65. In this paper, Kingsley Davis set forth his opinion that in the United States, "mental hygiene will probably fail as a preventive movement because it cannot overcome its defects, the free analysis and manipulation of invidious social elements never being permitted in an integrated society." The mental hygienist is a "practising moralist" in a "scientific, mobile world," and that is his dilemma, Davis says. He cannot give up his moralizing, but he must be a scientist to act preventively in the mental health field. H.S.P.]

And even though we were much better provided with 'good' facts, and reasonably clear about their broadly human implications, none of this may suit high policy here and there around the world.

Here in the United States, to quote Abe Fortas' appreciation of General Chisholm's White memorial, "We have smashed the atom and unleashed the terrible power of nature. We must smash the housing of preconceptions and prejudices which encases the mind and spirit of man, and set them free to cope with the forces of dissolution and disintegration which are loose in the world." *

This objective has never been approached thus far, even in the most isolated nation in the history of humanity. I think that we may well give pause to any optimism about its easy achievement in this new day and age of one, however cloven, world.

There is needed the best policy that can possibly be worked out by all the widely experienced and greatly gifted people whom we can discover anywhere in the world. There is needed, also, the most sustained of well-directed efforts to provide informed and responsible intellectual leadership in every community around the world.

By what dreary miracle of self-deception can psychiatrists longer ignore their call to a significant place in this leadership? And how can the great numbers of psychiatrists who have lived as cloistered custodians of the relatively disenfranchised rise to meet this call except they gain assurance from informed discussion?

This is the crux of the mobilization. We are called to fight destruction of the human future, not merely by finding and stating to the world the consensus which psychiatrists can reach with their other colleagues among those who study living, but by implementing with our personal efforts the *certainties* common to all these views, under the aegis of the United Nations organizations.

Man as a system of civilizations rises or falls in the near future. We go to unpredictable heights in realizing human potentialities, or we recede to pastoral isolations in which the ultimate renaissance of XX Century culture ends dark ages of pristine warfares

[* See p. 2 of Chisholm monograph, *op. cit.*]

and starts a new progress. Do we want nearly everyone to die in order that the human race may begin all over? Is it seemly that we, momentarily honorable among the builders of the future, shall further by irresponsibility a schizophrenic dream of death and rebirth?

By Whom?

For a psychiatrist to be qualified to serve in this effort, he must have some facts and opinion, some experience and knowledge, useful in promoting the greater harmony of human relations. It is not required that he shall be sure that he is thus equipped. The customary work of all too many of us is not conducive to a fair assessment of this phase of our social worth. Much will be discovered in the first stage of the actual mobilization.

Only rarely will a psychiatrist knowingly have lived for some years in close touch with a population of strikingly different culture. Even when this is the case, he may well have failed to observe a great deal of what went on, chiefly for want of suitable frames of reference with which to analyze and organize thought about the significant events in which he was participating.

Only occasionally will a psychiatrist have opportunity and interest to make searching inquiry into the experience of some one else who has lived for years in a significantly alien culture-complex, and here too there may be serious deficiency of certainly useful data because of the poor observational training of the informant.

The great majority of psychiatrists have had no opportunity to familiarize themselves with the conceptions and methods of either cultural anthropology or social psychology. They can be remarkably naive in their thinking about the representatives of ethnic minority groups who occur among their own patients. It is rather a far cry from this state of mind to the making of valuable contributions to improved group relationships in one's own community, and any actual concern with problems of world citizenship would seem both remote and didactic.

A good many psychiatrists might wonder, on reviewing their daily life, if they had anything especially valuable to say about the individual and even [about] so special a society as the one made up of their own most immediately recurring contacts; and quite a few of them entertain private regrets that they have been able to learn so little that is certainly true about family problems and the psychological disturbances that seem to be related to them.

This is all very grim, but its grimness is no monopoly of psychiatry. It is characteristic of the personnel in every field in the study of interpersonal relations, of select aspects of human living.

Doubtless no one in any discipline has much ready to contribute. Let us find what little each may have and make the most of it by mutual aid. . . .*

Some Notes on Collaboration **

The underlying principle of this attempt to pool all psychiatric competence is the following: People when adequately and appropriately motivated tend to understand each other and to collaborate to their mutual advantage. If this statement seems obviously true, let us see if it is important.

The conditional clause about the quality of motivation is the part that can be questioned. We may wonder if people are often adequately and appropriately motivated towards understanding and collaboration. Is this not, asks the cynical, a most exceptional characteristic of the interpersonal situations in which we find ourselves actually involved?

I am not particularly interested in real or fancied statistics about the commonplaces of current living. It may well be that the world as known does not demonstrate very conspicuously the essential goodness and illuminated foresight of man. If it did, there would be no pressing need to alter society—to start a cultural revolution to end war.

Everyone at least occasionally understands and collaborates with another. Everyone all too frequently fails, for a variety of reasons. One has to observe in a participant fashion if one is to understand another, and this can scarcely occur if one is but waiting the

[* At this point, the detailed plan for the collaboration of psychiatrists within their own discipline has been omitted. H.S.P.]

[** The next three sections were originally published as appendices to the main article. I have supplied my own titles for the headings and the subheadings in these sections, with the exception of this particular title, which is Sullivan's. H.S.P.]

socially decorous interval till one can "speak one's mind"—talk to oneself aloud in the presence of an embodied 'audience.'

The speaker who is finally understood has adjusted his communicative efforts to his increasing grasp on the experience embodied in his hearer. The hearer who finally understands has listened in terms of his own experience expanded by growing appreciation of differences in the experience embodied in the speaker.

Communication is an exquisite triumph of trial and profit from shrewdly observed error.

All the semiotic or semantic perfection conceivable in a statement is of no moment if the hearer is motivated to refute or misunderstand it. The "record" may look very well. What difference does that make in terms of understanding collaboration?

I have been concerned since 1927 with promoting collaboration of social scientists with psychiatrists. Dr. White took an active part in these efforts, and the William Alanson White Psychiatric Foundation established *Psychiatry* with that in mind. The Washington School of Psychiatry requires that every candidate in training to practice psychiatry shall study cultural anthropology and social psychology. It seems unnecessary to repeat here the excellent reasons for this requirement.

The fact that the International Congress has written this sort of collaboration into its central plan is extremely encouraging, but one has to realize that it takes more than conversational exchange to establish useful communication among representatives of the various approaches to understanding and helpfully influencing people and institutions. Facile use of words which under other circumstances are the terms in the special scientific language of one of the social sciences does not show any grasp on the conceptual structure of the science, and brief exposure of the social scientist to the field of psychiatry—here, truly, wittingly or otherwise, many have come to scorn and few have remained to pray.

Collaboration becomes vastly more probable when all those concerned know that, as Bridgman* has said: "A term is defined when the conditions are stated under which I may use the term

[* See "Symposium on Operationism," in *Psychological Rev.* (1945) 52: 241–294; esp. p. 246. H.S.P.]

and when I may infer from the use of the term by my neighbor that the same conditions prevailed." The import of this lucid statement is scarcely to be grasped by one hurried reading. It strikes at the very center of the difference between communicative statements and remarks which merely "express oneself." Interdisciplinary collaboration requires a maximum of communication and a continuing guard lest one be merely talking.

There are two patterns for achieving interdisciplinary collaboration. One is that of groups made up of people already skilled in two or more disciplines; these groups can be but relatively few. The other—to me vastly more important for many reasons—is the pattern of local groups in each discipline, first concerned with clarifying basic issues open to interdisciplinary collaboration, along with expanding liaison at the next level, and a subsequent change to interdisciplinary composition when and as this becomes obviously desirable to the participants. Each pattern has its place but the second requires mobilization—and promptly.

The Psychiatrist's Contribution

Some years since, when I was urging the imperative necessity that all the various students of living should collaborate, I tried to make clear the particular genius of psychiatry for helping to solve urgent public problems. I said then that, to become a psychiatrist "one goes . . . to the hospital for the mentally disordered and becomes familiar with the more striking patterns of aberrant behavior. One then seeks to understand the steps by which these have come about. It becomes evident that the peculiarities shown by mental patients are chiefly overaccentuated or unduly prolonged instances of relatively universal behavior. . . . [The psychiatrists' way of contributing to the understanding of morale] will be by way of observing demoralized people. We expect this to yield some clues as to what is significant [for a theory and technique for the positive protection and promotion of morale] . . . in comparatively healthy people." *

As then, so now the contributions of most psychiatrists to the critically urgent needs of humanity are to be sought in the con-

[* See "Psychiatric Aspects of Morale," *Amer. J. Sociology* (1941) 47: 277–301; pp. 278–279. H.S.P.]

sensual validation of what is known—from the study of the unfortunate—about that which works evil, as a basis for critical thinking about what would be better. Let us, then, see precisely what is the problem before us, and turn our energy into validating the data which we can offer towards its solution.

THE NEED FOR PRECISE INFORMATION
ON THE HUMAN YOUNG

The Charter of the WHO defines as its all-important field in mental health the fostering of *those activities which favor harmonious human relations*. It lays particular stress on the developmental aspect of personality, stating "healthy development of the child is of basic importance; the ability to live harmoniously in a changing total environment is essential to such development."

It follows directly that precise information is desirable about all favorable and unfavorable influences which bear on the developmental stages of personality, whether in infancy, childhood, the juvenile era, preadolescence, or in the long adolescent phase which should bring personal maturity.

The complex educational influences which convert the human young into more or less adequate persons are certainly first encountered in the primary, family group.

Any searching consideration of moulding influences exercised by the mother and other persons customarily or frequently in the home upon the evolving behavior patterns of the infant and child can be important *if* the study meets certain qualifications.

It must result in statements couched in terms of interpersonal action and the course of observable events. It must include reliable data on the 'emotional state' of the significant people concerned in the acts, for *anxiety*, in the sense in which I have defined it, is the first dangerously effective moulding factor brought to bear on the serially maturing adaptive capacities of the human young. Moreover, for immediate relevance to the crucial subject matter, the study should throw light on the outcome of the behavior-training in terms of its effects on the next stage of personal development, on its results viewed as better or worse preparation for the child's getting on with other children as he enters the juvenile phase and has to work and play with other young people of about the same age under more or less supervision by elders not of the home group.

These qualifications may well seem forbidding, preclusive of any probably useful agreements from group discussion of the factors in primary-group training which are significant in favoring or reducing the chances of harmonious living. Some groups may well apply themselves to determining if the qualifications themselves are necessary.

I presume that everyone will agree that the adaptive potentialities of the newborn human animal mature in a serial fashion over a term of years. I presume that a great many will agree that past educative experience has some effect on one's present and near future learning by experience. There may be a difference of opinion as to the importance of *operational statements* in the sciences concerned with human behavior. In this connection, I would like to recommend that each local group hear and discuss an informed summary of the symposium published in the *Psychological Review* for September, 1945, from which I earlier quoted Bridgman.

There may be wide difference of opinion on the meaning and importance of *anxiety*, and on the relation of unpleasant 'emotion' in the significant personal environment to infantile and childhood anxiety. My view in this connection is at least indicated in the *Conceptions*. In my seemingly never to be finished introduction to the theory of interpersonal relations this concept and that of *euphoria* are fundamental.*

There may be profound differences of opinion about the plurality of motivating forces which we require to explain interpersonal behavior, and about the developmental history of motivation as it can be inferred from participantly observed behavior and reported "inner experience." What, for example, of *envy;* how is it to be defined, at what developmental age is it first unequivocably demonstrable, and in what fashion is it related to basic anxiety, insecurity with significant others?

In view of the plethora of explanatory and descriptive terms

[* See index entries for Euphoria and Anxiety in the posthumous book, *The Interpersonal Theory of Psychiatry* (Norton, 1953). H.S.P.]

which one encounters in current psychiatric discourse—and with renewed emphasis on the previous quotation from Bridgman—I would like at this point to remind you that Gordon Allport and Odbert some years since found no less than 17,953 words which have been used to refer to alleged "traits of human individuality." *

THE DEVELOPMENTAL ERAS AS TRAINING AND
MISTRAINING FOR LIFE

The juvenile era of personality growth with its schoolroom and play-group settings and its often complicated repercussions in the home is obviously an excellent field for the participant observation of conjunctive and disjunctive tendencies in the young, and for the scrutiny of self-isolating techniques and ostracism. I presume that there is no serious opposition to the view that in some instances unfortunate trends of personal development have been remedied, and in other instances precipitated or aggravated, in this phase of growing towards maturity. Competitive and compromising techniques seem to be especially open to study at this time, and clearly have a bearing on harmonious living, thenceforward.

I am greatly impressed with the importance of the preadolescent stage of personality development, the time when some one else first becomes approximately as important to one as is oneself. It has seemed that people who had misfortune in achieving this growth are never at ease in dealing with strangers, just as those who were unfortunate in the next phase—early adolescence—are never at ease with strangers of the other sex. Being not at ease means that one is anxious, and the variety of disjunctive interpersonal processes in which anxiety manifests itself in these later phases of personal development is quite numerous.

Strangers become transformed into adequately and appropriately understood acquaintances by a variety of processes no one of which is facilitated by anxiety. If one is greatly susceptible to anxiety in new contacts, one never 'gets acquainted' with anybody. The outside world is populated with disturbingly strange

[* See Gordon W. Allport and Henry S. Odbert, "Trait-Names: A Psycho-lexical Study," *Psychological Monographs* (1936) 47:1-171. H.S.P.]

people, with whom one can never feel safely at ease, and about whom one can never correct one's misapprehensions.

A much more prevalent state of dis-ease in contact with others, a less extreme susceptibility to anxiety, is manifest in the remarkably prevalent practice of disparaging others, often under the guise of assessing their worth as persons with whom one has dealings. This practice of showing that one is "better than the other swine" does not increase one's durable self-respect nor facilitate harmonious human relations.

When it is expanded into prejudicial views about whole groups of one's fellow man, into massive disparagement of the alleged class of the rich or the poor, the educated or the ignorant, Jews or Catholics, Negroes or Irish, Russians or Japanese, Communists or Capitalists, Conservatives or Liberals or Radicals, Labor or Management, Republicans or Democrats, Psychiatrists or Social Scientists, it becomes an active menace to the community in which one lives. This community may be anything from the family group to the nation and the world, depending solely on the actual field of effect of one's prejudice. This does not alter the fact that disparagement in lieu of informed judgment is a manifestation of basic anxiety which can be rationalized as insecurity in one's self-esteem—a demonstration of the inadequacy of one's personality for living in the world of today.

It may be said of the practice of disparaging others and the entertaining of active prejudice to whole classes of people that, like the use of alcohol, they protect the person concerned from a more serious disturbance of personality; they are, in a word, the lesser of two evils, for the person who manifests them.

In one sense, this is but axiomatic. The uncomplicated, "natural" way of life would be free from anxiety, and no one is any further deviated from the self-respecting pursuit of satisfaction in living than necessary. All the recurring patterns of trouble two or more people have with one another may be taken to be complex performances for avoiding or minimizing anxiety, in turn the outcome of past mistraining for life as a member of society as it affects the perceived present and the more or less clearly foreseen near future.

In another sense, the idea [of the lesser of two evils] is dangerously misleading. It suggests that nothing constructive can be done; that *any* change would be for the worse—as many a life-course observed by the psychiatrist might seem to demonstrate. Fortunately, however badly a great many easy remedies have miscarried, some psychiatrists and some others have had opportunity to see that this does not have to be the case. My own work has convinced me that anyone who is not in despair can be led to show a striving towards less complicated, [less] anxiety-ridden living, an improvement in the adequacy and appropriateness of his performance with others. A variety of people with a variety of psychiatrists working with various sets of often self-contradictory ideas have in relatively infinite time come to much greater competence in living. Numerous others have undergone dramatic, if limited, favorable change in more or less understandable connection with everything from a nightmarish dream to an elaborately ritualized "new religion." I think it is safe to assume that many fewer people have gotten worse in the social sense than better in their years from eight to twenty-eight, not alone in this most privileged but in the most underprivileged parts of the world.

Community Opinion Leadership as a Practical Test of the Work of the Specialist

In a world mobilization towards enduring peace and social progress, there are certain technological problems—in contradistinction to the scientific policy problems.* The pressure of these technological problems is well reflected in the following quotations from a report made by the liaison officer of one of the local groups of psychiatrists, which has been at work for some time:

The group discussions . . . have indicated the inordinate amount of time and thought necessary to attain a relatively integrated approach to the problems, even when working with a fairly homogeneous and trained group. On the other hand, we already find a real demand for permission to participate from related professional groups. There seems to be an opportunity to organize a fair segment of the

[* I have slightly reworded this sentence. Sullivan reported in the original article that this section is a rewriting of an earlier editorial. It is obviously one of the editorials on opinion leadership, but I am uncertain which one. H.S.P.]

professional population. If this could take place in many communities, it would be well worth the effort. The distinctive feature emerges rapidly—that it offers the chance for people to discuss differences of opinion in a setting which tends to motivate them to find points of agreement. It is self-educational rather than a movement which seeks to indoctrinate. Feeling of participation seems to me to have much to do with the tendency to discuss and come to terms rather than to argue. It is a new experience for most participants and it has been interesting to know how the several groups have gone about finding a footing.

I suppose we will have to compromise and try to do both jobs. It may be well if you emphasize in your article the importance of organizing group discussions on Mental Health and World Citizenship, quite aside from the bearing it might have on any international conference.

This report clearly distinguishes two possibilities: the one may be called the working through in *intra*disciplinary discussion to the hard core of what the group has to offer to interdisciplinary collaboration and what it needs from it. As the writer indicates, this is anything but easy for psychiatrists.

The other is quite a different matter, and a form of activity which, I believe, may in general best wait upon the achievement of some results from the more grueling work of serious *intra*disciplinary discussion.

I counsel this delay for the seemingly self-evident reason that until a group has determined what it itself can agree on, *inter*-professional discussion can scarcely avoid the danger of mediocre or incoherent results.

This is in no sense a rejection of the writer's suggestion as to the importance of simply innumerable discussion groups concerned with the general topic of Mental Health and World Citizenship. It is instead a plea to safeguard this extremely important way of implementing our endeavor towards enduring peace and world-wide social progress, and of testing the practical worth of our progress in that direction, so that it may escape an early manifestation of the law of diminishing returns and, instead, grow indefinitely in real significance.

I am here laying before the reader some social psychological and psychiatric considerations which bear on the integration of all people of good will by the purposeful development of networks of *opinion leadership* to implement the work of specialists who are collaborating in the central endeavor, and to keep them alert to the practical aspects of their task—this on an explicit realization of the more important patterns of ability and limitation which are to be expected among the people on whom, in ultimate analysis, the maintenance of peace and world-wide social progress must actually depend.

I want to distinguish carefully the precise nature of this *opinion leadership* and will take as a point of departure the definition of political science as "the study of influence and the influential"— for which, as I recall, I should probably give credit to Dr. Harold D. Lasswell.*

Opinion leaders are people who exercise influence upon others *not because they wish to exercise political power, as ordinarily conceived*, but because they have come to function in their actual community—the group of people to whom they are thus significant—as people who respect themselves for the serious care with which they sift facts from prejudice, and study the probable consequences of alternative courses of action. Their judgment is respected, and their views are often accepted by those who for a great variety of reasons, find themselves unable or disinclined to "do their own thinking." They are, at the times and under the circumstances when they often unwittingly exercise fortunate influence, the relatively wise *and* broadly disinterested; not exploiting their fellows but discharging a perhaps but dimly recognized *social responsibility*.

ACTIVATING OPINION LEADERS AT
VARIOUS SOCIETAL LEVELS

The potential usefulness of [these opinion leaders] in an effort to remedy current disintegrative trends can scarcely be overestimated. The feasibility of activating this potential is by no means visionary. Its practicality has already been demonstrated in the work of the U. S. Department of Agriculture.

Something of this kind, applying at the *level of parent-teachers*,

[* See, for instance, Harold D. Lasswell, *The Analysis of Political Behaviour: An Empirical Approach;* New York: Oxford Univ. Press, 1948; p. 7. H.S.P.]

level, is the strategy for prompt implementing of good programs organized after the fashion of collaboration already discussed, and administered by the World Health Organization through appropriate channels. The developmental eras of preadolescence and adolescence seem to me to offer great opportunity for improving the ability to adjust to a changing environment, and thus better equipping the young for child rearing in the years that follow.

Something of this kind, applying at *the level of parent-teachers*, is the corresponding strategy to facilitate direct remedial action on the young.

Finally, something of this kind, applying at the *level of total communities*, seems to be the most promising way of making uninformed disjunctive prejudice and disparaging attitudes unpopular, and the rational assessment of personal worth the respectable way to handle corresponding anxiety born of one's earlier years. At this level, also, something of this kind should offer some hope of favorable change in the deeper elements of personal dissatisfaction and discontent which actually make a great many of the young more or less *tacitly desirous* of wartime adventure, and their elders anything but realistic in thinking about the frightfulness of another war.

The most dreadful aspect of the world today seems to me to reside in this widespread discontent and fatuous self-deception which at any moment can be used to destroy the peace and at the same time to stigmatize the thoughtful as enemies of the very people whose interest they are wise enough to seek to further.

17

Commentary

IN THE SUMMER OF 1948, Sullivan attended a series of international conferences in Europe. One of them, of course, was the International Preparatory Commission for the London Conference, which I have mentioned in the last Commentary. Another was the UNESCO Tensions Project, meeting in Paris, which took place shortly before the IPC meeting at Roffey Park.

The paper prepared as the end result of the Paris meeting constitutes the last paper in this book—"Tensions Interpersonal and International: A Psychiatrist's View." It is probably Sullivan's most comprehensive and important single paper. John Rickman, M.D., one of the eight participants in the Tensions Project, has commented on Sullivan's paper as follows:

One cannot read this contribution without a feeling of sadness at the death of a colleague who was so friendly and forward looking. In particular his early acceptance of field theory—a theory incommoding to one's complacency—puts him among the pioneers.

At the UNESCO discussions he quietly introduced this and other views on the problems before us with his native generosity of spirit and humor. [1]

The Paris conference of eight social scientists, representing six countries and at least five disciplines, used a special procedure, as reported by Hadley Cantril in the book *Tensions That Cause Wars*, [2] which grew out of the meeting: At the beginning of the first session, each participant gave a brief story of his life; and at the end of the two-week sessions, the discussants spent two hours discussing "bluntly and frankly" the tensions they had felt between themselves during

[1] See *Tensions That Cause Wars*, edited by Hadley Cantril; Urbana, Ill.: Univ. of Illinois Press, 1950; p. 81.
[2] See Cantril's Introduction, pp. 10–11.

the meetings, although this part of the proceedings has never been made public. This kind of systematic self-examination set a high standard for international interdisciplinary meetings and was importantly in the tradition of field theory. The Common Statement [3] issued by these men brought together by UNESCO "to consider the causes of nationalistic aggression and the conditions necessary for international understanding" remains an amazing document and a testament to the value of this kind of procedure.

After the UNESCO meetings, Sullivan went to Roffey Park in England to attend the IPC meetings. Twenty-seven countries had had Preparatory Commissions or discussion groups in preparation for the meeting, representing 5,000 people. The IPC consisted of twenty-five people meeting for two weeks. Out of this meeting emerged a statement agreed to by all members, which was presented to the Congress itself. At the IPC meetings, there was inevitably even more tension among the participants than at the UNESCO conference, since there were more people involved and the number of documents to be considered was very extensive. Following the pattern set at the Paris meetings, Sullivan opened the pages of the journal *Psychiatry* to comments from participants at the meeting in Roffey Park, even though some of the criticism centered on Sullivan's own participation in the meeting. He felt that the exploration of such tensions in international meetings was essential: "I believe that I can say quite positively . . . that each of the [conferences] showed that psychiatry as we understand it has a good deal to offer in group undertakings of this kind; as also that international, multidisciplined, groups are themselves an important field for psychiatric exploration. . . ." [4]

The last conference that Sullivan attended that summer was a UNESCO Seminar on Childhood Education Towards World-Mindedness, held in Poděbrady, Czechoslovakia. Ruth Benedict attended the same conference. For both of them it was the last summer of life. It seems somehow remarkable that they both had roots in the same small farming community, for both had completed their secondary education in Chenango County, New York State. [5] They

[3] See *Tensions That Cause Wars*, pp. 17–21.
[4] See "The School and International Prospects," *Psychiatry* (1948) 11: xvii–xx; p. xvii; [included at end of volume 11].
[5] See Sullivan's obituary of Ruth Benedict, in *Psychiatry* (1949) 12: 402–403.

had not known each other then. But they had both known isolation and deprivation of differing kinds in their early lives; and they must have both learned something of "world-mindedness" from their teachers: Sullivan's teachers in primary and secondary public school in Smyrna, New York, and Ruth Benedict's teachers in Norwich, New York.

When Sullivan returned to Washington at the end of the summer, I questioned him eagerly on what it was like in Czechoslovakia, behind "the iron curtain." He appeared sad when he answered me, quizzical and patient: "It is the same as it is here," he said. "Men fear. Over there, they call it the Pentagon; over here we call it the Kremlin." His concern was with that fear, wherever it was found: in the schizophrenic patient, alone and desolated on a hospital ward; or in a nation or ethnic group, living in a geographic or psychological ghetto. In the pursuit of some way to free men from their ancient fears, he was basically hopeful, even in the midst of a great World War and its aftermath. It was a hope based on science; and it sought for answers wherever they could be found. The fetters must be loosened whether culturally induced or personally determined. Through it all, men must begin to find across national boundaries some consensus. Perhaps this beginning consensus lay implicit in the sight of a newborn baby and the wish on the part of most people throughout the world that a baby would somehow have a good life, as I once heard him say. Mayhap in the years since his death, it is this simple beginning consensus about children and grandchildren that has, in the last analysis, deterred the hand of world leaders from the fatal destruction of life that has seemed at times so imminent in the continuing crisis of the cold war. Perhaps we shall survive by that beginning consensus, implicit in all of Sullivan's thinking.

Tensions Interpersonal
and International:
A Psychiatrist's View †

WHEN THE psychiatrist is asked to consider tensions affecting international understanding, and more particularly the influences which predispose toward international understanding on the one hand and aggressive nationalism on the other, he has to apply his accustomed reference frames to these larger problems and consider: (1) the interpersonal relations in which persons of different nationalities have face-to-face contact; (2) those in which this contact is mediate; (3) situations in which the people immediately concerned deal with personifications of persons of another nationality in the course of activities which are not primarily political; (4) situations in which personifications of persons of another nationality are dealt with to effect political ends; (5) the remarkable variant of the first mentioned, face-to-face relationships in which the persons concerned not only differ in nationality but represent as plenipotentiaries or other sorts of delegates the actual sovereignties concerned; and (6) the corresponding variant of the second case.

† Reprinted from *Tensions That Cause Wars: Common statement and individual papers by a group of social scientists brought together by UNESCO*, edited by Hadley Cantril; Urbana, Ill.: University of Illinois Press, 1950; pp. 79–138. [All quotation marks in this paper are double, following the form used in the Cantril book. In the original manuscript, Sullivan used single quotation marks to alert the reader to fringe meanings, following his usual style; but I do not have access to the manuscript now, and I have followed the form used by Cantril. H.S.P.]

It is of considerable importance to realize that some previous face-to-face contact between people currently in mediate communication may have important influence on the field processes; as may, for that matter, previous contact not with one's actual confrere, but with other persons of his nationality. We may then subdivide the second case into (2a) mediate contact between acquaintances of different nationality; (2b) the same between strangers at least somewhat acquainted with other people of the nationalities concerned; and (2c) the same between strangers unacquainted with any of each other's nationals.

Finally, to make the second case susceptible to thoroughgoing psychiatric analysis, one has to consider the zones of interaction that are concerned: whether, in particular, the channel of communication permits the hearing of each other, as by telephone; or of one only, as by radio broadcast; or if the medium is the written or printed word. While any system of symbols for speech tends toward an adequate substitution for vocal exchange, it is doubtful if there are many people anywhere who are able to use graphic symbols and the possibilities of a language's grammatic structure as skillfully as they can use speech—or could interpret the most skilled writing as surely as they interpret a conversation. The exception here is, of course, the precise referential languages of mathematics and the exact sciences.

Not that I would have you think that everyone is apt to speak "better" than he writes, or that conversing is ordinarily remarkably communicative. The voice is highly, if often obscurely, expressive quite apart from what is said, and conversation is a two-way process in which the pattern of the whole may greatly illuminate the purport of any particular of its parts.

Interpersonal processes, certainly so far as they are "contents of consciousness," are processes which involve *personifications* that may be relatively stable, or remarkably in flux, changing in the midst of the field processes of which they are a representational part. With perhaps not too common good fortune, two strangers' personifications of each other change in the course of serious conversation *in the general direction of improved approximation* to consensually verifiable fact.

Personifications are involved in listening to a speech, but the possibility of experimental intervention is lacking, and there is decidedly less chance of change being toward improved approximation to a "good" personification of the speaker; and while personifications are just as really involved in written interchange, there is very much less chance of their changing in this fortunate way. *

Training for Life in Society

The first task of the psychiatrist, when he is consulted by someone, is to try to get an idea of who the stranger is, how he came to be that person, and wherein his dealings with others are unsatisfactory to him—and doubtless to them. The psychiatrist has to seek, in other words, to discover the relatively durable patterns of recurrent interpersonal relations which characterize his client's living. He goes about this by participant observation of himself and the other as their relationship grows and takes form. He notices as much as he can of the course of energy transformations, activities, that go on in this two-group and infers from these data a series of hypotheses about the tensions that are ensuing in the behavior. He tests these hypotheses as opportunity offers and comes gradually to some reasonably probable conclusions about what would be helpful.

The psychiatrist never expects to know all about the other person. The psychiatrist regards personality as an actually undefinable dynamic center of various processes which have occurred, are occurring, and will continue to occur in a particular discrete series of interpersonal fields composed, as it were, of his subject-person and other people, real and illusory, past, present,

[* Here Sullivan included what he called "a long digression about the psychiatrist's view of personality and interpersonal relations, as a necessary preliminary to a frontal attack on the problems of international understanding and its absence." This "digression," originally published as an article entitled "Towards a Psychiatry of Peoples" (*Psychiatry* [1948] 11: 105–116), has already been reprinted as part of Chapter 22 (pp. 367–374) of *The Interpersonal Theory of Psychiatry* (Norton, 1953). It forms an important background for this paper, and should be read in conjunction with it by those not already familiar with the pertinent theory. In brief, Sullivan discussed the following subjects: psychiatry as the study of interpersonal relations, within the conceptual framework of field theory; the tension of anxiety; the stages of personality development from infancy to maturity; and security operations, in particular, selective inattention. H.S.P.]

and anticipated. There are patterns in this series of fields, and the fields of any particular pattern will have a history that is to some degree accessible to the person's recall.

The whole story about any person would begin around the time of birth of a particular human animal and would show the course of training for life among others of a wonderfully gifted creature as he had matured one after another of his inborn potentialities. As already indicated, the psychiatrist knows something about the serial order in which these innate capabilities for learning to live with others in this or that one of a variety of social organizations unfold themselves. This is the human schedule in biological time; but the further one goes from the date of birth the greater is the leeway even in this schedule, so that, for example, the chronological date of the puberty change can vary by several years of age from one to another of the young people in any social order.

With the help of the cultural anthropologist, the psychiatrist has gained some grasp on the variety of courses of training for life to which the young are subjected here and there around the world. In combination with the inferences about personality which have been gained from prolonged, intensive, therapeutic work after the pattern of Freud's epoch-making invention, psychoanalysis, this cultural diversity has taken on meaning of the greatest importance. It is now clear that nearly everything that one person does with another is to a remarkable extent a function of his past experience with people and of the particular chronology of that experience.

The inculcation of certain basic elements of any particular way of living is started long before the young are capable of understanding anything about the why or wherefore of the restrictions which are being imposed on the discharge of their impulses. The force that is available for use in accomplishing this entirely pre-rational phase of education, and a force that is certain to exert an extremely important if always somewhat obscure influence throughout the rest of life, is . . . the tension of *anxiety*.

I use the term, anxiety, to refer to one of the more fundamental conceptions in the theory of interpersonal relations. Anxiety, in this text, means something quite probably different from the reader's present understanding of anxiety.

Infants can be seen to show much the same interferences with their behavior when the person who cares for them is anxious, angry, or otherwise disquieted, as they do when they are frightened by painful events. Something which develops without a break into a tension state of later life that "feels like" *fear*, but has some very significant differences from fear, is thus seen to be capable of being *induced* in the infant by *interpersonal influence* which works through some obscure linkage between the infant and the mothering one.

I wish to stress the exclusively interpersonal nature of anxiety. Fear may be a fear of the hurtful potentialities of a person or, on the other hand, of something which is not in any way personified. This is never the case with anxiety, which is always interpersonal in a highly significant sense, even if this may be anything but immediately self-evident, as for example when a person has a "morbid fear" (a phobia) of soiling his hands.

Because the human animal is born long before he is able to fend for himself, the infant requires a great variety of *tender* actions on the part of the mothering one; such as the provision of food and water, the protection of body temperature, the removal of physiological waste products from his proximity, and, I am sure, physical contact with the mothering one. In an extreme sense, the infant needs to be free from anxiety most of the time—chronically anxious infants are known to sink into "primitive apathy" and perish from inanition.

The first of all learning, the initial discrimination in the previously all-encompassing, vague, and undifferentiated world of the infant, is called out to avoid recurrence of the extremely unpleasant tension of anxiety which is, and always continues to be, the very antithesis of anything good and desirable. I am sure that the first rudimentary personification that anyone achieves is one that may be named the personification of the Bad or Evil Mother, the manifestation of whose presence is the undergoing of anxiety. Discrimination of the Good Mother is not nearly so imperative, and doubtless follows after the other.

While sudden, severe anxiety is probably never much more educative than a severe blow on the head—offers nothing more than the possibility of recalling the circumstances which preceded the disorganization of observation and analysis it produces—the child soon learns to discriminate *increasing* from *diminishing* anxiety and to alter activity in the direction of the latter.

The child, as it were, learns to chart a course by the anxiety gradient. Simple performances which would relax the tension of some needs have to be made more complicated in order that one may avoid becoming more anxious. Before he is very many months of age, the child will be showing full-fledged *sublimation*,[1] in the sense of quite unwittingly having adopted some pattern of activity in the partial, and somewhat incomplete, satisfaction of a need which, however, avoids anxiety that stands in the way of the simplest completely satisfactory activity. The deficiency or incompleteness of the sublimatory satisfaction, the residue of tension, is resolved by *covert* activity of the sort later called reverie processes, and especially by this sort of activity in the phase of existence called sleep.

I need scarcely add that there are very real limits to the extent to which needs can be satisfied by covert activity alone, and therefore to the possibilities of sublimation; but these limits are wide enough so that this, so to say, "long-circuiting" of activities for the relief of recurring needs is generally a major factor in the earlier phases of learning to live. Please notice that sublimation includes nothing of witting "decision," no "conscious thinking" of the kind that I discuss elsewhere as experience in the syntaxic mode. Please note also that I have good reason for avoiding the term, *conditioning*, from the Pavlovian psychology, in discussing these beginnings of sublimation.

Whether it recurs in the second or the fifty-second year of chronological age, sublimation is, unwittingly, not a matter of conscious thought of a communicable sort, but rather the out-

[1] I continue to use the rather unsatisfactory term, sublimation, for this unwitting "long-circuiting" of energy transformation because I have not yet found a better word. "Socialization" ordinarily includes elements of witting and "reasoned" learning-processes in or approaching the syntaxic mode. The need for more observation and analysis in this area is suggested, for example, by the fact that the "overloading" of sublimatory processes can give rise to the clinical picture of so-called *excitement*, in contrast to the *disintegration* and *either* reintegration or reactivations to be observed when other more wittingly acquired motivational elements prove themselves wholly inadequate for resolving an interpersonal situation.

come of referential processes in the parataxic mode, in the service of avoiding or minimizing anxiety—and at the cost of some covert activity in waking reverie or in sleep. I repeat myself here because we shall consider presently the role of sleep and related sorts of relaxation in protecting man from long-continuing states of tension.

To return now to further consideration of the ways by which one learns to live up to the standards of his society, let me next mention the factor of *trial and success*, which is anything but an exclusively human factor, and go on then to the matter of *rewards* and *punishments*.

The rewards which encourage learning in the very young probably begin with *fondling*, pleasure-giving manipulation of the child. They take in general the pattern of a change from relative indifference to the child to more or less active interest in and approval of whatever he seems to be doing. The need for "audience response" becomes conspicuous remarkably early in human life.

The punishments are commonly the inflicting of *pain*, the refusal of contact or of attention, and, of course, the inducing of anxiety—a very special punishment. I know of no reason why punishment should be undesirable as an educative influence excepting it be anxiety-ladened. Pain has a very useful function in life, and loneliness and the foresight of enforced isolation, the "fear of ostracism," is bound to be an important influence from early in the third stage of development.

Well before chronological age two years, *trial and error learning by human example* puts in an appearance. This is probably exemplified in the patterning of facial expressions. It is certainly the chief agency in the acquisition of *language*. The phonemes of any system of speech have simply nothing to do with any but cultural necessity. The child learns to approximate, from among an indeterminately great variety of vocal sounds that he utters, the particular sound-areas that are used by the significant people around him. In the same way, he picks up the patterns of tonal melody in their speech; often being able to reproduce the tonal, melodic progressions of speaking well in advance of his "use" of any word.

Even the most spectacularly, but again not exclusively, human way of learning is quite probably evident under age two. I refer here to what Spearman called the *eduction of relations*.* The first instances of this sort of learning to live are purely matters of inference, but it is entirely reasonable to believe that some of the elementary mechanical-geometric relations pertaining to "parts" of a very important preconceptual "object," presently to be named *my body*, are prehended quite soon after birth.

Here, then, is a brief summary of the potentialities and in-strumentalities of education. What is it that the young are caused to learn? I must say that, despite a very great deal of data about child psychology and educational psychology, we are not yet well-equipped to answer this question. We know in a general way that whether chiefly from good wishes for the future of the child or from the threat of censure for being bad parents, or for yet other reasons, almost every home brings the child to the juvenile era ready to discover that the world is a much more complicated place than it had seemed thus far, and a place in which various other people, compeers and nonfamily adults, will subject one to anxiety and to pain. The experience of complex derivatives of anxiety, such as *guilt, shame, humiliation* by ridicule, and so forth, grows apace; and along with all this unpleasant experience, there goes the acquiring of more and more skill at various kinds of *security operations*—interpersonal activities for escaping from or minimizing anxiety.

We know that some social organizations, some cultures, treat the young so well, so to say, that but few of their juveniles are led to develop the "jungle" philosophy of which Dr. Allport speaks, ** while others produce but a minority still able to look upon their fellows as presumably simply friendly.

[* Spearman discriminates between eduction and *apprehension of experi-ence;* for example, "I-see-red" would represent apprehension of experience. But while *knowing* must begin in such actually occurring experience, ıt extends further, for relations and correlates are *educed* from the bare presenting experience. See Charles E. Spearman, *The Nature of 'Intelli-gence' and the Principles of Cognition;* London: Macmillan, 1923. H.S.P.]

[** Allport posits two types of personality that are likely to "be swept into the stream of national aggressiveness. One is the unintegrated, many-minded person, easily controlled through suggestion and momentary appeals by those leaders and publicists who paint the world for him in a

The more complex and incoherent the culture, other things being equal, the greater pressure the educational personnel will be under to whip the young into shape, and the less are the chances that any particular boy or girl will escape a great deal of anxiety-fraught experience and the learning of security operations that are far from the best manifestation of human adjustive ability.

But what we have not done in exploring the ways by which newborn infants are gradually converted into persons more or less competent to live in their own or even in quite alien types of social organizations is to observe and analyze the educative experiences of anyone's first ten years of life *as these experiences had to be*—not as we "intended" them to be, or presume that they were.

The brute fact is that even the developmental psychology that has grown out of Freud's work has but very recently paid serious attention to the extreme improbability of retrospective accounts of early experience which come up as "the patient's free-associations." It has been all too easy to think of the child as a little adult, equipped with the full complement of motivational possibilities that we posit in our chronologically mature selves. It has certainly been all too easy for the patients—who by definition are unequal to an adequate and appropriate participation in some field or fields of interpersonal relations—to convert reactivations of essentially vague past interpersonal situations into much less vague analogies from the recent past.

This misleading influence is chiefly responsible for delay in seizing upon the probable meaning of the strange performances of persons suffering the *schizophrenic* disturbances of living, and in utilizing the data from this *mentally disordered way of life* to provide clues to the nature of experience in, say, the first thirty months of life.

From this neglect, too, come the notions of a reservoir of a great many kinds of more or less primitive fantasies (a) with which everyone is born, or (b) which exists as a "racial uncon-

particular way. . . . The other type is the individual whose fears are such that he has himself developed a 'totalitarian' character structure. . . . Beyond the in-group he feels helpless. . . . To him the world is a jungle. . . ." See Gordon W. Allport, "The Role of Expectancy," in *Tensions That Cause Wars*, pp. 66–67. H.S.P.]

scious" or the like, with which everyone is in some fashion connected. My colleague, Dr. Rickman, has something of this in mind when he is discussing the tendency to try to match social realities to pre-existing personal fantasies; [this tendency] gives rise to some of the false images of the stranger, which are so much a part of our problem of international tensions. *

It is ever so much more probable that everything that can be found in the human mind has been put there by interpersonal relations, excepting only the capabilities to receive *and elaborate* the relevant experiences. This statement is also intended to be the antithesis of any doctrine of human instincts which is more ambitious than a mere statement that the human animal is capable of life after the pattern of innumerable schemes of dealing with people and their things—if and when he is trained to the particular scheme or schemes actually concerned.

I think that you can see what this statement must imply about any universal patterns in living; namely, that these patterns, if their existence could be verified, would be exceedingly important in that they must imply some universally effective patterns in the training for life which are essentially identical. Without concerning ourselves with anything quite this absolute, we can still find great profit in applying the same thought to the certainly demonstrable widespreading similarities in the interpersonal performances of people in one or in several culture areas. These can be read backward to give us insight into the functionally common meaning of the perhaps superficially different means of training to which the young were subjected. This insight would permit us to find the greatly helpful answer to the question: What are the young caused to learn by use of the various instrumentalities to which I have referred?

The psychiatrist knows a good deal about unfortunate outcomes of training for life, and some of his information may be helpful

[* See John Rickman's "Psychodynamic Notes" in *Tensions That Cause Wars*, especially pp. 182–185. Rickman notes: "The environment can aid an earlier and solider acquisition of stability or lead to a retardation of maturation. The effect of environment on this viewing is not so much a 'conditioning of reflexes' as a strengthening and enrichment or a weakening and impoverishment of this peculiar intangible thing—the fantasy life" (p. 182). H.S.P.]

in orienting one's thought about the influences which now make for cleavages in the interdependent world of man. Even here again, however, I must talk more about how everyone comes to be more or less incompetent to live in society than about how particular leaders come to direct the general discontent and distrust of others into international tensions and war.

Foresight, the functional activity which makes the neighboring future so important in human life, depends upon the adequacy and appropriateness of one's acquaintance with the past, as well as upon observation and analysis of the present. If one has been much influenced by anxiety in one's contact with significant people, the profit from these contacts in the way of useful understanding of what happened with them will be correspondingly small. This works both ways; one will not have very good grasp on oneself as a dynamic force in interpersonal relations, nor will one be clear about "who the other fellow is" or what he is "trying to do."

One will show a great many instances of . . . *selective inattention* as a result of which one fails to learn much of anything from a series of unfortunate interactions because one does not observe what was there to be seen or heard in the interaction, but instead goes on *as if* oneself and the other fellow were people quite different from that which the field processes show them to be. Thus "failure to profit from experience" is often the effect of anxiety, and the anxiety has to be eliminated before much learning can occur in the particular area of living.

I can perhaps best illustrate what I have in mind by discussing the *malevolent transformation of personality* as it is seen to occur in some juveniles. If one is led by consistent experience to expect rebuff and humiliation whenever one shows a need for tenderness, for friendly cooperation, it may become the case that one ceases to show any need for good treatment at the hands of others, but instead, when one would feel that need, acts hatefully as if to anticipate a presumedly certain rebuff. When such a deviation has occurred in developing one's potentialities for interpersonal relations, one can scarcely but become ever more firmly convinced that one is unlikeable and unattractive, that one is disliked and avoided, and that others are unkind and unfriendly and chiefly interested in making life unpleasant for one another. Selective inattention will almost certainly interfere with any helpful observation which might "open the mind" to negative instances and a beginning of discrimination of the more friendly from the less friendly among one's contacts. People of this sort are not very apt to undergo "spontaneous" favorable change.

Yet even these malevolent people, denied by early misfortune most of the profit from their associations in the juvenile era, sometimes encounter good fortune in the succeeding preadolescent phase. This points an observation of great importance in thinking about formal educational opportunities; namely, that there are remarkable new chances for favorable, curative, experience near the threshold of each developmental stage. The maturation of new capacities for relationship with others temporarily disorders, as it were, the self-system's power to govern one's profit from experience, for a time interferes with its power to resist change in the direction of one's development, so that greatly favorable—or unfavorable—"change in personality" tends to occur near these thresholds.

This is especially the case with the *preadolescent* phase of developing one's abilities for interpersonal relation, for it is at this time that the youth first becomes able to appreciate someone else as of approximately the same importance as himself. This is the time that something in the way of interpersonal relations that can reasonably be called *love* becomes possible. The conjunctive impulses that have been shown in the preceding stages are not of this egalitarian quality. Children do not love their parents, nor juveniles their teachers or their playmates, in the sense here meant. The quiet miracle of preadolescence, the changes in the character of interpersonal relations newly possible, include an interest in the satisfactions and security of another person which approaches or approximates one's interest in one's own satisfactions and security. This great increase in the field forces available to bring two people together makes possible an unprecedented personal intimacy, with relinquishment of many security operations and a great acceleration of the process of consensual validation of mutual personal worth. This is the time that firmly knit two-groups can be integrated into three-groups and, through members in common, into larger social units—"gangs" and "crowds" and whatever. The only thing in the way of social organization which cannot appear in at least essential rudiments is a truly heterosexual society. This last step calls for the final greatly important maturation, that of the genital lust dynamism with its initially almost incredible conjunctive power.

At least in the U.S.A., these days, many a person fails to complete the developmental phase of late adolescence, a good many fail to get through with early adolescence, all too many remain no further advanced than preadolescence, and, if I mistake not, a shockingly considerable proportion are arrested in the juvenile era. Rather than engage at this point in somewhat vacuous, invidious comparison of the people of other national areas, about which my information is grossly inadequate, let me invite the reader's attention to the meaning of *arrest in development*—about which one hears a shocking amount of nonsense even in superior psychiatric circles.

People are not ordinarily arrested in their progress in biological time. It may be that either specific deficiencies of nutritional growth elements or peculiarly vicious interpersonal influences may delay—conceivably entirely inhibit—the later maturational changes; but all this is definitely in the realm of gross pathology. What is ordinarily in mind when one speaks of an arrest—better, a deviation—of development of abilities for interpersonal relations [encompasses the] inadequacies and inappropriateness of living in the field concerned. This may be the result of factual deficiency of suitable educative experience, or [may] arise from experience which made the elaboration of one's further capacities too fraught with anxiety to be achieved. The authoritarian character to which Dr. Horkheimer refers, * who bears a close resemblance to people arrested in the juvenile era, in my nomenclature, does not fail to undergo the maturations implied in the preadolescent and the adolescent eras. He may come to have a very active sex life of one kind or another. What he lacks is sufficient freedom from anxiety to be comfortably at ease in intimate give-and-take relations of equality with people who have completed the preadolescent and the adolescent phases. His relations with more mature men are

[* See Max Horkheimer, "The Lessons of Fascism," in *Tensions That Cause Wars*, pp. 209–242. H.S.P.]

never of the kind meant by Dr. Allport's equal-status contacts;* his relations with more mature women, anything but greatly expanding to their feeling of personal worth. He may get on quite wonderfully with the young. Ordinary measures of "success" are not by any means simply a function of personality growth; the field of mutually satisfactory and respectful dealings with others is such a functional measure.

The extent to which one's capabilities for interpersonal relations have been realized is directly related to the character and timing of the anxiety-fraught experience one has undergone, and because of the functional activity of the self-system—itself evolved in order to escape or minimize anxiety in dealing with others— the extent of this realization has a direct relation to the particular sorts of inadequate and inappropriate ways in which one lives, whether in one's family, one's immediate community, one's sundry mediate communities, or as the citizen of a nation.

The immature cannot form useful personifications of the more mature; the insecure, of the more secure; or the unsatisfied, of those who are contented. These deficiencies are somewhat obscured by misuse of a useful human ingenuity, which I shall call negative conceptualization—the faculty of inferring polar differences, often manifested in the positing of subsistent entities and relations corresponding to terms created by adding the [prefix] *not-* or *an-* to a term standing for a conception derived from experience. This process, combined with selective inattention, nicely intervenes to spare the immature and the otherwise incompetent from any undue preoccupation with their limitations.

I hope that I have said enough to suggest what one *can* be taught, stage by stage; and what one *needs* to be taught, if one is to come to the adequate realization of his human potentialities.

As the older generation is the principal channel for inculcating the culture heritage in the young and no considerable number of people any longer achieve untroubled maturity in these times of

[* In *The Nature of Prejudice*, for instance, Allport reviews research demonstrating that if the white person has contacts with a Negro of equal status, he is much less likely to be prejudiced against Negroes and that prejudiced attitudes actually change under such conditions. See Chapter 16, "The Effect of Contact," in Gordon W. Allport, *The Nature of Prejudice;* Cambridge, Mass.: Addison-Wesley, 1954. H.S.P.]

startlingly rapid social change, the young—preadolescent and onward—are seldom encouraged to take an experimental attitude toward life, and any promising new insights into human probabilities that occur to them are seldom accepted as potential contributions to social progress. We have lived through some interesting phases of attempts to overcome this; I fear mostly by the *not*-technique to which I have just referred. Some experimental schools have not interfered with children and juveniles, in the name of progress—thus nicely cheating their charges of experience in social accommodation absolutely necessary for untroubled opportunity to amount to something socially useful in later life.

These and many another venture in formal education make me enthusiastic for follow-up studies of the achievements of the school. The current Hungarian study to which Szalai made reference is especially impressive because it seeks to uncover the effects on the foresight function that are resulting from the educational efforts. [a] The right idea is behind the study; namely,

---

[a] [In his Introduction to *Tensions That Cause Wars* (p. 11), Cantril notes that each of the eight men participating in the first UNESCO conference on tensions was asked "to comment in whatever way he liked on the final statement prepared by every other participant. These comments and their authors are indicated as footnotes in the text. No one participant saw the comments made by any other person on his own essay. Obviously, the process of rebuttal could become an interminable one." These comments are indicated by alphabetical footnotes. H.S.P.]

[Szalai comments:] Sullivan refers to a study which aimed to find out what ideals of life are held by adolescents in a certain school system. In the "free composition" lesson of Hungarian middle schools, the pupils had to write an essay on the subject "Looking back from the year 2000 A.D. I tell the story of my life." These fanciful life-stories were evaluated in the form of a catalogue of motives. For instance: "Makes an important invention and becomes a rich man living on his rent," "Becomes a hero of war and a statesman," "Tries to make a decent living," etc. Surprisingly— or not so surprisingly—such a catalogue of motives can be regarded as comprehensive (in a certain setting and in a certain school system) if it comprises some dozens of typical events. It is significant to note how a school system can change these "life expectations" in a few years. And it is interesting to see whether the ideal of life, provoked by a certain school system, corresponds to the intentions of the authority which supports the school, and to the teachings about a "good life" which are taught at that school. Allport is trying out this "Budapest experiment" on students in Harvard University.

that people might as well find out what their educational system is accomplishing, to see if that is what they want. But as a psychiatrist, I feel certain that inferences from the results will have to take into account the variety of trainings that pupils *brought to* the school system. Far-reaching and often very unfortunate limitations in freedom to develop adequate foresight are already established in some children before they enter into the juvenile era of formal training and education by contact with compeers.

It would seem to be very timely to investigate a variety of culture areas—if you must, ethnic groups within or composing nations—with the view to learning what is taught, and how, in the course of each of my developmental stages; what are the "normal expectations" of behavior-competence of the young early in each developmental stage after infancy; and what particular patterns of interpersonal inadequacy—mental disorder, delinquency, crime, addiction, and so on—are serious problems in each stage. It would seem that data of this sort would give us invaluable information about the limiting conditions of personality growth, and extraordinarily useful clues to the experience actually undergone by the young under a variety of circumstances. Needless to say, I would hope that these investigations would first be made in currently politically significant states, and only thereafter extended to temporarily politically insignificant, preliterate, or otherwise backward areas.

The reason for this hope is not far to seek. It is the inadequacies of the people in politically significant states, and in their leaders, which now imperil world peace and universal social progress. I do not believe that there are enough mature people anywhere in the world today to hold out great hope of dissipating international tensions by mere virtue of information about the common humanity of man. Perhaps it is because as a psychiatrist I see more of the unnecessary unhappiness of the world than of its contented success; but in any case, I fear deeply that the place of political leadership will always be open to persons who are restrained by no wide loyalty to man, as long as those who are led are incapable of dispensing with security operations which essentially seek to protect low self-esteem by protesting that "I am better than the other swine"—in whatever alleged respects not mattering greatly.

THE MATRIX OF "STEREOTYPES"

The psychiatrist, when he seeks to be of use to a person, participates with him in discovering the surviving anxiety-fraught *eidetic* or "imaginary" people—less accurately, the recollectable past interpersonal relations in which the patient suffered anxiety—that continue to be influential in distorting the personification of currently significant people "with whom the patient is dealing." Were so long a quest ever necessary, this retrospective reactivation of participants in anxiety situations would lead back to the personification of the Bad Mother of the developmental stage of infancy—an uncanny being of relatively cosmic if rather nebulous proportions, possessed of the nuclear essence of transcendental evil power, against the manifestations of which the infant's magic tool, the cry, had proved of no avail.

Reactivations of anxiety experiences in early childhood would bring up personifications of other only somewhat less bizarre "powers and principalities" of good and evil, including a nightmarish personification, Not-Me, linked in coincidence with the person's early sojourns in the realm of intolerable anxiety—and ever thenceforth growing along with "the rest of one," across the threshold of nightmare and schizophrenic psychosis; . . . one is always warned against [an approach to this threshold] by *uncanny emotion*.

Among the denizens of later childhood we would find a much better known shadow attached to the desirable; namely, the personification, Bad-Me, to prevent the unfortunate manifestations of which in interpersonal relations there is already developing what will soon become the greatest of all organizations of experience in personality, the dynamism of the self, the *self-system*, solely concerned with "living according to the rules" so that one will be spared any avoidable anxiety and its frustrating and complicating of activities in the pursuit of any and all satisfactions with which it coincides.

From these days onward, recall will show that in all interpersonal situations in which there has been smooth function of the self-system, whatever else may have been the case, the person concerned will have felt a comfortable *self-esteem*, an interpersonal security the very antithesis of anxiety.

Whenever this self-esteem was disturbed there had been at least momentary experience of anxiety; *and very frequently*—[and] immediately thereafter—whatever had been in progress was complicated or interrupted by [the] self-system processes . . . [that I call] security operations. These may have been no more obscure than a show of *anger*. They may have been as intricate as a years-long impulsion to degrade the other person concerned in "provoking the anxiety" to circumstances which will have divested him of his apparent power to provoke one's anxiety. In neither case, nor in the case of any other of the numerous kinds of security operations, is the personification of the anxiety-colored other person *apt to be like the personification of him before the anxiety-provoking event*. It will have changed to a closer resemblance to some eidetic personification in the patient's—probably recent—past.

So far as anything of a representational nature that can be recalled to awareness is concerned, everyone has come along a developmental course that began in the region of personifications that are truly nebulously cosmic in proportions, vested with the most extreme "felt" aspects of comfort and discomfort and essentially without relationships other than temporal coincidence and succession. These figures moved without anything approaching rhyme or reason in the growing framework of a center of awareness of vague but impelling recurrent needs which, as it were, stood out against a background of *euphoria*, a "state of empty bliss." There was in the cosmic center of events a magic power which evoked itself as needs became painful, and utilized its frequently successful tool, the cry. It gradually appeared that this magic was effective only in the presence of the Good-Mother—who could suddenly be replaced by the Bad-Mother with her aura of anxiety, against whom and which one was wholly powerless. Still later, Bad-Me was differentiated as that of the center which often evoked the Bad-Mother. Still later, techniques for avoiding or minimizing anxiety were evolved, including use of the still magically very powerful voice—ever *concealing* the presence of Bad-Me, often with ultimate success. *

[* This sentence originally read, after the dash, "ever ultimately often with success in concealing the presence of Bad-Me." H.S.P.]

From such a beginning, under the influence of the events—and nothing but the events—actually undergone, a gradual refinement in differentiating experience has progressed up to present. In this lifetime's work, Bad-Me has grown into some of the various personifications of oneself and into many of the personifications of other people who have hurt one or impaired one's self-esteem, *or who are foreseen as if they were threatening such damage.*

If one has been fortunate all along the developmental line, one has reached chronological adulthood with a great complement of referential tools for analyzing interpersonal experience so that its significant differences from, as well as its resemblances to, past experiences are discriminable, and the foresight of the related course of near future events will be adequate and appropriate to maintaining one's security and securing one's satisfactions without useless or ultimately troublesome disturbance of the self-esteem of the other person or persons concerned.

If one has been less fortunate in the developmental course, this state of mature competence will be lacking in some or in many areas of interpersonal relations. The handicap in these areas is apt to manifest itself in the phenomena to which I have referred as *parataxic concomitance*, of which "thinking in stereotypes" is a particular instance in the intergroup and international field. Personifications of the stranger are built around eidetic survivors from earlier experience, and anxiety and its complex derivatives prevent the progressive discrimination of significant differences between given persons and the inadequate, relatively stereotyped, personifications that are utilized in foresight and the observation and analysis of current events. Under these circumstances, the return in satisfactions and self-esteem which are derived from the relationships are inexplicably limited and this is rationalized by mostly disparaging and derogatory conclusions bearing on the personal worth of the alien persons. If the contacts, direct or mediate, cannot be avoided, anxiety-fraught states of being result, and these, because they interfere with repose and sleep, tend gradually to increasingly incompetent thought and action. This comes about because human life under any extant social organization calls for a good deal of sublimatory activity, the possibility of which in turn requires repose and sleep. Persistent states of considerable tension, whether of needs or of anxiety, make repose and sleep alike very difficult, unless and until the safety devices of *apathy* and somnolent detachment come into play. Neither of these protective transformations of living permits good observation and analysis of current interpersonal events.

Any but the most mature people who are living at a time when, one might say, the general level of interpersonal insecurity is increasing (e.g., at times of heightening international tension) may show quite generally a disintegration of their more recent developmental achievements—to which we refer as "chronic fatigue" and which is rather like the effects of alcoholic intoxication—such that their ability to observe events and draw useful inferences from them deteriorates progressively, and their "judgment" about the relative importance of alternatives becomes more and more defective, until finally anything that happens to be in the field of attention becomes of simply preoccupying importance. As a corollary to this motivational disintegration, these people establish interpersonal relations only with people similarly "reduced" in their state of being; everyone else is perplexingly troublesome, "unreasonable," if not seemingly ill-motivated.

These chronically tense people, often becoming more and more the victims of accumulating poorly formulated resentments—still another complex tension that contributes specifically to the feeling of overwhelming fatigue—fall readily into the immature types of interpersonal relationship reflected, for example, in being audience to a demagogue, associating with "calamity howlers," throwing oneself into radical-mystical "looking to the other world" for salvation; or turning away from the future to join in bewailing "the good old days."

As the regressive change continues, the actual contents of consciousness become less and less clear reactivations of earlier types of personifications, even these being oversimplified in keeping with the loss of refined grasp on the current situation, until these people become susceptible to entertaining the wildest extravagances, just so that these fictions approximate to the patterns of myths and misapprehensions which they once entertained.

The character of the myths and misapprehensions which come to have widespread currency among the less competent at times of intergroup or international tension is of chief interest to the psychiatrist along two lines: (1) From what particular personification in the developmental years do they derive their anxiety-fraught influence? and (2) By what combinations of overlapping verbalisms, rationalizations, are they given the semblance of group-wide acceptance so that they can be treated as consensually valid fact?

There is a good deal to be learned in the latter connection from study of the role of the *demagogue* in channeling the various insecurities of his audience into these mass security operations which interfere with the pursuit of information and improving foresight of possibilities and probabilities.

There is a good deal to be learned, also, from study of the constructive role of the *opinion leaders*—those whose expressed views in one or another field are adopted by many others as their own views—without any accompanying feeling of subordination, dependency, or requirement that they "give credit"—all this seeming to arise from the opinion leader's demonstrated status of being better informed, more skillful in sorting facts from mere prejudiced opinion, possessed of superior foresight and relatively *disinterested*.

No one knows better than I how great a gap there can be between the opinions one expresses and the motivation that one displays. Even if most people use their opinion leaders chiefly as a source of superior verbalisms, rationalizations, for their more inconsistent and incongruous actions—even if most immature people have an amazing congeries of relatively contradictory roles which they assume at different times with no feeling of discomfort—it still remains a fact that the opinion leader is a useful brake on the progress of social disintegration in the earlier stages of group or international tension.

While these relatively mature members of the community seldom aspire to the exercise of political influence in the governmental sense—perhaps because they appreciate the company with which it would imply their associating—they often act as the governing element in restraining political excess. They can be of great importance in bringing about a realization among parents and teachers (in the broadest sense, including those in youth organizations, labor unions, and so on) of "the extent to which their [these parents' and teachers'] own attitudes and loyalties— often acquired when they were young and when conditions were different—are no longer adequate to serve as effective guides to action in a changing world." *

Finally, there is a good deal to be learned from study of word-of-mouth transmission of information and misinformation, a field to the exploration of which *The Psychology of Rumor* by Allport and Postman,** provides a valuable outline.

Let me turn now to a brief consideration of some of the more important factors which have to be noted in anyone's attempts to gain valid information about living in an alien social organization.

Psychiatry Face-to-Face ***

While there is some reason to believe that a sufficient degree of novelty will always call out a disjunctive force the felt component of which we know as *fear*, a very great many otherwise illuminating observations of by no means intimidating novelty and difference fail entirely to inform us about the world we live in because of the equilibrating influence of the self-system—the tree that all too frequently reflects the way the twig was bent in the developmental years.

The extension of psychiatric theory beyond the confines of the familiar into the world of "foreigners" whose ways of life are alien to us calls for a sharp discrimination between fear and the various manifestations of anxiety and self-system activity, especially those of irrational *dislikes, aversions,* and *revulsions,* and the today so widespread *distrust of others.*

Current theory makes *hate* the characteristic of interpersonal situations in which the people concerned recurrently and frequently "provoke anxiety in each other," yet "cannot break up

[* From the Common Statement (Paragraph E) at the beginning of *Tensions That Cause Wars.* H.S.P.]

[** Gordon W. Allport and Leo Postman, *The Psychology of Rumor;* New York: Holt, 1947.]

[*** About six pages of this section have already been published, in a somewhat modified form in *The Interpersonal Theory of Psychiatry;* see pp. 375–382 *passim.* As far as I know, this is the only duplication of material in all of the posthumous books. In this instance, the continuity would be considerably damaged by the omission. H.S.P.]

the situation" because of some conjunctive forces which hold them together. [2] If the conjunctive force acts entirely outside of awareness, uncanny *fascination*, with moments of revulsion or loathing, may appear. If the integrating forces are not very strong; if the situation is "not very important," the milder manifestations of "more or less concealed," "actually unjustified," dislike and distrust are shown. The "actually unjustified" means that a consensually valid statement of adequate grounds for the dislike or distrust cannot be formulated. The unpleasant "emotion" arises from something more than what either person could readily come to know about the situation.

It is my thesis, here, that while no one can now be adequately equipped for a greatly significant inquiry into the fundamental "facts of life" of everyone, everywhere, there are many possibilities of greatly constructive efforts in this direction—if and only if instead of plunging into the field recklessly "hoping for the best" one prefaces one's attempt with a careful survey of one's assets and liabilities for participant observation.

Every constructive effort of the psychiatrist, today, is a strategy of interpersonal field operations which (1) seeks to map the areas of disjunctive force that block the efficient collaboration of the patient and others, and (2) seeks to expand the patient's awareness so that this unnecessary blockage can be brought to an end.

[2] Quotation marks are used to warn the reader that the thus-inclosed expression from common speech is being used as an expedient in pointing to a meaning which has to be much more precise than usual. This signal can often be interpreted as a warning against *voluntaristic thinking*, based on an implicit assumption that something of more or less transcendental power inheres in an alleged *human will*—an illusion exceedingly troublesome in that it discourages exploring the limits of man's analytic capacities, at the same time, serving to perpetuate archaic myths of the divinity of man, which in turn call for a belief in Divinity; the whole relieving the believer from any urgent interest in "doing the best he can" with the present moment and the neighboring probable future. Leaving it to God and seeking one's reward in the Hereafter seem to me to be among the most awful manifestations of perverted human ingenuity. The realm of Deity, if existent, might well be conceived as more than mere negating of human inconsequentiality.

[Sullivan is talking here about his use of *single* quotation marks (see footnote at beginning of this paper). In the version of this section published in *The Interpersonal Theory of Psychiatry* (*ibid.*), the single quotes have been maintained. H.S.P.]

For a psychiatry of peoples, we must follow the self-same strategy applied to significant groupings of people—families, communities, political entities, regional organizations, world blocs— and seek to map the interventions of disjunctive force which block the integration of the group with other groups in pursuit of the common welfare; and seek out the characteristics of [each] group's culture or subculture, and the methods used to impose it on the young, which perpetuate the restrictions of freedom for constructive growth.

The master tactics for a psychiatrist's work with a handicapped person consist in (1) elucidating the actual situations in which unfortunate action is currently shown repeatedly, so that the disorder-pattern may become clear; (2) discovering the less obvious ramifications of this inadequate and inappropriate way of life throughout other phases of the present and the near future, including the doctor-patient relationship and the patient's expectations about it; and (3) with this now clearly formulated problem of inadequate development . . . utilizing his human abilities to explore its origins in his experience with significant people of the past.

It must be noted that an identical distortion of living common to doctor and patient makes this type of inquiry, at the best, very difficult. Neither is able to "see" the troublesome patterns, and both are inclined to relate the difficulties to the unhappy peculiarities of the other people concerned in their less fortunate interpersonal relations. Each respects the parallel limitation in the other, and their mutual effort is apt to be concentrated on irrelevant or immaterial problems, until they both become more discouraged or still more firmly deceived about life.

For a psychiatry of peoples, these tactical requirements of good therapy—which is also good research—have to be expanded into (1) a preliminary discovery of the actual major patterns of tensions and energy transformations which characterize more adequate and appropriate living in that group, as a background for noticing exceptions—the incidents of mental disorder among these folk, uninformed study of which would be misleading; (2) a parallel development of skill at rectifying the effects of limitations in our own developmental background; in order that (3) it may become possible to observe better the factors that actually resist any tendency to extend the integrations of our subject-persons, so that they would include representatives of other groups relatively alien to them—a pilot test of which is the integration with oneself—and (4) thus to find real problems in the foresight of intergroup living which can be tracked down to their origins in our subject-people's education for life.

There is good reason to believe that all this is not impossible. These world-psychiatric inquiries are not at bottom particularly different from the already mentioned, all too common, instances where doctor and patient suffer approximately *the same* disorders in living. Let me say a word about the way in which one may proceed to reduce the handicap of such a situation, at the same time pointing to the answer to an oft-heard question: "What can I do to help myself?"

My conception of anxiety is in point here. While we may be unaware, at least temporarily, of milder degrees of any one of the other tensions connected with living, we are never unaware of anxiety at the very time that it occurs. The awareness can be, and very often is, fleeting, especially when an appropriate security operation is called out. The awareness can be most variously characterized from person to person, even from incident to incident, excepting only that it is always unpleasant. At the moment that anxiety occurs, one becomes aware of something unpleasant; but whether this seems to be a mere realization that all is not going so well, or a noticing of some disturbance in the activity or postural tone in one of the zones of interaction (a change in one's "facial expression" or in one's voice, as examples) a feeling of tightening up in some group of skeletal muscles, a disturbance of the action of one's heart, a discomfort in one's belly, a realization that one has begun to sweat—as I say, whether it be one or another of these or yet some other one of a variety of symptoms, one is always at least momentarily aware that one has become uncomfortable, or more acutely uncomfortable, as the case may be.

No matter what may have followed upon this awareness of diminished feeling of well-being, there was the awareness. It best serves in ordinary interpersonal relations to "pay as little attention to it as one can," and to "forget it." But if one is

intent on refining oneself as an instrument of participant observation, it is necessary to pay the greatest attention, at least
retrospectively, to these fleeting movements of anxiety. They
are the telltales which show increased activity of the self-system
in the interpersonal field of the moment concerned.

They mark the point in the course of events at which something disjunctive, something that tends to pull away from the
other fellow, has first appeared or has suddenly increased. They
signal a change *from* relatively uncomplicated movement toward a
presumptively common goal *to* a protecting of one's self-esteem,
with a definite *complicating* of the interpersonal action.

To the extent that one can retrospectively observe the exact
situation in which one's anxiety was called out, one may be able
to infer the corresponding pattern of difficulty in dealing with
others. As these patterns are usually a matter of past training or
its absence, detecting them is seldom an easy matter, but, I
repeat, it is by no means impossible—excepting there be an
actual *dissociation* in one's personality system, in which case
there will be prohibitively great difficulty in recalling anything
significant about the actual situation which evoked the anxiety.

Two things more remain to be said about this, shall I say,
self-observation of disjunctive processes in interpersonal relations.

Anxiety appears not only as awareness of itself but also in
the experience of some *complex* "emotions" into which it has
been elaborated by specific early training. I cannot say what all
these are but I can use names for a few of them which should
"open the mind" to their nature: embarrassment, shame, humiliation, guilt, and chagrin. The circumstances under which these
unpleasant "emotions" occur are particularly hard to observe
accurately and to subject to the retrospective analysis which is
apt to be most rewarding.

A group of security operations born of experience which
has gone into the development of these complex unpleasant
"emotions" is equally hard for one to observe and analyze. These
are the movements of thought and the actions by which we,
as it were, impute to or seek to provoke in the other fellow
feelings like embarrassment, shame, humiliation, guilt, or chagrin.
It is peculiarly difficult to observe retrospectively and to subject

to analysis the exact circumstances under which we are moved to act as if the other person "should be ashamed of himself," is "stupid," or guilty of anything from a breach of good taste to a mortal sin. These interpersonal movements which put the other fellow at a disadvantage on the basis of a low relative personal worth are extremely troublesome elements in living and very great handicaps to investigating strange people.

Disparaging and derogatory thought and action that make one feel "better" than the other person concerned, that expand one's self-esteem, as it were, at his cost, are always to be suspected of arising from anxiety. These processes are far removed from a judicious inquiry into one's relative personal skill in living. They do not reflect a good use of observation and analysis but rather indicate a low self-esteem in the person who uses them. The quicker one comes to a low opinion of another, other things being equal, the poorer is one's secret view of one's own worth in the field of the disparagement.

It is rather easy to correct interferences in participant observation of another which arise from one's true superiorities to him. It is quite otherwise with the baleful effects of one's secret doubts and uncertainties. We are apt to be most severely critical of others when they are thought to be showing an instance of something of the presence of which we are secretly ashamed, and hope that we are concealing.

This must suffice as an indication of the more pervasive, of the often unnoticed interferences with participant observation with representatives of somewhat unfamiliar background. I need scarcely discuss the role of linguistic difficulties or that of sheer ignorance of the culture patterns to which [my] remarks make reference. These latter are actually only somewhat more striking instances of similar interferences in getting acquainted with any stranger.

Progress toward a psychiatry of peoples is to be expected from efforts expended along two lines of investigation: (1) improving grasp on the significant patterns—and patterns of patterns—of living around the world; and (2) the uncovering of significant details in the sundry courses of personality development by which the people of each different social organization come to manifest more or less adequate and appropriate behavior, in their given social setting.

Each of these lines of investigation is a necessary supplement to the other. The first, which may be taken to pertain more to the interests and techniques of the cultural anthropologist, cannot be pushed very far, very securely, without data from the second. The second can scarcely produce meaningful data except it be informed by the provisional hypotheses of the former. The two provide indispensable checks upon each other, without which neither can proceed noticeably without running into increasing uncertainty.

The theory of interpersonal relations lays great stress on the method of participant observation, and relegates data obtained by other methods to at most a secondary importance. This in turn implies that skill in the face-to-face, or person-to-person, *psychiatric interview* is of fundamental importance.

While the value of interchange by use of the mediate channels of communication—correspondence, publications, radio, speaking films—may be very great, especially in case the people concerned have already become fairly well acquainted with each other as a result of previous face-to-face exchange, it must be remembered that communication in the psychiatric interview is by no means solely a matter of exchanging verbal contexts but is rather the development of an exquisitely complex pattern of field processes which *imply* important conclusions about the people concerned.

This is scarcely the place for a discussion of current views about what one can learn about the theory and practice of psychiatric interviewing; I wish chiefly to emphasize the *instrumental* character of the interviewing psychiatrist and the critical importance of his being free to observe—and subsequently analyze—as many as possible of his performances as a dynamic center in the field patterns that make up the interview.

Everything that can be said about good psychiatric interviewing is relevant to the directly interpersonal aspects of any work in the direction of a psychiatry of peoples. Every safeguard useful in avoiding erroneous conclusions about "the other fellow" becomes newly important when the barriers of linguistic and other cultural uncertainties are in the way.

Inquiries into the alien ways of educating the young must be oriented with close regard to *biological time* as it is reflected in the serial maturation of capacities; as to *social time* as it is reflected in the series of formulable expectations about what the young will "know how to behave about" from stage to stage of their development; and as to the exact *chronology* of presumptively educative efforts brought to bear on the young.

The spread of variations in each of these three fields is of great importance in understanding the people and their relationships which make up any community. Consider, for example, the effect of delayed puberty on the adequacy and appropriateness of subsequent behavior in many a youth in any of our urban areas. Consider, again, the effects on the living of the outstandingly bright boy from a small town when he enters a great metropolitan university. And, finally, consider the probable effects of early training in venereal prophylaxis in contrast with that of suppression of information in this field.

It is by chief virtue of [an ever] better grasp on the significant patterns in these series of events that we help patients to help themselves, at the same time becoming better and better informed about the factors which govern the possibilities of interpersonal action. To the extent that we have useful approximations to an undertaking of the actual processes of personality development which have ensued in the people with whom we deal, we become able to "make sense" of what seems to be going on. This must be the case whether one is a stranger in Malaya or host to a visiting Malay.

A last, peculiarly difficult, topic remains to be considered. I refer here to the *isolation* factor in interpersonal relations, particularly those which occur in situations intended to give information about unaccustomed ways of living. Something has been said, at least by implication, of the conjunctive forces that manifest complementary needs which "bring people together," and foresight of the recurrence of which needs serve to keep people together in more or less durable relationships of one kind or another. Much has been said of the disjunctive forces of anxiety and its derivatives, as well as fear, which "increase distance" between people, foresight of the recurrence of which disagreeable tensions "keep people apart" in more or less durable attitudes of dislike and distrust or of fear. What I have not discussed is that which one might call the specific absence of interpersonal field forces, the "neutral ground" of *possible* interpersonal forces which in a way sets off any particular pattern of field forces as different from another dynamically identical one; that which is apt to be most significantly different, for example, in the case of being a stranger in Malaya from being host to a visiting Malay.

This factor appears in the partition of living between waking and sleeping. The possible interpersonal relations which are wholly unrealized in the waking life call into being *dream-situations* which occur in the peculiar states called sleep and somnolence, the relations of which to subsequent events in waking life are often very obscure.

Dream processes are a part of living which may or may not be esteemed as important to waking life. The culture establishes this value attitude, and the attitude—the body of educative inter-personal experience which "makes up" this attitude in a given person—in turn affects the degree and character of the isolation of the person awake from his life in sleep.

Everyone on occasion has been "awakened by" a dream, often but by no means necessarily with recollection of some train of dream events marked with great "emotion." The events as re-called may have involved anything from an excellent simulation of a person known "really" in current life—an actual extant significant personification—to a bizarre creature or concatenation of events unknown to the world of science and unrecorded in myth or folklore to which the dreamer has had access.

The transition from deep sleep to full waking awareness may have seemed anything from sudden to so slow as to be almost imperceptible. It may on some occasions have been very trouble-some, as when the dream persists in some degree for a time after one has "gone to some trouble to wake up"—perhaps arisen and walked about. If it cannot be "shaken off," one has passed into the schizophrenic way of living, has become "acutely psychotic" as the Western psychiatrist is apt to put it, or is in a *fugue* or peculiar trance state.

It is from a combined approach to the understanding of events in sleep through the cultural anthropology of dream and trance phenomena and their role in daily living around the world, and the psychiatry of "remembered" dreams and of schizophrenic interpersonal relations as seen in our accustomed social setting, that we have gained our beginning understanding of the panoply of *unknown* referential processes that occur as preliminary steps in formulating an acquaintance with the really novel *but important* in the world of people and their doings with us—even (as witness the tale of Kekule and the "benzene ring" *) with the non-personalized world.

All that I can say, here, in this connection must pertain to the utilization of more or less—but in every case uncertainly—recollected dreams in developing one's acquaintance with oneself and others in current events. The psychiatrist who accepts his field as that of interpersonal relations works with reported dreams in a way quite different from the Freudian and other dream-analysts. In the first place, he does not encourage any dependence on dreams as a primary channel for communication, if only because of the isolation factor above-suggested. Second, he assumes that the intervention of sleep-processes in the work of participant observation is to be interpreted as *either* an isolation of the patient from expanding contact with the psychiatrist *or* a process for the overcoming of some such specific isolation. The first of these possibilities is well-exemplified when one encourages an actually schizophrenic patient to report his dreams: they grow more and more abundant and detailed as the patient sinks into more and more isolation from effective interpersonal relations, including that with the physician. I dare not take space to illustrate the second case. Third, he deals only with those reported dreams which he can convert into relatively simple statements, of situational characteristics in dynamic relationship, into rather simple *dramatic* statements. There is no search for "latent content"

[* According to Kekule's own account, he arrived at his formula for the atom composition of the benzene ring at a moment of waking, after he had been dozing in front of the fire. He observed, "If we learn to dream, we shall perhaps discover truth. But let us beware of publishing our dreams until they have been tested by the waking consciousness." See, for instance, F. J. Moore's *A History of Chemistry*, 3rd ed., revised by William T. Hall; New York: McGraw-Hill, 1939. H.S.P.]

in the dream figures, but instead a search *for the currently important factors in living that are isolated from current interpersonal events* occurring in the waking life of the dreamer. These are assumed to be possible interpersonal relations which are excluded from any approach to waking realization, whether because of dissociation within the personality system and the force of uncanny emotion, or by some other incapacity to foresee their possibility—such as gross ignorance, lack of any hint of their possibility.

For the psychiatrist or social scientist who is exploring alien ways of living, I would recommend respect for any occasional rather succinct and emotionally vivid dream that occurs to him, but I would also recommend that he look to an interpersonal context for any help from it. In other words, it is but seldom that the dream processes directly overcome the factor of isolation; they much more frequently present obscure data which, reflected as a reformulation in diagrammatic terms of situational characteristics *and* action by another, "open the mind" to the important possibilities that are being overlooked.

The Psychiatry of Sovereignty

There is still much to say in concluding my initial step in this analysis and in integrating my views with those of the other colleagues in this enterprise. I said in the introduction that interpersonal processes involve personifications which may be relatively stable or remarkably in flux. I did not add that the possible instability of those personifications is a matter of *change within limits*. Personifications are patterns, and patterns, for me, are the envelope of all insignificant differences. When a difference becomes functionally significant in its context of living, it is not within the same pattern but in another. If this seems to be a difficult idea to grasp, the trouble may reside partly in the fact that I am discussing *dynamisms* and not concrete, substantial mechanisms.

Gurvitch's insistence that nations are something specifically different from all other sorts of groups seems to me to be excellently in point.* Nations are those groups which, in the old

[* Georges Gurvitch, "A Sociological Analysis of International Tensions,"

way of thinking, require—as their necessary environing medium—other nations, and possess unique organization for functional activity in that peculiar environment. In language more suited to my way of thinking, they are dynamic centers in field processes so significantly different from those that can be observed in any other multipersonal fields that we can abstract from international relationships their specifically characterizing peculiarity, the manifestations of *sovereignty*.

Nations are particular dynamisms which are the locus of un-numbered other sub- or intra-national dynamisms, "groups," integrated into the national totality by the processes peculiar to and required for the manifestation of sovereignty. With all respect to the vigor with which Szalai * entertains the belief that change in social organization must precede change in "ways of thinking," and, I suppose, that therefore any great change in the international way of living calls for something radical like revolution or war—I must insist that the processes of sovereignty are a manifestation of inherent human potentialities and of their realization through the course of events in historic time.[b] The events were events that, so to say, impinged upon people and in so impinging upon or involving these increasingly numerous people, struck off or ensued in culture patterns that could transmit the past through the present into the future—but dynamically (that is, in flux, however low its speed), not statically. I can go with my Hungarian confrere [Szalai] far enough to say that one of the aspects of nations or of blocs of nations is, for very good reason, homologous with certain self-system manifestations in interpersonal relations of lesser complexity: namely, a marked resistance to

---

in *Tensions That Cause Wars,* pp. 243–256. Gurvitch points out that "because of their all-inclusive and suprafunctional character, nations are not very intensive social units" (p. 249). H.S.P.]

[* Alexander Szalai, "Social Tensions and Social Changes: A Marxist Analysis," in *Tensions That Cause Wars,* pp. 23–41. H.S.P.]

[b] [Szalai comments:] The whole concept of "sovereignty" is of quite recent origin. Every historian—not to speak of the sociologist or the cultural anthropologist—will very much doubt that it can be regarded as a manifestation of *inherent* human potentialities. Here again, as so often in this symposium, some attributes of class societies are regarded as inherent in human nature.

significant change of velocity in its directional sense; a, as it were, social inertia. This does not preclude great change of velocity, and I do not believe that revolution or war are the only ways by which these changes can come about.[3]

While more complex integrations can certainly manifest functional activities significantly different from the functional activities possible to any of their "parts," there are limits to the possibilities of these unique types of activity that are set by the functional possibilities inherent in the "parts," and the functional activity of the whole does not fail to involve some functional activity—if only changes in equilibration—of all parts.

The limits to constructive manifestation of sovereignty by social organizations seem to me to be all but reached at the present juncture of humanity, and, with Dr. Gurvitch, I hope for a rather prompt cultural revolution to end war, which would entail the widespread observation that manifestations of national sovereignty are no longer adequate processes for meeting the situation of continuing human progress, and that the world requires a change to something in the direction of an integration of all the peoples of the world.

Szalai's discussion of (structure and) superstructure in social organization—which, incidentally, seems to me in essence to say that I had somewhat more basic worth as a human being when I was cultivating carrots in my farmer father's garden than when I was cultivating implications in my forty-fourth floor office in that center of monopolistic capitalism, New York City—seems to take its departure from a dubious hypothesis about prehistory.[c]

[3] The herein treatment of *sovereignty* has been questioned by one of my greatly esteemed anthropologist colleagues on the basis of reference to certain historically isolated peoples who were a people, despite the absence of competing or threatening other peoples. These really utopian states can scarcely be said to be an important factor in current reality, and I am not here equating *ethnic group* with *sovereign power*. The passing of sovereign power as a superior, all-inclusive, integrating factor of very significant groups seems to me to be a prerequisite for achieving dependable understanding of all the conjunctive and isolating forces which will still be active in the early stages of one world of all peoples. [The anthropologist referred to here is undoubtedly Ruth Benedict. H.S.P.]

[c] [Szalai comments:] This must be a misunderstanding. No such thesis or anything like that was ever put forward by me or any Marxist. The solution for the crisis of capitalism is not a *Retournons à la nature*, a return

Can one doubt that the first *tool* of prehistoric man was an abstract idea and its associated name-sound, and not a piece of the physicochemical universe? [d] And is it not exceedingly probable that we can go on indefinitely improving our theory and technology—especially in the realm of the sciences of Man? I know no reason for thinking that Ikhnaton, Confucius, Galileo, Marx, or Freud, or any other of the people of great name in the history of thought, did more or less than expand the horizon of human possibilities in the realm of abstract thought and its related technological affiliations. As I hear of the "new" definition of freedom—freedom to take part in the common effort of people who are in one's own state of exploitation, as a step toward an ultimate freedom to develop the full potentialities of man—(besides recalling Remy de Gourmont's comment on *justice* in "The Dissociation of Ideas" [*]), I find myself moved to endorse with vigor the view expressed in Dr. Freyre's contribution to the analysis of social-scientific thinking from the standpoint of the

---

to a primitive or archaic form of economy. It is socialism, which can be *fully* developed only on the basis of increased production.

[d] [Szalai comments:] Is this question satirical or rhetorical? If Sullivan should think that the first tool was *not* a piece of the physicochemical universe, that it was an abstract idea, then we should emphatically assert that such a conception of human development is not only idealistic, it is also mythical or rather, fantastic. Quite apart from that: it may be doubtful whether abstract ideas are not really parts of the physicochemical universe. How else would they exert an influence on it?

[* See Remy de Gourmont's "The Disassociation of Ideas," in *Decadence and Other Essays on the Culture of Ideas* (authorized translation by William Aspenwall Bradley); New York: Harcourt, Brace and Company, 1921; particularly pp. 21–25. In this interesting article written in 1899, which Gourmont himself regarded as one of his more important essays, the author writes, in part, on justice as follows: "The moment an idea is disassociated and it enters thus, quite naked, into circulation, it begins to pick up, in the course of its wanderings, all sorts of parasitic vegetations. . . . A very amusing example of the way in which ideas are thus deflected was recently given by the corporation of housepainters, at the ceremony called the 'Triumph of the Republic.' These workmen carried a banner on which their demands for social justice were summed up in the cry: 'Down with Ripolin!' The reader should know that Ripolin is a prepared paint which anyone can apply, in order to understand the full sincerity of this slogan as well as its artlessness. Ripolin here represents injustice and oppression. It is the enemy, the devil. We all have our ripolin with which we colour, according to our needs, the abstract ideas which otherwise would be of no personal use to us." H.S.P.]

sovereignty-integrating factors that now influence it.*

I also find myself deeply sympathetic to Naess' interest in seeking out and making explicit the intrusions of sovereignty-integrating factors into the textbooks and other literature that are used in influencing the young.** It will not be easy to bring the current unsuitability of old doctrines and practices of national sovereignty to the attention of the thoughtful as long as they have been thoroughly prejudiced against attention to the problem at every stage in their development.

I often hear, these days, "You and your long-range programs; there isn't time, any more; can't you help at all right now?" Here again, I subscribe to views expressed by Gurvitch and Naess about intensive *action research* at major centers of conflict, and the use of international conferences none of the personnel of which are invested with any of the sovereignties primarily concerned. The major centers of conflict might be, at the moment, Palestine and India; on the other hand they might equally as well be, at the moment, high-level conferences which concern themselves with, say, particular aspects of the future of Germany. Our first contributions could scarcely be more than "fact-finding"—but perhaps "facts" about intransigent confreres, among others—and approaches to agreements in limited but not necessarily irrelevant or immaterial fields.

This venture toward utilizing psychiatry and the social sciences

[* Gilberto Freyre, "Internationalizing Social Science," in *Tensions That Cause Wars*, pp. 139–165. Freyre states (p. 140): "As 'human sciences' they [sociology and any of the other social sciences] should be free to develop according to the national cultural background of social scientists and not in some sort of vacuum. But this is different from admitting as scientific, or sociological, those 'sociologies' the contents of which are so narrowly and, sometimes, so aggressively nationalistic or ethnocentric, as to be propaganda or apology—national apology or race glorification." H.S.P.]

[** Arne Naess, "The Function of Ideological Convictions," in *Tensions That Cause Wars*. In this connection, Naess states (p. 285): "Between the world wars various international institutions took up textbook revision in their program. In the future such revisions should not only eliminate nationalistic exaggerations but any form of crude violations of the principles of critical attitude. There is scarcely any field in which international understanding can be more directly and intensively served than in the field of textbooks." H.S.P.]

in direct attack at focal centers of international disagreement would require of the scientists concerned an unusual clarity about *ethical* factors that would otherwise interfere quite seriously. I guess that I am dealing at this point with "the pluralism of morals" which disturbs Horkheimer and Szalai. Many years ago, I found myself defining *evil* as the unwarranted interference with life. This was not much of a definition but it seemed helpful in that it made the problem an operational one, and the process of tracing warranties for interference might be something at which one could ultimately become skillful. When I hear statements like "Nothing should be done to interfere with class warfare" or "There is no difference between the Nazi and the Soviet dictatorships—each has spilled the same amount of innocent blood," I have to lower my expectations of immediate highly communicative interchange, but I do not have to despair.e When, on the other hand, I hear propositions like "the Marshall Plan should be fought because it will delay the liquidation of U.S.A. capitalist monopolism—no basic change in society can be made without basic changes in the system of production," I know that I am in

---

e [Szalai comments:] Innocent blood has been spilled by the sentence "nothing should be done to interfere with class warfare." Where and when? And who has ever said "don't interfere?" Sullivan, a liberal man indeed, seems to be one of those who mean that class warfare is an attack of the proletarians against the capitalists and is something fought out exclusively on the barricades. This is a false conception. Class warfare is primarily fought out in the bureaus of factory managers, in the ministries of bourgeois states, by very civilized civil servants, against very uneducated and not at all gentlemanlike workers and peasants. The weapon is "hire and fire," "take it or leave it," "tuberculosis statistics," ignorance, bad schools, and—in some cases—the jury and the police. And if it is the suppressed and exploited class which takes over the initiative in this warfare, nobody says "Nothing should be done." The call is for strike-breakers, justice, the big stick and the like. The sentence "there is no difference between the Nazi and the Soviet dictatorship" is, first, a calumny and, second, the war-cry of warmongers. These examples of Sullivan were badly chosen indeed.

[Szalai's comment points up the difficulty of communication cross-cultural as well as cross-disciplinary. What Sullivan is attempting to point out in these two quotations is the difficulty of absolute right and wrong as a political slogan. He is in essence saying that there was, of course, a relative difference between Nazi and Soviet governments, even if both were dictatorships; and that perhaps *sometimes* class warfare should be interfered with. But he is depending on innuendo and exaggeration here; and his meaning did not carry to Szalai. H.S.P.]

pretty deep water; perhaps, unpreparedly, confronted with communication in my initial class.

There is no psychiatric technique that can be expected to reach behind a delegate and change his instructions. There is no swift-moving technique for changing beliefs held with intense feeling of their importance, as by a zealot. These flaming convictions are experienced as indispensably useful; one would be much less of a person if one were to relinquish them or open them to an assessment of their relative rather than absolute importance. In other words, these never-to-be-yielded convictions or never-to-be-compromised positions—and along with them sundry never-to-be-questioned prejudices—are functioning as *effective protection* against great anxiety, when, as nowadays sometimes is the case, they are not literally statements in a credo, assertion of the governing acceptance of which may be necessary for continuing physical survival and liberty.

So far as they protect one from severe anxiety they are so important a part of the self-system concerned *that they may rarely be attacked directly* with any result more desirable than a violent argument. Argumentation, if it is not of the mildest kind, includes so much that is parataxic that the psychiatrist expects nothing useful to come out of it. This does not apply to calm, succinct statement of a flatly contradictory view, but, here too, the possibility of usefulness is limited to greatly increasing the alertness of the person contradicted, a result sometimes much to be desired as a preliminary to other interpersonal operations.

Perhaps the most common technique for disposing of "highly emotional" beliefs which stand in the way of exploring an issue in quest for agreements lies in (1) becoming as clear as may be about how the belief can be stated *exactly*, with the assistance of (2) attempts to discover if some other statements are acceptable as being implied in the belief, (3) seeking to explore by the use of these other statements the limiting effect of the belief on the holder's freedom to participate in intelligent interpersonal inquiry, (4) from this limiting effect—and from hypotheses as to experience possibly anterior to the belief itself—to surmise *what the belief is concealing* or *disguising* which the believer would be "ashamed" or "guilty" or "embarrassed" to be judged to be.

(5) The fifth step is to explore the surmise as best may be, and when probability seems notable, (6) to inquire if the person, denied the belief, would feel that he were so-and-so—with something of formal suggestion that, if so, that would be a mistake.

All this is a tedious example of the psychiatric effort required to circumvent self-system function *in sole interest of the person in point*, so that he may become free from a major handicap in relations with others. He has to be led to observe closely, to catch on to the exact functional activity concerned—the "personal use" of the belief to him; then to see that the formula is by no means the best for achieving a useful end; and only then can he go about using his abilities to be "more realistic," less defensively vulnerable, in the field of collaboration.

My work with a stranger soon becomes a mapping of the areas in interpersonal fields in which he becomes anxious—which can be said to mean that he there tends to "pull away"; to explore many leads as to the historic why and distorted present that account for these incidents of anxiety; to elevate what I observe to lucid attention, when and if that can be done without a defeating degree of anxiety; and only then, by stating the problem as I have surmised it, [to] establish a beginning collaboration for its remedy.

This is a far cry from the blueprint for perfecting and then indefinitely preserving the peace of the world. I hope that it will not fail entirely to suggest some possibilities. Thirty years of work has taught me that, whenever one could be aided to foresee the reasonable probability of a better future, everyone will show a sufficient tendency to collaborate in the achievement of more adequate and appropriate ways of living. *

[* I have omitted at this point, two long evaluations of Sullivan's paper by Gordon W. Allport and Max Horkheimer. Allport's comment begins with the idea from which this book derives its name: "During his productive lifetime Sullivan, perhaps more than any other person, labored to bring about the fusion of psychiatry and social science. In this essay the reader catches a vision of the gain that would result from such a merging, and finds himself hoping that Sullivan's dream will become progressively realized." H.S.P.]

Name Index

Addams, Jane, xx–xxvii *passim*
Adler, Alfred, 13
Alcott, Bronson, 194
Alexander, Franz, xvi, 13
Allport, Floyd H., 66
Allport, Gordon W., xiii, xix, 16n, 284, 300–301n, 306, 307n, 314, 331n
Ames, Edward Scribner, xxii$n$

Barrett, Albert M., 16n
Benedict, Ruth, xxviii$n$, 16n, 56, 291–292, 326n
Berelson, Bernard, 147n
Bernheim, Hippolyte-Marie, 5, 8
Bertrand, Alexandre, 5, 8
Birkhoff, George D., 57–58, 60–62, 65
Bleuler, Eugen, 16n, 34n
Blumer, Herbert, 13
Bond, Thomas, 5, 7
Bradley, William Aspenwall, 327n
Breuer, Joseph, 5, 8, 204
Briand, Marcel, 5, 8
Bridgman, P. W., 58, 195–197n, 228, 271, 280, 283–284
Brill, A. A., 16n
Brush, Edward N., 16n
Bunker, Henry Alden, 233n
Burgess, Ernest W., xix, xxv–xxvii$n$

Cantril, Hadley, xiii$n$, 290, 293n, 307n
Castle, Henry Northrup, xx$n$, xxi–xxii, xxv$n$
Charcot, Jean-Martin, 8
Chiarugi, Vincenzo, 5, 7
Chisholm, G. B., 267–270, 273, 275, 277
Commager, Henry Steele, xx
Comte, Auguste, 58

Cooley, Charles H., xxi, xxii, 148n, 194
Cottrell, Leonard S., Jr., 215n

Daquin [d'Aquin], Giuseppe, 5, 7
Darwin, Charles, xxiii
Da Vinci, Leonardo, 153
Davis, Elmer, 163n
Davis, Kingsley, 276
De Gourmont, Remy, 327
Deutsch, Albert, 122
Dewey, John, xxi, xxiv, xxv
Dewey, Richard, 16n
Dix, Dorothea Lynde, 5, 7
Dunham, Albert Millard, Jr., 228
Dunlap, Charles B., 16n
Dunsany, [Lord] E. J., 22n
Dykstra, Clarence, 121–122
Dymond, Rosalind F., 215n

Esquirol, Jean Étienne Dominique, 5, 7

Ferenczi, Sandor, xvi
Fleming, Donald Harnish, xx$n$
Fortas, Abe, 277
Frank, L. K., xvii–xviii, 56
Frazier, E. Franklin, xxvi, 85, 86, 88, 96–99, 100–101
Freud, Sigmund, xxii, xxiii, xxvii, xxx–xxxi, 8, 16n, 24, 62, 204, 217, 233, 296, 301, 323, 327
Freyre, Gilberto, 327–328n
Fricke, Johann Karl Georg, 5, 7
Fromm, Erich, xvi, 16n
Fromm-Reichmann, Frieda, xvi

Galileo, 327
Gaudet, Hazel, 147n

333

Subject Index

†Sullivan's writings from 1937 through 1949, as cited in this book, are marked in this fashion. These items do not, however, constitute a complete bibliography for that period (see pp. vii–viii for explanation).

Norton Paperbacks on Psychiatry and Psychology

Adorno, T. W. et al.   *The Authoritarian Personality.*

Alexander, Franz.   *Fundamentals of Psychoanalysis.*

Alexander, Franz.   *Psychosomatic Medicine.*

Bruner, Jerome S.   *Toward a Theory of Instruction.*

Cannon, Walter B.   *The Wisdom of the Body.*

Erikson, Erik H.   *Childhood and Society.*

Erikson, Erik H.   *Gandhi's Truth.*

Erikson, Erik H.   *Identity: Youth and Crisis.*

Erikson, Erik H.   *Insight and Responsibility.*

Erikson, Erik H.   *Young Man Luther.*

Ferenczi, Sandor.   *Thalassa: A Theory of Genitality.*

Field, M. J.   *Search for Security: An Ethno-Psychiatric Study of Rural Ghana.*

Freud, Sigmund.   *An Autobiographical Study.*

Freud, Sigmund.   *Civilization and its Discontents.*

Freud, Sigmund.   *The Ego and the Id.*

Freud, Sigmund.   *Jokes and Their Relation to the Unconscious.*

Freud, Sigmund.   *Leonardo da Vinci and a Memory of His Childhood.*

Freud, Sigmund.   *New Introductory Lectures on Psychoanalysis.*

Freud, Sigmund.   *On Dreams.*

Freud, Sigmund.   *On the History of the Psycho-Analytic Movement.*

Freud, Sigmund.   *An Outline of Psycho-Analysis Rev. Ed.*

Freud, Sigmund.   *The Problem of Anxiety.*

Freud, Sigmund.   *The Psychopathology of Everyday Life.*

Freud, Sigmund.   *The Question of Lay Analysis.*

Freud, Sigmund.   *Totem and Taboo.*

Horney, Karen (Ed.)   *Are You Considering Psychoanalysis?*

Horney, Karen.   *Feminine Psychology.*

Horney, Karen.   *Neurosis and Human Growth.*

Horney, Karen.   *The Neurotic Personality of Our Time.*

Horney, Karen.   *New Ways in Psychoanalysis.*

Horney, Karen.   *Our Inner Conflicts.*

Horney, Karen.   *Self-Analysis.*

Inhelder, Bärbel and Jean Piaget.   *The Early Growth of Logic in the Child.*

James, William.   *Talks to Teachers.*

Kasanin, J. S.   *Language and Thought in Schizophrenia.*

Kelly, George A.   *A Theory of Personality.*

Klein, Melanie and Joan Riviere.   *Love, Hate and Reparation.*

Levy, David M.   *Maternal Overprotection.*

Lifton, Robert Jay.   *Thought Reform and the Psychology of Totalism.*

Piaget, Jean.   *The Child's Conception of Number.*

Piaget, Jean.   *Genetic Epistemology.*

Piaget, Jean.   *The Origins of Intelligence in Children.*

Piaget, Jean. *Play, Dreams and Imitation in Childhood.*

Piaget, Jean and Bärbel Inhelder. *The Child's Conception of Space.*

Piers, Gerhart and Milton B. Singer. *Shame and Guilt.*

Ruesch, Jurgen. *Disturbed Communication.*

Ruesch, Jurgen. *Therapeutic Communication.*

Ruesch, Jurgen and Gregory Bateson. *Communication: The Social Matrix of Psychiatry.*

Schein, Edgar et al. *Coercive Persuasion.*

Sullivan, Harry Stack. *Clinical Studies in Psychiatry.*

Sullivan, Harry Stack. *Conceptions of Modern Psychiatry.*

Sullivan, Harry Stack. *The Fusion of Psychiatry and Social Science.*

Sullivan, Harry Stack. *The Interpersonal Theory of Psychiatry.*

Sullivan, Harry Stack. *The Psychiatric Interview.*

Walter, W. Grey. *The Living Brain.*

Watson, John B. *Behaviorism.*

Wheelis, Allen. *The Quest for Identity.*

Zilboorg, Gregory. *A History of Medical Psychology.*